Introduction to Social Entrepreneurship

Introduction to Social Entrepreneurship

Teresa Chahine

CRC Press
Taylor & Francis Group
Boca Raton London New York

CRC Press is an imprint of the
Taylor & Francis Group, an **Informa** business

CRC Press
Taylor & Francis Group
6000 Broken Sound Parkway NW, Suite 300
Boca Raton, FL 33487-2742

Printed on acid-free paper
Version Date: 20151102

International Standard Book Number-13: 978-1-4987-1704-5 (Hardback)

Library of Congress Cataloging-in-Publication Data

Names: Chahine, Teresa, author.
Title: Introduction to social entrepreneurship / Teresa Chahine.
Description: Boca Raton, FL : CRC Press, 2016.
Identifiers: LCCN 2015039686 | ISBN 9781498717045
Subjects: LCSH: Social entrepreneurship.
Classification: LCC HD60 .C4195 2016 | DDC 658.408--dc23
LC record available at http://lccn.loc.gov/2015039686

**Visit the Taylor & Francis Web site at
http://www.taylorandfrancis.com**

**and the CRC Press Web site at
http://www.crcpress.com**

This book is dedicated to the social entrepreneur inside each one of us.

Contents

■ *Contents*

Preface: A Letter to the Reader

All entrepreneurship is social. As a mentor of mine once said, "Unless you're trading illegal or harmful substances, you're producing positive social outcomes by creating jobs, building the economy, and advancing human capacity."

The reason we use the terminology of social entrepreneurship, and the reason it has developed into a field of its own over the past decades, is that despite all the commercial entrepreneurship out there, despite all the industry and business and enterprise, there are still huge chunks of the human population without basic human needs. Water, sanitation, education, and basic health services and knowledge, which most of the world's population take for granted, are still today, in the midst of the third millennium, inaccessible for over a billion people.

Most readers would agree that governments carry the primary charge for meeting these basic needs and in most cases have already pledged in writing to do so. The purpose of this book is not to divert resources and attention away from the government sector. The purpose of this book is to acknowledge that individuals can make, and have made, a huge difference to underserved populations. Social entrepreneurs around the world have created and implemented effective, scalable, and sustainable solutions to the most basic of human challenges. While their work is unique each in its own context, we have gleaned lessons from their successes and failures.

Understanding the social challenges we are facing; co-creating solutions with the community; creating products and services in contexts not currently served by the markets; building resilient business plans around those products and services while adhering to the social mission; mobilizing financial, human, and other resources; and building initiatives and organizations that work to maximize social impact—these are the basic frameworks we have seen to maximize the chances of success of a social venture.

In this book, you will see many different models, examples, and ways of thinking about social entrepreneurship. These have been compiled into a framework that will help you start taking the first steps toward figuring out your own model. The only thing I need you to understand unequivocally is this: There is no *one* model that can solve all the world's problems. I don't know much, but I do know this for sure. We as a human race just have not figured it out yet.

So the purpose of this book is not to teach you how it's done or to present a winning formula. It's to share with you the collective human knowledge that has been created from numerous attempts, failures, and accomplishments to date. From here on out, it's up to you. The purpose is not for you to take these approaches, learn them, and copy and paste them. The goal is for you to completely disrupt them, question them, and find new ways of doing things.

What you are tasked with is taking this knowledge that we have collectively created up until now and completely hacking it! Knock it out of the ball park. Make it irrelevant. I want you to take this framework, apply it, and then discover new things that prove me entirely wrong and come up with new answers of your own. Leave no assumption unquestioned.

You might come up with something along the way that completely obliterates everything I have written in the book. I hope so. Because this is how human knowledge progresses. This is how we figure things out as a race.

Acknowledgments

This book was co-created by all the social entrepreneurs profiled here, and so many more. The only credit that would be accurate for me to accept is that I'm just the big nerd who sat down and typed it all out. The content is based on the work of countless people over countless years who have developed and implemented effective, scalable, and sustainable solutions to social challenges.

Most importantly, this book was co-created with my students. Based on my course at the Harvard T.H. Chan School of Public Health, each week was turned into a chapter, and chapters were read and commented on by students. The course content itself was also developed with feedback from students, which is further reflected in the book's content. Emily Holleran, who at the time of writing, was a graduate student at Harvard University Division of Continuing Education, has been a stellar collaborator and no words can thank her enough. Emily, I don't know what to say. At the time of writing, in this moment, you are literally my favorite person in the whole world. (Sorry, Mom!)

Because this book is based on a course, thanks are due to all who made that course possible: Jack Spengler, who kept me around for all these years (I'm still trying to figure out why!) and opened countless doors, the least and most humble of which was the funding of the course; SV Subramanian, who served as a long-standing mentor, supporter, and faculty sponsor without whom none of this would have happened; Nancy Turnbull, who helped me start the process by deciding that "yes, we need a course like that here!"; Michelle Bell, who guided me on curriculum; Rick Siegrist, who shared his expertise, guidance, intellectual, and moral support; Nancy Kane, who has been so generous with her time in helping me develop my writing and teaching skills. I'd also like to go a little more upstream than that to thank Jon Levy, Amy Cohen, and Donald Halstead, without whom I never would have gotten my doctoral degree in the first place to do all this.

Last but not least, the course on which this book is based was developed out of my experience at the Massachusetts Institute of Technology (MIT), as an honorary fellow (translated: tag-along) in the Legatum Center, thanks to Geoffrey Groesbeck, who was the fellowship director at the time. I wanted to replicate the experience for others at my alma mater who had not had the opportunity, and to create the same kind of knowledge at our home base where people convene from all over the world to solve the most pressing challenges affecting the well-being of our planet and its population. Thank you also to MIT's Elizabeth (Libby) MacDonald for your support in launching and participating in this course year after year as a guest speaker, for being so generous with your materials and content, and for providing a role model for my students and myself.

The secret I'll reveal here is that this textbook would not exist were it not for Professor Omar Bagasra, my mentor and friend, who turned to me as an afterthought as we were about to part ways following a meeting and said, "Hey, by the way, why don't you write a book?" He subsequently did much more than that by helping me structure the proposal, contact the publisher, and compartmentalize my time to get it all done. Most importantly, he taught me how to nurture my mind and my soul.

Without my family at Alfanar venture philanthropy, none of this would have any meaning. Thank you for providing me with the platform to practice what I preach and working to improve the lives of the most marginalized populations. This thanks goes both to the team, who not only tolerate but also appreciate and share my quirks and insanities, and to our investees, who are my day-to-day coworkers in Lebanon. *You* are what all this is about. Last but not least, I'd like to thank Bader Young Entrepreneurs Program and team and MIT Enterprise Forum Pan Arabia for hosting Alfanar Lebanon and me in their beautiful Coworking+961 space. I truly believe that place matters and that surroundings inspire. The opportunity to incubate my thoughts, and this book, in a serene oasis had a direct impact on what I produced, and I am infinitely grateful for that experience. Thank you for bearing with me and nurturing my need for deep concentration.

Tracing this all back to the root cause, ultimately, the largest thanks go to my parents. Realizing that not every student reading this book will have this ingredient to success, people who literally believe that you can do anything, I have tried to infuse this message into the book and serve as that person for my students. The source of all this is the two people who have infused me with this belief since my inception, constantly and repeatedly, without blinking. Thank you also to my dear sisters, who by far surpass me in their own writings, dreams, and achievements. I'm so lucky to have you, and you mean more to me than anything. Without you, I would not have done half of this, and I hope you know it. My friends and soul mates who have kept me sane, who not only humored me but also fueled me with their ideas, laughter, thought questions, and encouragement: I sometimes feel as if I've cheated, and one day someone will come up to me and recall you, because it's not possible to have scored the company of such celestial beings to share life's journey with. This is the meaning of life, taking care of those around you, and trying your best to collectively leave behind a world with more beauty and justice than when you started.

Author

Photo by Thomas Morgan, Reframed Pictures.

Teresa Chahine is the Social Entrepreneurship Program Leader at Harvard T.H. Chan School of Public Health, Center for Health and the Global Environment. She teaches social entrepreneurship at Harvard Chan School and Harvard Extension School, and trains social entrepreneurs worldwide. Dr. Chahine is also the director of Alfanar Lebanon, which she launched in 2012. Alfanar is a venture philanthropy organization that has been supporting social entrepreneurs in Lebanon and Egypt since 2005. To learn more about her work and how you can get involved, visit www.chgeharvard.org and www.alfanar.org.

Connect with her on Twitter @teresachahine.

Chapter 1

Introduction

Do you ever wonder what the world would be like if each person dedicated a large chunk of their brains, efforts, and resources to solving a set of social challenges? Have you ever wished that you could make a difference about the social disparities and injustices you care about? Many of us, whether living in one of the world's least developed or one of the world's most developed societies, find it hard to ignore suboptimal conditions that affect us and those around us. These could be local conditions or global conditions. They could include environmental degradation, pollution, corruption, lack of access to education or healthcare, and many others. In some cases, such conditions affect everyone; in most cases, they disproportionately affect the most vulnerable and underserved populations in our society.

How can we do something to change the face of these challenges? Each one of us has the potential to make a positive impact on a person, community, and social challenge. Certainly, the root causes of society's most pressing problems are complex, historical, and multifaceted, and it would be a gross simplification to say that one person can solve all the root causes. However, it is the lack of acceptance of the status quo that has driven many of the positive social changes and advancements over time. A systematic questioning and examination of why things are the way they are today, coupled with the tools and skills to investigate, formulate, and apply potential solutions, may allow us to take the first step in making changes.

If you envision a world that functions differently from what you see today, there is a social entrepreneur in you. Each one of us has the potential to apply our skills and resources to create better systems, services, and products that are lacking today or that are not accessed by a portion of peoples and populations. This book will help you get started in assessing the potential paths you can take to make the change you desire to see. Where you end up may be some place completely different from what you envisioned or ever thought you could imagine. The only way to find out is to get started... So, let's begin!

How This Book Works

This book is designed to help you create social ventures to address a social challenge of your choice. The word *social* here is used to refer to both social and environmental challenges. No matter your background, age, qualifications, or field of study, there is a core set of skills that can aid you in making a difference to improve the lives of underserved populations and help preserve or regenerate the earth's resources.

What social or environmental challenges do you care about? What resources could you mobilize to address those challenges? In this book, we will explore together the journey taken by a social entrepreneur in developing and implementing a solution to a pressing social or environmental problem or opportunity. In this introductory chapter, we will discuss the difference between social entrepreneurship and traditional activism, charity, or social work and the difference between social entrepreneurship and other forms of entrepreneurship. We will also review the blueprint of subsequent chapters and introduce some of the skills that will form the focus of our journey together.

Definitions

For the purposes of this book, we define *social entrepreneurship* as the process by which effective, innovative, and sustainable solutions are pioneered to meet social and environmental challenges. A social entrepreneur is someone who designs and implements an intervention, product, or service that improves the well-being of marginalized individuals and populations. A social enterprise is an organization (either nonprofit or for-profit) that is formed to meet a social or environmental challenge, that streamlines its operations and supply chain to maximize social impact and minimize the use of resources, and that uses a sustainable, replicable, and potentially scalable business model.

 Social entrepreneurship is a burgeoning field of study as today's generation of students and young professionals question the assumptions, work, and governance patterns set forth by previous generations. Why do we still have poverty? Why are we polluting and depleting our increasingly scarce natural resources? Many students and professionals today are applying a "can do" attitude of ending the social and environmental problems that have persisted for generations. With the increase in technology and access to information, it is not unthinkable that this may be possible. Increasingly, midcareer and seasoned executives and retired professionals are integrating social entrepreneurship into their careers or even launching new careers, applying the skills and experiences they gained over years and decades on the job to tackling social challenges.

As a field of practice, social pioneers have been implementing effective and innovative social interventions since the beginning of human society. However, only recently have the science and study of social entrepreneurship evolved and its terminology and methodology been integrated into general education and continuing professional education. Attention toward social entrepreneurship began to increase at the turn of the millennium as the successful entrepreneurs of Silicon Valley began to turn their talents and energies to tackling social challenges. It increased further with the development of microfinance techniques, which became popular both online (such as Kiva.org, pioneered by former Paypal.com entrepreneurs in Silicon Valley) and in remote rural areas (such as the Grameen Bank, which received worldwide acclaim and won the Nobel prize for providing banking to women living in poverty in rural Bangladesh). Today, business practitioners, nonprofit practitioners, governments, and grassroots movements worldwide are clamoring to join the social entrepreneurship movement, whereby private sector practices are applied to solving social problems.

Sustainable Development

In this book, we address social entrepreneurship in the context of sustainable development. In order to develop an intuitive understanding of what this term means, it is helpful to break it down

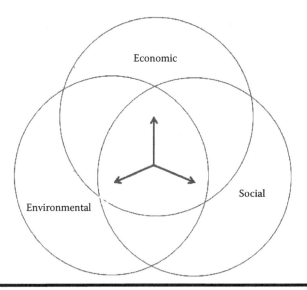

Figure 1.1   Growth in multiple directions and dimensions is the path to sustainable development.

into its parts. The word *development* is synonymous with *growth* (e.g., an embryo can develop into a full-grown adult, a start-up can develop into a large organization, a romance can develop into a lifelong partnership). The word *sustainable* means something that can last. Sustainable development means the growth of society in a direction that won't run into a wall. To keep growing, it is important to have an increasing or at least ongoing supply of resources, including financial, physical, environmental, and human resources.

Historically, it has often been that development of one component of society takes place at the expense of another, whether economic growth at the cost of environmental degradation, resulting in depletion of resources, or growth of one nation at the cost of another, or growth of social sub-populations at the cost of others within the same nation. This is still ongoing in our world today, but many people across sectors—in governments, in the corporate world, and in civil society and academia—are increasingly focused on ensuring that it is the sum of economic, social, and environmental growth that is considered as the ultimate goal (Figure 1.1).

Why Is Social Entrepreneurship Different from Commercial Entrepreneurship?

Many schools of thought point toward the positive social effects of any form of entrepreneurship. If an innovative and pioneering person or company produces a purely commercial product—let's take the initial creation of the mobile phone for use in developed markets—is this not social? Does it not produce benefits to society such as increasing communication, providing access to information, creating jobs, and many others? The answer is absolutely yes, most commercial enterprises do in fact produce the kind of positive social changes necessary for sustainable development!

Then why differentiate between social and other forms of entrepreneurship?

To clarify, social entrepreneurship refers to ventures and interventions targeting underserved populations, decreasing the gap between those who have access to social services and those who do not (see Figure 1.2). While commercial entrepreneurship often responds to a market opportunity,

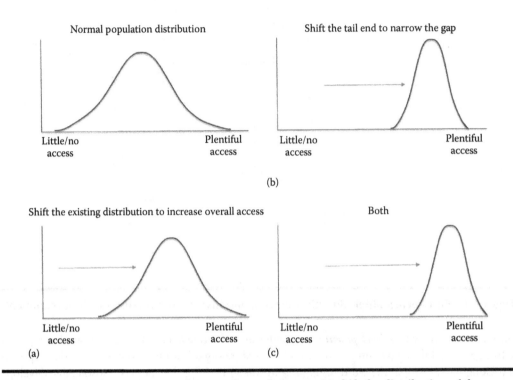

Figure 1.2 **Targeting access to underserved populations to (a) shift the distribution of the population curve, (b) shift the tail to narrow the gap, or (c) both.**

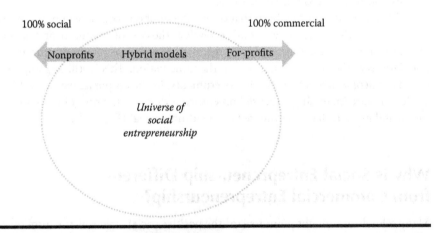

Figure 1.3 **Social entrepreneurship occupies a spectrum.**

social entrepreneurship often tackles a market failure. While the bottom line of a commercial enterprise is financial profit, the bottom line of a social enterprise is the social impact it creates (we will talk more about how to measure social impact in Chapter 7).

Before we proceed, please understand this: It is not black and white, and there is no neat line that cuts off social from other forms of entrepreneurship. Social ventures occupy the space between old-school commerce and old-school charity. In many societies around the world, there is a huge gap between social purpose organizations and businesses, and social entrepreneurship aims to fill that gap (Figure 1.3). So open your mind and don't be categorical. At the end of the day, what we're talking about here is a spectrum rather than a discrete category.*

How Is Social Entrepreneurship Different from Other Forms of Social Progress?

Social entrepreneurship is a form of social service and, like all forms of social service, is a path toward positive social change to improve the conditions, livelihoods, and standard of living of populations and ecosystems. Positive social change comes through multiple pathways, which can include advocacy, lobbying, awareness campaigns, policy papers, research, teaching, legislative changes, etc. Social entrepreneurship is simply one of these pathways and is characterized by the application of business methods to providing social products or services. While a researcher may write about a problem or analyze population data, an activist may create awareness through a social media campaign, and a case worker may accompany one person at a time or one family at a time out of poverty by connecting them with resources, a social entrepreneur will link these pieces of the supply chain together and deliver a service, product, or system that can be scaled to reach many people over a short period in a financially sustainable way.

This is well described in a short piece written by Dr. Larry Brilliant (who cofounded Seva Foundation, providing affordable technology to millions by driving down the cost of a sight-restoring operation) in a special series of essays published by the Stanford Social Innovation Review in 2013 on the 10th anniversary of its founding.[†] That is not to say that a social entrepreneur can solve all of the world's problems. Each piece of the supply chain and each of these and other different methodologies are a crucial component of the path to change. "No one can solve all the world's problems," as pointed out eloquently by Roger Martin, board member of the Skoll Foundation, in the same dialogue.[‡]

Social innovation can come in many shapes and forms. Oftentimes, a person working in an existing institution such as a government agency, large nongovernmental organization (NGO), or company comes up with or hears about a novel idea involving an innovative way of doing things differently from how they've always been done in that institution and decides to implement this new idea. That person can be an "intrapreneur," creating change within an existing entity and disrupting the status quo. Many of the leading corporate sustainability and corporate social responsibility (CSR; which we'll learn more about in Chapter 10) programs of the world's leading businesses were started by someone who stopped and asked, "Why do we do things the way we do?" Questioning the status quo, questioning all assumptions, and finding new ways of doing things are all possible without launching a new initiative or starting a new organization.

This is well captured in a story told time and time again by employees of the nonprofit organization City Year. This nonprofit was started by two college roommates looking to make a difference in the lives of inner city youth, who eventually built an organization around getting college graduates to work for one year in a public school in a low-income neighborhood; applying their skills, talents, and fresh perspective to transforming the lives of students in that school.[§] While the

---

* Gratitude goes to my wise friend and colleague Caterina Hill at Harvard Medical School, who responded with this beautiful blunt exclamation while I was explaining my topic of passion to her: "It's a spectrum!" thus helping me put it quite simply into words. Sometimes, the most obvious things are the hardest to put our fingers on!
† http://www.ssireview.org/articles/entry/fifty_years_of_social_change.
‡ http://www.ssireview.org/articles/entry/the_trouble_with_winning.
§ For more information on City Year, visit http://www.cityyear.org.

story takes its roots from an essay published in 1969 by Loren Eiseley, over the years, it has evolved as different employees and enthusiasts tell their own versions and add their own twists to the story. Here is one version: The story tells of a young girl who lived in a seaside town and was walking by the shore with her grandmother one day. She saw a beautiful starfish, with five bright tentacles, washing up onto the shore. The starfish eventually died, and changed color, and turned into stone. This upset the girl very much, and she asked her grandmother why this has to happen. Why does the starfish have to die? "Well, that's just how it's always happened around here," the grandmother replied. The girl thought about it and decided that was not reason enough for her. The next time she saw a starfish washing up onto shore, she lifted it and tossed it back into the water.

Decades later, that same girl strolled with her own grandchild by the sea. The grandchild looked over to the shore and noticed dozens of people all walking along the shore, bending down to pick up starfish and tossing them back into the sea. The child was puzzled and turned to his grandmother and asked, "What are those people doing? Why are they putting the starfish back into the water?" The grandmother simply smiled and replied, "Well, that's just how it's always been done around here."

Terminology

You may have noticed by now that the terms *social enterprise*, *social venture*, and *social start-up* are often used interchangeably to refer to an organization whose primary purpose or product advances social and/or environmental well-being and that operates using a financially sustainable model (Table 1.1). In this book, we will stick to the term *social venture* to emphasize the notion that it's up to you to create an entirely new model for social change—it can be a new initiative, an initiative within an existing organization, a new organization, or a project.

Institutions Supporting Social Entrepreneurs

You are about to embark on a journey that will hopefully last a very long time and evolve over the years. You should know that you are not alone! Many individuals and institutions believe in the power of social entrepreneurship to make a difference. There are numerous organizations, forums, networks, listservs, conferences, and events bringing together social entrepreneurs and those supporting them all over the world. Support can come in the form of investment, technical support, knowledge exchange, awareness, and advocacy. We will go into more detail about these different resources in later chapters, but for now, it's a good idea for you to surf around on the websites of some leading institutions in the social entrepreneurship space. Check out a list of a few popular examples in Box 1.1. Resources posted on these websites will prove invaluable to you as you develop your own venture, and once it is developed, you might be able to join one of the fellowship programs or other networks.

Common Characteristics in Social Entrepreneurship

At the end of the day, the distinction between social entrepreneurship and other forms of social innovation is not black and white, and oftentimes, these terms are used interchangeably. What is important to focus on are the characteristics that have been observed in successful social ventures. Whether you are starting your own new venture or creating change within an existing

At end: come up with
destructive idea for course

Table 1.1 What Is a...?

Start-up	A new company or organization
Social start-up	A new company or organization that was formed with the primary purpose of tackling a social or environmental challenge
Social enterprise	A company or organization that provides a social product or service at a fee. The main differences between a social enterprise and commercial enterprise are the nature of the product or service, the fee, and the distribution channels, all of which are crafted to maximize access for underserved individuals and populations
Social venture In this book we focus on social ventures — you decide the shape and form!	This term is used broadly to refer to any social initiative, which can include an organization, project, or initiative working toward positive social and environmental change. It is often used interchangeably with the above terms and has less defined attributes attached to it
Social entrepreneur	Someone who designs and implements a new method, process, product, or service that addresses a social or environmental challenge
Social intrapreneur	Someone who designs and implements a new method, process, product, or service within an existing organization to address a social or environmental challenge
Social innovation	The act of pioneering new methods, processes, products, and services that address social and environmental challenges
Social entrepreneurship	The act of pioneering new methods, processes, products, and services that address social and environmental challenges through the creation of new organizations or initiatives

Don't let these terms confuse you and don't get hung up on the hair-splitting differences among them!

BOX 1.1A SELECT INSTITUTIONS SUPPORTING SOCIAL ENTREPRENEURS

There are numerous institutions worldwide that were formed to mobilize resources (knowledge, people, funding) for social entrepreneurs. Below are some of the most active organizations which could serve as a resource for you. Check them out, and see if you can find others! (in alphabetical order):

Acumen. Impact investing fund based in NY, operating in East Africa, Southeast Asia, South America

Alfanar. Venture philanthropy organization based in London, operating in Egypt and Lebanon

Ashoka. Fellowship program and global network of changemakers headquartered in Washington, DC

Aspen Institute. Education and policy studies organization with fellowships and leadership networks

Echoing Green. Fellowship and Investment Program based in NY and operating globally

CASE. Center for Advancement of Social Entrepreneurship at Duke University, open to entrepreneurs worldwide

Nesta. UK-based innovation, research, and investment charity

REDF. Investing and knowledge building organization with online workshop containing resources and tools

Sankalp Forum. Annual summit and awards based in India, convening innovators and investors worldwide

Schwab. Switzerland-based foundation providing networking opportunities and platform for social entrepreneurs

SE Hub. Social Entrepreneurship Resource Hub at Stanford University, open to social entrepreneurs worldwide

Skoll Network. Includes Foundation, Awards, Global Threats Fund, World Forum, and Oxford Centre

SOCAP. Social Capital Markets, an organization bringing together social investors and social entrepreneurs an through annual event series, media platform, and online community.

Social Enterprise Coalition. UK national body for social enterprise, membership services and online advice

Social Innovation Forum. Boston-based accelerator program for innovators and investors

UnLtd. UK-based organization providing support and resources for social entrepreneurs nationwide and online

BOX 1.1B   OTHER POPULAR ONLINE RESOURCES

A multitude of online resources and repositories are available to support social entrepreneurs at various stages of their journey. Here are some of the most popular that we think you might enjoy! Check out these three websites in addition to those listed above:

D.I.Y. Toolkit. Social entrepreneurship planning tools and templates from various sources

Root Cause. Research institute generating valuable data and "how to" resources such as business planning

S.E. Toolbelt. Online hub where you can download resources on various topics

organization, it is helpful to be familiar with and keep in mind the key characteristics that are most likely to result in an effective, scalable, and sustainable social impact.

First, think of your social venture as a start-up. In the business world, a start-up is a new company that is formed to introduce a new product or service that aims to penetrate the market and gain a share of the existing consumers or add a new customer base to the market. Like any start-up, a social start-up is characterized by an *ambition* to impact a large number of lives, to *scale* rapidly, and to transform or *disrupt* the status quo.

An example of this is one of the first of many social start-ups growing out of Silicon Valley after the tech boom of the early millennium, Kiva, which linked people in high-poverty nations with people in high-income nations via the Internet, allowing them to lend and borrow money. By providing access

For profit /not for

to the savings of everyday people in the United States, who were returned their money after a speci-fied period of time with adjustments for inflation, this start-up allowed low-income individuals and communities around the world to lift themselves out of poverty by making the purchases necessary to increase their productivity and income. Founded in 2005, Kiva began with seven loans, which were repaid within six months. During its first year, the organization facilitated half a million US dollars in loans, scaling to almost $100 million in its fourth year. By its eighth year, Kiva had facilitated $400 million in loans, from one million lenders to one million borrowers in over 200 countries.*

This brings us to another important point. A social venture can be for-profit and it can be non-profit. It is not defined by the business model but by the *financial viability* of the venture and the allocation of revenues. Some ventures may have room for profit, whereby end users are charged a fee for the social product or service provided, and this fee is enough to cover the costs incurred in providing that product or service. In such cases, profits are reinvested back into the venture, to reach more people. That is not to say that the social entrepreneur and others working to provide the social good are not remunerated. To attract and retain top talent and provide the highest quality prod-uct or service possible, it is important to offer competitive salaries and other incentives. The main distinction is that after the predetermined salaries and remunerations are allocated, profits from a social venture go back into scaling the social impact, rather than benefiting the social entrepreneur.

HR

Other social ventures may not have room for profit; in many cases, the market value of the prod-uct or service or the willingness-to-pay of the target population may not be enough to cover the costs incurred in providing it. This is often the case in the social sector, as many of the problems we are trying to address result from market failures or externalities, and costs of reaching underserved populations are often disproportionately high due to weak systems and infrastructure. In such a case, the revenue generated by the social venture is complemented with external sources such as grants, donations, and crowdfunding. We will go into more detail about various business models and financing mechanisms for social ventures in Chapter 10. There are many business models for success in social change, and choosing the right one depends on the product or service in question, the setting in which it is pro-vided, the target population, supply chain, and many other factors. In Kiva's case, the lender is invited to add an optional "tip" of 15% while making a loan online, helping to cover operating expenses.

Social impact

While financial viability is a key to success, in social entrepreneurship, it is considered a means to an end and not an end in itself. The end goal and the only bottom line of a social venture is its social impact. What are the characteristics that determine whether the social impact is effective, sustain-able, and scalable? An effective social venture is built around a solution that is *evidence based*. This can begin with an idea that has not been tested and that has been developed through a small pilot project to determine what works and what doesn't before scaling into a larger growth stage. This involves collecting data to measure the social impact, in order to deliver the social product or service using the formula that has been proven to work best for the target population based on current knowledge.

> While financial viability is a key to success, in social entrepreneurship, it is considered a means to an end and not an end in itself. The end goal and the only bottom line of a social venture is its social impact.

When developing this product or service, a social entrepreneur will aim to tackle the *root causes* of a problem where possible rather than its symptoms. Many development efforts over time

---

* For more information on Kiva, visit www.kiva.org.

have tried and failed to solve a social ill by putting a band-aid on the wound rather than healing it. While the (metaphorical) band-aid is sometimes needed and sometimes the only choice, social entrepreneurs need to ask when defining the challenge we are setting out to tackle, why do we face this challenge today? Does my solution tackle the root cause, or is there an upstream factor I could reach for instead? One of the tools that social purpose organizations have used over time to build their programming is a logical framework, as we will see in Chapter 7. A helpful result of using such frameworks is that it pushes the planner to ask "why?" If a social entrepreneur aims to get more girls into school, the first question asked is "why are they not in school?" If, for example, one of the primary reasons is that they are spending hours each day collecting water for their families and are thus not able to attend school, the next question is "why are they spending hours a day collecting water?" What are some ways we can increase access to water for that population, or what are some ways in which we can design collection methods that decrease the amount of time collecting water? The answers to these questions require skills in design and in costing and most importantly require information about the local setting, geography, society, and culture.

> The number 1 rule of social entrepreneurship is: Do not let your desire to be a social entrepreneur become a delusion of grandeur, superiority, or supernatural powers!

This brings us to the next important point. For a social product or service to be effective, accessible, and scalable, a key factor that increases the likelihood of success is designing the product or service with input from the target population. Any social entrepreneur who thinks he or she can enter a community with the perfect solution in mind and implement it as is will most likely fail. The most likely solutions to stick are the ones that come from within the community. The number 1 rule of social entrepreneurship is: Do not let your desire to be a social entrepreneur become a delusion of grandeur, superiority, or supernatural powers!

To be effective, the social venture must be *accessible* to the target population. No matter how effective a solution is in design, or how powerful a new technology is, if it does not reach the last mile, it will not have a social impact. Oftentimes, this last mile can be quite literal, such as in the case of health products or services that cannot be delivered to the patients who need them because of inadequate roads. In other cases, bridging the gap between the intervention and the target population requires changing the design, cost, and other features of the product or service to meet the sociocultural and economic characteristics of the target population. This is also part of making it *acceptable* to the end user, within the local context and culture.

Beyond social factors, a key determinant in bridging these multiple aspects of design, cost, and delivery of the social product or service to the target population is the physical distribution channels—how will we actually deliver this? We will go into more detail about all these factors in the coming chapters and apply them to your own social venture.

What Are Some of the Basic Skills Needed for Social Entrepreneurship?

Many of the skills needed to start a social venture are very similar to those needed in starting a commercial enterprise. These include building the organizational structure, business planning, accounting, marketing, project management, human resource management, communications,

Social entrepreneurship is...	Skills required...
Disruptive Ambitious, scalable Financially viable	The Entrepreneurship Component: Innovation and Business Skills
Evidence based Accessible to target population Effective in addressing root causes of the problem	The Social Component: Social Service Skills

Figure 1.4 Defining characteristics of social entrepreneurship and corresponding interdisciplinary skills.

stakeholder analysis, and building external partnerships. In addition to these basic business skills, social entrepreneurs must further be able to characterize the problem they are trying to solve by collecting information on characteristics of the affected population, existing obstacles and infrastructure, and past attempts to solve the problem and why they have failed. A process to co-create the solution with the community then takes place to ensure that it is accessible, affordable, and acceptable by the community. Social entrepreneurs also set measurable objectives to monitor and evaluate the social impact they set out to create. Thus, the skill set required by a social entrepreneur includes skills from the worlds of both business and social services (Figure 1.4).

How to Use This Book

This book will guide you along the step-by-step process from characterizing your challenge to formulating your solution to implementing, measuring, and scaling the solution. It assumes no prior knowledge of social entrepreneurship and can be applied to various subject matter fields including science, commerce, law, education, health, and others. The contents of this book are based on the author's practical experience in working with social entrepreneurs around the world, synthesizing key tools, resources, and approaches to maximize the chance of success in producing the desired social impact. It is a nuts and bolts how-to guide that helps readers emerge from their silos to design and implement a solution.

This book is designed to function like a manual, to support a young social entrepreneur in developing and implementing a social venture from A to Z. (The word *young* here refers to the reader who is at the start of a new journey, regardless of your calendar age!) Exercises and learning tools are built into each chapter, including example boxes, discussion questions, planning templates, and assignments. Case examples of social entrepreneurship will be presented for various sectors including health, environment, energy, education, agriculture, and microfinance, representing various geographies and cultures from regions around the world, from both urban and rural scenarios.

We will also hear from a host of social entrepreneurs and thought leaders in the field. Each person will chime in with his or her own perspective and ways of doing things. The goal is to hammer home the idea that there is not one correct way of doing things, no magical model that will solve all the world's problems. It is up to each one of us to find the model that works for us and our challenge. The best we can hope to do is exchange success stories and lessons learned, to spread our impact, and together collectively change the face of the social challenges we are confronted with today.

Interview Box. Bill Drayton, Founder and CEO of Ashoka Innovators for the Public

TC: The term social entrepreneurship is often traced back to you. What do these words mean to you?

BD: An entrepreneur is someone who changes patterns in her field. A social entrepreneur is one who is committee to the good of all. This is a characteristic of the person, not the sector. Even in education, some people are in it for the money or for various reasons—trying to put a sector on it, or a business model on it, is not the way to go. Struggling with financial or subject matter structures is a losing game—the world is changing, and categories are shifting.

TC: What about the term social impact. What do these words mean to you?

BD: There are three layers of impact. The first is direct service: teachers in classroom, workers in factories, there are different measures of impact in service. This is where social entrepreneurs create their prototypes. Then, the second level is pattern change. Social entrepreneurs want to change society and the world—it's more than just how many people can you serve. Finally, the third level is mindset and framework change. Changemakers offer a new way of thinking and doing things, so that others can then apply it. That's their impact—the ripple effect.

TC: What advice do you have for someone about to embark on a social entrepreneurship journey?

BD: It's more than just having an idea and then implementing. How will you change your field? One aspect is your inner drive, something deep within you; you're looking for something you care about that you can change. Another aspect is how good you are at the "how-to." Are you thinking and iterating? Do you have an engineering (making things) mindset? It's an iterative process that goes on for years and years.

TC: You have been known to say that everyone is a changemaker. Do you think this can be learned?

BD: Everyone must be a changemaker because the game is changing. The world so far has been defined by repetition; that's how we've been raised, learned to read and write, trained for jobs. That will not do anymore. People reading this book have to master being a changemaker and have to aspire to be a social entrepreneur. A world in which everyone is a changemaker is a world where everyone is operating for the good of all—you need special skills to do that. Being a changemaker means everyone is powerful. Goodbye world defined by repetition—hello world defined by changemakers!

In the next chapter, you will be asked to pick a challenge of your choice and create a solution for it in the subsequent chapters. This will allow you to apply the different learning tools and concepts to developing your solution, building the skills you will need to implement it along the way. Don't panic if you have multiple challenges that you care about and want to address—Pick one to use along your learning journey, and you can tackle the others next, when your solution-building muscles are stronger. In choosing your topic, think about what you will most likely be able to realistically implement in the future. This will depend upon your knowledge base and experience, *social enterprise events*

location, and the resources available to you, including your networks. Because the nature of this work is already ambitious by definition, it is wise to start by keeping it simple, anticipating all the challenges and complications that will then unfold.

Conversely, if you do not have a topic of interest, don't panic! Spend some time reading about the social challenges that affect your community and learn more about their root causes. You will find something that speaks to you and that you feel you may be able to contribute toward solving. Get out there and talk to people! Social entrepreneurship is not something that takes place in a living room, classroom, conference hall, or in any ivory tower setting. You will need to roll up your sleeves and get your hands dirty! This book will equip you with the frameworks and tools necessary to dig deeper.

Most importantly, it is critical to keep in mind that social entrepreneurship is not linear. You can, and will, go back and start over, reassess, reconsider, and redevelop your solution and even your formulation of the challenge you are tackling. It is a dynamic process, so don't be afraid to take the first step; you can always come back and go in another direction.

The chapters in this book have been arranged in an order that is easy to follow and will facilitate the development of your ideas and the collection of evidence to build your venture. However, it is important to understand that this is not always the order in which social entrepreneurship takes place. Most of the time, there is no order! So keep in mind that while you go through the exercises prescribed in this book, you'll need to open your mind to the idea that solutions are born in many different ways.

Learning Tools

Among the tools and templates you will find in this book are some of the planning methods used in the fields described previously, carrying a combination of business and innovation and social service methodologies (Figure 1.5). In Chapter 2, one of the tools we'll share will be visual diagrams that you can use to help wrap your head around all the information you'll be digging up about your challenge. In Chapter 3, we'll talk about tools you can use during the co-creation process, such as a stakeholder analysis and asset mapping. In Chapter 4, you'll learn about user-driven design, rapid prototyping, and a template to help develop your theory of change. In Chapter 5, you will use a business canvas to assess end users, partners, channels, and other important components of

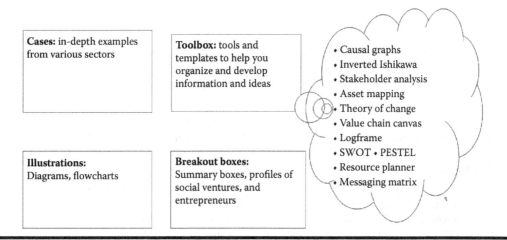

Figure 1.5 The different kinds of learning tools in this book.

building your supply chain. In Chapter 6, you will create a process map to outline the nuts and bolts of the operations you'll need to run to deliver your solution. In Chapter 7, you will use the logframe template to build backward from the social outcome you're working to create, starting with your ultimate goal based on the root causes of the problem you are trying to solve, and specifying your objectives, the measurable outputs you will produce to meet those objectives, and the activities and costs of producing those outputs. In Chapter 8, you will conduct a SWOT analysis and PESTEL analysis to analyze key threats and opportunities, and in Chapter 9 you will put it all together in a pitch summarizing your business plan. In Chapter 10, you will learn about a resource planning tool to help you navigate the various sources of funds and other information available to you; and in Chapter 11 you'll learn about different ways to institutionalize your venture. In Chapter 12, we will introduce a marketing matrix to help develop your messaging. Then we'll take a step back in the final chapter, Chapter 13, to assess the big picture and where we want to go with all this.

All the concepts and tools in this book were developed over long periods by multiple individuals and organizations in multiple sectors; the author does not claim to have invented any of them, and most can be found online in some publicly available format. References for these resources are cited throughout. This book is simply a repository and reference book for you to use as a guide to build your social entrepreneurship practice. You are strongly encouraged to be resourceful and conduct your own external research to identify different formats and methodologies that are more suited to your social venture as you develop it.

Along the way, you will also be reading the stories of social entrepreneurs who have taken the same steps you are about to take. They will share their stories of trial and error with you, what worked and what didn't work for them. These stories will give you ideas and encouragement and point out what to look for in formulating your problem and solution, building your organization and your team.

In summary, the learning tools we will be using in the coming chapters include the following:

■ A step-by-step guide for building your venture
■ Planning tools and templates for key steps along the way
■ Examples of existing social ventures in various sectors
■ Interviews with social entrepreneurs
■ Assignments for each chapter, which you will apply to your own social venture

Modules

Let's take a quick overview of the roadmap ahead. Steps to implement your own intervention can be broken down into learning modules, and over the coming chapters, we will go through these steps together one at a time. As you implement your social venture, you may need to revisit some of these steps multiple times. This is because social entrepreneurship is an iterative and dynamic process. It is almost impossible to complete the journey in a linear fashion, as each step along the way, you will collect new information and feedback that will continuously shape and reshape the outcome.

1. Define your challenge (Chapter 2)
   – What social challenge are you aiming to solve? It is recommended to start with the challenge and build the solution around it, rather than start with a solution looking for a problem (or as the saying goes, "a hammer looking for a nail").
   – What data and statistics are available about the challenge? What are its root causes?
   – Who is affected by it? Characteristics of the affected population include the following:

- Sociodemographic characteristics: age, gender, income, education, occupation, and others
- Geographic characteristics: where are they located, what is the physical infrastructure like, are there physical barriers to delivering a solution, are there environmental factors causing or affected by this problem
- Cultural characteristics: traditions or norms that affect the way people think or act related to this problem, and how they would react to potential solutions
- Other social characteristics: is the population isolated, are there social networks in place, what do they look like, is the population homogenous or is there a large amount of diversity, what other "co-challenges" are they facing
  - What has been tried before, why didn't it work; i.e., why are we still facing this problem today?

2. Co-creating and designing the solution (Chapters 3 and 4)
   - You'll need to work together with those affected most by this challenge to figure out what your value proposition to them can be. Then you build your solution around that.
     - What are the needs and preferences of the community? What opportunities are there to build a solution with available resources? What do we need to look out for?
     - What are the resources available based on the physical and social setting?
     - Who are the stakeholders that must be brought together for any solution that is developed to actually work?
     - What are the key considerations for delivering this product or service? What are the main barriers that need to be addressed in order to reach the last mile?
   - What might this solution look like? How will it work? What characteristics does it need to have?
   - How is your solution tied back to the challenge you are trying to change? What is your theory of change?
   - How can you develop new ideas and test them?
   - Who do you need to recruit to help you?

3. Delivering your solution (Chapters 5 and 6)
   - How can you build systems to deliver your solution effectively?
   - How will you reach your target audience? What is your marketing and distribution plan?
   - What will be the nuts and bolts of your operation?
   - Beyond the founders, what human resources are needed to build the organization?

4. Measuring your social impact (Chapter 7)
   - Measuring social impact is not something that happens at the end, it's one of the first things you think about because it informs your subsequent trajectory.
   - What does success look like? Define success and work backward from it to define your path to get there!
   - How will you know if you are making a difference? Set performance indicators, both in terms of processes and outcomes.

5. Ensuring financial viability (Chapter 8)
   - How will this all be financially viable? What is your business model?
   - What are the main costs and revenues? What are your financial projections, what resources will you need to invest, and how/when will you recoup them?
   - What are the strengths and weaknesses of your proposed model, what external opportunities can you leverage; what are the external threats to your success and how can you mitigate your risks?

6. Funding and structuring your venture (Chapters 9 through 11)
   - What resources do you need to make all this happen? We'll talk about both financial and other resources.
   - What funding sources are available to you?
   - What are the different funding vehicles and social investment approaches that you need to understand and navigate?
   - How will you roll your venture? Will it be within an existing institution or do you need to start a new organization?
   - If you do need to create a new organization, what are the various registration options available in different parts of the world?
   - What are the components of a healthy organization; what are the different systems and processes you need to put into place to grow sustainably?
7. Communicating and creating partnerships for scale (Chapters 12 and 13)
   - Who are the various stakeholders you need to exchange information with? These include your end user, your team, your partners, and others.
   - What pieces of information do you need to exchange with each stakeholder, and how will you get that information across?
   - Once you are up and running, you'll need a growth plan to help you work your way toward the definition of success you set for yourself from the start.
   - This definition might include reaching the largest number of people possible, or it might have targeted a very difficult to reach population that requires a very different trajectory from the general population.
   - As you grow, what needs to change? Starting your venture requires very different resources, skills, approaches, and strategies than growing.
   - There are numerous ways your social venture can grow and expand its reach, and many of these involve reaching outside of your own organization to maximize the total impact you can work with others to help create.

Learning Objectives

As you can tell from the nature of these modules, by the time you are finished with this book, you will be looking at the world in a whole new way. At many points along the journey, you might feel intimidated, overwhelmed, and tempted to toss everything into the wind. This is normal! It's a sign that you're immersing yourself and engaging in the learning process. Remember that each and every social entrepreneur has felt this way at multiple points along the road (or more like multiple points in the same day!). If we are going to let the scale, nature, and complexity of the challenges facing us today daunt us, then we will never be able to change them. Just take it one step at a time, and you will see for yourself, anything is possible.

As you progress through the sequential stages of the textbook, look at all the things you will learn how to do!

Upon completion you will be able to

■ Characterize a social challenge of your choice in an evidence-based manner using available data and statistics, describing root causes, barriers, and affected populations
■ Investigate localized settings, nuances, cochallenges, best practices in facing this challenge, and opportunities to change the status quo

- Develop a solution centered on the target population and taking into account existing infra-structure and networks, designed to maximize access and minimize costs
- Test the assumptions linking the solution to the social challenge and specify success metrics to indicate whether the intended changes are being made
- Build a business model to sustain the delivery of the solution, exploring multiple financing mechanisms and potential revenue streams in line with the overall mission
- Pitch and present the idea, exchanging information with the end users, funders, team, and other stakeholders
- Develop the organizational frameworks and team members to deliver the solution in a sus-tainable manner
- Develop a strategy to engage stakeholders and create partnerships to ensure success

Summary and Next Steps

Congratulations! You are about to embark on a life-changing journey. That part of you that has always longed to tackle the challenges facing our world today is about to become very, very alive. And have no doubt—we are aiming to create a monster! With the tools and concepts enclosed in this book, you will build the skills and mindset required to tackle the social challenge of your choice. Keep checking back in along the way, revisiting each step before, and ensuring that your solution cumulatively takes into account all the pieces of knowledge you will gather along the way (see Summary box).

Exercise: Your Assignment for This Chapter

The work starts now! Write down your answers to the thought questions below, using only *one sentence* per question. This is among the most needed skills you will need as a social entrepreneur! Spend a lot of time thinking and researching and then find a way to summarize your answers in a clear and concise manner. You might write pages and pages of notes before you're able to formulate your one sentence. This is good—hold on to these for later, you will need them.

Thought questions:

1. Thinking back to the information, people, and experiences you have been exposed to up until this moment in your life, what would you say are among the top social challenges you have spent time thinking about to date? (One bullet point or sentence per issue. Try to restrict yourself to the 3–5 social challenges you have interfaced with the most.)
2. For each challenge you listed, in one sentence per question please answer the following questions:
   a. What opportunities have you had to gain insight into this challenge over the course of your lifetime?
   b. Has your experience been personal or professional, firsthand or through reading/studies (or a combination)?
3. Think back to a failed attempt to tackle one of the challenges you've listed above. It could have been by you or someone else. Describe what was attempted. Why didn't it work? (2 sentences total.)
4. Each one of us holds one or more positions in society, whether as a student, professional, parent, or community member. In your current role(s), what opportunities and resources are available

to you that you can leverage to contribute to tackling one of the social challenges above? (These could include people, knowledge, events, physical or political or financial resources, or other.)

5. By the time you finish this book, what new knowledge, awareness or skills do you hope to gain more of? Are there any milestones or targets you'd like to accomplish?

CHAPTER SUMMARY

■ Social entrepreneurship is the process by which effective, innovative, and sustainable solutions are pioneered to meet social and environmental challenges.

■ This is implemented through a social venture, which can take many shapes and forms, designed to deliver a solution addressing a social challenge in a financially viable way.

■ This book approaches social entrepreneurship in the context of sustainable development: the growth of society in multiple dimensions, including economic, social, and environmental.

■ What distinguishes social entrepreneurship from other forms of entrepreneurship is that it serves marginalized populations, often responding to market failures. Financial viability is a means to an end, not an end in and of itself.

■ Skills needed by a social entrepreneur combine business, management, and innovation skills alongside research, social service, and communications skills.

■ This book provides tools, templates, and exercises to help build these skills. It also includes examples of social ventures across sectors, case studies, and interviews with social entrepreneurs.

■ As we proceed through the chapters, you will develop your own social venture, starting with a challenge of your choice and building an evidence-based solution tackling its root causes. Now, let's begin!

Social Ventures Mentioned in This Chapter

Company profile: Grameen Bank, www.grameen-info.org.
Founded in 1976 as an experimental project, in Jobra village of Chittagong district of Bangladesh. Later established as a specialized bank in 1983.
Product/service: Grameen Bank provides the impoverished in rural Bangladesh access to credit and other financial services without the need for collateral.
Goal: Alleviate poverty for the poorest of the poor by targeting and providing financial services to women in rural Bangladesh.
How it works: Grameen Bank has reversed conventional banking practices by removing the need for collateral and building a system built on accountability, mutual trust, creativity, and participation. Low income women in a community form groups of five, and several groups are federated into a "center" which meets weekly with a Grameen staff member. Loan proposals, collection of savings, and loan installments take place at the center meetings. It is the group and center that decide on whether to approve a new loan by a group member. The bank operates under the assumption that if the poor are given access to credit, they will identify and create viable income-generating businesses such as weaving, manufacturing pottery, raising poultry and livestock, cultivating vegetables and groups, running grocery shops, and sewing, to name a few.

Company Profile: Kiva, www.kiva.org.

Founded in 2005, San Francisco, California, USA.

Product/service: Kiva works with microfinance institutions in five continents to provide loans to people who do not have access to traditional banks. The company relies on over 450 volunteers worldwide.

Goal: To connect people by leveraging the Internet and a worldwide network of microfinance institutions, to provide microloans and alleviate poverty.

How it works: Created by executives from Paypal, TiVo, and other leading tech companies. Kiva allows anyone in the world to lend money online. Lenders pick a region or country and sift through the stories of those looking for funds to grow a business, go to school, implement clean energy, and more. Once a loan is given, the lender receives updates as the borrower works toward his or her goals and repays the loan. Lenders get back every cent—meaning that one $25 loan can be used to help alleviate poverty over and over again! Kiva proudly boasts a 98.75% lender repayment rate.

Company Profile: City Year, www.cityyear.org.

Founded in 1988, Boston, Massachusetts, USA.

Product/service: Education-focused national service organization dedicated to helping students and schools succeed.

Goal: To help students stay in school and on track to graduate from high school, ready for college and career success.

How it works: Diverse teams of highly trained City Year AmeriCorps members, who have been recruited through a highly selective recruitment process, provide high-impact student, classroom, and school-wide support. Using the holistic City Year "Whole School Whole Child" model, City Year AmeriCorps members provide individualized educational and emotional support to at-risk students and also work to establish a positive learning environment. A recent third-party study shows that schools that partner with City Year were 2–3 times more likely to realize math and English gains.

Chapter 2

Characterizing Your Challenge

PART ONE: INTRODUCTION

The very beginning of your journey starts with identifying and characterizing the challenge you are tackling. Before you even start thinking about developing the solution, it is important that you invest enough time and resources in understanding the challenge to the extent possible.

You are not alone in wanting to tackle all the challenges under the sun—we've all been there! But if you want to get anything done, you need to focus. The best way to get results is to proceed one step at a time.

This chapter will help you focus on one challenge to work on throughout the course of this book, to build your solution step by step. First, we'll start by characterizing the nature of what it is you are trying to change.

The best way to fail is to not spend enough time understanding the nature of the issue you are tackling. What other social entrepreneurs have learned before you is that this is something that changes with context. As we discussed in the first chapter, there are no one-size-fits-all solutions. And do you know why? The answer is quite simple. It's because there are no one-size-fits-all problems! While the core needs of the human race are shared by us all, the realities of each person's life depend on the context she or he lives in.

> Most social challenges we will talk about in this book do not affect everyone equally.

In this book, we will approach this by first collecting information that is already out there on the topic of your choice and then zooming in on the context in which you'll be working and collecting your own information. The next chapter focuses on the in-context immersion. In this chapter, we'll focus on how to frame your investigation, where to go about looking for information, and how to think about what it is exactly that you're trying to do when you first set out to characterize your challenge.

Because we are applying the social entrepreneurship approach, we start with the social part first: the people.

Let's start with some definitions. By social challenge, we mean anything about the world that you want to change that affects others. Most social challenges we will talk about in this book do not affect everyone equally. The people who are most affected are those who have already been disadvantaged by facing multiple challenges. For example, climate change affects us all, but it affects people living in poverty in remote rural areas more than most others. Air pollution and water pollution affect us all, but they affect people living in urban slums more harshly than most of us. Because we're applying the social entrepreneurship approach, we start with the social part first: the people. We try to understand who is affected by this issue, what the causes are, how it is manifested in their lives, and what they think should be done about it. You might already have an idea or a solution right now that you are already thinking about implementing. And you might stick with that idea throughout the course of the book! But you also might change your solution once you start your investigation. This happens very, very often in the life of a social entrepreneur. We go through many iterations before we find the right fit.

Characterizing a social challenge consists of two points of view: seeing the problem and seeing the opportunity.

Two Important Viewpoints

Characterizing a social challenge consists of two points of view: seeing the problem and seeing the opportunity. The problem is the issue you would like to change. The opportunity is the part that you think you can change about it. Sometimes, the opportunity is staring you in the face! Other times, you have to work hard for it. The reason it's important to understand these two aspects is that it's not uncommon for a social entrepreneur to start by seeing an opportunity first. You might see an untapped resource, and think about ways to mobilize that resource to solve a social problem. An example of an untapped resource that could be turned into an opportunity is a human resource, such as young people who could volunteer to improve their environment or society; or a group of women working in the same village who could be brought together to form a social fund. But even when you are working to meet an opportunity such as an untapped resource, you need to trace back the social impact you want to create, to the social challenge you are addressing. For the previous examples, this would mean understanding how these young people could be mobilized to prevent environmental deterioration and how household poverty in this village could be solved through a social fund led by these women. Understanding why the problem exists and the channels through which it manifests itself will allow you to more strongly build your solution around the problem. The reason it's important to start with the problem—or trace back the opportunity to the problem—is that there is something about the world that you are hoping to change. Understanding what that is and putting it at the heart and core of your social venture will help ensure that all the work you are putting into this will in fact create the impact you are trying to achieve.

Sometimes, the opportunity is staring you in the face! Other times, you have to work hard for it.

Seeing the Opportunities

As a social entrepreneur, feel free to unleash the visionary in you! Acknowledging the importance of having an in-depth understanding of why things are the way they are today does not mean putting aside the ability to imagine how they could be different. If you have a vision of how things could be better, that is a good place to start too! The main recommendation here is that you first ask yourself why things aren't like that already and what the challenges are that people face today, and then you can be better equipped to make things into what you think they should be.

Do you envision a landscape where everyone has access to information through Internet connectivity, so that they'll know what's going on in the world around them? You can make this change, anything is possible, just make sure to equip yourself with the knowledge of how things came to be the way they are today and who the players involved are. Tackling a great challenge is best done when you have assessed the landscape, the obstacles, the opportunities, and the resources available to you. Part of making your vision come true is to understand why things are like this today, and this could be one of the first steps to unlocking the path to a different tomorrow.

Social and environmental outcomes are multifaceted and there are no silver bullets.

Understanding the Challenges

It goes without saying that most social and environmental challenges are multidimensional. Environmental deterioration, poverty, lack of social safety nets, and unemployment are all due to multiple causal pathways that cannot all be solved with the same intervention. Many humanitarian organizations, foundations, private investors, and other funders often search for a "silver bullet" that will solve a problem with one solution. If only it were that simple! Social and environmental outcomes are multifaceted and there are no silver bullets. Social entrepreneurs working together to tackle various causal pathways will have a transformative cumulative impact if they can identify the exact challenge they are tackling, the pathways they are zeroing in on to tackle it, and the impact they will demonstrate as a result. We will talk more about charting your pathway and impact in future chapters; for now, let's focus on the first and perhaps the most important step: characterizing the challenge.

Scope of This Chapter

Providing information on the multitude of social and environmental challenges we face today is beyond the scope of this chapter. The focus of this chapter is to underscore the importance of building your solution around the challenge you are setting out to change. You will learn about what it means to characterize a challenge, what pieces of information you should be looking for, and where you might be able to find them. Different levels of evidence, data, and other forms of information will be described. We will also talk about the various dimensions you should look for in order to truly characterize a challenge from the inside out and get a 360-degree, 3D+ picture. Here, the plus sign refers to the notion that most problems have many more than three dimensions! Regardless of the source of data, you should be looking for the different faces of the challenge you are tackling. These include its geographic distribution (where it is) and its sociodemographic distribution (who it affects). It also includes the challenge's scope in terms of how widespread it is and how deep its impact is. Trend over time is another factor to consider, as are "co-challenges"—other challenges that are closely interlinked with the one you are addressing.

Data Is Power

In commercial entrepreneurship, it is commonly said that fewer than 1 in 10 start-ups succeed. In social entrepreneurship, the jury is still out, as experts continue to debate on whether there is a higher or lower rate of success. On the one hand, the basic social problems we face today are multifactorial and extremely difficult to solve. This is why they still exist! On the other hand, social entrepreneurs are armed with a weapon that can help inform their likelihood of success if applied properly. That weapon is data! A wealth of information and research has been collected and conducted on social problems facing various societies and communities to date. Researchers from government agencies, universities, think tanks, private consultancy firms, and NGOs have spent millions of dollars and person-years* characterizing the root causes, affected populations, and factors influencing the world's leading social problems. This is why it is so important to invest the time getting to know your problem inside out before you start attempting to solve it.

> The basic social problems we face today are multifactorial and extremely difficult to solve. This is why they still exist!

Why is it important to spend so much time characterizing the challenge? It may seem like a waste of time to many readers at first, who are eager to take action. We know the problem exists, you might be thinking—studying it to death will not help anyone; we need to start solving it! This is very true, and the textbook you are reading embodies the essence of taking action to solve social problems. However, it cannot be emphasized enough that before diving in to take action, time must be invested in ensuring that the social entrepreneur has all the information at hand. Data is power. The more you know about a situation, the higher your likelihood of success in making changes which result in tangible improvements to the affected population. It is absolutely not an option to start your social venture without taking the time to review the available information, synthesize it, and think about what changes are feasible to make and how.

> The more you know about a situation, the higher your likelihood of success in making changes which result in tangible improvements to the affected population.

Where does one start? Before you begin, it is important to understand the nature of the challenge and its underlying sources. "Know your enemies." If you are setting out to eradicate a certain disease

---

* A combination of time spent working on something multiplied by the number of people working on it.

in a certain community, find out what root causes are propagating it—you might end up tackling the challenge of getting clean water in that community instead! If your goal is to ensure that every child in this community is enrolled in primary school, you'll need to develop a deep understanding of why and how their parents make decisions, alongside understanding the general infrastructural challenges, like where the schools are, what the opportunity costs are, and what the student experience is like. Or your challenge could be reducing the carbon footprint of industrial complexes in an urban setting. Here, you'll need to understand what room you have to work with within the context of existing government policies incentivizing industries—or whether you can help change these policies—and what benefits you can offer to industries if they reduce their carbon footprints. What drives their behavior? If you don't have a solid grasp on these issues, then how can you change them?

Collecting information on a social problem can seem very time-consuming and overwhelming to a beginner, and for good reason. Do not rush this step. Take the time to familiarize yourself with key statistics and data sources, talk to people, and keep a record of each step you take and each resource and piece of information you find.

Approaching Your Topic

Think back to a previous time when you have explained a challenge to a friend or colleague. It could be a work challenge, personal challenge, homework challenge, or a plot in a book or television show. You probably did a good job of conveying the characters involved, the sequence of events, the physical and social setting, and the influence of various factors (relationships between characters, back story, twists in the plot) on the narrative. The person listening to you probably became extremely engaged, wanting to know more, and wanting to figure out how it's all going to end.

This is what you need to do when formulating your challenge. You need to have an in-depth understanding of why it exists, who the characters involved are, what the knowns versus unknowns are, how the surrounding environment (both physical and social) influences the challenge, what the back story is, and what the time trends are, i.e., where this is all going.

Most importantly, you need to be able to communicate this effectively. Thus, characterizing the challenge involves both (a) understanding the challenge for your own purposes and (b) being able to relay its importance for others to get involved. You will need others if you're going to effectively tackle this challenge. In the next chapters, we will talk about going out into the field to meet with the experts—those facing the challenge—and begin to investigate potential solutions together. In this chapter, we will talk about wrapping your head around the challenge, before you even take one step.

Resources available to you include Internet searches, peer-reviewed journal articles, academic dissertations, institutional reports, interviews with experts, and observation in the field (which we will talk more about in the next chapter). For now, start the old-fashioned way: by doing some online research. Start with a systematic online search (either of the general cyberspace and/or of a journal database) by identifying keywords to search for and gradually narrowing down your criteria. Most importantly, keep track of your research methods and your results. You can synthesize and analyze these later. In the coming steps, you will build on your results by speaking with the people directly involved and by immersing yourself to experience the challenge firsthand if you haven't already.

You will need others if you're going to effectively tackle this challenge.

Before you dive into your research, put your investigator lenses on. Look at everything with a fresh set of eyes, and don't take anything at face value. Two important things to keep in mind at all times are: question all assumptions, and think like a child!

> Keeping asking "why?" until you cannot ask it anymore.

Think Like a Child

The investigation stage can be fun! Just like a good old-fashioned detective, keep asking yourself "why?" until you cannot ask it any more. Dig out that investigative three-year-old in you that kept asking your parents "but why?" over and over again, regardless of the answers they gave you.

You may never understand in black-and-white terms everything there is to know about this challenge, but you will have at your disposal the facts that have so far been collected by humankind on it. The hard part is deciding what to do about the specific situation you are working in, and we will focus on that in the coming chapters. For now, focus on reading about, listening to, watching, and observing the previous work of others leading up to this moment. What have they found out that you can use in the future to build your solution? You won't be able to solve everything under the sun, but if you know the various pieces of information linked to your challenge, and if you are working with a community facing that challenge, then you will be able to put together the different pieces and connect the positive factors in a way that overcomes the negative factors.

Question All Assumptions

Assume nothing. This is another big part of asking "but why?" Just because things are run a certain way today doesn't have to mean that this is how they necessarily have to be run (remember the starfish story used by City Year)! Muhammad Yunus was an economics professor who was not trained in banking. Bankers had a good understanding of the minimum requirements to open an account and of why the banking institutions served only certain people in certain situations. Mohammad Yunus asked, "but why?" Others assumed that if you are poor, you will not be able to pay back a loan. Yunus and the Grameen Bank showed that in 98% of cases, microloans are in fact repaid (remember the company profile from Chapter 1)! He questioned the assumption that only wage-earning middle-class people could open a bank account. He believed that even people living in poverty should have access to financial services. Because he questioned these assumptions, he was able to break the mold.

PART TWO: A FRAMEWORK FOR CHARACTERIZING YOUR CHALLENGE

What Exactly Does This Mean?

Is it just another buzzword or catch phrase to say "start by characterizing the challenge"? What exactly does this mean? Characterizing the challenge means knowing exactly what you are facing. Narrowing it down to a manageable scope. Becoming an expert in the topic you are working on: both a subject matter expert and a field expert, the former of which we will tackle in this chapter and the latter of which we will talk about more in the next chapter on co-creating with the community. Right now, in order to characterize the challenge, you need to be able to answer the following questions:

■ *What?* What is the challenge you are narrowing in on? What is its nature and characteristics? What consequences does it have on people?
■ *Who?* Who are the affected populations? What are their characteristics? Does it affect some more than others?
■ *Where?* What is the distribution of the challenge, its causes, and affected populations?
■ *Why?* What are the root causes?
■ *How?* What are the pathways by which these causes affect these populations?

■ Dimensions:
  – Magnitude versus distribution (depth versus breadth) of the challenge
  – Sources, types, and quality of the data you are using to understand the challenge
■ Prior attempts to conquer this challenge:
  – What has been tried already, what has worked and what hasn't—And why?

What Are You Trying to Change?

Let's go through an exercise that will help you get started in characterizing your challenge. Start by writing down what it is you are trying to change. You should be able to state this in one sentence. This is an exercise that you are doing for yourself, so don't get stuck on the wording; you will have plenty of opportunity to circle back and edit, change, and develop it before you move on. But just to get started: write down your challenge sentence. What is it all about? Describe in one sentence the challenge and how it affects people.

Who Is Affected?

Next, write down who is affected by this challenge. Try to think of the different groups of people. Does it affect certain ages more than others? For example, some social challenges affect vulnerable populations, like the very young and the very old, the most. Air pollution is one such example: it affects the heart and lungs of infants and the elderly more than the average adult. Does it affect certain genders more than others? For example, some social challenges affect women more than men, or vice versa. Lack of access to water is one such example: girls and women in remote rural settings around the world spend hours each day walking to the nearest water source, collecting water, and walking back. In many cases, this has a detrimental effect on girls' ability to attend school. Age and gender are examples of what we call "sociodemographic indicators." These are descriptive data that indicate population characteristics. Other sociodemographic indicators are income level and occupation: many social challenges disproportionately affect those with low incomes or those with certain occupations. One such example is climate change, which dispropor-tionately affects farmers and food producers.

Where Are These People?

In addition to the sociodemographic distribution, you need to define the geographic distribution. Where is this problem observed? How widespread is it? Does it affect different people in different places, in different ways? Answering these questions will help you to think about where you might have the opportunity to change it. Don't be afraid to dig deep. Oftentimes, data are available only at the aggregate level. This means that you might easily find global averages, regional averages, or country averages. But there is so much variability at the local level, you need to look beyond the surface.

Another tricky aspect you need to think about in terms of geographic distribution is, are the causes and the symptoms observed in the same places? Knowing that there are multiple causes for each problem, it might help to ask the question: which causes are localized, and which stem from far away?

Why Has This Challenge Arisen, and Why Has It Persisted?

This brings us to the root causes. Understanding the root causes is the number 1 most important part of this journey. This is not to say that you will always be able to tackle them at the roots. But keep digging until you find the roots, and then you can step back and ask yourself how deep down your solution can go. Most social entrepreneurs would agree that if they have the opportunity to tackle a challenge at its root, they would go for it. If it is not feasible, then they would at least go as far down the causal pathways as possible, in order to maximize the resulting impact.

> Keep digging until you find the roots, and then you can step back and ask yourself how deep down your solution can go.

How Do These Root Causes Affect the Challenge and Its Outcomes?

Don't be satisfied with just listing the root causes without understanding as much as you can the mechanisms by which these causes result in the outcomes you are looking to change. Tracing the pathway of each root cause to its associated outcome is one way to do this. You might end up with a lot more information than you signed up for, but this is okay! Remember our mantra, data is power. Further in the chapter, we will talk about some ways to organize this information in a way that helps you step back and analyze the multiple causes and pathways, so that you can start thinking about which one(s) you will tackle and how. For now, putting on your investigator lenses and trying to explore multiple pathways leading to the same outcome will help you identify the different opportunities you have to change that outcome.

Dimensions of the Social Challenge

Try to think in as many dimensions as you can. This might sound abstract to you, but think about a circle you might see from far away. If you get closer and try seeing the circle from different points of view, you might find out it's actually a sphere. That changes the nature of the object entirely! Same goes for anything in life. When understanding a social challenge, it's important to think about its different dimensions. The *depth of impact* is one example. Is this a problem that's faced by many people, affecting different people in different ways? Is there a small number of people who are strongly affected, versus a large number of people who are impacted to a lesser degree? The spread of the challenge versus the depth is one important dimension for you to think about when getting to know your challenge.

Think about a circle you might see from far away. If you get closer and try seeing the circle from different points of view, you might find out it's actually a sphere.

Examining *trends over time* is another way to investigate your challenge more deeply rather than taking it at face value. Is this problem decreasing, increasing, or staying the same? Are the trends different in various parts of the world, or in different populations? What is causing these changes and variations?

Uniformity versus variability is yet another way to look at it. Is your challenge manifested in more or less the same way everywhere, or is it highly variable? This is critical to designing your solution and to scaling it: understanding to what extent the challenge differs in various places and among various peoples, and what factors influence this variability.

Dimensions of Data

It is also important for you to think about the characteristics of the data you are using to build your knowledge about this social challenge. What are the sources of information? Is there consistency in your results?

Different types of research studies result in different types of data. One type is observational data. Observational studies can provide a snapshot of the situation, or they can track it over time. The data can be collected prospectively, such as by signing up a group of people to participate in a study. Or they can be collected retrospectively, such as by looking into existing archives like hospital records, government census data, etc. Observational studies attempt to draw links between different factors.

For example, they may observe that in countries with certain policies, girls get educated more. They may also observe that in these same countries, maternal child health outcomes are more positive. Does this mean that education is the root cause of positive health outcomes? We can only be certain in cases where individual women were tracked for both these pieces of information, and other factors in their life that could also influence these results were also accounted for. In this example, it turns out that yes, it is indeed a root cause.

Ecological data are information we have at the large-scale level, such as country statistics. It is more difficult to reliably infer relationships between different factors from ecological data because there are so many other different factors that could be responsible for these results. So be careful when making your own inferences. Read about the work of others who have been studying this field for years and decades and immerse yourself in the scientific debate of the leading researchers on the topic.

Another type of study is a randomized control trial (RCT). This is used by researchers when they want to control the setting in which the social outcome in question is observed, to be sure that the factors they are studying are indeed the cause of this outcome. This results in experimental data rather than observational data. If we have enough people in the experiment to ensure that the results are not likely to be a coincidence or an exception in this small sample, and if the experiment follows proper protocol to make sure the results are not biased, an RCT can be a powerful study design in understanding root causes of social challenges.

Why is it important for you to understand the different types of data and the type of study they came from? It's important because you need to be aware of the different implications of various study designs, and the different dimensions of data, to assess whether and how the results can inform the setting you're working in.

Immerse yourself in the scientific debate of the leading researchers on the topic.

Causality is an important concept to understand because if two factors are related, that doesn't mean one causes the other. Understanding the *directionality* of relationships is important in identifying opportunities. If two factors are related, but the first doesn't necessarily cause the second, then changing the first will not necessarily change the second! The second might affect the first instead—the arrow might go the other way! Or, they might have a common root cause, which means you have to keep digging.

Generalizability is another dimension you should be aware of. If a study is conducted in one town or one country, are the results generalizable to any setting? Or could they potentially be attributed to the unique qualities of that setting?

Different Types of Data

Different types of data also include quantitative versus qualitative, primary versus secondary, and raw versus aggregate. *Quantitative* data refers to numbers, such as statistics. Quantitative information can tell you how many people are affected, what proportion of the population this is, and what their outcomes are, such as health or education test results for example. Many of the above study types result in quantitative data. *Qualitative* information is descriptive and results from interviews, surveys, and other field-based methods. It can tell you how people feel about a certain challenge and how it affects their lives and provides examples of personal experiences with this challenge.

Primary data are that which you collect yourself, while *secondary* data are that which have been reported by someone else. At this stage, you will most likely be collecting secondary data. Last but not least, all of these types of data, with the exception of data from the ecological studies described previously, can be either raw or aggregate. *Raw data* means the original information you initially collected, such as what this person said or measured or earned. *Aggregate data* means that raw data have been grouped and summarized over many people; for example, percentages, averages, sums, and other statistics are aggregate data.

The type of information you will be accessing at first will largely be from sources that have already compiled, synthesized, and analyzed multiple studies. This will make it easier for you to get a general introduction to the topic of your choice before you dive deeper. But it's still important for you to keep in mind all these different dimensions of a social challenge and dimensions of the data used to describe it so that you can decide for yourself what the knowns and unknowns are.

Prior Attempts to Conquer the Challenge

Last but not least, what has been tried before? What has worked, and what hasn't? So many prospective social entrepreneurs have jumped headfirst into a challenge without doing their homework. Don't reinvent the wheel! There are individuals and organizations worldwide that have dedicated their lives to figuring out what works and what doesn't, so at least start with this knowledge base as your foundation.

Again, as in all the previous points, go with the data. Following your intuition is not enough if your intuition is not well informed with evidence. Be objective, open up your mind to the possibilities, and start from fresh like a true detective would. Don't forget, people's perceptions may differ from the reality. And many get caught up in trends or hot topics. You need to spend a lot of time thinking about which challenge you want to address, learn everything you can about the multiple dimensions of that challenge, and investigate what others have tried before you. By taking these steps, you can help ensure that all the time, effort, and resources you will be putting into developing and implementing your solution will be more likely to make a difference.

Interview Box. Matt Flannery, Kiva Cofounder and Former CEO; Branch Founder and CEO

TC: You are often cited as a leading example of a social entrepreneur. What does this term mean to you?

MF: Entrepreneurs who are building business with a social purpose as a primary metric and financial as secondary.

TC: Kiva.org and Branch.co are two different models—does your definition encompass both?

MF: I use the word *business* to refer to recurring, scalable, repeatable value streams. These can come in the form of income, revenue, or donations. Those relying primarily on donations from foundations or individuals in large amounts, I wouldn't really consider a business. A lot of for-profit enterprises that we never think of as social entrepreneurship are really motivated by social change. It's a blurry line used to describe something that's been done forever.

TC: How did you first get started as a social entrepreneur?

MF: Growing up, I always wanted to start my own company and had idea after idea and literally made lists of ideas. None of these ever got implemented or really took off the ground. What made Kiva different was that this time, it wasn't about me. It was about the people whose lives we were changing—they really wanted this and needed this. When we first got back from Uganda after our first scoping trip, the community we had spent time with kept reaching out, following up, and persisting. We realized we have to do this, for them, we had to find a way to make this happen. It wasn't about us, or our idea. It was about them, their needs, and it had to get done.

Photo source: http://tulane.edu/socialentrepreneurship.

Photo from Kiva's press center. Image provided by Kiva to advance its mission of connecting people around the world through lending to alleviate poverty.

PART THREE: HOW TO SELECT YOUR TOPIC

One of the first questions that many readers ask is, "do I need to have a specific topic in mind?" You might already have a clear idea of your topic of interest or even a preliminary idea of your solution—or, you might simply be interested in the general idea of social entrepreneurship without having a specific challenge in mind. This is completely okay—even those who think they already know what they're going to work on often end up implementing something completely different! It is definitely recommended that you spend a generous amount of time exploring your interests before honing in on a topic. Oftentimes, it can help to choose a learning topic, which you can apply toward the exercises in this book, to gain practice and skills before graduating to a topic you will work on after the book ends. You may even end up learning so much about your topic that you decide to keep it for good, and implement a winning solution!

In thinking about your topic for the remainder of this book, a few helpful questions to ask yourself are the following:

■ What sociodemographic and geographic settings am I most familiar with?
■ What are the needs in these settings? What are people asking for?
■ What resources do I have access to, which I can mobilize in a helpful way?
■ What skills and characteristics are my strengths and weaknesses?
■ What are my passions, what drives me in life?

Subject Fields of Interest and Expertise

You will notice that your subject area of specialty did not appear in this list. This is because you do not need to be a subject matter expert when you start. After you select your topic, you need to mobilize the experts to help you bring together existing knowledge and create new knowledge about your topic of interest. In fact, it is often those who are not specialized in a topic who are most able to tackle it. Oftentimes, being trained in a subject area means that you have been habitualized around existing practices—as a social entrepreneur, you want to question existing practices and find a better way of doing things!

Sociodemographic Setting

Being familiar with a particular location and a particular population is a key strength in establishing a social venture. That is not to say that it is impossible to succeed in unfamiliar territory—on the contrary, social pioneers do just that, chart new territories! This is simply to say that a good place to start when thinking about your topic is asking yourself which places and which peoples you have experience with. If you have experienced a social or environmental problem firsthand, chances are, you'll be better positioned to work with the community to co-create a solution.

Needs-Based Framework

Thinking about your own characteristics is helpful in choosing your topic, but don't forget, this isn't about you. Social entrepreneurs respond to the needs and preferences of the people they are working with. In the setting(s) you are exploring, what have the people asked for? Do you have any firsthand information or secondhand accounts on what they actually want and need? We will talk more about this in the next chapter, but it is also crucial for you to be thinking about it from the very start, and framing your thinking about choosing your topic based on the needs.

Access to Resources

Making a mental map of the resources that you have access to right now is another way to start honing in on your topic. If you work in a large company offering a product or service to society, the processes and resources that go into creating that product or service could be extended to meeting the challenge you identify. If you are stationed in a university setting or a specific department, the knowledge and skills of your peers and professors may be an untapped resource you want to leverage. Of course, once you identify your challenge, you will still need to mobilize resources you may not currently have access to. But thinking about the resources around you and how you can leverage them for positive impact is a great way to start.

As a social entrepreneur, you want to question existing practices and find a better way to do it!

Strengths and Weaknesses

Knowing yourself is the first step to becoming a leader. While we are dynamic beings and our strengths and weaknesses evolve over time, assessing your current skills and characteristics can help you think about what you have to offer. Are you a person who enjoys research, digging up facts, and exploring different options before you take action? Are you an ideas person, who gets excited about potential solutions but may not always follow through on your leads? Are you a great communicator, do you enjoy working with people, or do you prefer to work quietly in a less social setting? All of these characteristics can be extremely valuable—there is no one winning formula. The reason it is important to assess yourself is because in choosing your topic, you are effectively matching yourself. Are you well matched to venture into a tropical forest? Are you well matched to code software that can be used for a mobile app? What activities do you excel at? It is completely okay to get out of your comfort zone and tackle a challenge that might not be an easy feat for you, but it's important to know your propensity so that you can surround yourself with the people, knowledge, and other resources needed to complement your skills and strengths.

Knowing yourself is the first step to becoming a leader.

Passion and Motivation

What drives you in life? If you wake up every morning thinking about a certain topic, then you should definitely follow that lead! Most people don't necessarily have one topic they wake up every morning thinking about, but they do have certain parts of the living experience that they tend to gravitate to. Some people enjoy working with others. Some people enjoy being in nature. Some people feel the most alive when they are solving a complicated arithmetic problem. Ask yourself what you would spend your time doing if you could do anything. Don't be paralyzed if you can't think of one thing—make a list of all the different options and then think about the various options on that list, perhaps narrow it down to a shortlist. Discuss with your peers and mentors. Then you can look up information on each option, weigh it against the questions listed previously, and start to get closer to your challenge.

> Don't be paralyzed if you can't think of one thing—make a list of all the different options and then think about the various options on that list, perhaps narrow it down to a shortlist.

Again, it is important to drive home the importance of thinking about all these questions within the context of what is needed. Being a social entrepreneur is not about building your legacy. As you will observe from the cases and interviews throughout this textbook, a key characteristic of social entrepreneurs is that they leave their egos at the door. Being a social entrepreneur is about responding to the needs and opportunities presented by others. So when thinking about the previous points and aspects, think of them in the context of assessing yourself as a resource for others. Where could you best serve?

> A key characteristic of social entrepreneurs is that they leave their egos at the door.

PART FOUR: DIGGING DEEPER

Collecting Information

In researching your topic, it is crucial to (1) be systematic and (2) keep track of everything. A good way to do this is to get a logbook and record each step you take, gathering information one step at a time. Even in conducting the most basic Internet search, record the keywords you entered into the search bar and the number of hits or pages of hits that you surfed through. Out of these, how many were relevant to your search? Take notes from each one, recording the website and key points, so that you can go back to them as needed. This is crucial as a first step and simple to execute. Otherwise, it is all too easy to lose track of your results, become overwhelmed with all the information you will find, and not be able to go back and review key findings. Not to mention, you may need your references and citations when you share your results with others! So this way, you will already have a record of everything.

Common sources of information that you can draw on when first starting your investigation are international development agencies, universities, think tanks, and other NGOs. International development agencies can often serve as a helpful source of information on various social and environmental challenges because they often dedicate a large amount of resources (both human and financial) to gathering the existing evidence on any one topic. The World Bank, regional banks, and various United Nations (UN) agencies (World Health Organization [WHO], UN Children's International Emergency Fund [UNICEF], UN Development Programme [UNDP], UN Environment Programme [UNEP], Food and Agriculture Organization [FAO], and many others) have focused on various topics and challenges over time. Most of these agencies have created portals containing information and resources collected from other agencies, nonprofits, governments, and universities worldwide on their topic of interest.

One such portal is the sustainable development knowledge platform, which consolidates information on the UN's Sustainable Development Goals (SDGs). These were created by the global community in 2015 and agreed upon by world leaders. They stem from the historical Millennium Development Goals, which were drafted at the turn of the millennium when the global community decided that it was time once and for all for us to eradicate poverty, achieve universal primary education, achieve gender equality, make drastic reductions in child mortality and improvements in maternal health, combat major diseases, and ensure environmental sustainability. These were the overarching goals of the human race at the turn of the millennium, to ensure that basic human needs were met for all. While some progress was made, we are nowhere near successfully tackling these challenges, and more entrepreneurial approaches are needed. Reading about the information that was collected around each problem, the interventions that were designed to solve these problems in various settings and by various players, what worked and what didn't, is a helpful way to have a general overview which could provide a useful background to your thinking about the social venture you are building.

> While some progress was made, we are nowhere near successfully tackling these challenges, and more entrepreneurial approaches are needed.

A wealth of information has become available on the social problems included within the SDGs as a result of the resources pledged by the world's leading development institutions, academic institutions, and all the world's countries to meet these goals. Further information has been created as various stakeholders (spanning the governmental, academic, civic, and private sectors) develop programs and interventions to reach the targets specified within each goal. The challenge you take up could be included among the SDG targets, or it could be something completely different. In both cases, it is well worth your time checking out the portal (https://sustainabledevelop ment.un.org) and its predecessor (www.un.org/millenniumgoals).

> A good way to approach your investigation is to start at the global level, then look for regional sources of information, then zoom down to the country and local levels.

Another similar global portal is the World Bank data portal (http://data.worldbank.org), where you can look up statistics from countries around the world. You can also find information on national datasets, where most countries will also have household surveys and other national information available on sociodemographic indicators and environmental and economic indicators. Local NGOs may also have more small-scale data that will serve to be extremely valuable to you in completing the picture and assessing variability in your social challenge at the local level. A good way to approach your investigation is to start at the global level, then look for regional sources of information, then zoom down to the country and local levels. Global foundations and think tanks are another useful source of information, as they often invest time and resources into thinking about and learning about the challenges they aim to tackle. Various examples from around the world include the Clinton Foundation, Gates Foundation, Qatar Foundation, Agha Khan Foundation, and many, many others.

Both of these types of institutions rely on academic and field researchers to produce and analyze the data they consolidate. Thus, universities and local researchers (whether contractors or

NGOs) are often the source of these data. These groups will also have their own websites and centers dedicated to their topics of specialty. Many organizations also lie at the intersection of academia and grassroots work, collecting evidence on what works and what doesn't from out in the field, analyzing and disseminating this information broadly for others to use in their own work. These organizations are especially valuable to you. Two such examples are Innovations for Poverty Action (www.poverty-action.org) and Millennium Villages (www.millenniumvillages.org). Such organizations design and implement programs based on data collected by academic researchers and evidence from the field and in turn share their results to add to the evidence base for further analysis and dissemination.

Being your own investigator, it is important to know that it is very rare for any one source of information to contain the complete picture. More often than not, even in peer-reviewed scientific journals, for every scientific article, it is possible to find another article with contradictory findings. Therefore, a top rule to keep in mind while characterizing your challenge is to always get a "second opinion" (or a third, or a fourteenth)! Just like you would diagnose your health by meeting with more than one health professional and doing your own reading, the same goes to diagnosing and characterizing the challenge you are setting out to tackle. So whatever you do, remember to *be your own investigator*.

Analyzing Your Results

If you do a good job of asking why over and over again and of recording this systematically as we discussed previously, chances are, you'll end up with a whole load of information! When you are ready to step back and collectively examine the body of information you have gathered, a few analysis tools and techniques might come in handy here.

Data analysis refers to the process of sorting through data to recognize patterns. What story do the data tell? Because you are collecting secondary data at this stage rather than primary data (which you collect next during the co-creation stage), it might be helpful to start with visual tools. Researchers collecting primary data use other tools, which range from laboratory analysis to statistical analysis. The good news is, they have already done this for you! At later stages in your venture, you will most likely want to collect and analyze primary data of your own, to contribute to the body of knowledge out there on this topic. But for now, let's talk about some visual tools you can use to organize the information you have collected stemming from others' research and to help you think about it in a way that will allow you to get to the bottom of it.

Tables are one way to organize your findings visually to help synthesize and analyze them. This can help compare different pieces and sources of information across different subjects, factors, or scenarios. For example, if you are conducting a literature review, or even a series of informational interviews, a good way to organize the information is to type it into a table listing each source, website or contact info, and key points. Then you can sit back and view them collectively, noticing commonalities and differences in the key points or gaps that you need to find other sources to fill.

Diagrams are another, if you want to show the association between two or more different factors. One example of a diagram is a new take on the old DAG, or direct acyclic graph. This is a tool used in epidemiologic studies (those which study the pathways of disease) that can be adapted for a general investigative purpose. Creating such a graph entails writing down the different factors that are related to your challenge and then connecting them with arrows where the body of evidence indicates that a relationship exists between two factors. The direction of the arrow shows which

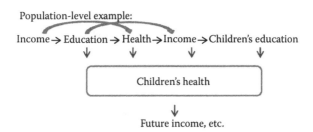

Population-level example:

Income → Education → Health → Income → Children's education
↓   ↓   ↓   ↓   ↓

Children's health

↓

Future income, etc.

Individual-level example:

Poverty → Poor sleep → Lowered productivity → More poverty

Figure 2.1 Examples of diagrams to help organize information.

factor influences the next (sometimes the arrow goes both ways), and a dotted arrow indicates that you have reason to suspect there may be a relationship there but you're not sure yet. Above the arrows or next to the graph, you can list the sources of information for each relationship.

Of course, while drawing your diagrams, you may find that some relationships can be cyclical too, with either positive or negative feedback loops (Figure 2.1). This is especially the case in social outcomes, where the presence or lack of one factor leads to more or less of another factor, which then further reinforces the presence or lack of the first factor. We have already seen one earlier in this chapter: higher levels of education lead to higher levels of health. You can add to this on both ends: on the back end, higher levels of income lead to higher levels of education and health. On the front end, higher levels of education and health lead to higher levels of income, which further reinforce the cycle in subsequent generations. This example is at the population level. At the individual level, another example is sleep. Poverty is correlated with poor sleep, which in turn is correlated with reduced productivity, leading to more poverty.

A similar tool to organize and build on your thoughts about a challenge is also a new take on an old technique, the Ishikawa diagram—also known as a fishbone diagram because it looks like a fish's skeleton. In this book, we'll use a "flipped" Ishikawa diagram called the "Inverted Ishikawa" to help visualize root causes. The original version was initially used in industrial business and subsequently adapted to studying social and environmental problems.* The Inverted Ishikawa starts by writing out the central challenge in a circle at the top of your page and then drawing a line down from that circle. From that line, various off-shoot lines emerge, linking various factors related to the challenge. Because every challenge has multiple factors influencing it, and thus multiple solutions, this will help you flesh out the various possible scenarios to set the stage for deciding in the coming steps how you and various other stakeholders might possibly work together to tackle it, either from various angles or by focusing on one factor (Figure 2.2). At the very bottom of the line will be the root causes: when you are not able to identify any further branches, when you are not able to ask "why" anymore, this is where you have found the roots.

---

* Ishikawa, K., & Loftus, J.H. (1990). *Introduction to Quality Control.* Tokyo, Japan: 3A Corporation. Wong, K.C. (2011). Using an Ishikawa diagram as a tool to assist memory and retrieval of relevant medical cases from the medical literature. *Journal of Medical Case Reports,* 5, 120–123. See: Andrews et al. (2012) https://research .hks.harvard.edu/publications/getFile.aspx?Id=841.

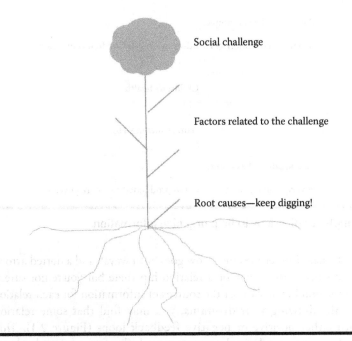

Social challenge

Factors related to the challenge

Root causes—keep digging!

Figure 2.2 Visualizing root causes using the Inverted Ishikawa.

Let's examine the following example on maternal mortality.* Let's say you are working in a rural area in a low-income country. Some of the factors influencing this outcome are lack of prenatal care (visits to the health clinic by the expecting mother before birth), unattended births (those which take place in the absence of a health worker), and lack of medical facilities (such as clinics or hospitals that can respond to emergencies taking place at or after delivery). If you keep asking "but why?" you can tie these questions even farther back to limited resources at the government level (weak health systems and infrastructure) and limited time and awareness at the household level (mothers who need to work, don't have time to travel to the nearest health center, and don't have knowledge about health-related needs and services). You could even keep asking "why?" until you traced it back to geopolitical and historical forces that led to the poverty of this nation (Figure 2.3).

At this point, naturally, you are feeling overwhelmed. "What can one aspiring social entrepreneur do about all these major forces?" you might be asking. Don't forget, at this stage, you are not yet attempting to tackle this challenge. You will have plenty of opportunity to think about at which level you want to tackle this challenge, as well as the feasibility of your solution, in future stages. For now, your task is to understand the problem to its core. Understand who it affects, where, how, and why. If you keep asking why until you get to the roots of the challenge, then you will at least be closer to getting a sense of the full picture. In the next chapter, we will step back and assess at what level you might actually be able to intervene. You may not have access to the government systems or larger geopolitical forces, but you may have access to knowledge and services you can help get to the mothers. For now, you are charged with combining the informational resources at your fingertips to learn as much as you can about this challenge.

---

* You can view a short talk by Professor Matt Andrews of Harvard University on this exercise using a fishbone diagram here: https://vimeo.com/91733930.

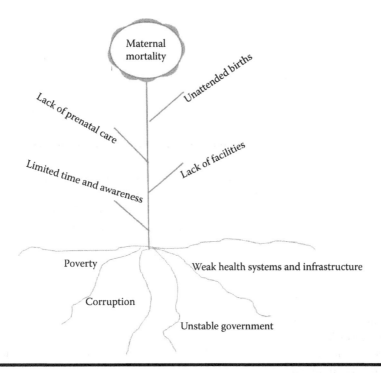

Figure 2.3   Example Inverted Ishikawa visualization for a maternal mortality scenario.

Summary and Next Steps

In this chapter, we have taken the first steps toward building the solution—understanding the challenge! The hardest part might be choosing one topic to focus on for the rest of the book. Give yourself time on this, but then pick something and stick with it. Remember, you are doing this as a learning exercise. You can, and will, go back and apply all the learning tools and skills you'll acquire in these chapters to other topics over time. For now, follow your passion and follow the need—ask yourself where you can serve as the most valuable resource.

We have gone over the basic framework for characterizing a challenge and the basic types and sources of information. If you have done your homework right, you will find yourself faced with a huge amount of information! Now, it's time to apply the framework above to help you synthesize and analyze that information and look at this challenge from a holistic point of view. Time to step up and deliver your milestones for this chapter:

Exercise: Your Challenge

At this point, you are tasked with identifying and characterizing your challenge. Now, you'll start building your knowledge base, upon which you'll create your solution. Provide the answer to the following questions using only one sentence each, unless otherwise specified. (Yes, it's difficult to summarize the wealth of information at your fingertips in one sentence only! This is an important skill to master. Moreover, you'll notice that the more you understand something, the more concisely you'll be able to convey it—when you're unsure, you tend to ramble on, hoping you've covered everything! So think first, and answer second.)

1. Describe what social challenge you will be tackling moving forward. How does it affect people?
2. Who does it affect? Include statistics on the number of people affected.
3. Where is the affected population? Include information on the distribution.
4. What are the root causes, and what are the pathways by which these causes affect this population? You can either provide a diagram here or write it out, using up to a sentence per cause if needed.
5. What data sources and types have you used? List at least eight references.
6. Challenge question: In 800 words or less, describe previous attempts to tackle this challenge, what has worked and what hasn't. (Make sure to specify by whom and where these attempts were implemented.) Think carefully to yourself and review your answers to the first five questions before answering this question. Reviewing the evidence and arming yourself with data will serve as your number 1 weapon moving forward in developing a solution that actually works!

CHAPTER SUMMARY

- The first step in a social entrepreneur's journey is to identify and characterize the challenge she or he is tackling.
- Building your solution around the challenge and the people it affects is the best start you can get in making it work.
- This includes familiarizing yourself with what others have tried before you.
- This chapter provides a framework for characterizing your social challenge, focusing on *what, who, where, why,* and *how.*
- At this stage, you'll be primarily dealing with secondary data collected and analyzed by others, and in the next stages, you'll head out to talk to more people and build your knowledge base even further.
- Familiarize yourself with the different data sources and types described in this chapter and how they might affect the results you are reading about.
- We've reviewed some key repositories of data including international organizations, universities, and local organizations. Many of these are connected and build on each other's work.
- A good way to approach this challenge is by starting with the global knowledge and statistics, then zooming down to the regional, national, and local levels to explore different sources.
- Most importantly, across all sources of information, keep asking "why" and digging deeper until you reach the roots. A DAG or Inverted Ishikawa can help you visualize this. Don't forget to question all assumptions!

Chapter 3

Co-Creating with the Community

Now that you've zoomed in on the challenge you're addressing and learned everything you can about it, the best people to figure out a way to solve this challenge are the ones most involved and most affected. You can help facilitate, organize, and bring resources to the solution, but you can't create it from scratch all by yourself.

Ideas are easy to come by, but implementable ideas are not always as straightforward as you might think. To find the idea that has the best chance of succeeding, it's important to first live and experience the challenge yourself. This chapter focuses on co-creating a solution working with the people it's being tailored for.

The best way to ensure that your solution is feasible and helpful to implement for a certain target audience is to develop it hand in hand with that person and that community. This is part of the research and development stage, a natural extension of the problem formulation stage you've already started on, and a bridge to the solution you'll implement. Before you're able to design and implement the solution, a careful assessment and co-creation process is in order.

For this, we'll draw on different fields of study and practice in defining what it means to co-create and how to go about co-creating your solution. From the field of community-driven research, we will explore different steps toward participatory planning, identifying solutions and assets in the community and exchanging knowledge and capacity. From the field of human rights, we'll discuss what it means to ensure accessibility, affordability, and acceptability in any basic social product or service. We'll also draw on key principles from the field of leadership skill building and well-known best practices. Finally, we'll review an example of community-driven planning that resulted in a viable social venture.

"Community"—What Does This Mean?

A community is a social group bringing together individuals sharing one or more things in common. They could be either living in the same place and facing the shared challenges and opportunities associated with that place, or they could be a subpopulation with a shared culture and way of living. Within any community, there are always diversity and variability. A community is a good starting point to understanding the social challenges faced by different groups of people and how each group interacts with that challenge. Once you are immersed within a community, you will gain an understanding of the individual variabilities that lie within.

Piecing Together Pieces of the Puzzle

In most cases, you will discover that the solution you are seeking to formulate is not a mysterious and elusive nor necessarily a complex or sophisticated new idea. Rather, the most likely solution you will find is a simple one that brings together existing pieces at the community's fingertips. As the social entrepreneur, you are adding value by bringing together the pieces of a potential supply chain that already exist in some shape or form. The solution is out there; its different components are already in the community or an arm's reach away, and the job of the social entrepreneur is to build a new vision of putting them all together.

This is why your solution is not likely to be a head-scratching new concept that requires a genius mind nor rocket science. It's definitely not something you are going to find in the library. You need to get out there and figure out how people are interacting with this social challenge, what resources are available, and how people can come together to interact in a more positive way with this challenge, resulting in a more positive outcome. You don't need to start from scratch or reinvent the wheel. Even if—especially if—your solution involves a new technology, it is important to be aware that there have actually been very few cases where a new advanced technology developed entirely in a lab or institution of higher learning has been scaled to effectively solve a social problem in different settings far away from that lab. The most impressive and effective cases have involved a simple mobilization of existing resources, including human resources, to work within the existing framework of a community and put together the different pieces of the puzzle (Figure 3.1). The different pieces are already there; the most challenging aspect is often simply identifying them and finding a way to put them all together into a complete solution.

The Social Entrepreneur as a Connector

Have you ever heard of the game "six degrees of separation"? A common parlor game that builds on the theory that all humans can be connected by six degrees of separation, it challenges the player to link together two seemingly impossible people. When piecing together the different parts

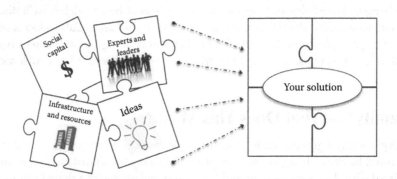

Figure 3.1 Putting together the different pieces of the puzzle.

of the puzzle in your social challenge, think about the connections that might already exist, which you just have to put together. What are the six degrees of separation between Ana, an inhabitant of a remote village, and the healthcare services she needs? Of course, there may be more than six, or even less. With your Inverted Ishikawa from Chapter 2, you will have already explored many of these. Which of these do you have the opportunity to bring together?

During the co-creation process, try to think of your role as a Connector, as described in the book *The Tipping Point* by Malcolm Gladwell. After all, aren't you trying to tip this challenge? A Connector is someone who knows a large number of people and who can connect others through a smaller degree of separation than the average person can. For those of you thinking, "what if I don't know that many people?" this concept can be extended further than just one's social network, by considering the common characteristics of connectors: Connectors often exhibit curiosity, versatility, confidence, and energy for new links between people and ideas. They see things in others that others themselves may not see. Their work spans many different worlds; they occupy diverse communities, subcultures, and niches. They have an instinct that helps them relate to different peoples and populations. Chances are, you probably exhibit at least one or more of these characteristics!

In this sense, as a social entrepreneur, one of your most important roles is to serve as a connector—keenly observing the different resources, stakeholders, opportunities, and gaps in your community and finding ways of putting them all together. Keep your eyes open for those untapped resources, talk to as many community members and stakeholders as you can, and build your base of supporters who will champion your solution. Also keep in mind which of these characteristics you have and which you'll need to look for in others you'll want to recruit for your team!

In describing the power of the connector, Gladwell points to the social power conferred by social acquaintances, who we rely on to open up new worlds to which we don't belong and give us access to new opportunities. This underscores the importance of going beyond your own network to *find the existing connectors inside your community*. You are not the only entrepreneur out there! Whatever field you are venturing into, find out who's been doing things differently in that field.

Who has pioneered new ways of interacting with the social challenge you're facing and of facilitating more positive ways for others to interact with it? Who are the local entrepreneurs and leaders that people turn to? This is a good place to start when connecting the dots. Find the sources of social capital, to extend the leverage you already have yourself as a connector.

Catalyzing Change

By connecting the existing pieces of the puzzle, you are acting as a catalyst. Just as an enzyme brings together different molecular components and catalyzes the formation of a new molecule, the connector brings together different people, ideas, and resources and catalyzes the formation and implementation of a new social solution. "The closer an idea or product comes to a Connector, the more power and opportunity it has."[*]

The key point to remember here is that you need others. The enzyme is only serving to bring together the components of the molecule; without these components, the new molecule is not created. Just as we rely on connectors to put us together with new people, we rely on others to put us in touch with information and other resources.

---

[*] Gladwell, M. (2002). *The Tipping Point: How Little Things Can Make a Big Difference.* Back Bay Books, p. 55.

Just as an enzyme brings together different molecular components and catalyzes the formation of a new molecule, the connector brings together different people, ideas, and resources; and catalyzes the formation and implementation of a new social solution.

Who Is Your Starting Team?

Before you venture out to collect more information on your challenge and the people it affects, put together a "starting team." This team will change and grow as you add members of the community and other players to the picture. It will continue to evolve as you search for specific talents and skills along your journey to help you formulate your solution and build your venture. But for now, what is your starting point? Don't go at it alone. It could be colleagues, classmates, friends, or other contacts. It could be local leaders, grassroots organizations, and other social networks. As you think about what steps need to be taken, think about who needs to be by your side to help make sure you don't drop the ball!

A practical way to assemble your starting team is to recruit those already around you. If you're building your social venture within the context of an existing organization, tap into your human resources department, colleagues, volunteer groups, and interest groups and assemble a starting team who will hit the pavement with you and support you. If you're working on this as part of a university course, look for resources inside your university. Are there teachers, researchers, staff members, student groups, or others who would be interested to help?

If you're starting out on your own, what existing groups and resources can you tap into? These could include interest groups, study groups, youth groups, faith groups, professional networks, or a multitude of other social structures bringing together like-minded people. Is there anyone you've worked with or volunteered with in the past who might be able to help? Have you contacted the research groups whom you read about over the course of your research during the previous chapter? You might think you are alone, but chances are, there are multiple people out there trying to tackle this challenge, and your best shot is to find ways to join forces with them.

What skills do you need? Look not only for those whose interests match yours but also those whose skills complement yours. If you are a numbers person, you'll definitely need to take along a people person—and vice versa! Look for diversity in age, background, gender, and other characteristics because it will help you to have multiple people looking at the situation with multiple perspectives.

Interview Box. Libby McDonald, MIT CoLab Director of Global Sustainability Partnerships*

TC: Libby, you are best known for building businesses with waste pickers in Central and South America. What has your work with waste pickers taught you?

LM: What I've learned is that you can design systems for zero waste by building many businesses and linking together. To do this, you need to co-create with the existing local entrepreneurs in the community. Finding your local entrepreneurs is the most important step. You have to work alongside someone.

TC: How do you go about finding the people in the community to co-create with?

LM: I followed the trash, and that's where the entrepreneurs were! These were single women with eight or more children, and they had to make a living. When I go into a community, it's really the women and children that are the poorest, and they are also the game changers. Innovation exists at the margin because people who have nothing, have to survive, and so I work with these survivors.

TC: You recommended the waste pickers' social enterprise case study. Why do you think it's important to study this example when learning about the principles of social entrepreneurship?

LM: Solid waste management is one of the most pressing problems worldwide and affects the most marginalized people. Globally, there's a growing movement around waste pickers; there are about 20 million people worldwide collecting and sorting garbage; and they have organized into municipal, national, regional, and international unions, sharing strategies for how they were growing waste sector businesses. Corn Island just outlawed plastic bags and they're about to outlaw plastic bottles. This was their biggest problem and they solved it through social entrepreneurship; they created a water purification social enterprise and cloth bags made by women.

TC: How do you build a business out of waste picking?

LM: The first thing you need to do is an assessment: you've got to figure out your supply chains. It's really a volume enterprise. If you put together enough municipalities, you can get the volume needed. We had to build networks of waste enterprises. One business wasn't going to make enough money for these women, so we had to launch several. We started by serving local institutions: we mapped out their locations and took care of their waste needs. We now have a waste-to-energy business. We built a biodigester. The only way we could survive was to diversify.

TC: What is the hardest part of co-creation to you?

LM: The ability to imagine and the ability to have confidence to realize your dreams. It's like a Polaroid picture where it first comes out and you can barely see it; you have to shake it, and then the image becomes clear. Many of the women I work with, when we first start, haven't found the voice yet to be able to say, "This is what needs to be done, this is why we should be the ones doing it, and this is why you should be paying us."

---

* Title at time of interview (Feb 2015). Current title is Executive Director, Prosperity Catalyst (as of Apr 2015).

Interview Box. Albina Ruiz, Founder and CEO, Ciudad Saludable, Lima, Peru

TC: Albina, you've been working in the waste sector for 30 years, but you only formed your organization 13 years ago. Why did you wait so long?

AR: I wasn't sure I could manage my own organization! Plus, it takes so much time to build results. First, we just needed to focus on doing the work. It took years to build trust within the waste pickers community, and even more years to build partnerships with the local businesses and municipalities.

TC: Tell us more about how this all started, 30 years ago.

AR: I grew up in the jungle, my parents were small farmers. I begged them to send me to the city to study, and in the end, they saved up and bought me a one-way ticket. When I got to Lima, I was shocked. I had never seen or heard of garbage before. In the jungle, we don't use plastics. And our food waste, we don't think of as waste. It's a resource, we are very careful with it, it has great value and we use it for our livestock, fertilizer, etc. In Lima, there were literally mountains of garbage! I couldn't believe my eyes. I lived in the slums, and I noticed that the garbage was the worst where the poor people were.

TC: What was the first thing you did?

AR: I talked to the government workers and asked why they didn't remove the garbage in the slums. They said the poor people don't pay for their services, they like the dirt. I said it's not true, I am one of them! I went to the dump to talk to the waste pickers. There were mosquitoes, rats, cockroaches, dogs eating garbage. It was a horrible situation. I made it my goal that there would be zero waste pickers working in the dump.

TC: So how did you get from that situation to where you are today?

AR: It took a very long time. The waste pickers were afraid to work in the city. They don't believe in the municipality or anybody. I told them, "You are the entrepreneurs." We had to talk to the municipality, to the businesses in the city, to offer our service. Now, each year, we have a convocation with the municipality. We worked with the government to give financial incentives to municipalities to work with waste pickers. We had to advocate for new law. Today, there is a national program to sort garbage; we wrote this law! Now, they are not waste pickers anymore; we call them recyclers. It was a long, long road.

TC: What are the next steps?

AR: Next step is for families to pay directly to the recyclers. The neighborhoods and families believe in them. We are already starting this in one neighborhood. We have ID cards for each recycler, and people trust them.

TC: Working with the government, didn't you ever face any corruption?

AR: We did! Big companies offer services to municipalities and get a lot of money but don't want to recycle. But after we made this law, municipality has to work with waste pickers. It took years to approve, and more years to implement. Now, we are getting the

Ministry of Economy to provide incentives program for municipalities and to citizens to separate their trash.

TC: How will you expand beyond your first sites?

AR: We can only do this by working with others. We made three toolboxes for other organizations like us to work on the different things we do. To do the landfill studies, work with waste pickers, recycling factories, local law, and national law. We made a national round table on recyclables, where big companies sit side by side with the waste pickers micro-enterprises "rueda de necogios."

Step 1. Assessing Stakeholders for Knowledge Exchange

One of the ways in which you can act as a catalyst is to bring together local knowledge and global knowledge (Figure 3.2). This knowledge exchange is the first step in building your solution. The number 1 experts are those interacting most closely with the challenge you are taking on. So the first question to ask yourself is, what are the different segments of the population that are faced by this challenge? What is the experience of each one? Segments of the population refer to the different sociodemographic groups we talked about in Chapter 2. Do people of different ages, genders, income, backgrounds, locations, etc., interact with this challenge in different ways? What insight can you gain from each one? We will talk about different techniques for gathering this information in the pages to come.

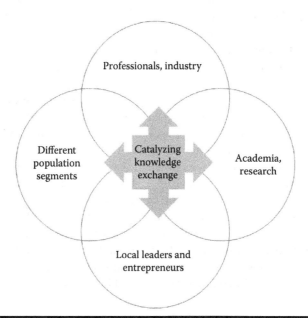

Figure 3.2   Generating new knowledge.

Who Are the Key Players?

Now that you've identified your starting team, the next step is to identify who exactly you're going to be co-creating with! Each community you work with will have multiple stakeholders within and external to the community. A stakeholder is anyone who will influence or be influenced by the process or outcome of your intervention. This includes individuals, organizations, business, policymakers, and government. Anyone with an interest in this social challenge, anyone who has a stake in it, is a *stakeholder*. You may have been focusing on those affected by the social challenge up until now—but what about those who are part of its root causes? It is not enough to co-create with your potential end users, who will be your customers for your end product, you also need to work closely with those who will be part of the supply chain—the different parts of the solution—they will be part of designing, building, and implementing your solution. All of these groups of people are considered stakeholders in your social venture. Therefore, before we proceed any further, let us take a deeper look at stakeholder analysis.

Tool: Stakeholder Analysis

A good way to prepare yourself to organize the information you have about your stakeholders is to equip yourself with a stakeholder analysis table to fill out as you progress. This lists all the potential customers, suppliers, competitors, collaborators, partners, and other types of stakeholders. Spend some time sorting through the potential individuals, groups, and institutions who interact with this challenge. How would they interact with a potential solution? What is the potential role they could contribute to your development and implementation of the solution? You won't have most of the answers to these questions when you first start; they will help give you a sense of what information you should be looking for along the way.

As your picture of the challenge and potential solutions forms and solidifies, you will need to update your answers as they may apply to potential ventures you may be developing. At each stage in your venture in the future, make the time to stop and ask yourself what the current attitudes are. The answer might be constantly changing each step of the way! Are various stakeholders supportive, antagonistic, neutral, or undefined as yet? And what is the role we want them to play? Do we want them to go from being a competitor to being a collaborator? If they are neutral, what steps can we take to move them across to being supportive? This will depend on the potential benefit or harm of any prospective solution to each stakeholder. As you progress with your research, you may change your mind about the positioning of one of the stakeholder groups and have to adjust your plans and resources accordingly—or better yet, you could change their minds!

Stakeholder analyses can come in many different sizes, shapes, and forms. They can be a full-length narrative document with one section for each of the previously mentioned questions, or they can be summarized in a simple table for an early-stage start-up. Some organizations have intricate diagrams depicting their numerous stakeholders, while others have a few bullet points. At this stage, you will want to keep it simple yet comprehensive. Many helpful templates for this analysis are available online.* An additional dimension to think about is the level of influence of each stakeholder. A common way to do this is using a simple four-way table (or nine-way table, if a middle level of "moderate" is inserted), as depicted in Figure 3.3.†

---

* One example template is available at http://www.setoolbelt.org/resources/2031, adapted from the WHO and other original sources.

† For more ideas and information, see http://www.institute.nhs.uk/quality_and_service_improvement_tools /quality_and_service_improvement_tools/stakeholder_analysis.html.

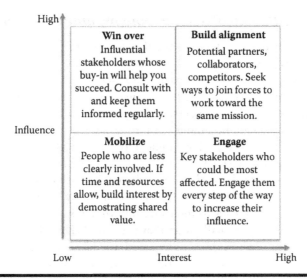

Figure 3.3   Stakeholder mapping to plan for action.

Step 2. Community-Driven Research

Defining the Agenda

Thinking about your stakeholders will help make sure you've identified the key players and started to prepare the primary questions and feedback you'll be asking of each one. You may have already started to form a vision for what challenge you'd like to tackle and what changes you'd like to see, but your vision will only solidify into an actionable mission and venture once you hear from the various people affected by this challenge. What are their priorities? What are their needs? Has the way you've been approaching this and thinking about it been aligned with their realities? What can you do to learn more about it, experience it firsthand, and figure out how you're going to start building a solution?

There are existing social change agendas for each stakeholder. Don't form your own without understanding these and understanding the different ways you can contribute.

Before you start, make sure you think about sensitivities you should be watching out for. These could be social, cultural, or political. Various groups of people have various backgrounds and dynamics underlying their relationships and behaviors toward one another. Whatever you do, you need to proceed cautiously. This is why it is impossible to hammer home enough the importance of working in a setting you are familiar with or investing the time to familiarize yourself deeply with a setting when venturing into new territories. Being part of the community, living in it, and experiencing for yourself the social challenges it faces are always, always the first steps. There are existing social change agendas for each stakeholder. Don't form your own without understanding these and understanding the different ways you can contribute.

Understanding the People, Places, Problems, and Potential

Once you have identified your stakeholders, you'll need to carry out different approaches for the first knowledge exchange with each group. Some might be more amenable to one-on-one meetings. This will most likely be the case with local NGOs and other grassroots organizations, which may offer opportunities for in-depth and rich exchange of information and experience. With others, such as the multiple population segments, larger gatherings such as conferences, round tables, or town-hall-style meetings might be a more comfortable fit.

A general rule of thumb is to keep a low profile in the initial stages, especially during introductory meetings with the various stakeholders. This will help make sure you don't unintentionally activate sensitivities and help you slowly build a deep understanding of community issues and dynamics before you start gaining momentum. Once you have that sturdy foundation, you will feel more confident holding bigger and more high-profile meetings with less of a risk of a faux pas as they say!

Think about a community or small group that you have belonged to in the past. It could be family based, school based, faith based, activity based, friendship based, etc. Think about all the dynamics, history, and nuances that characterized the interactions between people in this group. This is the level of familiarity you need to have with any setting you are working in!

Research Tools

What defines community-driven research is that it is conducted *for*, *by*, and *with* the community. It's not just you and your starting team as a group of outside researchers studying the community! Most people don't like to be studied.

It's you as a catalyst and connector, bringing people together to exchange knowledge about their interaction with this social challenge. Ideally, you'd like to put together a research team bringing together members of various stakeholder groups to carry this out.

Tools and techniques needed to gather information from multiple stakeholders are summarized in Figure 3.4. Depending on the situation, topic, location, and social preferences, you will craft your own combination. These include door-to-door surveys, focus groups, town hall meetings, one-on-one meetings, and other creative ways to exchange knowledge. Contests, conferences, and workshops might be used in some cases. Outdoor events bringing together different groups in the community might be another. It depends on where you are, what your topic is, and what people are accustomed to. Ask for people's feedback on what techniques they suggest and what they think would work best. Your technique will also differ on whether you are bringing together like-minded people to get their feedback (which is more common in the earlier stages)

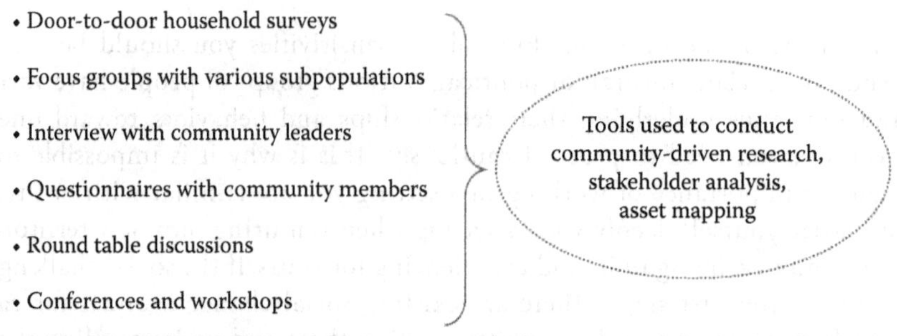

- Door-to-door household surveys

- Focus groups with various subpopulations

- Interview with community leaders

- Questionnaires with community members

- Round table discussions

- Conferences and workshops

Tools used to conduct community-driven research, stakeholder analysis, asset mapping

Figure 3.4 Community-driven research.

or bringing together diverse groups to exchange knowledge between themselves (which is more common as you progress).

> Ask for people's feedback on what techniques they suggest and what they think would work best.

All of this requires ongoing ties to the community, connectedness between the stakeholders, and active relationship building. This is one of the most important investments of your time. In fact, as your venture develops, building relationships with end users and other stakeholders may end up consuming the majority of your time, while technical aspects are delegated to others.

This is especially the case in the co-creation phases, before you get to the design and business planning phases. This is because the end users themselves inform the design and costing and other factors, by having a role in the development of the solution. As such, community-driven research requires not only multiple sources of expertise but also a large amount of flexibility and creativity in bringing people together to develop the methods that you will use to collect and exchange knowledge.

> Community-driven research requires flexibility and creativity in bringing people together to develop the methods that you will use to collect and exchange knowledge.

Research Tips and Techniques

You will likely be using a combination of multiple research tools from Figure 3.4 to gather the different types of information you're looking for. A few tips to keep in mind across research techniques are as follows:

■ **Keep it simple**

When preparing your questions, whether written or oral, keep them finite in number. One consideration here is that you want to start with general questions in order to avoid overwhelming people. A second consideration is that you want to leave room for the unknown to emerge. If you have too many questions that you need to get through, there's no space for your participants to bring up questions of their own! While it's important to come prepared in order to provide a structure for the conversation, it's also important to be flexible, open, and encouraging for participants to divert the conversation or add new topics or perspectives.

■ **Listen!**

The number 1 thing you are trying to do here is *hear* people. If you're coming in with prejudgments or predeterminations, you won't hear what people have to say. Start with an empty slate and an open mind each time you talk to someone. Each person and each group will have completely new perspectives and experiences to share. Your role is to talk less and listen more. Also, debrief with your team afterward, to learn what they heard too. Each person has a way of noticing nuances in others, and your teammates might have picked up on observations you may have overlooked. Stay focused while conducting your research, and then share your observations after each piece of research is conducted. This will multiply the information you are able to collect.

■ **Diversify**

Sometimes, it's helpful to ask the same question in different ways, to different people, using diverse methods. This is why you will most likely want to use more than one of the tools listed previously to understand your challenge. Each tool has its advantages and disadvantages. For example, conducting one-on-one interviews with community members has the advantage of creating more privacy for the person being interviewed. Maybe she or he wants to share information, experiences, or perspectives with you that she or he doesn't necessarily feel comfortable exchanging in a group setting. On the other hand, focus groups allow for people to build on one another's contributions, reinforce or conversely bring out points of differences, highlighting group dynamics, and reaching more people. A focus group is basically an interview conducted with more than one person at the same time. Focus groups usually include less than 10 people; depending on the situation, they could include a small handful such as 4 or 5 people, or they could include up to 12 or 15. Once you start getting closer to 20 people, you'll find yourself more in a "town hall" type of situation. Here, you're less likely to be able to go into as much depth on any one topic as in a focus group, but you're more likely to gain different perspectives and reach a large number of people. Using more than one of these techniques, while keeping in mind the cross-cutting tips, can help make sure you gain a more comprehensive understanding of the challenge you are tackling from different perspectives and dimensions.

Step 3. Creating Collective Capacity

Key questions you want to be asking yourself during this time are the following: What are the characteristics of the local community that can be leveraged as strengths in building your network, solution, and distribution channels? Who are the key resource people? What is the existing infrastructure that you will be operating in? No enterprise operates in a vacuum, and this is especially the case for a social enterprise. Your added value as a social entrepreneur is to identify those assets that are currently not being tapped toward providing a solution and bringing them together to bridge the gap between your challenge and the available resources that can be leveraged to tackle it.

One of the outcomes of co-creating with the community is building collective capacity. By bringing people together and transfusing knowledge across boundaries, you are breaking silos and generating new resources. You are not simply taking an existing solution and introducing it in a new setting. You are taking an existing challenge faced by this community and working with them to develop a solution. There may be similar forms of this solution that exist elsewhere, but by co-creating it with the target audience, you are in effect creating local capacity to deliver it in this setting (Figure 3.5). It is not only the product or service which you are creating, but also the human capital.

This approach that you are using in the co-creation stage will stay with you throughout your social venture. Each step of the way, rather than thinking what resources you'll need as input, you will be thinking of what resources you're creating as outputs, which will have a ripple effect.

All too often, organizations think of human capital as an input into their work. How many people do we need to hire, what skills must they have, and how much do we need to pay them are commonly asked questions in building a new venture or growing an existing one. If you challenge yourself, however, to think of human capital as an output, your social impact will be multiplied many times over. By implementing your social venture you are not only leveraging existing human capacity but also growing it and building capacity, building productivity, creating new skills, and

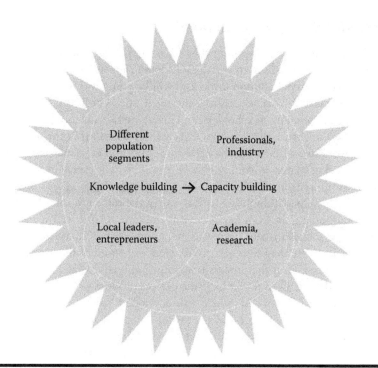

Figure 3.5 Creating collective capacity.

creating new markets. Thus, accounting for human resources should take place not only when accounting for your inputs but also in thinking about how to characterize your outputs and what you want to contribute to that community.

The Goal: Conceptualizing the Solution

Understanding who your stakeholders are, what their needs and preferences are, how they do things, and what they feel are different opportunities to do things differently is the first step in working together to identify potential solutions.

You may be working on your own as a student or midcareer professional—or you may be part of an existing organization that is aiming to develop a product line as a social business. Or you may be working as a group of individuals aiming to make a social change in your community. In all these cases, there are many factors involved in determining whether you will be able to develop a solution that will stick. The most likely scenario is that the solution you are aiming to develop will involve a lot of moving parts. The implementation, the supply chain, the end user, the competitors, and collaborators and other stakeholders—these must all be taken into account during the first stages of preconceptualization. Because you alone cannot determine the success of your solution's implementation, by extension, you alone cannot conceptualize it. Any stakeholder who will be remotely linked to the success of your solution must be part of its conceptualization in some shape or form.

> Because you alone cannot determine the success of your solution's implementation, by extension, you alone cannot conceptualize it.

The Process: Mobilizing the Community

Many leaders fall into the trap of thinking they have the perfect solution and no time is to be wasted in implementing it. Rushing to get the job done, they assume that once it is complete, everyone will see what a worthy solution it was and will be grateful that it has been done. In reality, the more likely scenario is that successful solutions to social problems and opportunities will require the collaboration of many stakeholders, and involving the stakeholders from the beginning is one of the best ways to ensure that they have a sense of ownership in the solution and a vested interest in its success. Thus, while a leader's drive for results and efficiency may tend to cause her or him to act first and ask later, it would behoove any social entrepreneur to invest the time in mobilizing the community from the start.

In the field of leadership skill-building, this is one of the top rules voiced by leadership trainers: time spent obtaining buy-in from key players at the start is time well spent. No matter how well thought out your solution is and no matter how high your estimated social impact, if your stakeholders do not feel that they were part of its creation, you will likely encounter resistance. This is because satisfaction with the process is as important as satisfaction with the outcome—and can even overshadow it. Even if you have the perfect product or service, if your community feels disgruntled with the process with which you developed it, they most likely will not adopt it. Conversely, if you are not able to build the perfect product or service due to restrictions in the environment in which you are operating, but the community understands how and why you ended up with this product and service as it is being offered, they will be more likely to accept it and feel that it meets their needs.

> While your drive for results and efficiency may tempt you to act first and ask later, it behooves you to invest the time in mobilizing the community from the start.

The Key: Incorporating Local Infrastructure

Beyond exchanging knowledge at this stage, it is critical for you to map out the landscape you're working in. What is the infrastructure like—both in terms of social networks and physical strengths and limitations—and how will you design your solution accordingly? Defining what you will change and what you will work with is one of the most valuable thought questions you can go through from the start.

Asset mapping is an exercise that can help you organize information on this level. As discussed previously, human resources are one form of assets that exist in the community, which you will need to characterize and which you will need to grow. Physical resources are another form of local assets that will inform the development of your solution. What physical resources are available to you that are relevant to the needs and opportunities you are addressing? These could include natural resources (water, vegetation, soil), and they could include infrastructural resources such as roads, factories and their products, and built structures. Financial resources are also a key input and a key output at the same time. In order to determine during the business planning stages down the line how these resources will flow in and out of your social venture, it's important to conduct an inventory before you start. Asset mapping is an exercise whereby you identify the different resources available to you and evaluate what resources you need, where you will get them from, and how you can leverage the strengths of your local setting and incorporate weaknesses.

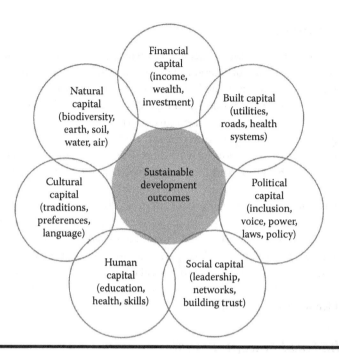

Figure 3.6   Examples of community resources identified through asset mapping.

Examples of the different types of resources you may identify are depicted in Figure 3.6, which is adapted from the community capitals tool and framework for evaluating strategic interventions. This framework was developed by a group of community researchers based on their analysis of entrepreneurial communities.* They observed that communities that were successful in demonstrating sustainable development not only addressed and incorporated these different types of capital into their work but also took into consideration opportunities for synergistic interaction building on the different types of resources.

In order to determine during the business planning stages down the line how these resources will flow in and out of your social venture, it's important to conduct an inventory before you start.

Your challenge is to co-create a solution that is feasible within the local context, culture, environment, infrastructure, and economy. Not only that, your goal is for it to thrive in that setting. Therefore, an important step in co-creation is to assess that setting and thoroughly characterize it so that the solution you develop will be the right fit and will operate based on resources that are the right match. Asset mapping can help pave the way by identifying available skills, points of leverage, and strategies to diminish deficits.

---

* Flora et al. (2008). See http://www.soc.iastate.edu/staff/cflora/ncrcrd/capitals.html. A helpful handout can also be downloaded at http://wp.aae.wisc.edu/ced/wp-content/uploads/sites/3/2014/01/204.2-Handout-Community -Capitals.pdf.

Participatory Planning

The types of community-driven research depicted previously are the foundations of your participatory planning process. Setting your action plan moving forward will depend on the resources available to you and how things are done in your community. How can you build a system that puts together the different assets and links them together sustainably? What are your strategies for effectively engaging your community in a deep dive participatory process?

A popular way of bringing together different stakeholders to identify resources and ideas for potential solutions is to organize a visioning workshop. This is an event that usually lasts more than one day, whereby people affected by and interested in solving this challenge are brought together. They start by identifying needs, priorities, shared interests, and preferences to establish common grounds. They then work together to formulate common objectives and a larger vision for social change. This can be a powerful way of building a sense of ownership over potential solutions from the start and more importantly tailoring those solutions to meet identified needs and priorities. The key here is to have multiple stakeholders partner to organize and implement the event.

Once you have mapped out the assets of your local context, create a learning plan. What questions remain to be solved? At what point is it okay to begin? If there are various ideas arising, how will we decide which idea(s) to test out?

Where Are the Local Entrepreneurs?

Most importantly, remember what we said at the beginning of the chapter, about not reinventing the wheel. One of the first questions you set out to answer was, what are the different ways in which things are done in this community? In understanding how people interact with the social challenge you are investigating, have you identified any solutions that have been applied on a small scale by local entrepreneurs that can be built on?

In every community, there are people who are already implementing solutions. By now, you will most likely have identified them through your community-based research, stakeholder analysis, asset mapping, and participatory planning. How can you learn from these individuals? Sometimes, their innovations are simply band-aids, and sometimes, they have the potential to be built into larger systems. In both cases, they will almost certainly contain clues for you to dig deeper into.

Examining Local Supply Chains

First, what are the characteristics of the solutions they are implementing? Are they low cost, are they easily accessible, are they user-friendly and simple to understand? On the flip side, where are there spaces for improvements? Do they easily break down, are end users noncompliant with high dropout rates, are there characteristics that make these solutions hard to scale beyond a microlevel? Learning from what is already being used is often the first step in building your solution!

Second, there is most likely a rich mine of data made available to you from examining the entire supply chain. Where do the local entrepreneurs get their supplies from, where do they sell their products or services, and who buys from them? Are they at capacity, is the demand high or low, and is there room for growth? What are the growth barriers? How much are people willing to pay, how much is it costing the local entrepreneurs, and how much are they profiting? What are the social and cultural obstacles they are facing? Your field research will give you not only answers to these questions—beyond insights to inform the ideas behind your solution—but also data to inform your business planning as you proceed.

Join forces with others on the ground, if and when this is possible! There will still be plenty of opportunity to innovate, build social business, create value, and disrupt the status quo by working with others.

Last but not least, don't fall under the delusion that social entrepreneurship means starting from scratch. If you find someone who is already tackling this social challenge and it is possible for you to work with them, don't start your own shop! This is one of the key pieces of advice offered time and time again by social entrepreneurs all over the world. Join forces with others on the ground, if and when this is possible! There will still be plenty of opportunity to innovate, build social business, create value, and disrupt the status quo by working with others—in fact, the opportunity will be greater in most cases, rather than each one working on her own.

Checklist: AAAQ

In implementing community-driven research and participatory planning, we can draw lessons from interventions and programming in the field of human rights. When you are co-creating with the community, you are following what we call a rights-based approach to sustainable development. This has been reflected by the participatory aspect of your work and by your assessment and incorporation of local context and landscape, including political assets such as policy frameworks and conflicting national laws. Exhibiting transparency and accountability to your stakeholders is another aspect you have laid the groundwork for at this stage and must continue to do so by sharing information at each step along the way as you implement and grow. Taking into consideration and including all possible stakeholders, you have taken measures to build the foundation for a solution that is nondiscriminatory. Together, all these characteristics and approaches you have been applying reflect a rights-based solution building process.

Beyond these, one way to ensure that any solution you build will continue to follow a rights-based approach is to apply the AAAQ checklist. This refers to the criteria of accessibility, availability, acceptability, and quality.

Accessibility ensures that your target population will be able to reach and consume the product or service you are creating. One subcomponent of this is affordability. Another is physical accessibility, ensuring that it reaches the last mile. Durability is also included, as it will not be accessible if its usability has expired by the time your target customer needs it. Availability refers to the provision of the product or service. Acceptability refers to the social and cultural aspects that may foster or inhibit the uptake of, and benefits from, your product or service. If you have made it available but have not ensured that it can be accessed in a socially acceptable way, then how can your end user benefit? Last but not least, quality is a cross-cutting component in any field of work. For your solution to produce the social impact you are setting out to achieve, it must maintain an optimal level of quality.

Finding this optimal level can be tricky for the social entrepreneur who is aiming to produce the most affordable solution. Affordability is often associated with the lowest cost possible, but is the lowest cost solution always the highest quality? It is often not. Where does one draw the line and find the right balance between maintaining the lowest possible costs and prices and maintaining sufficient quality to result in the desired outcome? While affordability is a component of accessibility, so is durability, which is affected by quality. This is why applying this checklist is so important! None of these characteristics alone will build the winning solution. Finding the solution that provides value after taking into consideration these multiple dimensions—low-cost, high-quality products that are durable over time—is the key to effectively tackling your social challenge. Otherwise, you will be asking your end users to invest in a product or service that will only perpetuate the existing status quo. We will talk more about this in the next chapter, when we discuss the S-shaped curve and related concepts.

Values and Characteristics of Various Stakeholders

By now, if you are following these steps, you will be aware of the fact that "community" does not refer to a homogenous block of people. Rather, each community is composed of various subgroups and individuals representing a vast amount of diversity in values and practices. Looking around at the community in which you are sitting today, it is likely to be composed of various ethnic groups, potentially various socioeconomic levels, and in most cases, various age groups. In most cases, gender analysis will also be a huge part of developing your solution.

Therefore, no matter which community you are a part of and you are operating in, take into consideration the values, preferences, and practices of other members in your community. Depending on which part of the world you are operating in, this may involve presenting yourself in a certain way, following specific social protocols, and recognizing existing social hierarchies. This includes a range of behaviors down to the way you dress and the way you greet people! Most social challenges are cross-cutting and involve multiple subpopulations, so it's crucial to keep in mind that finding ways to collaborate across stakeholders is your number 1 priority. Do everything you can to make sure that you, and others, go out of your way to demonstrate and earn each other's respect.

Reflective Practice

Social entrepreneurs have the tendency to charge through the planning process without stopping for breath. Set aside a time each day for reflective practice on your own and with your starting team. What have you learned from your community-driven research? What new insights were gleaned from talking to the different stakeholders? Have any red flags arisen? What have been the unexpected elements, containing surprise or confusion or even alarm, that need further investigation? More often than not, your learning path is not a clear-cut one that leads you to a predetermined point. Stopping to fully ingest and digest all the information you access along the way is crucial in incorporating it into any future solution you may develop.

Summary and Next Steps

On the topic of reflective practice, let's take a moment to recap the journey we've described so far. In Chapter 1, we talked about the meaning of social entrepreneurship, the differences between social entrepreneurship and other forms of social service, and the differences between social entrepreneurship and other forms of entrepreneurship. In Chapter 2, we focused on characterizing the social challenge we're setting out to tackle. What are the root causes, who are the populations affected, and what has been attempted to date and why has it not worked? In this chapter, we introduced the steps that a social entrepreneur can take in the process of co-creating a solution with community members and other stakeholders.

This involves community-driven research, which can take place in the form of workshops, conferences, round tables, door-to-door surveys, focus groups, and one-on-one interviews with stakeholders. Stakeholder mapping is a process that helps the social entrepreneur and starting team to identify key players influencing the success and the characteristics of any solution to be implemented. Asset mapping is a process that helps identify key sources of knowledge and other resources that can be leveraged toward creating and implementing the solution. By exchanging knowledge with community members who have a firsthand experience with the problem at hand, and experts who have technical knowledge on the problem and potential solutions, the social entrepreneur thus acts as a facilitator in the process to build local knowledge and capacity toward creating and implementing a solution.

These steps ensure that the community is mobilized in a participatory planning process so that all stakeholders can have ownership of the solution and a vested interest in its success.

Exercise: Your Homework

You are only three chapters in and have already come a long way! Let's build on the research you conducted in the previous chapter to add your own take to the challenge characterization, based on fresh work you've conducted with the community you're addressing. The first step of co-creating a solution is to understand the different ways that people interact with this challenge and the different opportunities that this community provides to bring together and build on existing resources. In this context, it's time to prepare the following:

1. Prepare your stakeholder analysis. You have the choice of simply listing stakeholders and adding one to two sentences next to each, describing their level of interest and influence; or summarizing in a two-by-two table as illustrated in Figure 3.3. Note to yourself where you'd like each stakeholder to be. What can they contribute to your solution?

2. Prepare your asset map. Again, this can be either a simple list of assets that fall within the eight categories described, or a visual diagram summarizing them as illustrated in Figure 3.6. Note to yourself any opportunities you've identified for different assets to interact with each other and build on one another. How can you leverage these assets to tackle your challenge?

3. List the sources of information behind the two analyses you've produced. Who are the different people and groups you've met with and spoken to? Is there anyone missing? How can you bring these people and groups together in a visioning workshop or other forum to exchange knowledge and ideas? Make a list of steps taken, and next steps for yourself. If and when needed, go back and adjust your stakeholder analysis and asset map as you proceed.

4. Last but not least, write out your AAAQ checklist. What characteristics and qualities will any solution you develop have to exhibit in order for it to be acceptable, available, and acceptable to the community you are working with? What considerations will you need to make in determining the optimal level of quality needed to produce your desired outcome while ensuring these attributes?

CHAPTER SUMMARY

■ The best way to start building a winning solution is by co-creating it with those most affected by the social challenge.

■ The social entrepreneur serves as connector, bringing together existing resources and catalyzing an exchange of knowledge to start identifying potential solutions.

■ A community is a social group bringing together individuals sharing one or more things in common, whether living in the same place or sharing a common culture and way of living.

■ Community-driven research is characterized by being developed and implemented with and by the people affected by the social challenge.

■ Conducting a stakeholder analysis and asset mapping exercise will help ensure that you are including and leveraging key players and resources.

■ Using a rights-based framework means including everyone in the planning stages without discrimination, demonstrating transparency and accountability to all stakeholders, taking into account legal and policy frameworks, and ensuring the AAAQ checklist.

■ Remember, find the local entrepreneurs and build on their work; don't reinvent the wheel!

■ These co-creation techniques will help you pave the path toward finding a winning solution.

Social Ventures Mentioned in This Chapter

Company profile: Ciudad Saludable, www.ciudadsaludable.org.
Founded in 2002, Lima, Peru.
Product/service: Ciudad Saludable means "Healthy City" in English. Healthy City is a nonprofit organization that strives to build inclusive, harmonious cities where all have equitable access to opportunities and social justice. To enable this vision, they developed a new solid waste management model that is interdisciplinary, participatory, progressive, and innovative all the while considering economic, social, and environmental impacts.
Goal: Ciudad Saludable's mission is to contribute to the sustainable environmental management of cities through the implementation of solid waste management systems that holistically consider the environment, the economy, and society.
How it works: Ciudad Saludable creates efficient solid waste management systems that demonstrate how sustainability and profitability can be aligned across a variety of industries. By enabling the development of microenterprises that collect and recycle waste in Peru, they have empowered and improved the livelihoods of waste pickers. The microenterprises reduce waste volume in municipal landfills and generate income by separating and selling recyclables. Their programs are designed around the concept of sustainable development and focus on integral public policies, equity, and sustainable management of solid wastes.

Case Study: Ciudad Saludable

We will now examine the case example of a social enterprise that was built to tackle the challenge of solid waste management in Lima, Peru. Like many cities in emerging or developing nations, solid waste (what we refer to in layman's terms as trash or garbage) is a challenge. Incomplete and inefficient disposal and management by governments and municipalities or by private companies contracted to do the job commonly lead to overflowing garbage containers, landfills, and unhealthy practices such as incineration. In Lima, like in many similar settings, an informal waste management system grew in parallel with this formal system, whereby waste pickers would scavenge through the overfilling containers and/or dumpsites. Waste pickers commonly earn a living by collecting recyclable material from garbage sites and selling it to a middle man or point person, who then sells it to the recycling factories. This has been documented in diverse settings around the world.[*] In many of these settings, the waste pickers have come together to organize an existing community into a social business, transforming themselves from scavengers to service providers.[†] We will examine the case of Ciudad Saludable.[‡]

This was a long and multifaceted process with many moving parts and players; for educational purposes, it can be summarized and simplified into a stepwise process that could be applied in many different settings across the world and adapted to many other social problems and sectors. The first step was for the waste pickers to come together, to meet and discuss the challenges and opportunities they were faced with on a daily basis. To start with, their work was physically hazardous, as they commonly used their bare hands to sort through garbage, which contained hazardous material including broken glass, medical and industrial waste, heavy metals, toxic chemicals, and even dead animals. The improper management of this waste resulted in environmental and public health consequences in addition to the injuries and illnesses experienced by the waste pickers. The municipality at the time was collecting less than half of the total waste dumped into garbage containers in many neighborhoods. Waste pickers were often working alone and moving around by foot. By coming together, they could scale their operations and find ways to make them more efficient.

Thus, the second step was the formation of a social venture to regularize and expand their work. They took a loan from the bank and invested it in pushcarts and pickup vehicles, building their own carts, which were attached to motorcycles. They began collecting waste at the source, by going door to door. Clients were asked to sort their own waste, but compliance was not high to start. Secondary sorting shelters were created for service providers to go through and sort the collected waste again after aggregating many households. Scrap shops were then created to aggregate recyclables collected by the members, selling them to the recycling factories and assuring the members a fair price for the materials they collected.

When a waste picker works alone, he or she sells his or her collected recyclables to an intermediary every day, earning low prices. After organizing and creating a storage center, waste pickers were allowed to aggregate and sell at larger volumes straight to the recycling factories, manufacturers, or exporters. These large businesses only accept large volumes, and they have to be clean. Working alone, one person in one day cannot accomplish that. But by forming an association the waste pickers—now dubbed recyclers—are able to meet these requirements.

As an example, if a kilogram of plastic is sold to an intermediary, the price earned is 0.5 sol per kilogram.[§] But if the same kilogram is sold directly to the recycling factory the price is 1.5 sol

---

[*] Example: Report on informal SWM sector in Beirut, Lebanon, pp. 75–79 (http://planbleu.org/sites/default/files/pub lications/gestion_dechets_liban_en.pdf).

[†] Example: SWacH case study in Pune, India (http://no-burn.org/downloads/ZW%20Pune.pdf).

[‡] www.ciudadsaludable.org.

[§] 1 sol = US$0.3 at the time of writing.

per kilogram. That's three times the revenue! Most importantly, the recyclers have gained dignity, recognition, and protection in their work.

Other organizations have achieved similar results in different parts of the world, each with their own business model. In Pune, India, the SWaCH cooperative collects monthly fees directly from households, with differential pricing depending on the neighborhood, also increasing the daily income of each recycler by threefold on average.* In Malang, Indonesia, a social enterprise founded by medical students invites people to bring in their recyclables in exchange for healthcare insurance rather than cash.† And these are just a few examples; there are many others.‡

What are the business practices that allowed them to attain these achievements? Investing in equipment allowed them to increase in efficiency and volume. The sorting shelters and scrap shops built a supply chain to connect the service providers from the source (households) to the recycling factories. Customer service practices were also implemented: members wore uniforms, ensured punctuality, and learned to professionalize their appearance and their interaction with clients. In summary, their profit margins increased because they were able to introduce new components along the value chain, which enabled them to aggregate their individual production levels.

The driving factor behind this group's ability to foster success and sustainability was their community-based approach (see interview with Albina Ruiz, founder and CEO). Starting with the people affected by this problem, and empowering them to be part of the solution and reap the benefits on multiple fronts, was the core factor for success. This came hand in hand with the involvement of various stakeholders, from the consumers to the municipality. Finally, building the social enterprise one step at a time, from community-based research to stakeholder analysis to incorporating available assets to adding different components and best practices, allowed the group to co-create a sustainable, viable, and thriving new community-based venture.

Conclusions

The co-creation process is not a start-and-end procedure, but rather an ongoing approach that will characterize the formulation, development, implementation, and growth of your social venture. Involving your target audience and other stakeholders from the start, identifying and incorporating local capacities and other assets, and engaging the community in creating an action and learning plan are all part of ensuring that your solution is effective, viable, and scalable. Key principles to adhere to are creating a shared vision, managing expectations, preparing adequately by assessing your capabilities, and understanding your partners and key players. Establishing processes and building the framework for information sharing will pave the path for the transparency and accountability that is essential for you to maintain this sense of ownership for your stakeholders. Continuous communication and immersion are essential. Most importantly, collecting and constantly reflecting on data and information will ensure that you do not miss out on opportunities to fill the gaps that have been overlooked or simply not linked together in the past. Thus, you will effectively fulfill your role as the connector. In the next chapter, we will expand on ideas and tools to help you refine and test the design of your product or service and develop your theory of change to link this design to the social change you seek.

---

* SWaCH case study, available at http://no-burn.org/downloads/ZW%20Pune.pdf.
† Garbage Clinical Insurance, see https://www.facebook.com/pages/Indonesia-Medika/194273577406528.
‡ Example: nine case studies: http://www.no-burn.org/downloads/On%20the%20Road%20to%20Zero%20Waste.pdf.

Chapter 4

Designing Your Solution

Co-creating with the community is not a finite step that's completed and moved on from. It's a continuous way of doing things, and the tools and methods we learned about in Chapter 3 are just the start. Now that you've initiated your community-driven research, stakeholder analysis, asset mapping, and other key steps, it's time to zoom in on the design aspect. How can you design your solution to fulfill all of the attributes you've identified in the last chapter?

Now that you have a sense of these basic attributes, it is time to put them all together into a product, service, or system that will change the way people interact with your social challenge. You've developed an in-depth understanding of your stakeholders, and now the time has come to decide who your end user will be, how you're going to build this solution around them and their needs, and how to ensure that the solution you're building will indeed tie back to the social challenge you're setting out to tackle. Get ready to hack this challenge!

In this chapter, you'll learn about innovation and design tools and methods used by leading organizations, from nonprofits to Fortune 500 companies, working to develop cutting-edge products and services. When most people think of the word *design*, they think of the fine arts, graphic design, or the fields of architecture, urban design, or interior design. Many people do not know that organizations working on sustainable development have "designers" in them. These people work to design a wide range of programs and products from poverty alleviation interventions to consumer products with environmental solutions.

This chapter will be divided into three key areas. The first will focus on design and innovation, sharing tools and techniques to generate ideas based on the information you gathered in your research phases. The second introduces the theory of change, a crucial planning tool that helps ensure that you effectively design your venture around the challenge and end user you've identified, test your assumptions, and communicate clearly the connection between your solution and the problem. The third walks through a case study of design for affordability, quality, and scale, providing an example of a social entrepreneur who developed a venture that effectively tackles a social challenge and is innovative, scalable, and financially sustainable.

Levels of Innovation

At this stage, you are focused mostly on formulating the solution in terms of how you are going to come up with the actual product, service, system, or process that you will use to change the social challenge. But it's important to point out that this is only one level of innovation! Innovation is not a step, or something that happens during only one stage of the process. Innovation means finding new ways of doing things, and this is something a social entrepreneur applies each and every step of the way! Right now, we'll talk more about innovation in designing your solution, and in future chapters, we'll talk about innovation in building your business model, building your operations, building your distribution systems, and many other aspects which will help you create the largest social impact possible (Table 4.1).

Failing Is Part of the Process

Rule number 1, don't be afraid to fail! If you are truly going to embrace innovation at every step of the process and create a social venture that knocks your social challenge out of this world, you cannot be afraid to fail. The only way it is even possible to create something new is to try something different—and 9 out of 10 times, you will fail! So be brave, put your pride away, and make sure everyone on your team does the same.

Table 4.1 Levels of Innovation

Level	Description
Product or service	The product or service itself contains elements that have not been applied to this social challenge before and that increase the effectiveness by which this product meets the challenge. • Examples are designs that make a product more affordable, more durable, more tailored to the target audience, or more effective in producing the desired change.
Business model	The enterprise has created financial viability through a business model that has yet to be employed in addressing this challenge, mobilizing resources that have not yet been leveraged. • Examples are creating multiple resources streams, differential pricing, combining different funding sources or vehicles, identifying new untapped resources.
Distribution (external)	The product, service, or system penetrates the target market through distribution channels that have yet to be achieved and that allow the product to reach the most underserved. • Examples are supply chain innovations; creating a market of providers, transporters, manufacturers, retailers; creating social impact through their provision, not just the customers.
Operations (internal)	The social venture employs processes that allow it to deliver the highest social impact possible at the lowest cost, in a way that will allow it to scale. • Examples are setting up internal systems and processes to increase efficiencies, setting up innovative monitoring and evaluation systems, and creating effective feedback loops.

Tangible progress does not always mean success—it also means failures and lessons learned. It means you tried something, worked toward something, and put everything you have into making it succeed. You need to share those stories too, as they will help others build on your trials. Expect to fail; it is part of the process, and remember, each and every failure is one step closer to success.

Each and every failure is one step closer to success.

Innovation and Design

User Driven Design

As a continuum of the co-creation process, developing the solution centers around the end user. Designing around the end user is not only the recommended approach in social entrepreneurship but in developing any product or service in the commercial world. Software is designed in a way that makes it "user friendly." Refrigerators, baby strollers, video games, bikes, and clothes are all designed to meet the needs and preferences of their target audience. It is this type of thinking that you want to internalize as you develop your solution.

The first question you need to ask yourself is: Who am I designing this for, and with? Now that you're familiar with the various segments in the population that are most affected by this challenge, which one are you targeting? As illustrated by the previous examples of commercial products, no product can serve everyone. You need to tailor it around and build it with your end user. This needs to be one segment of the population whom you are focusing on for now. If you want to reach multiple segments, then you'll probably need to design multiple products, services, or systems to reach each one. Remember, there are no one-size-fits-all problems, so it's not likely you'll find a one-size-fits-all solution.

User-centered design refers to the process through which products, services, and systems are created for and around people's needs. This has been used in government, law, health, education, consumer products, community services, and many other fields. It starts with the characteristics, needs, and preferences of the end user and builds around that. You are taking this one step further by building your solution with the user, and this is why we refer to it as user-driven design (Figure 4.1).

User Driven = Data Driven

Remember a couple of chapters back when we said data is power? Well guess what—by now you will have collected quite a lot of your own data! All the steps you've taken have provided you with data to inform your design—from talking to different stakeholders, to immersing yourself in the community, to building and exchanging knowledge on the preferences, experiences, and needs of the different segments of the population. How can you now use these as data to inform the design of your solution?

Your collective experience forms the basis of your user-driven solution.

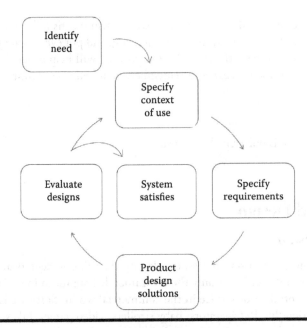

Figure 4.1 User centered-design. This is an example of how user-centered design is applied across sectors—believe it or not, the source of this diagram is a government website dedicated to improving user experience with government, like understanding and accessing healthcare in America! (From http://www.usability.gov/what-and-why/user-centered-design.html.)

Leaders in the field of social entrepreneurship, public heath, and other population-based fields often debate the issue of individual stories and anecdotes versus population data. While individual stories are powerful in conveying the human experience, population scientists, funders, and other players often voice the concern that individual stories do not provide a complete picture and sometimes can be biased. This is why so much effort and resources are put into gathering representative data at the population level.

However, when used collectively, stories from the field can also be a powerful tool for you to use in designing your intervention. If you have taken all steps necessary to ensure that all segments of the population you are working with have been represented, then their joint voices can paint a picture for you of the landscape you are operating in. Your collective experience forms the basis of your user-driven solution.

One note of caution to consider is that giving different people equal opportunity to share their stories does not necessarily mean they will equally execute on that opportunity. Social and cultural divides and dynamics may inhibit some individuals and groups—whether due to gender, age, social strata, and other complex factors—from voicing their experiences in the same way that others might. You will be more likely to gain a sense of these dynamics and variations by working with members of the community who represent these different subpopulations and who can help you not only extract but also interpret and weight the different stories.

You can even assign different degrees of uncertainty to each population segment, to carry forward in developing your product or service, and to test at every opportunity. By maintaining this awareness of the nuances in the community you are serving, you can increase your likelihood of ensuring that your product or service will sufficiently penetrate existing gaps to fill the needs of your end users.

Generating Ideas, Models, and Solutions

How can we move forward from the current state of the challenge we've described and understood in this community to envisioning future possibilities? Solutions may be possibilities that are implemented within the current framework and infrastructure of the society you are operating in or that may require disrupting the current framework and building completely new systems.

Full Immersion

Generating ideas, models, and solutions is not something you can do most optimally or effectively while sitting at your desk at home or in a university or office building. Identifying opportunities requires a blend of group dynamics and reflective practice, as we discussed in the last chapter. Immerse yourself and your collaborators in the middle of the social challenge you are tackling! If it is improving healthcare, you need to spend time on the frontline of healthcare delivery, working to provide access to your target population and experiencing firsthand the barriers to access, quality, and reach. If it is improving education, you need to be engaged in a learning institution or other organization working to increase access and quality of education. This could be as simple as being a tutoring volunteer. The important thing is you need to be right in the middle of the situation you are trying to improve, not observing it from the outside and designing potential solutions there.

Blended Perspectives

Try to include various perspectives such as those who have been working on this topic for a long time versus those who are fresh to the topic. This latter point may surprise you, but it is often those who approach a challenge with a fresh new perspective who are the most able to question existing assumptions. It may be daunting to find the right balance between working with experts and challenging existing ways of doing things—at the end of the day, your key out of that conundrum is realizing that the number 1 expert is your end user, and the only way you will learn whether a new way of doing things might work is to first think outside the box and then test it out with the user.

Experiment with Different Ideas

During the design phase, you'll have to get comfortable with disorder, as you turn everything inside out to generate different ideas and formulate your solution. You might end up with something completely different from what you started out with, but we'll make sure you tie it all back to your challenge using the theory of change tool later on in this chapter. For now, embrace the unknown!

Let's start with a few basic principles that others have tried in various fields. Get together with your team and your end users and brainstorm different options. Build on each others' ideas and try out different scenarios! Multiple models and versions of ideas are generated as you try out different things through iterative brainstorming and prototyping.

Brainstorming means generating ideas—literally like a storm in your brain, with lightning, thunder, and disruption! First, you immerse yourself, reflect deeply, and build your understanding of the challenge—and then you let your brain cells loose to attack it! This is the *exploratory* stage of idea generation. No idea is too big or too small, and none are discarded just yet. Brainstorming is done best in multiple stages—on your own, with your starting team, with your community and other stakeholders. After this exploratory phase, a few ideas are selected to move forward with based on stakeholders' feedback. *Prototyping* means developing "practice runs" of the initial versions of your solution that you can test and iterate until you hit the home run.

Ask the Right Questions

This is the time when you compile all the data and insights you've gathered from the field. What have people told you they need and want? What would *you* need and want if you were in their shoes? Trying out different ideas is a part of the co-creation process; it's not something to be intimidated about. Kick off the brainstorming and prototyping with questions that will help plant seeds of ideas that will snowball and grow as you proceed. Ask yourself and your team, "What would it look like if…?" or "How would I…?" Start your discussion with "Let's imagine…" or "I want to…" Don't forget to keep applying the basic principles you've been using from the start, when you first set out to tackle this challenge. Think like a child, question all assumptions, and ask "why?" and—more importantly—"why not?" Let your creative juices flow, shake things up, and let your imagination run wild! Remember, the sky's the limit.

Brainstorming Rules

This type of brainstorming and questioning will keep happening at various stages down the road, not just during the design stage. So get comfortable with chaos! When brainstorming, there is no need to determine whether an idea holds promise, is feasible, or might work. It is simply a way of reaching into your own brain and seeing what you can find. Simple ways of brainstorming include sitting around a blackboard, flipchart, or piece of paper and sharing ideas. Group energy allows you to build on others' ideas or propose the complete opposite of others' ideas or to generate multiple ideas of your own! It is important to create a safe space: do not criticize or discuss the different ideas, simply note them and return to them later. No idea is too big or too small—encourage everyone to contribute thoughts, which may at first seem random but more likely than not will lead to others—this is how you explore different parts of your brain that have been awakened by the co-creation process in this whole time.

Check out the brainstorming rules posted on the wall at the Hippocampus Learning Centers in Bangalore, India, which we'll read more about in the case study at the end of this chapter (Figure 4.2).

Deep Reflection vs. Group Dynamics for Design

In the last chapter, we also talked about the importance of reflective practice and daily debriefings. In the design stage, you want to continue to build on both of these. Deep thinking is required to dig out innovative ideas from your brain! Encourage each and every member of your design team to spend time reflecting calmly on a daily basis out in the field and back home after information collecting excursions. Time in solitude allows one to explore thoughts, stories, and observations stored in various parts of one's mind. Record your observations from the field and review them, noticing patterns and noting down your questions. This will allow you to synthesize the information you've collected, which builds the foundation for you to generate solutions.

Once you've spent time in silent reflection and/or small-group discussion, report back to the larger group of stakeholders with these insights. This will help you create a catalytic space to build on each other's ideas, and do this sequentially and cyclically until you have generated new insights, ideas, and solutions together. The surest way to make progress that is long lasting is to

IDEA KILLERS...

REASONS WHY CREATIVITY AND INNOVATION DON'T FLY IN YOUR ORGANISATION

Yes, but... It already exists! Our customers won't like that!

WE DON'T HAVE TIME... **NO!** It's not possible...

It's too expensive! Let's be realistic... That's not logical...

We need to do more research... THERE'S NO BUDGET...

I'm not creative... We don't want to make mistakes...

The management won't agree... **GET REAL...**

It's not my responsibility... It's too difficult to master...

THAT'S TOO BIG A CHANGE. . .

The market is not ready yet... Let's keep it under consideration...

It is just like... The older generation will not use it...

WE ARE TOO SMALL FOR THAT...

It might work in other places but not here...

SINCE WHEN ARE YOU THE EXPERT?... That's for the future...

There are no staff members available...

IT IS NOT SUITABLE FOR OUR CLIENTS...

Poster from the book: Creativity in Business
Download your own poster at: www.ideakillers.net

Figure 4.2 "Idea killers" to avoid—posted on the wall of HLC's headquarters (see case). (Poster from the book: *Creativity in Business* by Igor Byttebier and Ramon Vullings. Free download available at http://www.ideakillers.net.)

inch forward, one step at a time. By iterating back and forth and combining these approaches, you'll be able to leverage the power of deep reflection and build on it with the power of group dynamics.

> The surest way to make progress that is long lasting is to inch forward, one step at a time.

Tips and Tricks to Try

When you first start, you'll inevitably feel optimistic that you are going to find a solution. You'll try out a few things, brainstorm and prototype and test and iterate, and the solution might start to solidify. Other times, it might start to feel even more and more elusive and beyond your reach. This is not where you give up. This is a familiar feeling to every social entrepreneur. Know that the mere fact you are feeling this way means you are deeply immersed in the process and this is actually, literally a step in the right direction.

When it feels like nothing is working and you have run out of ideas, try a few fun exercises:

- Reframe: Change the way you're framing the challenge. Are you imposing restrictions on yourself by surrounding your topic with a set of predetermined assumptions? Are you associating certain features of your checklist with qualities that they may not necessarily be associated with? What would you create if this feature was not an issue? If you're getting stuck, try that first and then see what new ideas might come up along the way. You can always go back and adapt later, this is just a way to temporarily remove different restrictions that could be blocking different ideas!
- Reposition: To help get a new perspective, try looking at it from a different angle—literally, try changing your mental and physical positioning. Maybe you need to step back at this point and see the forest from the trees or, vice versa, zoom in on one particular aspect and see it up close in a way that you never have before. Have you experienced the challenge from different perspectives? Try shadowing people who might be interacting with it in a way that you haven't yet considered. Try asking others to propose solutions to you, and you can test them out! Being on the receiving end puts you in a completely different position and that might give you a whole set of fresh ideas.
- Ask yourself what you could possibly do to make it worse: this is another way of looking at things from a different point of view. Can you invent a way to make this social outcome go in the opposite direction from where you're trying to get it? What would it take? Many creative teams in innovative organizations conduct a "premortem" on a challenge: rather than asking what success would look like, they ask what it would look like to *not* deliver this solution. Identifying the trigger points that will take the social outcome the wrong way might help give you ideas on how you could do things differently and reverse those trigger points.
- Break it down into smaller mini-challenges: It might help to break down the challenge into multiple aspects, rather than tackle it as one giant intangible topic. What are the different aspects that have emerged as opportunities for improvement during the co-creation process? How might you tackle each aspect separately, before putting them back together again? This might help you get a fresh insight into multiple opportunities, which you can then combine into one product or service. Thinking about it in a different way, examining different parts of the problem can help plant seeds of ideas, which will lead you to the solution you're looking for. Don't forget, it might be completely different from what you start out to create!

Don't rush the design phase. After all, you're creating the solution here that you'll spend the remainder of your venture building systems around. You'll keep innovating right through the business model, delivery model, organizational aspects, and growth. But before you start, make sure you're not rushing into things until your solution is ready. Focus on creating the best possible product or service for your end user. Most of the time, it will be something painfully simple. Once you've conceived it, you might not even be able to wrap your head around the fact that this is something that didn't exist before you started!

Give yourself as much time as needed for this stage. If you don't feel satisfied with what you've come up with yet, check out the resources in Boxes 4.1 and 4.2 to explore further possibilities, thought questions, and design methods to push your creative boundaries even further than you thought possible.

BOX 4.1   TIPS FOR USER-DRIVEN DESIGN

1. Learn everything you can about the situation and the people it affects. Immerse yourself by playing a part in the existing system or supply chain, either as a provider or end user.
2. Recruit others to design with you—You cannot do this alone. Make sure to include both experts from the field, who have been working on this topic for a long time, and newcomers with fresh ideas and perspectives.
   ★Remember that the number 1 expert is your end user.★
3. Leverage both the power of deep reflection and the power of group dynamics. Both on your own and with your design team, ask questions like "why?" and "why not?" Start sentences with "Let's imagine…" "How might we…" "What might work?" "I want to…"
4. Think outside the box and don't disregard ideas that might sound crazy (even if people tell you that your idea is crazy—You won't know if it works until you test it)!
5. Test out your ideas with your end user. This will require you to prototype them. Many designers use a rapid-prototyping method to test out multiple ideas before developing a more focused set of prototypes to test in the field.

BOX 4.2   POPULAR RESOURCES

For further ideas and inspiration, check out these popular tools and courses, which are freely available online:

www.designkit.org
plusacumen.org/courses/hcd-for-social-innovation
itunes.apple.com/us/course/creative-listening-with-ideo/id886724883
https://hbr.org/2013/11/three-creativity-challenges-from-ideos-leaders
www.ted.com/talks/david_kelley_how_to_build_your_creative_confidence

Who Is Your Design Team?

In the last chapter, we talked about assembling your starting team, those who would head out into the field with you and engage in the co-creation process with you. To that starting team, you then added various stakeholders as you got to know the community. Now, let's take a step back to ask yourself: is your starting team the same as your design team? Is there anyone missing? Do you want to recruit specialized people based on the information and needs you have gathered? By now, you might have started formulating some preliminary ideas on what your solution will look like. For example, is it likely to involve specialized subject areas such as coding or manufacturing, or is it likely to involve training a new service corps and setting up a new service system? In some cases, the answer could be more than one of these—or something entirely different! As you proceed, make sure you start thinking about who you might want to add to your team. Also, at certain points in the process, you might want to break up into smaller more specialized groups to tackle certain steps in more depth.

Building Your Solution

Analyzing and Organizing Your Options

At some point, the sheer number of ideas generated becomes overwhelming. This is where you allow yourself to step back and apply your own judgment and the judgment of your team members and stakeholders to different ideas. Your research in the field is the key driver that will inform your process of taking forward different options. Think back to what others have tried, what's worked and what hasn't (and why or why not), what your end users have taught you about the way they experience the social challenge, and the different resources available to them and to you. This is where you really need to engage your stakeholders in assessing the feasibility, desirability, and potential of various options. Some ideas are simply stepping stones to reach your solution and can be eliminated from the pool. Once you've narrowed it down to a manageable number of potential models, you can prototype them and test them out, in order to gather data to inform the solution you will be building your social venture around. Remember, at the end of the day, the solution you are looking for is the one that was generated by the end users—what did they tell you, what is their experience, what are their needs and preferences?

Prototyping

Think of prototyping as a step that allows you to communicate your idea in a more tangible way in order to test the concept and gather feedback. It's also an exercise for you to develop your ideas further by solidifying them into something concrete—whether a physical object to serve as a model for your product or a diagram to chart out your service or system. Rapid prototyping is a useful tool to help you use existing resources and information to put together a sample model of your solution. Rapid prototyping is an iterative way of generating multiple sequential models, each incrementally building on and improving the previous.* Try rapid prototyping with your team and see what ideas you generate (or discard)!

Even if your solution is a process or system rather than an object, you can still prototype it using the same concepts and methodologies. Let's use the example of a new framework for a hospital waiting room to better triage patients and reduce waiting times in emergency settings. You can start prototyping it by writing out the framework, hanging it on the wall, and going through a series of tests whereby various stakeholders are asked to go through the procedure as if they are in a waiting room and give you feedback. Ask your testers not only about their use of your model but also about the supply chain on either end: what transportation did they use to get here, how long did it take, did they have to leave their work, how much are they willing to pay for this service, would they come back for a follow-up, what concerns do they have about the clinical staff they are interacting with, what information do they wish you would provide them with before, during, and after the emergency room experience?

Test your model with both prospective patients and prospective service providers, such as in this case, clinical and administrative staff. Give them multiple options to test out, in order to create the opportunity for comparing and contrasting. Think of it like administering a survey—you want to benefit from answers given by both open-ended and multiple-choice questions.

---

* A fun example on the use of rapid prototyping from the commercial sector is the following TED-ed talk (thanks to Catlin Powers for suggesting this): http://ed.ted.com/lessons/rapid-prototyping-google-glass-tom-chi.

Prototyping your model is a useful exercise after you have undergone community-driven research and collected a variety of ideas for your solution: obviously, you'll need to test more than one idea! Brainstorm with your team about the various options, and don't build your solution based only on ideas on paper. Create models and test them out, and most likely your solution will integrate components from multiple ideas and prototypes that you've tested.

Testing

Test, Test, Test! Test It 'til You Break It

Testing your prototypes with your end users in a cyclical fashion (model it, test it, and model it again) through an iterative process is how you will get from challenge to idea to solution. "Tried and tested" is the only way your product or service will work in the real world. This is referred to as establishing proof of concept.

Multiple stages of testing include (1) gathering feedback on your experimental prototypes, (2) developing multiple versions and testing them as you get closer and closer to your end product, and (3) pilot testing your end product before attempting to build an organization around it and scale it. Gathering feedback on your experimental prototypes is part of the iterative process of selecting and developing your winning ideas by testing them out on your end users! Prototypes are representations of your idea that are not completely developed. As you collect initial feedback, you will start generating the first version of the fully developed product or service, such that you could potentially introduce it to the market. Even then, you will want to go back and collect feedback on the fully developed version, which will likely result in a second, third, or multiple versions (Figure 4.3).

A pilot can be one small cluster of end users (such as one school, one hospital, or one village, depending on your venture) or a small number of clusters.

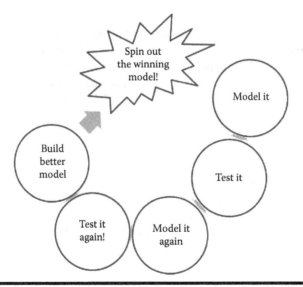

Figure 4.3 Iterative prototyping.

Piloting Your Product

Once your feedback is largely positive and user comments have been incorporated over several cycles, you will have a marketable product or service. When you reach this stage, it is rarely advisable to roll out your product or service before piloting it. A pilot can be thought of as a "test run" of your final product or service. This will inform the processes, people, and value chain around the product or service. Customer service, transportation, storage, dealing with emergencies, and unexpected situations are all part of delivering (as opposed to developing) your solution. These multiple moving parts are referred to as your supply chain. A pilot can be one small cluster of end users (such as one school, one hospital, or one village, depending on your venture) or a small number of clusters.

An example of the value of testing can be learned from D-REV, a nonprofit product development company whose mission is to improve the health and incomes of people living on less than $4 per day.* After gathering information on the social problem at hand, D-REV generates various conceptual solutions and then dives into several rounds of rapid prototyping, assembling various iterations of their product and collecting feedback from users. In the case of their newborn health product "Brilliance,"† the team collected feedback from various stakeholders along their supply chain, including procurement officers (people responsible for purchasing products in a hospital), maintenance officers (who will need to address the situation when a product breaks down or the end user experiences difficulty applying it), and healthcare officers (doctors, nurses, and other medical practitioners responsible for applying it). In this case, an interesting twist is that while the end user is the healthcare provider, the target beneficiary is newborn babies. Therefore, the medical needs of the target beneficiary informed the development of the product initially, but the characteristics of the end user and the environment in which she operates were key to further refining and delivering the product.

Interview Box. Umesh Malhotra, Founder and CEO, Hippocampus Learning Centers, Karnataka, India

TC: Tell us how you pilot tested Hippocampus Learning Centers.

UM: The question was not are we piloting to see if it works. It has to work. The pilot was to make sure it worked at scale. We had to break it—do enough scale that you can't manage—that's how you build it. Then you steady the ship and demonstrate the basic ingredients of scale.

TC: How did you phase this out over time?

UM: Year 1, we piloted 17 centers; year 2, went up to 78. Then in year 3, we introduced new processes, pushed the teachers to see what would make them leave, what are characteristics we need for teachers to have, to develop our selection criteria. Finally, in year 4, we can demonstrate profit by increasing the average enrollment per center.

TC: What elements did you innovate, and how did you find out what works?

---

* http://d-rev.org/.
† http://d-rev.org/projects/newborn-health/.

UM: To start with, the educational curriculum is nothing superior to what traditional NGOs are already using; it's just been simplified and designed in a way so that it can be standardized and scaled. The management is also streamlined. A core factor that drives results for us is that the teacher is the boss of the classroom. We don't want to impose an external interaction.

TC: What are some other design elements that you had to test before scaling?

UM: Curriculum length, monitoring and evaluation frequency, and the rate of growth and expansion. We had to ask ourselves, what is the lowest cost that can deliver quality? This is a dollar-a-day situation here; families in these villages earn, on average, $100 per month and have more than one child. We assessed price over time and went up from charging $2 per month to more than three, which was an 80% increase and the kids didn't drop out. The government provides free daycare for 1–6 year olds with milk and lunch, but villages are still asking for our preschools.

TC: What external factors did you need to take into consideration in designing for scale?

UM: The main external factor we realized early on is that we'll never reach our end goal through our work alone. We partner with as many stakeholders as possible: government, NGOs, many schools, libraries, and teachers. We provide our curriculum to other organizations to apply in other states. If you want to reach 150 million children, you can't work alone.

Photo courtesy of Hippocampus Learning Centers.

Designing a System around Your Product or Service

Results from testing your product or service will most likely point to the need for building multiple systems around it. In the commercial space, we see companies building an entire world for their consumer, selling not only a mobile phone but also the apps, accessories, chargers, technicians, software, and complementary products such as tablets and computers with the same software, drawing in the customer for the long-term and penetrating the customer's life to the deepest and widest reach possible. In social business, this has been exemplified by the Grameen group, who added one component after the other to the design of their interventions. What started as a social fund for women to increase their access to financial tools grew into a group of organizations to increase their access to healthcare, education, and other social goods. As a simple starting point, the women in each lending group were also provided with health awareness seminars and support to enroll their children in school, as part of the group benefits that came along with accessing the microloans.

In the case of D-REV, after finalizing the design, they partnered with a well-known local manufacturer of neonatal medical equipment, which allowed them to leverage an existing distribution network and piggyback on the existing customers, in addition to accessing data on key customer needs and markets. The manufacturer already had access to hospitals and healthcare practitioners through its existing products, so D-REV was able to integrate itself into an existing system, in addition to expanding the market and sales for the manufacturer. In the case of HLC, the system included an array of products and services to complement the core curriculum offered by the early learning centers, which allowed them to build a pipeline of customers at various stages of the life cycle.

So once you've prototyped your solution and are testing it, think about what systems could go along with it to support and amplify its delivery and its impact!

BOX 4.3   ELEMENTS OF DESIGN FOR AFFORDABILITY

(Extracts from Out of Poverty *by Paul Pollack*)*

1. Go to where the action is, talk to the people living with this challenge, listen to them and learn everything there is to know about the specific context
2. If you come up with a solution to a problem, there is no reason to be modest Be ambitious!
3. Think like a child (to find the obvious solutions)
4. See and do the obvious (immerse yourself in the problem)
5. If somebody already invented it, you don't have to

* Pollack, P. (2009). *Out of Poverty*. Berrett-Koehler Publishers.

BOX 4.4   COMMON FEATURES OF INITIATIVES THAT HAVE TACKLED EXTREME POVERTY*

1. Listening to customers and understanding the specific context of their lives
2. Design and implement extremely affordable technologies or business models
3. Market-based solutions whose implementation is driven/supported by the private sector
4. Last mile distribution while maintaining low costs succeeds through decentralization
5. Design for scale from the start

* Warwick, M., & Pollack, P. (2013). *The Business Solution to Poverty*. Berrett-Koehler Publishers.

Beyond Design

Design is only one aspect of innovation, and innovation is only one aspect of social entrepreneurship. When developing your solution, it is critical to stay focused on the core challenge you are tackling and the community you are co-creating it with. You will cycle back to various stages of innovation and design as you begin to grow and implement your solution, but the challenge and community will remain at its core. A few rules to keep in mind were well summarized by Paul Pollack, the founder of International Development Enterprises, which creates income and livelihood opportunities for poor rural households by designing and delivering technologies for improved agriculture, sanitation, and hygiene.* In his two books *Out of Poverty* and *The Business Solution to Poverty* with Mel Warwick, Pollack presents a commonly understood framework synthesizing best practices from his own experience, which reflect and mirror also a multitude of success stories from development ventures worldwide (Boxes 4.3 and 4.4).

These common principles emphasize extreme affordability, but it is important to remember that this only pertains to the extent that it fulfills your central mission. Sometimes, the lowest-cost

* http://www.ideorg.org/.

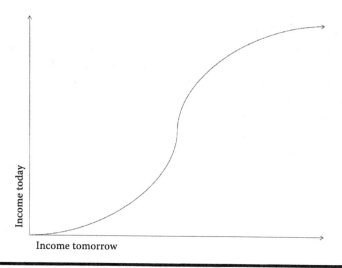

Income today

Income tomorrow

Figure 4.4 Poverty trap.

option is not that which will allow your customers to escape poverty. This was pointed out by Dr. Catlin Powers, cofounder of One Earth Designs. "Why would I ever buy a lead shoe?" she was asked by one of her field testers, pointing to the fact that a lead shoe may be more affordable than a lightweight shoe but would defeat the purpose of increasing mobility, the driving mission behind making shoes! One Earth Designs manufactures and distributes solar-powered cook stoves, originally designed for nomadic communities.* If the cook stove is designed for extreme affordability but is not lightweight and is not durable, then the social enterprise would be defeating its purpose. This points to a new definition of affordability, incorporating not only the dollar cost of the product but also the opportunity cost of failing to deliver on your mission.

This is elaborated in the S-shaped curve of poverty as taught by Professors Banerjee and Duflo at MIT's Poverty Action Lab (Figure 4.4).† The S-shaped curve represents the observations that living in extreme poverty lends itself to behavioral economics that propagate poverty, thus creating a poverty trap. Buying the cheapest product (in this hypothetical anecdote a pair of lead shoes) rather than the most effective or most durable product is one way in which household poverty is often perpetuated, since the purchase will have to be made over and over again. This underscores the importance of studying your social challenge and learning everything there is to know about your community, their lifestyle, and the way they make their decisions. It also emphasizes the need to be able to frame the design of your product within a theory of change that connects it to the challenge you are tackling and the impact you aim to create for your end users, specifying the assumptions underlying each step along the way.

Design is only one aspect of innovation, and innovation is only one aspect of social entrepreneurship.

---

* www.onearthdesigns.org.
† Banerjee, A., & Duflo, E. (2012). *Poor Economics: A Radical Rethinking of the Way to Fight Global Poverty*. Public Affairs.

Your Theory of Change

As you narrow down to the winning prototype, honing and refining it through multiple testing, you also want to make sure you have a bulletproof, tried and tested explanation on how your solution will change the social challenge you are facing! This is what we call your theory of change. Is this prototype going to address the social challenge you are aiming to meet, or is it going to be a pair of lead shoes? The theory of change is the explanation and justification for why you are about to embark on this social venture you are planning, why it will work, and why people should join you and invest resources in your solution. It is the essence behind the design of the solution, which will bridge the gap between the challenge you have characterized and the measurable change you are aiming to achieve.

So what is your theory of change? So far, along this journey, you have started with the challenge you're tackling and are building your solution toward that end. Spending time developing and testing your theory of change at this point will help make sure that you are truly developing your solution in a way that will create the change you want to see.

How can you match your design to a set of targets you want to reach? A good way to start thinking about your targets is to start by describing the current state of the challenge you are tackling, then describe how you would like to see it. How far toward that ideal scenario do you think you can reach with your solution?

Your target will be based on certain assumptions. Let's say you are working to reduce preventable infant deaths in your community. If your intervention is a medical device, then your target will be influenced by factors such as the clinical efficacy of the device, the health system in which it will be applied, the human resources, and the capacity of clinical staff to apply it. If your intervention is based on sociobehavioral changes such as the responsiveness of mothers to text messages reminding them of vaccination appointments for their children, then your target will be based on mobile penetration rates, literacy rates, psychosocial factors influencing the efficacy of receiving such reminders, and barriers to response such as transportation and work or family schedules. Gender patterns may also influence the impact of such reminders in settings where there may be one mobile phone per household, which is not always with the mother.

See where we're going with this?

You could be designing, innovating, and prototyping with the best of intentions, only to find out that your solution fails the test.

This is why clarifying your assumptions from the start is crucial—they will inform your target and will help you determine what steps you need to take to reach there.

What design features can optimize the sociobehavioral response in the previous example, given what you know about the end users? Going back to the medical device example, what features can be optimized to increase clinical efficacy, make it user friendly for the staff you're relying on to apply it, and make it feasible to implement within the health system it will be applied in? These may include language options, use of layman's terms rather than medical jargon, use of graphics and images, and other options that increase the user-friendliness.

So, where your theory of change comes into play is in determining how the solution you are developing will meet the needs of your target audience in the setting you are operating in. Stating your assumptions at every step will help you evaluate whether you are designing your solution optimally. Specifying the assumptions allows you to test them and determine whether your theory holds! The theory of change is a concept used most often in the nonprofit world but is applicable to for-profit social ventures too.

Tools to Develop Your Theory of Change

Your theory of change can be as simple as a few paragraphs of narrative outlining the key pieces of information described previously. You can also turn to a number of interactive tools to help you and your team brainstorm, discuss, build, and strengthen your theory. Many larger organizations use diagrams to map their theory of change and represent the multiple players involved. Others try to summarize their theory in an "if, then" sentence. "If we provide a rigorous yet simplified curriculum charging low prices within walking distance, then we can improve educational outcomes in young children in rural India."

To help you get there, one of the most basic tools is the theory of change table. This is simply a series of columns and rows that walks the user through the different pieces of the theory of change puzzle. Once you've described the challenge you're tackling and the changes you're setting out to create with your solution, this tool helps fill in the steps needed to get from one to the other. You can fill it out in whichever order makes sense to you, then go back and revisit each column to make sure it fits in with the rest (see Figure 4.5). Many social entrepreneurs start by filling in the first column, which specifies the challenge they're trying to tackle, and listing underneath it the key assumptions and data points available to them regarding the challenge they've identified. It might help to then pencil in the last column, which specifies the long-term change you're setting as your goal. Then, keep your eye on this last column as you go back and fill in the steps to reach there.

Moving to the second column to the right of the problem: who is your target audience? Who does the problem affect, and which segment(s) of the population does your solution serve? Again, list underneath the key assumptions about this population. The testing that you put your prototypes will inform these assumptions. Have you explored the barriers between you and your audience? Are you assuming that they will be open to and interested in adopting your solution? If you are sending text message reminders to mothers to bring in their children for vaccination, you are assuming that (a) the mother has access to the mobile telephone number recorded in her file (oftentimes, the father receives the message and does not relay it to the mother), (b) she is able to read and understand the message, (c) she is physically and logistically able to respond to it and

Problem	Audience and entrypoint	Steps needed to bring change	Measurable effects	Wider benefits and long term change
Assumptions:	Assumptions:	Assumptions:	Assumptions:	Assumptions:

Figure 4.5   Example theory of change template table.

get her child to the appointment, and (d) she is open to responding and wants to vaccinate her child. A simple yet very important assumption is that mothers want to vaccinate their children. Vaccination has been debated in many societies and there may be multiple social and cultural factors to consider along with the science.

Next, how will you reach your target audience? What is your entry point? Since you have spent time on community-driven research and participatory planning, you will have a better idea of the context in which you're going to operate and you'll have already refined your assumptions regarding your entry point to reach the target audience. It could be an existing supply chain. It could be partnering with an existing organization. Going back to previous examples, if your goal is to introduce a new medical device which will lower infant mortality, options for your entry point might include local clinics, physicians' associations, nurses associations, hospital managers, or the ministry of health. These are all very different entry points, and your choice will differ depending on the setting you are working in. For the vaccination text message reminders example, such an intervention would work best building on an existing healthcare provider with records for all its patients. Mobile numbers could be collected from or added to each patient's record, and an automated system could be set up in collaboration with an existing telecom provider.

> What needs to happen for your solution to work?

Now, to get from here to your goal, what steps are needed? Once you achieve your entry point, how does your solution work? Walk yourself through each node of change. Note down the possible outcomes at each node. What needs to happen for your solution to work? This will lay the foundation for your future business plan, which will require you to think about what you will do if things don't go according to plan. It is impossible to emphasize enough the importance of fleshing out your assumptions at each junction, so that you can continue to collect data to back these up and assess to what degree they will hold and be prepared with a contingency plan for what you will do if and when they don't.

Finally, what is/are the measurable changes(s) your social venture will produce? Identifying the measurable outcomes you will be looking out for to assess your success is critical. The challenges you're facing are sticky stuff; otherwise, someone else would have solved them a long time ago! So arm yourself with these data tools to amplify your chances of success. You've already identified the long-term change you see as your goal, but what intermediary changes do you need to create in order to get there? How will you know if you're making progress or need to step back and reassess what you're doing? Sticking to the text message reminders example, if your goal is to reduce child mortality before the age of five, the measurable effects you'll directly produce from your intervention are that more mothers will bring in their children for vaccination, the number of missed vaccination appointments will be reduced, and the number of children vaccinated will increase.

Incremental Innovation and Disruptive Innovation Are Not Mutually Exclusive

People talk about incremental innovation and disruptive innovation as if they're mutually exclusive. A common misperception is that to build new markets, we need to invent things that didn't exist before. That's actually not true most of the time. Building evidence-based solutions requires, by definition, that you are exercising some form of incremental innovation. Tackling challenges most likely brought about by market failures means, by definition, that what you are doing is disruptive. So, by definition, you are doing both! And you will hack this challenge to death.

So don't be afraid to proceed one step at a time. You can still be disruptive and ambitious and make a phenomenal change, taking what others have done before you and building on their results. Whether positive or negative, i.e., whether building on what has worked or what hasn't, you are maximizing your chances of success if your solution is based on evidence.

That's not to say you shouldn't pursue bold ideas if you have come up with something entirely new—go for it! This is just to say that whatever you do, test it first, pilot it first, and make sure it really works in the way you want it to. The stakes are high. Whatever you do will affect others. And often, there are unintended consequences that can be either positive or negative. So proceed with care, and don't play God.

Remember the importance of building on what others have done before—learn from those who have attempted to solve this problem before you—dig up the evidence collected about your key assumptions. This is where the research you've been so arduously conducting will come in handy! The only way we can go farther than those who came before us is to "stand on the shoulders of giants," as the famous saying goes. This means that in the majority of cases, rather than reinventing the wheel, social entrepreneurs will build on the incremental progress achieved by those before them and push that progress further by using all the knowledge they gained.

It's not a sprint to the finish line.

Summary and Next Steps

We are really getting there! You're starting to get an idea of how to tackle the challenge you set out to change, what your product or service will do, and how it will work. You might not have it all figured out yet, and that is completely okay. Don't think at this stage you're supposed to already have all the answers. You're simply supposed to take the time and space required to brainstorm different ideas, test them out with your team and stakeholders, and develop them further until you're able to identify a solution that has the potential to work.

It's not really fair to represent all this in one chapter, as the development phase can take months, if not years. Don't rush it. Your goal is not just to come up with something—it's to come up with something that *works*. That's why the theory of change is so valuable—because it keeps you in check and doesn't let you get away with proceeding any further until you can really prove that the solution you're proposing will have the intended effect.

Get out there and talk to people and see what they think! If you're not being met with reactions along the lines of, "This has to be done!" then you might want to go back to the drawing board. You want to come up with something that people *want* and *need*. And you want to make sure the people who want it and need it are those you've designed it for and with! Stay immersed, stay focused, and don't be afraid to come up for air when you need it. This takes time, it's not a sprint to the finish line. There's no magical button you can push or formula you can follow to build your solution. You'll never feel fully equipped, you just need to unleash your brain cells and start working.

Exercise: Your Deliverables

You'll need to go through multiple iterations to come up with your deliverables, so take your time. Just make sure that when you're ready to deliver, you can summarize your answers in one sentence, and with one diagram:

1. Sketch out your product or service. What is it? How will it work?
2. Test it out with potential end users. Who is your audience? What is their feedback? How did you incorporate it?
3. Fill in your theory of change table, listing the underlying assumptions beneath each step. Has your research and testing validated each assumption? What else might you need to do to prove this will work?
4. Last challenge: summarize your solution in an "if–then" sentence!

CHAPTER SUMMARY

■ Starting with the checklist of attributes we created in the last chapter, this chapter is all about making them come to life.

■ Working with your end users and bringing in new skills needed to your design team, you'll need to experiment with potential ideas and go through multiple iterations of trial and error.

■ The most important thing to keep in mind is that by definition, in trying out different things to see what works, you'll need to fail. Failing on purpose is how we learn and discover new solutions!

■ Start by brainstorming potential ideas, avoiding idea killers, and considering all options with your team and your end users.

■ Then, prototype a number of potential winners, testing them out with your stakeholders to get feedback.

■ One of the first steps in testing your solution is putting it through the theory of change test. List out all your assumptions and validate them. Can this product or service actually bring about the changes you're aiming to create?

■ Before you launch forward with building an entire venture around this potential solution, you'll need to organize one or more pilot tests. We'll add the components needed to test this out more fully in the coming chapters, such as impact metrics and business plan components.

■ Most importantly, make it fun. The design phase is one of the most creative stages in social entrepreneurship. Explore different options and push yourself beyond conventional boundaries … who knows what you might find!

Social Ventures Mentioned in This Chapter

Company profile: D-Rev, www.d-rev.org.
Founded in 2007, US 501(c)3 nonprofit organization.
Product/service: D-Rev is a nonprofit product development company that designs and delivers medical technologies that lose the quality healthcare gap for under-served populations.

Current projects include a high-performance knee joint for amputees in the developing world and jaundice treatment devices for newborns.

Goal: Close the quality healthcare gap for under-served populations.

How it works: It is rarely viable for for-profit companies to design and develop products for the 4 billion people living in under-served populations. D-Rev closes this gap by subsidizing research and development and working with a global network of partners to design disruptive and profoundly affordable products aimed to improve health. Their products are world-class, market driven, and user obsessed. By relying on grants and private-sector contributions (such as from the Bill and Melinda Gates Foundation), they own the research, design, and development stages and then partner with industry leaders to manufacture and scale the product for maximum impact.

Company profile: One Earth Designs, www.oneearthdesigns.org, www.oneearthdesigns.com. Founded in 2009, registered in the United States, China, Hong Kong, Norway.

Product/service: SolSource is a miniature solar power plant that provides solar cooking, heating, and electricity generation in one elegant and affordable system. The SolSource product roadmap also includes add-ons that enable water purification, desalination, solar autoclaving, food dehydration, home cooling, and refrigeration.

Goal: To replace polluting cooking fuels (which currently kill 4.3 million people each year), with affordable solar energy for cooking, home heating, and electricity.

How it works: SolSource was inspired by and developed in collaboration with rural Tibetan families in the Himalaya. Prior to SolSource, these families often cooked indoors with yak dung fuel in adobe stoves which contributed to severe health problems, high death rates, and reduced economic opportunity. By using highly reflective panels that direct sun light toward the bottom of the pan, which is placed in the middle (similar to the shape of a satellite with the pan replacing the antenna), SolSource harnesses solar energy seven times more efficiently than competing technologies, enabling families to access clean energy to replace polluting traditional fuels.

Company profile: Hippocampus Learning Centers, www.hlc.hippocampus.in. Founded in 2010, Bangalore, India.

Product/service: Provides preschool (under age 6) and after-school (over age 6) educational services for children in rural India. Carefully selected and trained local women use fun and interactive methods to help children learn and ultimately do better in school.

Goal: To create high-quality, low-cost educational programs for children in rural India, making learning available, affordable, and fun

How it works: HLC focuses on highly efficient, streamlined operations and scaling to 600–700 centers. Each learning center is independent, autonomous, and financially sustainable. All performance monitoring and assessments are simplified into efficient checklists systems that are the responsibility of each center, reducing travel costs of headquarters staff. Headquarters is highly selective in their recruitment and training of new teachers. They hire only local women who may lack formal training and experience but have a vested interest in the success of the community's children. They personally train each teacher in the skills required and provide basic, standardized packages containing all necessary educational materials to teach the children.

Case Study: Hippocampus Learning Centers

Designing Impact, Scale, and Sustainability

The Hippocampus Learning Centers (HLC) were designed for scale. The vision is to create learning opportunities for children and youth in rural India, thus enabling power of choice.* Headquartered in Bangalore in the state of Karnataka, India, HLC has 104 learning centers at the time of writing. The design of this social venture, on multiple fronts spanning organizational, content, and delivery levels, was developed to streamline operations and maximize results.

The challenge identified by the HLC team was a learning deficit in India and especially in rural areas, where children were not exposed to a literacy environment until they entered public school at the age of six, already putting them at a disadvantage in their cognitive and social ability. This was manifested by poor learning outcomes, with ripple effects throughout the life cycle. The HLC team asked, "What if we could provide children with the best chance at a fair shot in life?" They did this by developing a preschool system that fulfilled the criteria of availability, accessibility, acceptability, and quality. Innovation at multiple levels was a key to ensuring that both the educational model and the management model of each center were robust enough for them to be applied and replicated in hundreds of centers at large scale without sacrificing quality. Through user-driven design, the team identified two key factors that made this possible: the profile of the teachers recruited and trained, and the nature and content of the curriculum. Both were simplified and streamlined to allow for application at large scale.

Rather than recruit teachers with training and experience in the existing public school system, the HLC team recruited women from the village in which each center operated. The women did not necessarily need to have any formal training or experience as teachers, nor was it required for them to be proficient in English. HLC's team trained them in the complete package of skills required. A large portion of an average day's curriculum and communication in a Hippocampus center could be delivered using the local language, with certain keywords, phrases, and lessons in English. HLC's team found that it was more efficient and effective to train a fresh new learning and teaching corps rather than to work with pre-trained, experienced teachers who would then have to unlearn their existing habits.

HLC teachers had a certain degree of autonomy in running their own center, and gained a sense of independence. A large portion of the curriculum was not only on language, math, or other academic topics but also on following instructions, behaving in a classroom, working as a team, and functioning within an orderly system.

Independence of the learning centers on multiple levels was a key factor to success: each center as its own unit is financially sustainable (surpassing 100% cost recovery) and the only nonrecoverable costs are those of the central headquarters. Teachers at the center level are responsible for recruiting students and have the freedom to tailor and adapt the learning material and style to a degree, incorporating local contexts and cultures. The role of the central headquarters is to

---

* http://hlc.hippocampus.in/hlc/about/our-vision/.

develop and update the curriculum, branding, marketing, monitoring, and assessment. This cost can be covered by increasing the number of centers, so that their small profit margins will add up to surpass the running costs of the central headquarters. Thus, in designing the organization, it was essential to ensure that the size of the central headquarters would not need to greatly increase over time in proportion to the number of learning centers. This could be accomplished through a combination of factors.

One is decentralization and automation of monitoring and assessment. It would be too costly to send staff members from headquarters to monitor the performance of each center in the rural areas. Instead, field coordinators are recruited and trained to serve this role. Each field coordinator monitors a cluster of centers within a defined geographic area, allowing her or him to conduct daily site visits to centers within the cluster, ensuring that each center is visited once per week for two to three hours. Automation of the data collection was also developed by equipping each center with a low-cost tablet, allowing for a more streamlined approach to the recording, collection, and analysis of performance indicators recorded during the field officers' site visits.

Additionally, many centers operated both as an early learning center in the mornings, hosting children aged under six, and operated a remedial English program in the afternoons, hosting children over the age of six who had gone on to enroll in the formal school system. For the remedial English program, HLC's team researched existing reading programs from all over the world and created their own reading program, which simplified elementary-grade English into six levels (as compared with over 20 levels in other programs from around the world). They ordered low-cost booklets coded by color to reflect the levels. They called the program "Grow by Reading," where the first two words represent the six levels of advancement: green, red, orange, white, blue, and yellow. Thus, the system was simplified and made easy to understand by teachers, children, and parents.

Another design factor was the development of a package of physical resources for each center. In order to ensure standardization across centers, a basic package of educational materials (books, chalk, toys, seating mats, etc.) was created to supply and equip each teacher with the core range of essential teaching materials. Thus, each time a new center is opened, the characteristics and costs are known in advance, and the procurement of supplies takes place according to a preset system.

Beyond design, in growing the organization, an essential ingredient to smooth expansion was the development of robust systems that could withstand the strain of rapid scale. It was calculated that in order to become financially sustainable as an organization, HLC needed to scale to 600–700 centers. How could the team maintain quality of performance at each center and manage the exponential increase in workload at the central headquarters? The former was ensured through decentralization and automation of monitoring and assessment. The latter required a clarification of processes and simplification of roles, in order to streamline operations.

That is to say, during the start-up phase of any organization, a large number of roles are played by a small number of people. The founding team is responsible for building the content, recruiting, assessing, marketing, accounting, and keeping up with growth. As the organization scales, these roles are simplified. Rather than having one person responsible for the teacher recruitment and student recruitment required to open each center, the mature organization will have a recruitment officer specialized in recruiting new teachers and a marketing officer specialized in recruiting new students. Similarly, during the start-up phase of an organization, many procedures and decisions are taken in an ad hoc fashion, on the spot, depending on each scenario and on a case-by-case basis as the team develops their approach. As the organization scales, these processes and procedures are evaluated and put into a system.

HLC was initially piloted with 17 centers. This is highly unusual in traditional development fields, where one center may be a more common initial pilot. The founder of HLC, Umesh Malhotra, insisted on designing it for scale from the start. He wanted to "test it until it broke." From the initial 17 centers in the first year, he grew the organization to include 78 in the second year, until things started to go wrong and teachers started dropping out. His test question was "How would I need to run this in order for everything to go wrong?" And then he fixed it so that these things would not go wrong again when the organization grew. His goal was to design it for scale because his end users were the millions of children without access to affordable quality education.

Education and healthcare in high-poverty populations have always been a challenge in terms of delivering affordable services at high quality using a sustainable model—the international development and philanthropy world has been debating for decades whether it's possible to deliver education in high-poverty populations using a self-sustaining financial model. Just as we'll see many examples in healthcare that have proven that it is in fact possible, HLC serves to demonstrate with their data and results the real possibility of delivering education using a for-profit model. What are the characteristics that allowed them to achieve what no other education organization targeting low-income children has ever achieved before?

The key to their success was not only the business case. It was that they built a system of products and services using innovative methods and designed for scale, envisioning a target from the start that reaches thousands if not millions of end users and piloting a system with the vision to grow it to that scale. This has involved a simplification and standardization of the core educational materials and concepts and of the management of the learning centers themselves. It has involved a decentralization of the monitoring and assessment process using an efficient checklist system, which is now also being automated using low-cost tablets at each center, to further streamline the quality assurance process. Finally, it has involved building systems for scale. This includes simplifying roles as the organization grows, where at the start-up phase one person is responsible for carrying out various roles and making various decisions as the founding team develops their approach; and as the organization grows they evolve into a more specialized division of labor. This allows them to reach large volumes with each person in charge of one specialized part of the process: marketing, recruitment, content development, product development, delivery, and evaluation. At the time of writing, the HLC team is undergoing a process mapping phase whereby each step taken within this operation is evaluated to assess how that step can best fit into a system that's streamlined and efficient and can function as a well-oiled machine, all the while keeping in consideration how to conserve the organizational culture and hold on to the mission as the organization grows.

Chapter 5

Market Strategy

The Multidimensional Market

This Little Solution Went to Market

Now that you have a basic idea of what your solution looks like, who it's for and how it works, it's time to take the next step in the design challenge. How will you actually get it to them? How will you price it? Where will it be provided? Let's start building your supply chain and your value chain.

You've learned a lot about how people interact with the social challenge you're tackling. Now, it's time to find out how they're going to interact with your solution. Your market strategy basically answers the question, how will you reach people? How will they find out about you? Who are you serving, and where? This is a continuation of your testing phase, to ensure that the solution you're proposing is truly what's needed.

In this chapter, we'll start building the basics of your business model so that you can take the first step in building a venture around your product or service. How will your solution penetrate people's lives?

Compass: Vision, Mission, Values

Before we start, let's make sure you know where you're trying to get to. This is a time when you'll be testing out your theory of change and building your vision and mission, which will drive your work for years to come.

Every venture has a mission, vision, and core set of values. These drive the work of the organization or initiative, and every person, process, decision, or output related to the venture always refers back to these driving factors.

You've already started to form a vision of how things could be different from the way they are today. Now, that vision is starting to take shape. It's time for you to start thinking about how you will put into a clear, concise statement a description of the world you are trying to create. This helps ensure that all stakeholders are clear on what you represent and why you are doing what you are doing. Most importantly, it helps you and your team keep your eyes on the prize!

Vision

Your vision is a description of how things could be different from the way they are today. Describe the world that you would see if you were able to completely transform your social challenge! All your work, everything you have done up until now and everything you will do from this point onward, is driven by your vision. It can sometimes be daunting to put it into words! Keep it simple—sometimes, the most effective vision statements are simply a counterfactual description of the world as it is today—a statement saying what it would be like if your social challenge was knocked out of the ball park. For example, your vision could sound something like this: "A world in which every child has the opportunity to fulfill their love of learning."*

Your vision should be aspirational. It is what drives you, and you want it to drive others to join forces with you. Many people might have similar visions, each working in their own way to help that vision come true. Clarifying your vision will help you find like-minded people whom you can work with to collectively achieve larger progress toward that vision than you would alone.

A world without poverty is a vision that many organizations work toward, each with its own different mission (increasing the earning power of farmers in Kenya, increasing access to capital for immigrants in the inner city in New York, and educating female heads of households in the slums of Egypt are three separate missions that all work toward this same vision).

Mission

Your mission is the assignment you have tasked upon yourself. How are you going to make this vision possible? The mission is the path you are taking to reach your vision. By developing your products and services using user-driven design, testing them out and fleshing out your theory of change, you've already taken the first steps toward charting that path.

For example, if your vision is a world in which every child has the opportunity to fulfill their love of learning, then how are you going to work toward that vision? The mission statement needs to be more specific and tangible than the driving vision. There are many potential ways of fulfilling your vision: the mission specifies the what, who, and how of your work.

A strong mission statement will capture your desired outcome and target population, and what it is that you do. It is your organization's introductory statement to the world! Just like when a friend or colleague introduces you at a reception, "Ms. X does _____," your mission statement is how you introduce your organization, "We do _____."

A common rule of thumb for the mission statement is the 4Ms: memorable, manageable, measurable, and motivational. Another common rule of thumb is keep it short. You don't necessarily need to go into too much detail about "how" you will do it, but be extremely clear about "what" you are doing: "Save kids' lives in Uganda. Rehabilitate coral reefs in the Western Pacific. Prevent maternal–child transmission of HIV in Africa. Get Zambian farmers out of poverty" are all hypothetical examples of mission statements that are less than eight words.† Don't panic if you need more than eight words of course; these are just a few very concise examples—the important thing is that you keep it clear and concrete, filtering down to the core of what you do.

---

* This is a real-life vision statement that was drafted as part of a business planning process with Ana Aqra Association and Alfanar venture philanthropy (http://ana-agra.org/).
† Quoted from http://www.ssireview.org/blog/entry/the_eight_word_mission_statement.

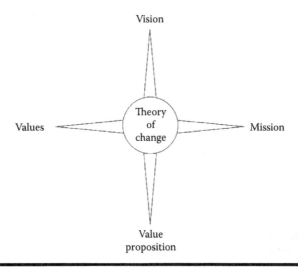

Figure 5.1   Organizational compass.

Values

While the mission and vision of your venture refer to the social outcomes you're working toward, values refer to the characteristics and processes your work will adhere to. Thinking about these with your team is key to building your market strategy, and your venture moving forward, in accordance with your values. You'll need to refer back to these at multiple points down the line when making decisions that could result in potential trade-offs.

What values does your organization follow? Examples of common values are transparency, equality, integrity, empathy, quality, safety, and innovation. Others are teamwork, respect, partnerships, patient centeredness, student centeredness, and client focused. Some organizations use nouns; others use phrases or expressions, and yet others use sentences. Your organization's values will inform the decisions and prioritizations you make and the behavior of your team.

Social entrepreneurs serve as leaders in embodying the values of their organization and inspiring everyone in their organization to internalize these values and demonstrate them in all actions. In HLC's case, the organization's mission, vision, and values extended to anyone who was part of the supply chain; not only the teachers at the field sites and managers at the headquarters but also the cleaning team who were hired to maintain the centers, the parents who dropped their children off at the door, anyone who had any interaction with the centers, were encouraged to embody its goals and values.

The reason it's important to spend a lot of time thinking about mission, vision, and values at this point—and continuously in the future as you chart your path—is that together with your theory of change and value proposition they form the compass for your social venture. Your decisions will be made based on how you will affect people's lives. Your vision is the underlying force that led to your creation of this solution. And your theory of change was built around that and gave birth to the mission, values, and value proposition of your social venture (Figure 5.1).

Value Proposition and Unique Selling Point

Building on the previous section, your value proposition captures how this vision, mission, and set of values translate into benefits for your end user. What are you offering people? How will you make their lives better? Quite literally, what value are you proposing? Why should people give you their attention, time, and money?

Your value proposition is the added value you're contributing to peoples' lives. It is important to be able to clearly and concisely describe what your product and service are, who your end user is, and how you are making their lives better. This is because you are going to be building the components of your social market strategy around this value that you are trying to create. This is how you will take your solution to market!

As part of articulating your value proposition, make sure you've captured your *unique selling point* (USP). What makes your product or service better than the alternatives? What are you offering that no one has offered before, or how is what you are offering better? Is it more affordable, is it more effective, is it more user-friendly, is it all of the above? Is it simply the first of its kind, with data demonstrating the demand? Your USP will explain why your end users should turn to you, rather than the best possible alternative out there.

The main advantage you have compared with others who have tried to build social solutions in the past is that you've built it with your end user. By now, you know that people will likely not be interested if you just come up to them and try to introduce a product or service by informing them that this will make them healthier, more productive, or replenish their environmental resources for the future. The thing about social outcomes is that they are long-term concepts. People are focused on their immediate needs and their lives in this moment.

This is why articulating your value proposition is very different from articulating your vision and mission. Stay focused on the product or service itself. How is it making people's lives better right now? We help children perform well in school by providing top-of-the-line preschool at prices parents can afford. We help you save time and money and come home with a healthy meal for your family. We help mothers deliver safely by providing low-cost, high-quality care.

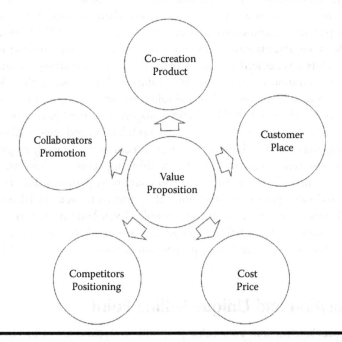

Figure 5.2 Multidimensional market: the 5Cs and 5Ps of social entrepreneurship.

Ask your end users and testers to put it into words themselves, as a continuation of your co-creation and user-driven design! Then you can communicate it to others and build your social market strategy around it (Figure 5.2).

Market Size: Defining Your Denominator

An important part of building your business model is estimating the number of people you are trying to reach. So far, we've thought a lot about *who* your end user is and *what* their characteristics are. Now it's time for you to calculate *how many* people you're targeting.

This is different from what you did at the start of your journey while characterizing your challenge. At that stage, you were researching how many people are affected by the social outcome you're addressing. But now that you've developed your solution and are working on your business model, how many of them do you think you can reach?

This is your denominator, against which you'll track progress moving forward. In the coming chapters, you'll piece together the operational pieces and distribution channels required to reach your target, figure out the success metrics you'll use to measure whether and when you achieve the changes you're aiming for, and determine how you'll design and manage the financial flow in and out of your venture.

Estimating your market size is extremely challenging, but it's critical to know what kind of denominator you're dealing with here. Billions of people around the world may be affected by the social challenge you're addressing. Are you aiming to reach them all? Let's start by narrowing down on the customer segment(s) that your value proposition speaks to.

Let's walk through an example together. In this example, let's say you're serving pregnant women. You've co-created your solution with women and their families in a rural setting in Kenya. How many pregnant women per year are there in similar rural settings in Kenya? Do you want to make the assumption that your solution can be adapted and offered in similar rural settings in other countries, or do you want to put that aside for now until a later expansion stage? You are already narrowing down your numbers by making these decisions. Now, depending on how much this solution is costing you and how you are going to price or finance it, you can narrow it down further based on the number of people who are willing to pay. Then, depending on where you are going to sell it and how you will promote it, you can set a target of the number of people you might be able to reach.

It's important to realize that the size of your market speaks to the need and potential. How much you can grow to fill that need and potential depends on a host of other factors including your resources, external environment, and internal operations. We will discuss these in more detail in the coming chapters.

Let's take a look at the different dimensions of your potential market, in order to help form a more complete picture.

Social Market Strategy

In this chapter, we'll use the 5Cs and the 5Ps to encapsulate the key components of a social market strategy. All these components center around your value proposition, which is at the core of your venture. You'll notice that you've already dedicated a substantial amount of time and resources toward building many of these components! The co-creation process, the customer, the product, and the place were the focus of the past three chapters. Now, we're going to start thinking about the cost and price aspects. Then we can go into more depth about positioning, promotion, competitors, and collaborators. Going through these different dimensions one at a time and then putting them all together will help you determine whether and how your solution will be feasible.

This is all a continuation of the testing process you started in the last chapter—prototype, test, iterate, until you find the combination that works. Don't forget, innovation happens at multiple levels; it's not just the product that needs to work, but also the price, the distribution channels, all the nuts and bolts of your solution. So let's test and iterate each component until we can get that solution to market!

Co-Creation

That's right, co-creating with the community was the first step you took in developing your social market plan! This is because it made sure that your product or service is user driven (Figure 5.3). Marketing gurus often talk about using a "push" versus "pull" strategy, i.e., aggressively or preemptively entering a market versus responding to cues from customers. Co-creating with the community was your first step in the "pull" process. Both are needed, and we will talk about some "push" strategies further in the chapter.

Product

The product or service you co-created through user-driven design is the core of the marketing strategy. What are the key attributes of your product or service that will make your customers' lives better? What is your core offering? This will define your branding, which we'll talk about a little bit later. It will also inform how you want to position yourself in the market. Your identity as a social venture and the image you want to project are based on the solution you are offering.

Customer

We talked about population segments in Chapters 2 and 3. Who is your core customer? You may be offering your product or service to more than one population segment, but you need to be clear on this when developing your marketing strategy. In the most simple and basic of cases, a social venture will target one core customer: expecting mothers in remote rural settings with lack of access to health information, young children in villages in India, nomadic tribes in the Himalayan plateau, overworked underpaid mothers in US cities with lack of access to healthy

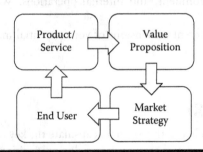

Figure 5.3 Co-creation as a cornerstone.
Understanding your target audience informs your solution, value proposition, and market strategy.

foods (see interview box). It's important to understand both the characteristics that tie your customers together and any variations and heterogeneity that will result in diversities of behaviors and preferences. In other cases, you might have a huge amount of customer segmentation, in which case you'll have to tailor your messaging—and the options that are offered with your solution—around multiple core groups.

Try to put numbers on this dimension of your social market strategy—how many end users are you aiming to reach? How much will it cost to reach them? How will you retain them? Intentions are not enough to grow your customer base. People will try your product once out of curiosity or because it has been co-created in a way to maximize social impact. But they will only become repeat customers if it makes their life easier and if it makes them happier.

Place

Where are you going to offer your product or service? Tell us more about the part of the world you're working in, and what the unique features of this context are. What kind of market is it? Are you working in a dense urban setting, a remote rural setting, or something in between? What is the infrastructure like, and what are the distribution channels like? Is your social venture mobile, or is it stationary? Are you opening a new distribution channel (store, website, clinic, school) or piggybacking on existing channels? In either case, are you asking your customers to come directly to you, or are you making your product/service accessible to them vis-à-vis a place or activity they're already passing through? Your place of distribution is affected by and will affect your value proposition, customer base, costs, competitors, collaborators, pricing, and promotion channels— this is to say, it is a central component of your social market strategy. Ultimately, the leading factor will be your target audience's preferences and needs, which you have collected information on early during the co-creation process. In the next chapter, we'll talk about various distribution options to expand the reach of your solution in different places.

Cost

Measuring and optimizing your costs will be key to your success in both maximizing your customer base and ensuring your financial sustainability. As we saw in Chapters 3 and 4, while it may seem that the lowest cost formula is always the desired option, this is not always necessarily the case in achieving your mission. Your goal is to make the product or service as affordable and accessible as possible, and that means offering the value needed to produce the desired social outcome in the most affordable manner. If making it low in costs results in a lower quality or durability product, which does not result in the desired outcome, then it defeats the purpose. So when thinking about affordability, think beyond lowering costs. Sometimes, your end user can't afford a low-quality, low-durability product; they might require other aspects that will get them to where they need to go in terms of escaping a poverty trap (remember the S-shaped curve).

Affordability isn't necessarily always contingent just on how you manufacture your solution, it can also be attained through financing the product, for example, through creative payment schemes or through creative distribution schemes, as we'll see in future chapters. These multiple aspects should all be reflected in your marketing plan and your business plan. A great example is water.org, which experimented with different payment options to make water affordable.*

---

* http://water.org/solutions/watercredit/.

Remember Catlin Powers of One Earth Designs?* She pointed out that in building their business, they had the option to choose between lowering their costs or lowering the weight of their solar-powered cook stoves. Their mission was to improve health and environmental outcomes in a low-resource setting, but if they went for the lowest-cost solution, it wouldn't have attracted their target audience. They had to select the cost that optimized their value proposition by providing customers with a less costly but also more convenient alternative to what they were already using: wood-fuelled cook stoves. If their product was heavier and less convenient, why would a prospective customer make the switch (remember the lead shoes)?

Affordability does not necessarily mean choosing the lowest-cost option.

Once the value proposition has been fulfilled, however, minimizing costs is generally desired. This is especially the case in a social venture, where your target audience is most likely a low-income population. You're not designing a luxury good or attempting to sell a "VIP" service. Therefore, as long as it does not interfere with accessibility, lowering costs is usually key to reaching as many people as possible.

Price

While the cost refers to what you're paying to produce, promote, and distribute your product or service, the pricing component refers to what you're charging your customers or clients. Not only the price you set but also how you'll communicate it is part of your marketing strategy. After all, you are pricing and promoting this product or service in a way that will allow you to penetrate your target market to the largest extent possible. Your target market is the end user you've described in your customer section. In most cases, a social entrepreneur's goal is simple, to make the product or service affordable for as many people as possible. In this case, the pricing is a reflection of the cost of production and distribution, adding only the administrative costs of running the organization to make sure that you break even.

In certain cases, you can price your product or service below the cost of production, if you're able to subsidize it with other activities or sources of revenue. These may include donations from fundraising, corporate sponsors, or the addition of multiple revenue-generating activities that can cover the costs of one another. An example of the latter is when an organization offers multiple products or services to multiple customer bases, some with higher profit margins than others. This is called *differential pricing*, and it allows the organization to cross-subsidize the lower-priced items using the profits from the higher-priced items. Famous examples of differential pricing include the Aravind Eye Hospital and Narayana heart health centers, where patients with higher incomes are charged more and patients who cannot afford to pay are provided with the same high-quality service at no charge.†

What do people want, how much will they pay for it, how would they like it packaged, and where would they like it sold? Listen to your end users and you will find the answers.

---

* https://www.oneearthdesigns.org/.
† www.narayanahealth.org, www.aravind.org.

If your research suggests that your end user is willing and able to pay more than the amount resulting from the previous formula, then you might want to consider charging more. This does not necessarily conflict with your mission, as long as charging a higher price is reflected by a corresponding increase in your social impact. If you're able to produce a product or service at extremely low cost but want to value it at a higher price depending on the purchasing psychology you're experiencing in your target audience, this increased profit margin may in fact allow you to scale your operations and reach more people. If you're not sure, you can go back and conduct market research similar to the community-driven research you conducted at the start—it's all part of the co-creation process. What do people want, how much will they pay for it, how would they like it packaged, and where would they like it sold? Listen to your end users and you will find the answers. If you're dealing with a diverse target audience and some may be able to pay more than others, you may consider differential pricing.

> If you're not sure, you can go back and conduct market research similar to the community-driven research you conducted at the start—it's all part of the co-creation process.

Competitors

Understanding your competition is part and parcel of understanding your customer. Even if you think your product is unique and is fulfilling an unmet need, there is most likely another organization or service provider your target audience is turning to at this very moment. You want them to come to you instead in the future. If you've conducted your community-driven research thoroughly, you'll have all this information at your fingertips already. If not, go back and put yourself in your target audience's shoes.

Literally, physically go to the other organizations and service providers, or call them on the telephone. Find out exactly what they are offering, how much they are charging, and the other costs associated with accessing this product or service (transportation, time off from work, etc.). Ask your target audience who they go to, and why. Would they be interested in your product or service, and what characteristics would make them become your customers or clients?

Oftentimes, your product or service is truly unique and is offering a solution for the first time to this target audience, that no one else has offered before. Still, you're competing with something else for their time and money. What alternatives have they been turning to, to deal with this social challenge and related cochallenges? Even if it's been a band-aid rather than a solution—or on the flip side, something that has been making it worse!—you are asking them to abandon old practices and develop new ones. Getting to know people's activity patterns and decision-making processes is part of characterizing your customer and also part of characterizing your competition. Where are they putting their time, thought, attention, and money right now, which you want them to be putting on you instead?

Positioning

If your solution is competing with existing products or services or with other alternatives that people turn to in the absence of a solution, people will choose you if you can convince them that you offer more value. This is why you need to understand who your target customer or client is and how they make their decisions. Are they looking for the solution that's the easiest to understand, the easiest to access, the most effective, the lowest cost, or more likely, some combination of these? Who else is offering them related solutions, and what are you offering that others aren't? It helps to compare yourself with other alternatives via a positioning matrix. The traditional matrix compares price versus quality, as illustrated in Figure 5.4. How do other alternatives compare to you? Some may be cheaper but poorer quality, while others may be higher quality but more expensive. Try to think of other dimensions as well—what affects your end user, other than price and quality? Figure 5.5 provides an example of this more multidimensional analysis.

Filling out a positioning matrix will help you see who your closest competitors are. These will be the ones literally positioned the closest to you on the matrix. It might help to start with just a two-axis grid comparing price and quality to first do a "kitchen sink" analysis of all potential competitors. Then, once you've identified your closest competitors, you can do a multidimensional analysis to figure out where your USP is that distinguishes you from them.

Promotion

How will you build a relationship with your potential customers? Whether you're trying to penetrate an existing market with existing competitors or creating a new market where there is no comparable product or service, you still need to attract the customers' attention and provide the necessary information to make it easy for them to adopt your product. This goes back to understanding your customers' behaviors and preferences, as you've been doing throughout the co-creation of your solution. It's also very much tied to the resources at your disposal. If you're bootstrapping your start-up (funding as you go), you might not have a budget for advertising. Word of mouth, social media, and other inexpensive promotion channels may be your best option.

It's also important to understand the sociocultural components of building ties with your customers. What is acceptable and desirable in your specific setting? Do people prefer electronic, paper, or human/in-person advertisements? Will you be working through existing channels (e.g., placing an advertisement in an existing clinic, supermarket, website, or social service center) or

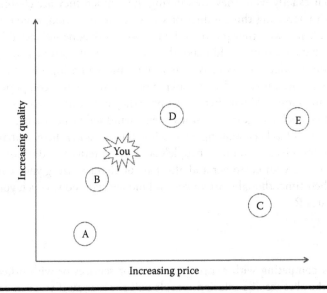

Figure 5.4 "Kitchen sink" analysis of all possible competitors. (A–E represent five other products or services).

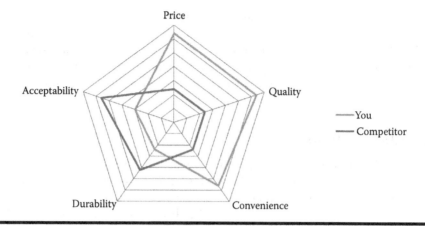

Figure 5.5 What dimensions are important to your end user? Where do you position yourself?

advertising independently (e.g., sending SMS advertisements, advertisements by mail, going door to door, etc.)? We'll talk about these a little more in the communications chapter, but for now, it's critical that you think of this important dimension of your social market strategy and how it will affect your business model and use of resources. Mapping out your promotional strategy involves centering it around your customer's behavioral and movement patterns, your available resources (i.e., team and funding), and the social preferences and customs within which you are operating.

Learning from best practices in the private sector in developed markets can help inform your promotional strategy. Many companies offer their product or service for free to first-time customers, to hook them into coming back. Another common practice is to offer packages, like discounted prices for multiple purchases. Other ventures offer promotions for repeat customers when they bring in or recommend new customers, providing discounts to both as an incentive. Just for fun, try popping into a gym in any metropolitan area to experience firsthand some typical promotion techniques (and good luck getting out)!

In other settings, people have turned to local culture to help get the word out, especially in remote rural settings. Examples have included advertising through local musicians, troubadours, and traveling theater troops! One social enterprise realized that people in the local community love receiving free calendars and started printing out calendars with ads on them to promote their products. In these cases, no private sector best practice could have been more effective than just working with local culture.

Collaborators

Who else is taking on this social challenge and related co-challenges? Other than your customers and competitors, what about your partners and collaborators? When working toward a social purpose, you will find that you are not alone. Your mission is most likely aligned with the missions of other organizations and initiatives, and it is not a zero-sum game. That is, others have something to gain by helping you achieve your mission: they will get closer to achieving their mission too.

Because you have done your research on stakeholders, competitors, and the other products/ services available, you will likely have a lot of information at your fingertips about potential partners. Are there resources you need that others have? Are there ways you can cut costs by tapping into these resources? Are there ways you can reach more people by tapping into the client bases of others?

A helpful tool to organize these relationships is the social business canvas (Figure 5.6). This allows you to examine your central value proposition, key resources needed, and potential partners to help bring these resources together. Put in all your notes about your product or service, customers, place, promotion cost, and price and examine how they start fitting in together into a preliminary business model. What pieces are missing that you still need to figure out?

Tool: Business Canvas

Once you've developed the different components of your social market strategy, it helps to put it all together in the same place to start assessing your business model. The business canvas is simply a visual way to organize the information you've already been hard at work collecting and put it together in a way that makes you assess it as a whole. This will force you to stop and take a quick step back to make sure that all the pieces of your puzzle are fitting together to create your social value chain.*

Key Partners	Key Activities	Value Proposition	Customer Relationships	Customer Segments
→→		←← →→		←←
	Resources		Channels	
List your key costs here:		List your revenue streams here:		

←← ←← Your Social Value Chain →→→→

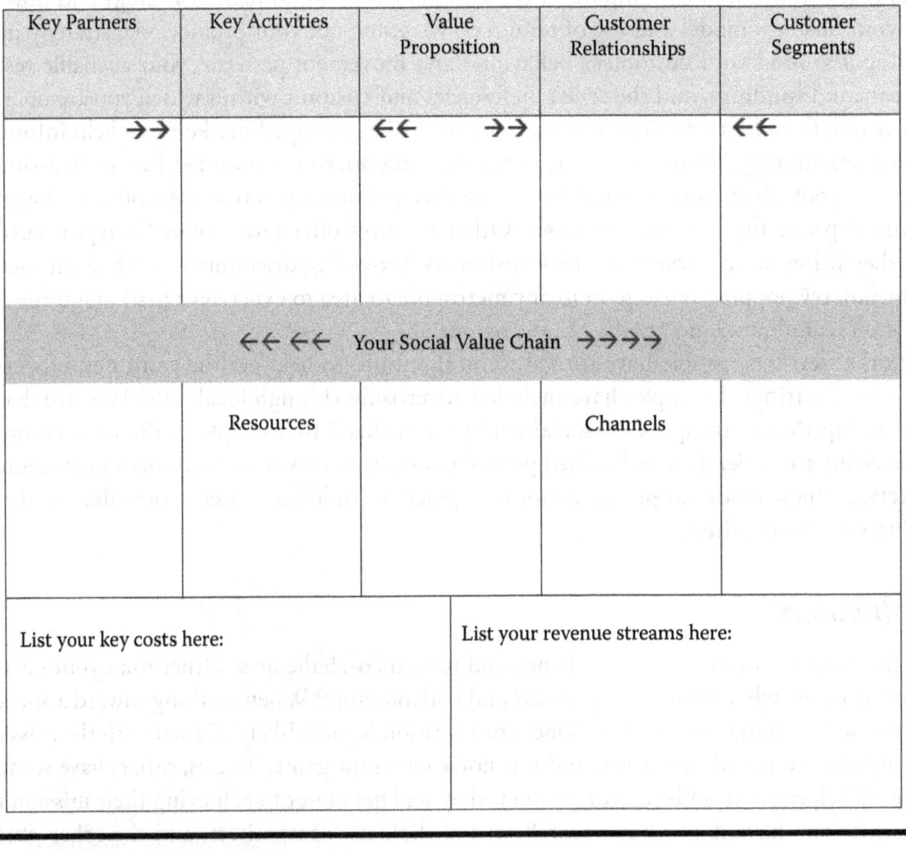

Figure 5.6 Your business canvas.

---

* This visual tool was developed by Osterwalder et al. and is publicly available. You can read more about it at www.businessmodelgeneration.com/downloads/businessmodelgeneration_preview.pdf.

Branding

Key Concepts

Branding is how you present your social venture, the image you want to project, and how it's captured in all your messaging and more. Picking the name of your social venture is a huge part of this! One of the reasons the Kiva founders went with this name, other than its meaning, is that it's short and has a nice ring to it—they pointed to the theory that the two-syllable name has been a successful formula for many popular brands. Starting with your name, logo, colors, abbreviation, packaging, and including your behavior, the terminology and tone with which you present information, the style of interaction your team has with customers, even the way your team answers the phone—these are all a part of branding. It's your image. Consistency is key, and this goes down to every detail, from your letterhead, type font, website, business cards, to your delivery vehicles, uniforms, and every piece of your venture. These are referred to as the "identity" of your venture.

A great way to present your brand is by having a tagline. This is a short statement presenting your value proposition in a catchy way. "TED: Ideas worth spreading"[*] is one you might be familiar with. "One for one" is another well-known tagline, for Tom's[†] brand. "Generation Good" and "Redefining disposable" are two other great examples from environmental businesses.[‡] "Real fish. Real flavor. Real easy" is yet another from the sustainable seafood industry.[§]

> Your branding is something that sticks with you and remains consistent across messages, audiences, and channels.

Your brand and identity are developed according to the target audience specified in your theory of change. Who are you trying to reach with your social product or service, and what is your entry point? Revisit your core value proposition when branding your product or service. Stick to this brand when representing your social venture, even if the communications content and channels may differ when speaking to audiences and stakeholders other than your target customer. Your branding is something that sticks with you and remains consistent across messages, audiences and channels.

Your branding is your first opportunity to convey your value proposition. When people look at your name or logo, it conveys something to them. It might convey "trustworthy," "tasty," "healthy," or even "exclusive." Don't think that social ventures can't attract people based on perceived exclusivity! All people, no matter what their socioeconomic status, want the best for themselves, want to feel special, and want to be convinced that acquiring your product or service will make them a happier person.

Examples

How have some of the social ventures we've come across built their brand and company identity? HLC has a fun, colorful, happy logo and sign attached to all the early learning centers, field officer's vests, website, and various other components of the organization. They are targeting parents

[*] www.ted.com.
[†] www.toms.ca.
[‡] www.seventhgeneration.com and www.gdiapers.com.
[§] http://fishpeopleseafood.com.

as their end user and want to convey a safe, happy, fulfilling environment for their children. This includes making sure that all their staff members embody this spirit, from the cleaning team to the executive team. Part of their company identity is cleanliness. Their centers are always freshly painted, their signs are always clean, their field coordinators' vests are always freshly laundered, even their vehicles are well maintained and regularly cleaned. They need to emanate an aura of trustworthiness and professionalism. We bring international standards to your town to brighten your children's future.

Another social venture is Jacaranda Health, which targets prospective mothers who will come and deliver there. Its value proposition is that it is offering high-quality, low-cost health-care to mothers to help them deliver safely in a country where the only two options so far have been low-quality, low-cost healthcare provided by the public sector versus high-quality, high-cost healthcare provided by the private sector. In this case, Jacaranda wants to brand itself as having all the qualities associated with the private sector, while offering affordable prices. The center's colors, logos, staff uniforms, signs, transportation vehicles, waiting rooms, clinical settings, and bedside behavior need to differentiate it from the public clinics and hospitals. Awareness and advertising about the center's existence and its services must reflect the values associated with these details: reliable, fast, customer-friendly, high-quality care at affordable prices. At the end of the day, their goal in developing their brand is for expecting mothers to look at them and feel safe. You are in good hands, we will take care of you, and your baby will be healthy.

Similar qualities have been associated with health ventures in the United States, such as the MinuteClinic. Its branding is based on its value proposition of being available to take care of you whenever you need and to get the best care without the wait. Customer service and interaction (from taking phone calls, greeting customers, following up, to obtaining feedback) are all part and parcel of conveying that value proposition.

We will also hear from the Aravind Eye Care System in the next chapter, which caters to both paying and nonpaying customers, offering the same services for both but using differential pricing. They brand themselves as providing the best medical care you need—they don't tell their paying customers that they are actually subsidizing someone else's care. Even if you think that might be an added advantage that would make some people want to sign up for this hospital's services, at the end of the day, people don't choose a hospital to help others—they choose it to get the best treatment they can possibly afford for themselves. Aravind sets their pricing, and their messaging and branding, accordingly.

One last example is Newman's Own. This is a brand of food products ranging from break-fast cereals to salad dressings, condiments, etc., that was created for the sole purpose of generating money for social programs. It leverages the brand of the famous actor Paul Newman but doesn't rely only on that brand to sell. It relies on taste, quality, and packaging based on market studies of what people look for in their supermarket purchases. It mentions that all profits go to social programs but doesn't rely on that as a selling point for people to purchase. This tactic is based on the knowledge that a shopper may make a one-time purchase to support a social cause, or a limited number of purchases, but what it takes to get a repeat customer is a great-tasting, great-value product. This is the advice given by Doug Rauch, founder and president of Daily Table.*

---

* dailytable.org.

Interview Box. Doug Rauch, Founder and President, Daily Table; CEO, Conscious Capitalism

TC: What were your guiding principles in building the brand and identify of Daily Table?

DR: Know your customers. This is just good business sense. The money will follow—the bottom line should come last, everything else will lead to it. If you put it first, it's like driving with your rearview mirror. Put your people first, and that means treating both your customers and your employees well.

TC: What promotional practices have worked best in your setting?

DR: I find that samples of product are powerful. If a picture speaks a thousand words, an experience of our food speaks ten thousand. And let your customers choose. Studies show that if you give someone an apple, they'll toss it, but if you get them to choose it themselves, then they'll value it more.

TC: How can a social entrepreneur craft their value proposition to get the message across?

DR: Narratives really matter. Hone your narrative, hone your narrative, have a story. There's a great TEDTalk on practicing your pitch thousands of times. Also, the presence of positives outweighs the absence of negatives in motivating customers. Examples from the food industry are abundant—"contains whole grain" is more inviting than "doesn't contain GMO." What they sell to their customers is healthy food replacing junk food.

TC: How do you convey the positive health and environmental benefits of your venture?

DR: We talk about the amount and nature of food recovered, the number of customers served, the basket size—how much they bought. We track all these things, and we track their growth over time. So they're all part of our market strategy. One thing we decided not to do was directly measure health effects in our customers. People don't want to be measured. They don't want to feel they are part of a program. This goes back to listening to your customer and going with what works for them.

TC: Are there any common mistakes a social entrepreneur should watch out for while developing their business model?

DR: Short termism. Five 1-year plans cannot do the same as one 5-year plan. It's also crucial to understand the nature of your problem—and it's certainly more complex than you think. Another piece of advice I'd give is building an internal culture of innovation, a culture of risk taking, that permeates your organization from the start. If you try to introduce a new strategy to the wrong culture, it's like transplanting a new organ into the wrong system. You have to embrace or at least tolerate failure. Share your failures internally, fail "on purpose," fail around your purpose, to learn; this is how we discover things we need to know.

TC: How did you build your market strategy to rally people to help make this possible?

DR: You need to build mission alignment—and that means all your people. Who are the people that already have a stake in this? Cold calls never work. Use your network, ask who they know. Make sure when you get that one shot, you give it your best shot.

Market Research

Needless to say, when you set out to define the different dimensions of your social market strategy, you probably won't have all the answers. You'll have a good idea based on your previous steps of characterizing the challenge, co-creating the solution, and the user-driven design of your product or service. But you might have to go out there with these new questions, test out different options, and ask your end user what works for them. By now, you have engaged an army of stakeholders and they are as invested in this as you! So don't be afraid to keep testing and iterating together until you get it right.

Market research is just like any other stage of the co-creation process you have gone through. You can conduct surveys, focus groups, town hall meetings, visioning workshops and one-on-one interviews. The only major difference is that now you're asking people to respond to your proposed solution, which you've already formulated. One other key difference which may arise is that the person you have designed your solution around may not be the same as the person you're building your marketing strategy and business model around. For example, if your end user is a child, you will have designed and tested your product with children. But the pricing needs to be designed and tested with the parents!

Market research means collecting information to assess consumer habits. We already talked about how to assess the competition. Now, how much are people willing to pay for your solution? What are they already paying for different products or services? What form of payments do they use, is it a cash-based market or do other systems work better (such as prepaid, credit, or some other form of payment)? Are you going to finance the payment, allowing them to pay small amounts over a long period of time, to make it more affordable? And how will you package your product or service—will customers pay per unit, or for a group of units bundled together? Find out what places and delivery methods work best for people—do they want to come to you or do you need to go to them? These are some of the questions you will head out there to find out.

Remember, innovation happens at multiple levels, it's not just a step in the process. So keep innovating, keep iterating, and don't forget that every research point and every question is an opportunity—your market research might introduce new insights and opportunities to improve upon your design; seize this! Nothing is written in stone, and you should be prepared to come out with answers for questions you didn't even ask.

Summary and Next Steps

Solution, meet world! World, meet solution! In this chapter, you've taken the design stage one step further by figuring out how you're going to get your solution out there and how people are going to interact with it. This is all part of the co-creation process and user-driven design, and now you're starting to put a business model around it.

This involves working with your end user to gain insight on the answers to your multidimensional marketing questions. Each dimension of your market strategy needs to be built with your end user, tested, and iterated until you get it just right. And you'll keep making improvements as you go—a marketing strategy is dynamic and nothing is written in stone.

You've now taken the first few steps in building your business plan. In the next few chapters, we're going to continue the design process by thinking some more about distribution and operations. But before we go any further, let's make sure you've taken the time to conduct the market research you need to formulate your market strategy and put it all down in one place.

Exercise: Taking Your Solution to Market!

Before proceeding any further, please write down your answers to the following questions, using one sentence only per item unless otherwise specified. If you need more time to conduct market research then get back out there and do it! When you are ready to put your thoughts down on paper, then you can tackle this chapter's assignment:

1. Write down your vision statement and your mission statement (one sentence each).
2. Write down your social venture's values. What values will you ask your team to live and work by? (Use bullet points.)
3. What is your value proposition? How does this make you different from any other?
4. Who are your customers, and what is the total number of potential customers?
5. Where are you selling your product or service?
6. How much are you pricing it at? Is it priced per unit or are you offering it as a package?
7. How will you promote your product or service?
8. List your top three to five competitors and what distinguishes you from them.
9. List five potential collaborators that you could partner with to reach your audience.
10. Once you're done writing down your answers, put it all together in a business canvas using the template from Figure 5.6. This will help you see it all in one place and identify potential synergies between different dimensions of your market strategy. It will also help you notice if you've missed anything or can tighten up and strengthen certain aspects.

CHAPTER SUMMARY

- In this chapter we take your proposed solution to market to test it out and continue the user-driven design process. This requires ongoing prototyping and iteration of your solution and how people will interact with it, to determine whether it's feasible, what your potential market size might be, and what your market strategy will look like.
- The first step is to create a compass for your social venture, to guide its development and growth. This starts with your vision, mission, values, and the value proposition you are offering to your end users—all driven by the underlying theory of change.
- Your market strategy is then assembled around your value proposition. We use the 5Cs and 5Ps to summarize the multidimensional market, bringing together customer, place, cost, price, competitors, positioning, promotion, and collaboration.
- Building your brand means defining the customer experience you want your end users to associate with your product or service. This needs to be clear, catchy, and consistent.
- Market research uses the same research techniques you've already applied to previous questions, to define the different dimensions of your market strategy.
- At the end, write down all these dimensions in a business canvas to see how they will come together into a value chain. Step back and assess yourself. Try looking at it like a painting or any other canvas—up front, from a distance, at different angles, and over an extended period of time. This will help you notice nuances and connections and build synergies between the different dimensions.

Social Ventures Mentioned in This Chapter

Company profile: Water.org, www.water.org.
Founded in 1990 as WaterPartners, became Water.org in 2009 after merging with H2O Africa, US registered 501(c)(3) nonprofit organization.
Product/service: Water.org has created new financing models to increase access to water and sanitation.
Goal: Driven by the challenge that every minute a child dies of a water-related disease, nearly 1 billion people lack affordable access to safe drinking water, and more people in the world have a mobile phone than a toilet, Water.org's goal is "Safe water and the dignity of a toilet for all, in our lifetime."
How it works: Water.org fosters fresh and innovative ideas by applying the best thinking from the private, public, financial, and technology sectors. Their WaterCredit initiative provides microloans for affordable water and sanitation access. Customers are able to repay the loans through cost savings, as the cost-per-liter from the municipal water system is significantly lower than what they would otherwise pay street vendors.

Company profile: Jacaranda Health, www.JacarandaHealth.org.
Founded in 2011, operates in East Africa, and also registered as US 501(c)3 nonprofit.
Product/service: Jacaranda is a maternal health service delivery organization for low-income women. They strive to provide respectful, patient-centered obstetric care, safe delivery, family planning, and postnatal care in East Africa.
Goal: To transform maternal healthcare in East Africa and make pregnancy and childbirth safer and affordable for women and newborns.
How it works: Jacaranda's first maternity center, which opened in 2012, currently operates in the outskirts of Nairobi, Kenya, "in the backyards of the women who need them most." Their model provides high-quality, comprehensive maternity care at a fifth of the cost of other private hospitals in the area. Their goal is to create a replicable maternal healthcare model that is adaptive and innovative, and integrates the best technologies, protocols, and systems while remaining affordable. They put an emphasis on building networks and sharing lessons learned and tools with the global healthcare community.

Company profile: Newman's Own, www.NewmansOwn.com.
Founded in 1982, US-based.
Product/service: As of the writing of this book, Newman's Own sells almost 200 food products across 20 categories including salad dressing, pasta sauce, frozen pizza, microwave popcorn, cookies, pet food, and more.
Goal: To sell great tasting, high quality food and give all profits to charity.
How it works: Newman's Own is a food company created by actor/philanthropist Paul Newman. From the company's first product, Olive Oil and Vinegar Dressing, all after-tax profits and royalties have always been given to charity. Together, Paul Newman and

Newman's Own Foundation have given more than $450 million to thousands of charities around the world. Although Paul passed away in 2008, the food company continues his original commitment to two basic principles: quality trumps the bottom line and all profits go to charity. Newman's Own Foundation focuses its giving in four areas where it can have meaningful impact: children with life-limiting conditions, empowerment, nutrition, and encouraging philanthropy.

Company profile: Daily Table, www.dailytable.org.
Opened June 4, 2015, Dorchester, Massachusetts, USA.
Product/service: Daily Table is a not-for-profit retail store that offers ready-to-eat meals and a selection of produce, bread, dairy, and grocery items. Meals are priced to compete with fast-food options, making it easier for families to eat healthier within their means.
Goal: Reduce both the effects of poor eating habits caused by challenging economics and the impact that wasted food and its precious resources have on our environment.
How it works: Daily Table works with a large network of growers, supermarkets, manufacturers, and other suppliers who donate their excess, healthy food or provide special buying opportunities. In this way, prices are kept affordable for all customers.

Case Study: Daily Table

Many innovations in both the commercial and social sectors are first conceptualized in response to a need and an opportunity, with the business model and commercialization to then follow at a later stage. This was the case with Daily Table. Doug Rauch, the former president of Trader Joe's, a supermarket chain in the United States, saw that a huge amount of food was being thrown away on a daily basis across the United States. He also noted that a large proportion of the population had no access to fresh and healthy foods. In the inner cities and other low-income neighborhoods across the nation, families relied largely on fast, affordable meals that were high in calories and low in nutritional value.

Putting these two problems together, he saw an opportunity to redirect wasted food from supermarket chains, to make it available in low-income neighborhoods (Figure 5.7). However, he was acutely aware that ideas are a dime a dozen, and the devil was in the details. The details of the implementation at first seemed beyond his grasp.

Rauch considered various options. One of the first questions he asked himself was, who is already working on this? What has already been tried, what has worked, and what hasn't? His first thought was that he could potentially join forces with existing initiatives, and learn from the past attempts of others.

Among those who were already working on this were food banks. However, food banks were run by volunteers, and their operations were not streamlined and predictable. Feedback from the supermarket chains was that if corporate managers were to take the time and resources to put aside food, they wanted to make sure it would be picked up in a timely and consistent manner.* More importantly, feedback from prospective end users indicated that food banks were the last

---

* Rauch, D. Solving the American Food Paradox. Harvard Business School Case Study 9-512-022.

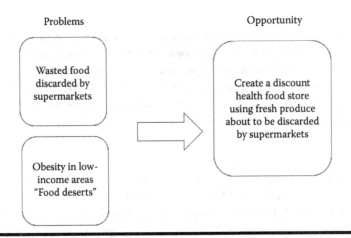

Figure 5.7   The conceptual innovation.

resort. According to Rauch's research, the working poor would rather buy low-quality fast food than accept a handout meal. They wanted to provide for their families, not think of themselves as recipients of charity.

Exploring other options, Rauch realized that another possibility would be to join forces with a corporate partner such as an existing supermarket chain. This would allow him to leverage that company's human resources, operations, distributions and products supply. However, after looking into that option, Rauch realized that it would present a challenge to piggyback on existing resources that were in place to serve the corporation's primary mission and bottom line. This is because he would be competing for people, products, and infrastructure that were needed to fulfill the corporation's primary work. He needed to build a social enterprise staffed with people who woke up every day thinking about one mission, and one mission only: getting healthy food to low-income neighborhoods and providing high-quality service, taste, and value in those neighborhoods.

Rauch decided to build his own business. The next step would be to figure out key components of the business model, including costing, pricing, and marketing. He wasn't going to give handouts, he was going to charge his customers, and he needed to make sure he was providing them with the best value possible in order to compete with their current food choices. His goal was to provide them with the highest quality and service at the lowest price. Thus, he sought to lower his costs as much as possible.

Iterating the Business Model

The highest costs for supermarkets are the cost of goods they procure and sell. Rauch first tried to see if he could eliminate this cost completely. He met with multiple supermarkets to create a system whereby his team would pick up perishable items that would otherwise have been thrown away. These consisted mainly of items that were nearing their "best-by" date. Supermarkets purchase their supplies in bulk, leading to a certain percentage of groceries that are not sold by the time fresh supplies come in. The unsold groceries are thrown out because the marginal revenues that would be gained by taking the extra time and effort to sell them are outweighed by the opportunity cost for a large supermarket. For Daily Table, if these unsold groceries are procured at no cost, then it is well worth the investment creating delicious meals out of the ingredients, even if it is time consuming. Thus, the first iteration of Daily Table's business model was tested: Rauch aimed to secure his inventory at only the cost of transportation and staff (Figure 5.8).

Rauch registered as a charity (U.S. 501c3) so that supermarkets could receive tax deductions for giving away rather than throwing away their unsold goods. This step presented a whole set of challenges of its own. While the proposed business model of the organization was in effect nonprofit, it was unconventional in its innovative business model, and as a result, the registration took more than two years to come through. Authorities could not figure out why this seemingly regular neighborhood enterprise was trying to qualify as a nonprofit! After all, Rauch was proposing to charge his customers for the goods he sold; in effect, it seemed to them he was just running another business.

Rauch then turned to the careful consideration of pricing. In order to compete with fast-food options, he needed to offer better value. He would tackle taste, customer services, and other components of the value experience, but first and foremost, he needed to tackle price. At first, he considered pricing the goods such that revenues from the sales would cover the cost of sales and the general/administrative costs of running the enterprise, without incurring any profit. But then he realized that the most effective way to gain market traction in the neighborhood was to price based on willingness to pay. What would be the best price you could put on this item, to make it extremely attractive to shoppers? This is the question he now asks himself, and his staff, every day.

Rauch's value proposition to his customers was that he would provide a friendly neighborhood place where they could buy great-tasting, fresh, and healthy food at affordable prices. His USP was the healthy aspect because he was opening his store in a neighborhood where no other fresh products were available.

But would the people want it? How would he know their needs and preferences? Rauch conducted several focus groups in his target neighborhood to obtain feedback from his target customers. This was his key into the neighborhood. He realized that while people did want to feed their families healthy food, they didn't want to be bombarded with health information. They wanted fresh food fast, and it had to taste good. They wanted food that they knew the name of, not alien ingredients they had never heard of.

A key marketing challenge was to convey the message that this was high-quality food, not someone else's leftovers. If you conducted an Internet search on Daily Table in the years leading up to its launch, you'd see headlines from multiple media outlets describing this social enterprise as selling garbage. Rauch needed a way to make sure that all safety concerns were met and that his customers knew he wasn't selling them anything he wouldn't eat at home. He realized that even the simple wording of a message can make a huge difference. If you describe his business model as

	Typical supermarket		Daily Table	
	USD ($)	% of sales	USD ($)	% of sales
Sales	100	Sales	25	
Cost of Goods	75	75% Cost of Goods	0	0%
Gross Profit	25	25% Gross Profit	25	100%
Operating Costs	22	22% Operating Costs	25	100%
Operating Profit	3	3% Operating Profit	0	0%

Figure 5.8   Estimated income statement for initial Daily Table business model.
(Reprinted with permission from HBS case (512022), "Doug Rauch: Solving the American Food Paradox" by Jose B. Alvarez and Ryan Johnson. Copyright 2012 President & Fellows of Harvard College; all rights reserved.)

employing food waste, you'd be using *waste* as the noun and *food* as the adjective. However, if you use the term *wasted food* instead, then the noun becomes *food* and the adjective becomes *wasted*. Selling food that would otherwise be wasted was much more socially accepted than selling waste that was composed of food.

Rauch also realized that price was not everything. People did not only buy fast food because of the lack of availability of fresh produce. People also had limited time. He realized that poverty was not only financial but was also related to time and knowledge. Rauch cites a Harvard researcher who calculated that you can feed your family a fresh meal for $2.30 a day. This study assumed that people have time to find the right ingredients and prepare them, which can be even more time consuming and which requires knowledge about how to prepare fresh meals. According to Rauch, the working poor are constrained not only by financial limitations but also by limitations on their time and knowledge regarding this subject. A mother who is working two jobs and getting home just in time to put food on the table needs a place where she can go in, buy the food, and have it on the table within minutes of opening the door.

For these reasons, and also to underscore the lack of safety risks, Rauch decided to offer cooked meals at Daily Table alongside fresh produce. He recruited a chef who was from the neighborhood where he was first piloting his social enterprise, who had trained and worked for many years preparing food to meet a variety of culinary tastes. They conducted tastings and samplings in the neighborhood, and that was when the neighborhood population really got excited about the newest arrival in their neighborhood. After tasting the new chef's food, they started asking Rauch how soon the Daily Table would open.

After getting to know the community, Rauch realized that his initial business model idea wouldn't fly. He needed to find a way to procure his own fresh produce, rather than basing his business model on donations from supermarkets that want to get rid of produce nearing its best by date. His customers were just not attracted to that model, and he had to listen to his customers. After much head scratching and soul searching, Doug came up with a way. Today, his team picks up fresh produce from bulk sellers, each morning. The same producers that sell bulk items to large stores, always have a small amount left each morning that nobody buys. Daily Table purchases these on a daily basis at discounted prices, and sells them at a fraction of the market value. With this final iteration, Doug Rauch and the Daily Table were finally ready for business.

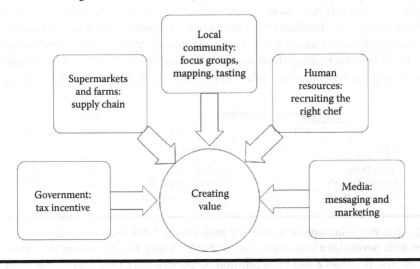

Figure 5.9   Connecting stakeholders to create shared value.

The development of Daily Table from idea to implementation took more than three years, which is a common statistic in business planning. Entrepreneurs with great ideas often underestimate how long it takes. Even after implementation, it will take a while to break even. This underscores the importance of planning and forecasting and analyzing your social, financial, legal, and other risks. It also speaks to the importance of getting to know your target customer, finding out what drives their decision making, what they really need from you, and what will get them excited (Figure 5.9).

At the time of writing, Rauch is now piloting the first Daily Table in Dorchester, Massachusetts. He aims to launch two more pilots before even thinking about how to go to scale. To him, the most important thing is to demonstrate knowledge about how to effectively bring together the need and the opportunity. In entrepreneurship, it is often the first entrant into the market who learns all the lessons, whereas new entrants later take these lessons learned and achieve greater success. According to Rauch, his goal is to establish a proof of concept, to be that first mover that gets "clobbered." His advice to social entrepreneurs is to "dare greatly." "Don't just nibble at the corner. You have to inspire and aspire. Put your heart and soul in it, put yourself on the line. Challenge the status quo—Be the irritant, the sand in the oyster that makes the pearl."*

---

* Doug Rauch, speaking at Harvard T.H. Chan School of Public Health, Friday, February 27, 2015.

Chapter 6

Delivering Your Solution

Operations and Distribution

Developing a market strategy is not enough to get your solution across the last mile. Careful consideration is needed on the nuts and bolts of operations and distribution. This is where many social interventions have failed! In this chapter, we will focus on different distribution channels, processes, and considerations needed. In the next few chapters, we'll talk about different aspects of organizational foundation building, compare the financial viability of different options, and analyzing risk. Just like we left no stone unturned in characterizing the challenge, we'll leave no stone unturned in finding the best possible way to make the implementation of your solution a success.

You may have heard the phrase "reaching the last mile" a lot. But what exactly does this mean? In some cases, it may be physically the last mile—reaching locations that are logistically challenging to get products and services to. It's the distribution costs that have prevented large global corporations and/or central governments (among the other factors we discussed in Chapter 2) from reaching the most marginalized populations with basic human needs and services. In other cases, it may mean bridging the gaps in information and knowledge that prevent some people from accessing solutions. And in others, it means finding creative ways to put together the different pieces of the supply chain—the information and knowledge required to create demand, the logistics required to supply the solution, and the payment or financing to make it all possible.

What Is Operations?

Management of the different pieces of the supply chain is what we are referring to when we use the word *operations*—it's the functioning of your social venture, the processes required to get to the outcomes you're aiming for. Operations refers to the day-to-day activities required to produce and deliver your solution. These will depend on your distribution model and other aspects of your multidimensional market strategy.

> Operations are the processes required to get to the outcomes you're aiming for.

Prototyping and pilot-testing an idea are completely different from rolling it out. How can you create systematic processes through which you provide your social product or service to your target audience? This not only helps you ensure the results that are so critical to reaching your social impact targets, it also helps you set up your venture in a streamlined way, minimizing resources and maximizing output.

Here's where it gets really juicy! Here's where you tell us how you are actually going to *do* this. Now, we're starting to get into new components of the business planning process that you haven't reached yet in your journey. This is the nitty-gritty of the execution. So, let's dive in!

Process Mapping

Process mapping refers to the clarification of how exactly the moving parts of your product or service will flow between these different components to get to the final end goal. The result is literally a step-by-step description of your core operations, similar to a recipe or instructions manual for your team.

This includes distribution. At the start of your journey, you defined the "last mile," that missing gap that is preventing your end user from overcoming this social challenge. How are you going to get your product or service across the last mile? The process map includes each and every step taken from A to Z.

As your organization grows, you might end up having more than one process map for the different departments and subsections of your venture. But for now, let's focus on your main operation, the primary product or service you offer. How is your social product or service produced, how is it offered to the customer, who is involved at each step, where does it take place, and when? This is how you map out your operations.

An example is shown in Figure 6.1.

You'll notice that this process map describes a system providing a social service. A process map for the provision of a product is much the same. Person X purchases ingredient Y. They hand it

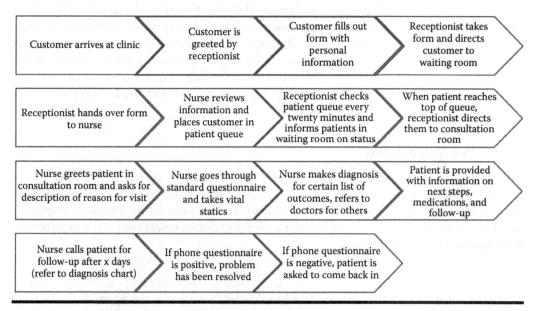

Figure 6.1   Process map for community health clinic.

over to person Z, who takes it through procedure A...all the way to the distribution, transportation, and customer service. Where do the customers go to, who do they buy it from?

This is just one simple example using a basic word processor diagram, but you can also use more specialized software and symbols. There are also free web-based tools that you can use to create more sophisticated flowcharts, and many process mapping softwares provide a free trial in case you'd like to try it out for your own process map!

Process maps can help you make sure that nothing falls through the cracks; they also help you chart out the resources you'll need and the room for growth. Process maps need to be revisited in the future as your organization grows to figure out what redundant steps can be eliminated, enhanced, or improved. They may also change as you refine your distribution channels. Going into the nitty-gritty details of how it will all work will help you ensure that you don't drop the ball when it comes to delivering.

Distribution Models

The simplest model of distribution entails taking the same package—your core product or service—and offering it to more people. To do this, you'll need to carefully think through the processes this would entail. Do you have enough resources to reach more end users? How will the increased operations affect and be affected by economies of scale? What geographic areas do you aim to cover, and will you need to tailor your package to the local context as you spread? Even if you have created a standardized package that does not need tailoring and can be replicated across subpopulations and geographies, you may have to customize your marketing, pricing, or other aspects that vary across location. In this chapter, we will cover all of these considerations, providing information for various options you may be considering. Depending on your product or service, you may pick and choose the most relevant components for you.

Expanding Your Reach—Different Mechanisms

Once you've assessed the different variables and factors for success through pilot testing, it's time to assess the various mechanisms available as options for reaching your audience. How will you actually carry this out? Before we explore different options, let's put a disclaimer out there. Here's how this is *not* going to go down: *Don't* expect to read through the various models and examples like a menu, pick an option, and hit the ground running. *Do* expect to try out different options and analyze different scenarios to assess what the (1) impact will be and (2) resources needed will be for each of the options, before you start.

This is one of the major differences between thinking about scale as an afterthought—as in "okay now that it works, how do we scale it?"—and being a strategic social entrepreneur who sets out to create that measurable change from the start. Let's look at some different options now, and in the next two chapters, you can start building an organizational framework to assess which options work best for you, and as a result, you may just end up creating your own new way of doing things! Don't forget, operations and distribution are yet another step on the innovation ladder.

Expanding Central Production Volume

The first option is to keep doing what you are doing, and do more of it. Did your pilot provide your product or service to 100 people to test your processes and outcomes? The next step might be to offer it to 1000 people. How do you decide on the numbers? This depends on the need and the market, the resources available to you, and the nature of your intervention. Before you expand, it's important to evaluate your results from the pilot. What could you be doing better? What worked and what didn't? Multiple pilots may be necessary before you can go to full scale. Don't make these decisions alone. Your team and your board can help provide their perspectives from their viewpoint, which will be different from yours. Your team might have different views to offer from the battlefield, and your board might have different views to offer from the bird's eye view.

Expanding your central production volume can carry the advantages of increasing efficiencies and reducing costs per unit produced or transaction served. Key challenges to look out for are building systems to maintain quality assurance and creating feedback loops between management and the frontline. On the former, hiring team members specialized in monitoring and evaluation (M&E) and creating a data management and analytics platform for them can help you ensure consistent quality. As we'll discuss in the next chapter, you'll want to monitor both your operations (how things are done) and your outcomes (the results you are getting). On the latter, make it a priority to ensure that if expansion of the central unit is the route you take, this does not result in a heavy, bulky, bureaucratic organization.

The important thing to note here is that a natural characteristic of economies of scale is that at one point, they start going back down. Economies of scale increase until you reach your optimal production level, and then they decrease. In commercial business, one might just stay at that optimal production level. But in a social venture, you probably won't want to stop there! You'll need to think about what to do next to reach end users that you are not yet serving—either open a new production unit or a satellite branch or explore further ways of replicating your success.

Opening New Branches

Replicating your pilot by opening new branches at various locations, rather than—or in addition to—increasing operations at the original location is also an option. As we will see in the Aravind case, even though they were successful in achieving economies of scale in their hospitals, they also had to venture out and open new branches to reach people where they were. New branches might be very similar to the original branch or might have different characteristics. They might offer modified products or services or additional products or services. This depends on the nature of the population you're trying to reach, the influence of local context on the nature of your work, and the test results at each location. Don't forget—you have to test the market before each step! In many ways, it's like going from one pilot to several new pilots (Figure 6.2).

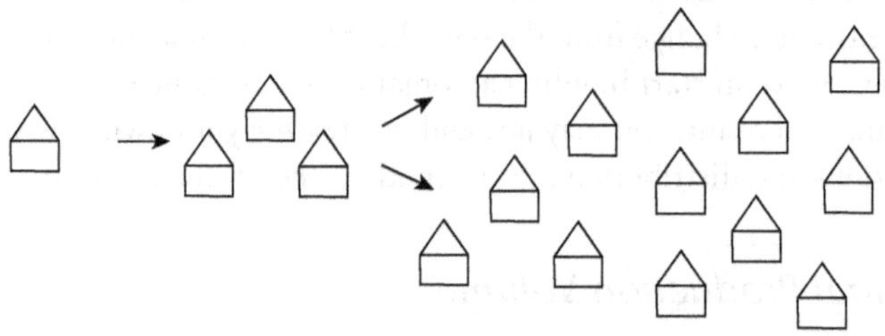

Figure 6.2 Replicating your pilot.

Franchising

Franchising means that rather than trying to produce more yourself or serve more yourself, you partner with other organizations to replicate your model. In the commercial sector, you can franchise your venture to an individual willing to take it on and build it from scratch. In the social sector, it is recommended to franchise to an existing organization that has already determined viability as a social purpose organization. By viability, we mean that the organization has sustained itself over time, demonstrated social impact, and built trust in its community. This organization will then take on the responsibility of manufacturing or implementing your product or service in its community. In most cases, you will receive a franchising fee from the organization, which it will pay out of the revenues generated from your product or service. You will be responsible for continuous guidance and training to ensure consistency and quality in your brand, its output, and the social outcome that is your ultimate goal.

The decision to franchise might come later in the game, or you might design your social venture around this model from the start. Advantages of franchising are that it requires fewer resources to deliver your solution to a larger audience because the franchisee is carrying the burden. It also allows you to leverage existing networks, relationships, and systems in communities you have not entered yet. Key challenges to look out for when franchising include the importance of selecting a franchisee with a mission that is aligned to yours, and an organizational culture that is amenable to replicating your impact. If your organization invites innovation and creativity from its staff but your franchisee does not, then it is not likely they will be able to replicate your model. If your business model requires you to operate in a lean and efficient manner to reduce costs, but your franchisee has high administrative costs and operates inefficiently, then you need to diagnose that from the start and step out. Another key challenge is the importance of recognizing that franchising requires you to have the time and capacity to provide management guidance and training. You have to first perfect what you're doing at your pilot site and have your operations running smoothly there before you replicate to the first franchisee site. So franchising is not something that happens early on in a social venture. However, the same could be said for any mechanism of expansion!

Microfranchising

Microfranchising is a distribution model that differs from the social franchising method described above. As its name suggests, microfranchising entails much smaller units of replication. Rather than franchise the venture as a whole, it is usually the last mile distribution that is franchised. That is, your core organization is still responsible for a large portion of the operations and production, while the franchisee is responsible for interfacing with the end user. The franchisee is usually an individual or, in some cases, a small organization.

The microfranchising model has been used to provide access to basic goods and services at affordable costs and foster job creation. Microfranchising examples from emerging economies around the world include SPOT taxi in India, Fan Milk in Ghana, Natura in Brazil, Kegg Farms in India, and BlueStar Ghana and Coca Cola's Manual Distribution Centers in Africa.* These are traditional franchises that have fostered job creation and asset creation at the base-of-the-pyramid microchain. Social ventures have also employed microfranchising to provide social goods and services around the world. Examples include VisionSpring Eyeglasses, Living Goods, HealthStore

---

* www.templeton.org/newsroom/in_the_news/docs/091215_frontiers_markets_summary.pdf.

Foundation, PlayPumps, KickstartPumps, Drishtee, and Grameen Phone. Microfranchising may be seen more as a business model than a distribution strategy since it's something that needs to be decided much earlier on in the process. However, the same could be said for any of the distribution strategies discussed in this chapter.

Nonmonetized Methods

Another option available for your consideration when choosing your distribution methods is sharing your core package with other organizations without incorporating any financial transactions. This can be employed in combination with one of the other previous methods to expand your reach through the work of others, even if it's not under your structure or your brand. One way to do this is to create an open-access platform where people can access the knowledge and skills needed to provide your product or service to their own end users. You can also license your work free of charge through legal tools such as those provided by Creative Commons, which allow you to set conditions on the use of your work.*

Some social ventures take this one step further and also provide training to other organizations interested in applying their model, to help ensure that the desired social impact is achieved. These kinds of options may not work for everyone, as they require you to have a robust revenue stream from other sources. However, some organizations have made it work by diversifying their revenues—for example, adopting a hybrid model where revenues from one market support activity in another market, or by complementing revenue-generating activity with fundraising, or through financial support from their board. In some cases, it could also serve as a marketing tool to attract enough paying customers to compensate for the freely shared material, thus balancing out your venture's financial viability. In these cases, social impact growth takes place at a higher rate than financial growth, but the organization remains financially viable.

Success Factors across Distribution Models

Whatever distribution model you end up choosing, make sure you're aware of the control knobs you can adjust to influence your reach. While these differ by organization, success stories from around the world suggest that there are a few that are important for you to think about no matter what field you work in and no matter how you end up setting up your social venture.

Define Your Core Package

Part of evaluating your pilot is identifying the main factors responsible for creating the outcomes you're looking for. These make up the core package that you want to get to your target audience. The contents of your core package are determined by the results of your pilot testing and are informed by iteration after iteration and prototype after prototype of your product or service.

Until there is further evidence from your future results down the line to suggest that they should be modified, consider them your "nonnegotiables." The next step is to figure out how to get this core package to as many people as possible, within the context of your theory of change.

---

* http://creativecommons.org.

Standardize

In many cases, in order to expand your reach, you need to standardize the processes by which you produce and offer your core package.

What exactly are the elements that have proven to be responsible for the social impact you are reaching for? How can you ensure that these elements are effectively delivered to each and every customer as you grow and expand distribution? As we will see further in the chapter, not all elements of your social venture will be standardized—many will be tailored and customized—but before you design your distribution model, it is essential to determine what needs to be maintained across your offerings and how to ensure consistency in your operations.

Standardization can take place through training, through automating, and through quality control. Creating protocols, checklists, and procedures focused on ensuring the key characteristics of your core package that are tied to your social impact is one way to do this.

Automate

One way to standardize and to boost your organization's ability to offer its core package as efficiently as possible in general is to automate certain processes. The key is to select the right processes. This helps you open up resources (people, time, funding, physical assets, and facilities) to take on larger volumes and serve more people. Not all processes can be automated, but it is worth your while to spend some time figuring out which steps can be automated. We're not talking about the people part here! We're talking about steps that take away from the people part.

As an easy example, data entry and analysis are usually low hanging fruit, inexpensive steps to automate. Rather than have your monitoring take place on paper, have it take place electronically, so that data do not need to be manually entered into a system. At each site, you can record the data in an electronic system (whether using a phone, tablet, or other computing device), which allows it to be added to your database immediately. Data analytics software is easily accessible and can help you identify the trends in your data. This will help you determine which sites are performing well, whether you are reaching your social impact targets, what equipment or inventory you need, and other crucial factors needed to optimize both the social outcomes (where you're trying to get to) and the operations (how you're getting there). Many other "back-end" processes of your management systems, such as managing supplies, are logical parts of your social venture to automate. They can then be overseen and interpreted by a qualified person, but there's no need to waste time and talent and overhead on steps that don't need to be taken.

Shorten the Last Mile

What if a part of designing your delivery model around reaching the last mile was finding new ways to make that last mile shorter? Might you be able to innovate your supply chain to excel in distribution? How can you turn the distribution challenge from being your enemy into being your best friend? Let's look at some examples of how successful social ventures have done it.

Decentralizing the production unit is one way some successful ventures have done it. Rather than having a central headquarters churning out the product (like a factory) or offering the service (like a hospital), social ventures aiming to reach the most marginalized populations have brought the actual production unit or service unit to those populations and created the social good there. Aravind eye care system is a good example, which we'll read more about in the case study.

Determining whether this might be an option for you requires testing, like anything else. It took Aravind several rounds of trial and error before they reached their vision centers model. At the time of writing, it is being tested for effectiveness and scalability, and the next iteration might lead them to a new improved model. A second example is the host of new social entrepreneurs around the world aiming to make sanitary pads for adolescent girls and women more affordable, available, and accessible. The theory of change behind these new social ventures is that lack of access to affordable sanitary pads in many countries leads adolescent girls to miss school days, and that making sanitary pads more accessible would improve their educational outcomes, with all the ripple effects that entails. These social entrepreneurs realized that manufacturers of these pads do not find it profitable to sell in rural areas because the transportation costs are so high. They designed new machines to produce high-quality, affordable pads and instead of producing the pads themselves in a central factory and facing the same distribution/transportation dilemma, they instead provided the machines to women in decentralized locations. These women then became the manufacturers and distributors. This model is currently being tested by social entrepreneurs in Rwanda (http://sheinnovates.com), India (www.newinventions.in), and many other settings.

Foster Local Leadership

These manufacturers are not the only examples that relied on local capacity to build a network of production and distribution. HLC made the teachers the business leaders at each learning center site by recruiting young women from the surrounding villages, training them in HLC's core package, and then giving them the responsibility to manage the center and recruit the end users (children and their parents). This is another form of decentralization! Nuru International, which will meet in the next chapter, also relies on recruiting and training local leaders. The local leaders then take the helm of building Nuru's program, monitoring and evaluating social impact, and running the operations after Nuru's core staff exited. Without such a model, Nuru would not be able to scale beyond its first site. Thinking back to the waste pickers' association we read about in Peru and other locations around the world, they formed alliances and unions and spread their impact by finding local leaders who could serve as catalysts in both direct service and advocacy for improved laws and policies.

Whatever your operations entail and your distribution model calls for, the experience of others before you shows that if you find and work with the local entrepreneurs and leaders, this could be your best shot at reaching your end users.

Decentralize Operations

The previous examples point to the importance of decentralizing operations, one through manufacturing and sales, the other through working with local leaders. There are yet more ways to maximize this beyond manufacturing, distribution, and recruitment. M&E is yet another component of your operations that you can decentralize. HLC exemplified this by recruiting and training field coordinators to conduct the M&E of the learning centers, rather than conducting this step from the central headquarters. This streamlines the process and lowers cost, just like the local manufacturing lowered costs by eliminating the need for transportation and warehousing. More importantly, it increases the "surface area" of the interaction between the team and the end user.

Do you remember in middle school science how we learned about the surface area of an object, through which materials like air or water can be absorbed or transmitted? The surface area of an organization can be thought of in the same way! The more opportunities and surfaces built in for interaction between you and your end user, the better. You don't want to be a tight round sphere that is centered upon itself; after all, you were built from the ground up, so it's important as you grow that you don't lose that important touch.

Even communications and marketing will be optimized through decentralized teams because the content and channels can then be more finely tuned and tailored to the local setting. This includes customer service and feedback. Aravind vision centers are a prime example of the inside-out approach, rather than outside-in. After relying on satellite mobile vans to go out into the community and bring people back in to the central hospitals (outside-in), Aravind's team realized that a more effective way to reach more people would be to take the services to them (inside-out). Today, they are focusing more on growing the number of decentralized eye care units (see more in case study at end of chapter).

Tailor to the Local Population

Further beyond the local distribution, management, and communications, there are ways to tailor your offering to the local population to ensure that you are able to optimize impact wherever you spread your reach. As your organization grows and more distance is created between the central unit and the decentralized unit, you need to leave a certain degree of freedom and flexibility to tailor both what you are offering and how it is offered.

Let's look more closely at customer service as an example. While it is critical that all staff members are trained in the core components of your model and its implementation, they also need the skills and competencies required to personalize your offering. This also applies to nonstaff members of your supply chain. Some ventures choose not to hire but rather to contract out certain elements of their supply chain. An important way to maximize your social impact is to ensure that each step of your supply chain is integral to your mission, from the suppliers to the vendors. This gives your venture the power to adapt and respond to local customs, preferences, and needs. Even behaviors, mannerisms, and social protocols adopted by staff members interfacing with your customers can be tailored to provide the best customer experience possible.

Leveraging Existing Channels

What are the existing distribution channels that exist in the community you're working with? What products do they already have? Regardless of your distribution model, you can always find ways to creatively piggyback on existing channels rather than starting from scratch in creating your own. This can work in various settings—from dense urban areas to remote rural areas. Each setting has its own challenges but also its own opportunities!

As always, the key is to test out different theories and see what part of your model delivers impact and what part actually doesn't so much. A striking example is Cola Life, which designed a product for oral rehydration therapy, aimed at combating diarrhea, which is a leading cause of childhood mortality in many areas. The initial idea behind Cola Life was to package the product in pods, which were shaped to fit in the spaces between cola bottles delivered to small shops in both cities and villages. This was inspired by the fact that you can buy Coca-Cola in every village in Africa, but you have to travel several kilometers in most cases to access health products through rural health centers, which are often out of stock when you get there! The packaging idea sounded brilliant, but when the team tested it, only 4% of the rural retailers actually used the cola crates to transport the product. So it turned out this was not the key to their success; however, the idea of creating and selling this product through rural retailers just like Coca-Cola does was in fact a success. People were willing to pay for it, and it increased access by bringing the product to the retail shops. The team is still constantly finding new ways of packaging their offering to reduce costs and tailoring the contents based on results from field tests which gave insight into how it was being used and what the customer needed—and didn't need.*

Interview Box. Thulasiraj Ravilla, Executive Director, Aravind Eye Care Systems

TC: We have seen a lot of success stories coming out of India on scaling social ventures. Do you think that the lessons learned from Aravind Eye Care Systems might be applicable to India only, or can they be generalized to other settings?

TR: India is certainly a large market amenable to high-volume systems, but our experience shows that the models developed here can be adapted to other settings too. Our team has already helped implement similar models in many countries around the world. For example, in many African countries, the doctor population is low, and this model can increase access to basic eye care services.

TC: What about in other sectors? Do you think your model is applicable beyond the healthcare sector?

TR: Yes, I do think it can be applied across sectors. My only warning is that adopting a cross-subsidization business model may not be the right fit if your social product or service is not equally needed by paying and nonpaying customers. Eye care is needed by both and is especially sought after by paying customers; but other services may not be.

TC: What other pieces of advice would you like to share with aspiring social entrepreneurs?

TR: Most importantly, social entrepreneurs need to recognize that their customers are smart and know what's good for them. It's about the process and the prices, but most importantly about the people.

Photo Source: Schwab Foundation Social Entrepreneur Profiles.

Strategic Partnerships

In order to find these results, Cola Life needed to partner with private sector, government sector, NGOs, international agencies, and universities to design and test their ideas. Ciudad Saludable, whom we met in Chapter 3, now operates in 11 countries at the time of writing but emphasize that they did not—and could not—start from scratch in each one. They found other entrepreneurs who were already working in those settings, and joined forces with them. Strength is in numbers—and you'll find that out very painfully when you start crunching your numbers! If you're going to reach the people you need to reach and make your solution as affordable as possible while remaining financially viable, you'll need to be very creative about how you're going to leverage resources along the way.

---

* http://www.colalife.org/2014/02/11/seven-of-the-headline-findings-from-the-colalife-trial-in-zambia/.

Your Biggest Resource: Your Team

Now that you have a more concrete and detailed idea of what needs to be done, you need to make sure you have the right people surrounding you to execute it! Your starting team and your design team might not necessarily be the same people who will launch your venture with you. This is one of the hardest parts of building a social venture. It depends on who's invested and who has the right skill set.

By "who's invested," we mean who is in this with you for the long haul. You will get financial investors at a future stage to fund your venture, but that's not what we're talking about right now! If you are going to do this, if you are really committed to make this happen, then you may likely not get paid for a while. There will be a lot of sacrifices you will have to make. You need to make sure that the people who have been by your side up until now are committed to making those sacrifices.

By "who has the right skill set," we mean who can be a true partner in complementing your strengths and weaknesses. You will get a lot of compliments for your work, but that's not what we're talking about right now! You need to think about the competencies needed to build a venture and make sure your founding team includes those competencies: someone who can be outward facing and build bridges, someone who can be inward facing and build systems, someone who's good at the business side, and someone who's good at the programmatic side.

It's time to start thinking about who is going to take this dive with you. The composition and structure of your team moving forward is one of the most critical factors which will determine your success. Finding the right people is not easy. You've already done it once when you first started, so go back to those rules. Start within your organization, company or university, or other existing social networks. You might stick with your starting team—chances are there will be a huge overlap. But not everyone might want to continue, and you may need to recruit one or more others through external professional networks.

Building the Team

A common mistake that social entrepreneurs make while building their venture is trying to do everything themselves. When you first begin, this is naturally what happens. You go out into the field to collect information, learn from others, and get input from stakeholders. You meet with potential funders, with scientists and experts who have researched your topic, with practitioners who can help you produce and measure the impact you're after. You find people to support you in aspects you're not able to do on your own, such as coding or manufacturing or delivering technical services like medical care, education, etc. You eat, breathe, and live your social mission. And for this very reason, you're often hesitant and scared to build the executive team you need. To let go of the reins or share responsibility with others, to depend on others, to relinquish control, and to create the space for someone other than you to take action can be a daunting proposition. But if your goal is to scale your impact, then you need to think ahead and act accordingly.

Envision yourself 10 or 20 years down the line. Where do you want your organization to be? At that point, how many people are working in this organization? What are the roles? Once you have this picture of what you want the organization to look like in the future, you can ask yourself what is needed to get there. Someone is needed to help you recruit, hire, train, and manage future team members. Someone is needed to help you manage finances. Someone is needed to help you liaise with others.

No entrepreneur can possibly foresee on their own all the different roles and positions that will be needed as their social venture unfolds. This is why it is recommended for you to focus on thinking about the executive backbone, which is composed of the core functions. Then, you can work with these core members to determine how their future teams need to grow. There is no formula for the composition of an executive team; it varies from organization to organization depending on the needs and functions. However, there are certain roles that are found more commonly than others, and it may be helpful for you to familiarize yourself with these and then tailor them to your needs.

Composition of the Executive Team

Most often, one of the cofounders takes on the role of the CEO. This is the person who carries forward the mission of the organization, serving as its representative. The chief executive is the face of the organization and works to garner support from others and also is most often the person who is held accountable for the organization's performance. This is why it is crucial for the chief executive to surround herself/himself with the right team to build the organization.

The chief operating officer (COO) is often known as the right hand of the chief executive. This is the person who makes sure that the operations of the organization run smoothly and that it is able to produce the product or service it provides to its target customer. The role of the COO often involves building management systems and administrative systems to ensure that the organization runs smoothly; in many cases, it also may initially include human resources (i.e., ensuring that the right personnel with the technical skills to produce your organization's product or service are recruited, trained, and managed) until an human resources person or team is hired.

The chief financial officer (CFO) is responsible for the financial bottom line, which includes financial management and reporting, financial modeling, and pricing. Often, there is also a chief communications officer or chief marketing officer (CCO or CMO), who is responsible for getting the word out about the organization and getting feedback in. This includes building an internal and external communication strategy, overseeing social media, following up with individuals and organizations who have a vested interest in the company, building the base of customers, supporters, and other stakeholders. While the chief executive is the main proponent of the company and is responsible for breaking new frontiers in terms of getting the word out and building relationships, without a communications or marketing officer, the growing network of relationships is challenging to manage and optimize.

Last but not least, a chief program officer (CPO) of some form is needed. This is the person who manages and optimizes the social impact of the organization in terms of technical programming. Thinking back to your theory of change, this is the basis of your programming, i.e., the planning and implementation of the products and services you provide, how you provide them, to whom, and what they consist of. As your organization grows, so will its programs, products, and services. If your organization works in health, your CPO may well be known as the CMO, or chief medical officer. If your organization works in technology, then this person will more likely be known as the CTO, or chief technology officer. Depending on your topic area, this is the person who focuses on the subject matter expertise and ensures that all programs, products, and services are technically robust and are built to maximize the impact to your target audience.

Different organizations refer to these roles using different nomenclature; for example, in some organizations, the chief executive is referred to as an executive director, while in others, this role is referred to as the CEO. The COO, CFO, CMO, CPO, etc., could also be referred to as a general manager, director of finance, director of communications or marketing, and director of programs.

Also, not all organizations have the exact same structure and combination. Each organization builds its own team according to its own needs and functions. You have a creative license to draft the job descriptions and titles that you need!

At the end of the day, make sure all the core competencies required to build your venture are there: in most cases, you need someone with strong people skills to champion the organization, someone with strong management skills to build processes and ensure that everyone is using their time well, someone with subject-specific skills to make sure you are at the cutting edge of your field, someone to make sure your organization has strong financial health, and someone to make sure that your internal and external communications are helping you reach your goals.

Do You Have to Be the CEO?

Do not make the assumption that the founder of the organization necessarily needs to serve as the chief executive. The founder may instead hire someone to play this role. The chief executive is someone who has long-term vision and can carry the team forward toward that mission, building partnerships and accruing supporters along the way. Traits to look for in this person are strategic thinking, the ability to not get lost in details, and the ability to forge alliances and win supporters. Sometimes, the founders find that they feel more comfortable playing a more technical role and need to recruit someone to be their external pioneer and people-person. Some social entrepreneurs find that the more their organization grows, the less time and opportunities they have to interact with their target audience because of the outward-facing nature of the chief executive's role, and they prefer to recruit someone else to play this role.

Whatever your preferences, make sure that you have one person for each of the key roles outlined previously. Of course, your set of executive team members may not exactly follow this general outline because your organization has its own unique needs and attributes. When you first start, one person may be playing more than one (or all of) these roles. The important thing is to revisit your plans for the future and think about where you want to be further down the line and envision what roles will be needed when you get there, and before you get there, in order to achieve these goals. Make sure to invest the time and resources getting the right people on board who can help you get there. It might be tempting to plug along in your work thinking that you can't afford the luxury of time needed to find someone else to take the load off you because of the urgency of the work itself. But taking this time will allow you to have a larger impact in the future, and you are most likely harming your own mission if you don't prioritize finding the right team to help you carry your venture forward.

Summary and Next Steps

Let's take a moment to step back and reframe. In the last couple of chapters, we've designed our product or service with the end users and conducted market research to assess who we're targeting, what our value proposition is to them, and how we're going to get this solution into their hands. In this chapter, we focused on how those plans will be operationalized. How will that solution be delivered? We explored various options for distribution channels, to get products and services across the last mile. Last but not least, we started thinking about how to put together the executive team to take this forward.

In the next chapter, we'll talk about impact metrics. Where are we going with this, and where do we hope to reach? Then we can complete our business model by assessing costs and revenues and conducting a risk analysis. After that, you'll be ready to go out there and start securing resources to help make all this happen!

Exercise: How Will You Deliver Your Solution?

It's time to put down on paper your thoughts about operations, distribution, and team:

1. Draw out your preliminary process map. What steps will be needed, from sourcing raw materials, to assembling them, to delivering your solution to the end user? Who is responsible for each role?
2. What distribution channels are viable options for you, in the context you're working in? What are the pros and cons of each one? What information do you need to collect to figure out what will deliver the highest impact possible at the lowest cost?
3. What key positions will be necessary in developing your venture further? Were there any core operational fields that you identified in your process map? How many of your team members are already present from your starting team and your design team, that fit these roles? Do you need to recruit new ones?

CHAPTER SUMMARY

■ A critical part of designing your solution and developing your market strategy is figuring out the nuts and bolts of implementation. In this chapter, we talked about how to design your operations, distribution, and team.

■ Operations are the processes required for your social venture to function. These are the day-to-day activities required to produce and deliver your solution. A helpful way to visualize what your operations look like is to sketch out a process map. This is a step-by-step description of the core operations behind your social venture: the where/when/how of all that needs to happen.

■ Your distribution model refers to the mechanisms and set-up of your venture to reach the last mile. Challenges in developing your distribution model include cost considerations, physical logistics and transport, and information gaps. Common models used by social entrepreneurs include centralized production, branches, franchising, microfranchising, and open sourcing.

■ Success factors across distribution channels include the importance of knowing what aspects of your operations to standardize and automate, shortening the last mile, fostering local leadership, decentralizing where possible and tailoring to the local population, and leveraging existing channels. This requires strategic partnerships to build value chains and leverage local resources.

■ Your team is one of the most critical success factors moving forward. The composition of your executive team depends on how your social venture operates—most teams need an outward-facing chief executive, an inward-facing operations lead or general manager, a financial lead, a marketing and communications lead, and a technical lead specialized in the subject matter you're working in. As you complete your business plan in the coming chapters, you'll need to make sure your team is complete too.

Example Social Ventures from This Chapter

(only a sample of the microfranchising examples are included, as many were listed)

Company profile: Cola Life, www.colalife.org.
Open-source approach licensed under Creative Commons, registered in 2011 as UK charity.
Product/service: Antidiarrhea kit containing oral rehydration salts (ORS), zinc supplements and soap, packaged in an easy-to-use kit, distributed via existing private sector supply chains using the same principles and networks as soft drink sellers and other producers of fast-moving consumer goods (FMCGs).
Goal: Save children's lives, improve caregivers' access and knowledge of health issues. Diarrhea-related dehydration is a leading cause of under five mortality in developing countries.
How it works: Cola Life studied Coca-Cola's techniques and applied them to the design, marketing, and distribution of a life-saving diarrhea treatment kit built on established global recommendations. This was achieved through the twin approaches of redesigning a basic product to better meet the needs of customers, and the development of existing distribution channels to remote communities, already used for fast-moving consumer goods. This proved more important than the original Cola Life concept of piggybacking the product within cola crates—although that original idea helped unlock other innovations. Preliminary results include increased coverage from <1% to 45% during the pilot year, improved preparation of ORS from 60% to 94%, and reduced distance to ORS and Zinc access point from 7.4 km to 2.3 km.

Company profile: Living Goods, www.livinggoods.org.
Founded in 2007, registered as U.S. 501c3, employs hybrid model operating in Uganda, Kenya, Zambia, and Myanmar at the time of writing.
Product/service: Network of health entrepreneurs who go door-to-door to teach families how to improve their health and wealth and sell life-changing products such as simple treatments for malaria and diarrhea, safe delivery kits, fortified foods, clean cook stoves, water filters, and solar lights.
Goal: To lower child mortality, improve nutrition, and create livelihoods for thousands of enterprising community health workers.
How it works: Living Goods' model empowers health entrepreneurs through a direct-selling approach of "Avon-like agents," to deliver life-saving products to the doorsteps of the poor. Community health promotors (CHPs) live in communities they serve and earn an income by providing products and services that improve the lives of their customers. CHPs visit families in their homes to check children's health, support pregnant mothers, and advise parents on improving at-home health practices. Customers can call their CHP day or night to help when a child is ill. Living Goods partners with district health teams, Ministries of Health, and other NGOs such as BRAC.

Company profile: KickStart, www.kickstart.org.
Founded as ApproTech in 1991, later became KickStart in 2005.
Product/service: KickStart designs, develops, and promotes affordable irrigation tools that poor farmers in Africa adopt to no longer wait for the unreliable rains, but rather make their own rain.
Goal: To lift millions across Africa out of poverty by creating a sustainable solution to the rural poor's most important need—a way to make more money.
How it works: KickStart uses farmer-centered design to develop their irrigation products in Kenya. To sustainably distribute and sell the pumps and spare parts to farmers, KickStart developed a private-sector supply chain throughout Africa. Farmers who adopt these pumps go from not growing enough food to feed their family to growing enough year round to start a profitable business selling their surplus crops. These low-cost ($70 and $170) pumps enable farmers to increase their annual farming income through irrigation by ~500%—from $150 to $850. Additionally, through investments in livestock and poultry, and the ability to afford better seeds and fertilizers, farmers increase their total net annual household income by ~400%.

Company profile: Vision Spring, www.visionspring.org.
Founded in 2001, formerly Scojo Foundation.
Product/service: Accessible and affordable eyewear to restore vision for a productive life.
Goal: Strengthen the economic productivity of individuals by up to 35 percent, ensure students learn, and working poor can work, through corrected vision.
How it works: Vision Spring is testing innovative business models to forge new distribution channels for the delivery of affordable, high-quality eyewear. Vision Spring began with a microfranchising approach with individual sellers and evolved into a franchising approach with organizational partnerships, later taking a step further to test out a referral system with optometrist hubs.

Company profile: Aravind, www.aravind.org.
Founded in 1976, India.
Product/service: Network of eye health care centers providing affordable high-quality eye-care services.
Goal: Eliminate needless blindness through hospital services, community outreach, education and training, research and mentoring other eye hospitals.
How it works: Aravind eye care centers treat high patient volumes and offer patients the option to pay the market rate, a subsidized rate, or no fee at all for their services. To address awareness challenges among the patient base, Aravind opened mobile eye screening camps, which built trust and generated demand. Aravind leadership attributes success to keeping costs low, decentralizing services, training in-house all the clinical staff, and providing high-quality services equally to both the poor and rich.

Case Study: Aravind

Aravind Eye Care System started out with an 11-bed hospital inside a home in the Tamil Nadu state of India. Founded by Dr. Govindappa Venkataswamy (Dr. V), an eye surgeon who was employed by the government for many years and there he initiated the mobile eye camps. The business innovation was based on his experience of more than two decades at the town, state, and national levels. The mobile eye camps that Dr. V had led for so many years had focused largely on cataract surgery to prevent blindness in the older adult population, but over the years, he noticed other causes of blindness that could be prevented, such as nutritional deficiencies in children, which led him to start India's first residential nutrition rehabilitation center.* By the time he reached the mandatory age of retirement from government service at 58, Dr. V had performed over 100,000 eye surgeries, trained hundreds of young doctors, and managed countless community outreach initiatives. He asked himself why, when the technology and knowledge existed to prevent blindness, were there still millions of untreated patients in India. In a country with one government hospital for every 2 million people, Dr. V asked himself whether it was possible to provide cataract surgery at a cost most people could afford.

Together with his family, he formed a trust which allowed him to found the first Aravind eye hospital. Records of the start-up phase recall challenging days for many years. To start, the founders took a risk by self-funding, which involved mortgaging Dr. V's house, selling family jewelry, and pooling their life savings. This was further compounded by obstacles that resulted from limited knowledge of business planning, costing, and budgeting.† At the start, the founding team, which was composed entirely of medical doctors, was responsible for all administrative and maintenance tasks—down to cleaning the patients' rooms and restrooms.

At the time, there was a great need for cataract surgery, but low demand. This may sound counterintuitive, as a reasonable assumption would be that low treatment rates were due to lack of supply, rather than lack of demand. While lack of supply was certainly a reality, with only one eye doctor for every 100,000 people—and many districts without any doctors at all—understanding and acceptance of eye care treatment were also a challenge. Many people were not aware that blindness could be prevented or cured, and many were afraid of surgery, leading to a poor response to outreach efforts. Other challenges included the multiple costs of eye treatment: not only the cost of surgery, but also transportation, time, lost wages, and the need for food and accommodation, not to mention the anxiety and mental costs associated with surgery.

Eye screening camps were Aravind's way of addressing these challenges, by visiting communities to provide information and support, including transportation to the hospital and back as well as surgery costs, food, and medication. The camps allowed Aravind's team to reach out to patients in rural areas, building awareness and trust, and generating demand.

Aravind's business model involved providing a menu of price point options to patients arriving at the hospital. Patients could choose to pay either market rate or a subsidized rate or no fee at all if they could not afford it. All patients would receive the same clinical services regardless of payment and the same quality. Staff rotated and alternated between paying and nonpaying patients to ensure an equal level of quality for, and understanding of, all patients' needs. The key to financial sustainability was twofold: to serve high volumes of patients, which would decrease the cost per

* Mehta, P., & Shenoy, S. (2011). *Infinite Vision: How Aravind Became the World's Greatest Business Case for Compassion.* Berrett-Koehler, p. 65.
† Mehta, P., & Shenoy, S. (2011). *Infinite Vision: How Aravind Became the World's Greatest Business Case for Compassion.* Berrett-Koehler, p. 69.

patient, and to have enough paying patients to balance out the nonpaying patients. Both targets required building demand in the surrounding community and building systems to allow for maximum efficiency in dealing with high volumes.

The Aravind founders were able to innovate on the processes because they placed constraints on themselves, which required them to find solutions that were out of the ordinary. Their constraints were as follows: "We cannot turn anyone away; we cannot compromise on quality; we must be self-reliant." Achieving these three goals simultaneously required them to keep resource use at a minimum. An example referred to in the book *Infinite Vision* demonstrates the waste mitigation and down-cycling common at Aravind. Bed linens no longer in use are converted into tablecloths, and then into washcloths, going into multiple cycles of use. When the first hospital was founded and resources were especially scarce, the team used to make their own cotton swabs and cut packaging material into sponges. Today, resources are more readily available, yet the Aravind team manages to avoid unnecessary costs and increase the usage out of every resource. Spare parts and repairs for medical equipment are managed by an in-house maintenance team, which implements cost-cutting measures such as manufacturing locally made spare parts and identifying local substitutions and innovating ways to safely reuse expensive equipment that would otherwise be used once and discarded.

An important factor in building trust to grow the customer base was no hidden costs. Anyone who has ever been to a hospital or a bank can identify with this. Aravind's team did not add charges for each test or service added but charged only one consultation fee, which was valid for up to three months if the patient needed to return. The fee for outpatients is 50 rupees, which is the equivalent of less than one dollar. Amongst those coming directly to the hospital, the paying customers outnumber nonpaying customers by 3:1 for outpatient services and 2:1 for surgery.

The price was set by the market, and the costs were lowered to the degree that revenues would exceed cost. Doctors were paid a fixed fee rather than a per-patient fee so that when they treated large volumes of patients, the profit went back into the organization. To make this all work, intensive monitoring and scrutiny were required on both the cost front and the quality front. The tiered pricing system expanded and diversified the customer base, serving not only those who can't afford to pay but also those who can afford it and have a choice on where to get treated. This model would only work if the highest quality is provided for all customers.

Aravind's team sees the patient as customer with choice, even those patients who cannot afford to pay. Zero is one price point they can choose from, and the market rate is another, with subsidized rates offered in between these two price points. Letting the patient choose the price helped build demand across customer segments. Approximately half of the nonpaying outpatients come to Aravind on their own account, and half come in after Aravind's outreach efforts.

However, uptake in the rural communities where the eye camps were held was still under 7% of the population who needed eye care.* It became clear to the management team that providing access to service to the rural communities through outreach alone was not enough to create the impact they sought. Exploring potential reasons for the lack of uptake, their initial conclusion was that it was simply not a priority among the rural population, who had poor acceptance of eye treatment and fear of surgery. Referring back to the AAAQ framework of health and human rights (see Chapter 3), they came to the conclusion that while they had succeeded in addressing affordability, they had not succeeded in addressing awareness and acceptance, nor in fully bridging the gap to access.

---

* Aravind Eye Care System: Providing Total Eye Care to the Rural Population. Ivey Publishing, Teaching Case W11212-PDF-ENG.

Initial responses focused on marketing and communications. How could they explore different promotion options in rural markets? What were different ways in which they could change the perception of the target population? The key assumption was that Aravind's need to increase rural customers' acceptance required education, the creation of trust, and reduction of the associated costs (not just the cost of service). This is what Aravind's executive director Thulasiraj ("Thulsi") Ravilla referred to as their pull strategy: drawing customers in.

Over time, Thulsi realized that in this case, the demand side required both a pull and push strategy. The solution was *not* to assume that customers did not know what they wanted or what was best for them and to concentrate efforts on convincing them. It was the organization that needed to change its way of thinking and behaving. Achieving their vision of universal coverage required adjusting their mix of services and also where and how they interacted with patients. If not everyone was coming to the eye camps, then perhaps the eye camps were not the best way to fulfill the organization's goal of reaching everyone.

It was the organization that needed to change its way of thinking and behaving.

Aravind's team was able to crack the case only by setting up a network of permanent primary eye centers (vision centers). Using population coverage as their key metric, they calculated that each vision center would cover patients within a five-mile radius, based on the data on attendance at the eye camps. At the time of writing, there were about 50 vision centers in Tamil Nadu, covering a total population of 3 and a half million people. These centers cumulatively had registered over 900,000 patients, well over 20% of the total population. This translates to universal coverage of that population, according to Thulsi and the Aravind team. Plans are in place to add a 100 more centers, scaling to a population of 10 million.

Looking back, Thulsi identifies a number of factors that were key in building the organization and scaling its impact. He is careful to point out that "hindsight is 20/20" and that these factors were identified only by doing the work and listening to the community—there was no blueprint from the start with perfectly laid out plans. Many of these keys to success echo similar patterns we have seen in other cases in this book.

First, basic services can be provided by a basic workforce with a basic level of training. In the case of Aravind, not every patient needed to see an ophthalmologist, as the majority of clinical needs of patients presenting at the vision centers could be diagnosed and treated by optometrists who have two years of training after high school. Technical support was provided by the central team, and centers were telemedicine enabled. This allowed Aravind to keep costs low, charging 20 rupees per consult, which is less than the bus fare to the nearest eye hospital. Each center was able to break even as a stand-alone financial unit. This is similar to the case of HLC from Chapter 4. Decentralization of the services, freshly trained young graduates rather than highly specialized teachers, low costs, and technical support from the headquarters allowed for each center to break even and to produce the desired educational (in the case of HLC) or health (in the case of Aravind) outcomes.

Second, scaling the services require that the processes be tightly packaged for easy replication. Quality management, standardization, and a detail-oriented approach were necessary. Personnel were disciplined, accountable, and responsive to patients. To deal with large volumes, it's necessary to find the right balance between the "factory" approach of standardized processes and the need to tailor the human interaction to the local context and the person. While the Aravind Eye Care

System can be thought of as "mass production" and the goal of its founder was to serve millions, its services are still tailored to multiple populations. These include children with congenital problems or infections, workers with refractive errors, diabetics with retinopathy, and adults with cataracts, glaucoma, and other clinical needs. Process innovations also helped drive the costs down across the different services, such as the assembly line approach to clinical care.

> It's necessary to find the right balance between the "factory" approach of standardized processes and the need to tailor the human interaction to the local context and the person.

Third, tailoring your services to your customers' needs is the cornerstone of your social venture. Thulsi's message draws parallels with the case of Daily Table in the United States, the need to understand your customer and to offer them the ability to exercise choice. Aravind's perspective is that customers are driven by value for money and quality of care and that charity is not always associated with quality. They don't advertise to paying customers that they are subsidizing those who are not able to pay. Customers come to you because they want to get a high-quality, high-value service for themselves, not because they want to help others.

Aravind has quadrupled its growth every decade, making an operational surplus of 50% on revenues of tens of millions of dollars, a performance "worthy of any commercial venture."[*] Says Thulsi: "Self-sustainability emerges from a complex interaction of organizational, technical, and human factors." Careful consideration must be given to pricing structures, patient volumes, standardization and effective resource use, and an extremely cost-conscious leadership is needed.[†]

---

[*] http://www.forbes.com/global/2010/0315/companies-india-madurai-blindness-nam-familys-vision.html.
[†] Mehta, P., and Shenoy, S. (2011). *Infinite Vision: How Aravind Became the World's Greatest Business Case for Compassion*. Berrett-Koehler, p. 75.

Chapter 7

Measuring Impact

Targeting Success

This can be one of the most exciting times in developing your social venture. You've learned everything there is to know about the challenge and context you are tackling and your target audience. You've designed an exciting and innovative new solution that emerged from your end users and built a theory of change around it to penetrate that market and that audience and change the face of the challenge at hand. The first step of implementing your solution and manifesting that change is setting your performance metrics. Before you start, you need to ask yourself, "How will I know when I succeed?" To set your strategy, you need to define what success looks like and how you will measure your impact. Then you'll work backward from there!

Your social impact is the basis of all you do; it is the purpose of your work. It defines how you spend your time, allocate human and financial resources, build external partnerships—every component of your work and your organization. How will you know when you've reached your goal? How will you monitor your progress as you work toward that goal? How will you decide where to spend your time, money, human, and other resources? And how will you convince others to support you and invest in you? This is why it's critical to be able to measure and communicate your social impact.

> To set your strategy, you need to define what success looks like and how you will measure your impact. Then you'll work backward from there!

The reason impact metrics is so fun in social entrepreneurship is it's so challenging! There's lots of room to get creative in imagining what changes you'll see and how you'll measure them. Most of the time, in a typical commercial venture, profit is the main indicator of success. This is used to evaluate the growth of the start-up, its customer base, its sales, and its penetration into the market. In a social venture, your goal is social change, and you need to find a metric to capture and track that! Determining whether social outcomes have improved and people have been empowered requires a lot more creativity. And, on top of that, you're still tracking your financial viability to make sure that this venture is financially sustainable! So, you'll need more than one indicator to measure the health, growth, and success of your social venture. Let's dive in and see how others have done it and how you want to do it for your own social venture.

Theories to Results

We'll start by building on the wealth of work that you've already done. You may not know it, but you've already built the foundation to measure your success. In Chapter 4, we talked about your theory of change and how you define the change you want to see. You've already set your desired ultimate outcomes and the intermediary effects of your work, which will lead to those outcomes if your assumptions hold. Next, we'll take the theory of change one step further, building on it to create the logical framework of your organization. The logical framework will lay the foundation for your building your organization, operationalizing your theory of change, specifying how you will execute on your vision, and forming the blueprint of your work. It sets the stage for budgeting and business planning, which we'll focus more on in the coming chapters. Most importantly, it sets the stage for forming your social impact metrics.

In this chapter, we'll focus on the characteristics of robust social impact metrics, providing examples from existing social ventures. You'll find as you read more about this topic online and in other publications that the term *social impact metrics* is often used interchangeably with other common terms, including *success indicators, success metrics, impact metrics*, or *performance indicators*. The idea behind these terminologies is that the act of *achieving* success in your social venture comes hand in hand with the acts of *measuring* and *demonstrating* success.

An easy way to internalize the meanings of these different terms is to go back to the core of the words: a metric is simply a measure. It is used to indicate success. *Indicators* and *metrics* are different words with the same function: capturing results.

Different Metrics for Different Fields

Different organizations in different fields of work have measured success in different ways. Educators measure educational outcomes, like the learning objectives in a course you've taken, and the assignments you've performed that are graded to reflect whether you're reaching those objectives. Healthcare providers measure health outcomes, like your heart's functioning and the test results that indicate whether it's functioning well. Financial investors measure investment outcomes, namely, the financial return on their investment. One measure they use that has been applied in the social entrepreneurship world is return on investment (ROI).

What Is ROI?

This is a way of assessing what you are getting out, compared with what you are putting in. An example with financial metrics is that if an investor puts in $1 million into a venture and gets out $1.4 million, then this is a 40% return. ROI is used in many fields to compare various options of where you should put your money. For example, in the field of public health, ROI is used to highlight smart investments that produce positive population outcomes and quantify the impact per dollar invested. A bicycle helmet can result in a return of almost $50 for every $1 invested*!

---

* By preventing medical costs. See http://www.nphw.org/assets/general/uploads/APHA-NPHW2013_Sec_ONE_4b _noTOC.PDF.

Knowing exactly what you are putting into your social venture and what you are getting out of it is crucial to expanding your impact.

ROI is only one way to communicate your impact, and you can use measures other than monetary value on the outcomes side. For example, the social ROI can be the number of students who stay in school per *x* dollars invested, the number of cases of a certain disease prevented, or the number of jobs created. Even without converting these into their estimated monetary value, this measure still allows you to compare different routes or different ventures. The cost of keeping a child in school, the cost of preventing one case of disease, or the cost of creating one job is another way to evaluate different options when forming your plans or approaching different investment opportunities.

Quantifying Your Social Investment

Further in the chapter, we will discuss what to do in settings where it is hard to collect data, how to make sure your impact metrics are easy to communicate and useful for your stakeholders, and describe a few examples of commonly used metrics. You can refer to these examples or invent your own metrics! These examples are just to give you an idea and help get your thought process flowing.

To start thinking about various metrics that others have used, a useful introduction can be the IRIS catalogue developed by the Global Impact Investing Network, a nonprofit organization dedicated to supporting social impact investing. Flipping through this catalogue will help give you a few starting ideas of the types of metrics you might be able to use for your social venture. Ultimately, the number 1 pointer to keep in mind when selecting your metrics is to keep it simple. As a social entrepreneur, your main purpose in collecting data on your social impact is to know whether you are achieving your goal. Therefore, if your goal is well defined and tied into a set of smart objectives (more on this further in the chapter) then your impact metrics will naturally follow.

Which Metrics Are the Right Fit for You?

There are no one-size-fits-all success indicators. On the one hand, it is practical to use simple, clear-cut indicators that are common in your field of practice. This will enable others, such as investors, to assess you and compare you with other social ventures. On the other hand, each situation is unique, and it's up to you and your stakeholders to decide what measures of success best reflect your goals and the social outcome(s) you're trying to change.

If, at any point in the process, you start to feel that measuring your social impact is getting complicated and overwhelming, then you are most likely doing it wrong. Don't panic—this is an experience most social entrepreneurs go through—it's all part of the process of finding your metrics. Take a step back, revisit your goals, focus on what you want to achieve and what the obvious indicators would be that would let you and your stakeholders know if, when, and to what degree you have achieved your goals.

> Focus on what you want to achieve and what the obvious indicators are that will let you and your stakeholders know if, when, and to what degree you have achieved your goals.

Before You Start

A few tips to keep in mind while thinking about how you'll measure success.

Decide Early On

You want to measure the change you are creating from the moment you start. One of the very first decisions you need to make before launching is to decide what you are going to measure—what pieces of data will indicate success. The reason it is not recommended to leave this to a later stage is that defining the indicators you are working to achieve will help you define your work plan and business plan. You can always revise your success indicators at a later stage in your journey if evidence points to a need for adjustment. This may happen if you find that the indicators you have set are not truly reflective of the change you are achieving or if the data collection is not feasible or takes up too much time and resources and needs adjustment. But doing the work and then deciding what to measure is generally not a good idea. This is why we start early on by defining the metrics. They are the core drivers of our work, not an afterthought. Building your business model and work plan and then deciding on your metrics may run the risk that your organization or initiative goes in a different direction from what your mission, vision, and theory of change have set out to accomplish.

Measure Inherently

Ideally, you'd like for the measurement of your success indicators to be a part and parcel of your work, rather than an extra step. Think about what steps your team, suppliers, providers, end users, and other stakeholders are already taking. Discuss with them what they feel and observe are the important pieces of information that can be gleaned from their roles and processes. What information can you collect through your core operations? Streamlining the processes, human resources, time spent, and associated financial costs are all keys to your success, across the board! This applies to all components of your work, first and foremost measuring your success.

Don't Measure Too Much

An easy pitfall to fall into is setting too many indicators. This will result in a cumbersome and inefficient data collection process that will be labor-intensive and require more time and resources than necessary. A general rule of thumb is that the smaller the number of indicators you deem sufficient to demonstrate success, the better. What statistics do you want to show to your funders, customers, team, and other stakeholders in 1 year, 5 years, 10 years, and 20 years? What statistics do you want to reach as your core mission and the ultimate reason for your work? Oftentimes, the ultimate outcome is just one statistic. A simple example is the reduction in infant mortality in a community from the baseline rate to a target.

Refer to Baseline Data

Because change by nature is relative (we are changing from the current situation to a future situation), ideally, we would want to compare our future statistics to current statistics. This can sometimes be tricky in settings with a dearth of baseline data. In Chapter 2, we talked about the importance of characterizing the problem you are trying to solve or the situation you are trying to build on. The work you have done at that earliest stage may be the most valuable resource to inform your comparative statistics. In an ideal situation, you will have statistics available to you on the current status in your target population (such as infant mortality rate). In a less than ideal situation, you may have to refer to average statistics, citing reasons that point to your target population being above or below average.

One powerful step you can take is to collect your own statistics when starting out on your social venture. This is often the most valuable use of your time and resources, not only to have a reference point to compare to in the future but also to better understand the setting you are working in and tailor your intervention to be as effective as possible. It might represent an extra step, but this will be a one-time investment, so it's worth considering.

What to Look for in Your Impact Metrics

Earlier, we talked about the multidimensional causes and consequences of the many social challenges we face. Education, for example, has been linked to improved earning power, health outcomes, peace-building, and other social outcomes. Let's take for example an organization aiming to improve the level of education in a community, having identified low levels of schooling in that community. The approach of the organization and the way it measures its impact will relate directly to how the problem was characterized in the first place. If the initial research in that community suggested that enrolling children in school at an early age was not the problem, but keeping them in school was, then the organization's work would focus on identifying and tackling the causes of school children missing school, failing, or dropping out. A simple impact metric to evaluate success could then be the percentage of students advancing from one grade to the next each year. The number of children enrolling in school in this case would *not* be the best metric.

Another example we've visited was the text message intervention, which improves health outcomes by reminding mothers to bring in their infants for vaccination. A simple metric in this case could be the number of vaccinations given after the intervention, compared with before, assuming no other major changes have taken place that might be responsible for this change.

The Comparative Factor

Both these examples point to the fact that impact relies on comparison. It is rare that an absolute value can inform the user as to its impact. If a number of children are brought in for vaccination the first year in which the text reminder intervention is applied, some questions we might ask ourselves are as follows: How many children were brought in last year? Or, how many children are there in this community? If there was no increase from year to year, then there is no evidence that the intervention worked. If there are a large number of children in the community and only a small fraction have been brought in for vaccination, then the social entrepreneur would want to think about how to expand the reach of this intervention.

Baseline Data

This brings us to the importance of collecting baseline data. You can measure your impact only if you have adequately characterized the situation before you implement your venture. Oftentimes, you can do this as part and parcel of implementing your venture. For example, you can interview mothers bringing in their infants for vaccination, asking them either whether they brought them in last year or whether they missed their last appointment. Other times, it might be necessary to take the extra step of collecting baseline data before implementation. This could entail implementing measurement systems before implementing the intervention—for creating or strengthening the existing medical records system to track the number of missed appointments. Another approach is to select a comparison site where the intervention is not being implemented.

Controlling for Other Factors

Collecting data on other factors influencing your target outcome is also important. While characterizing your social challenge you may have identified factors along the causal pathway to your outcome. For example, going back to the text message intervention, forgetting to bring children in for appointments was recognized as one of the causes behind lack of vaccination, which this example social venture decided to focus on. But other factors were most likely also identified. One example could be the challenge of transportation. If transportation were improved at the same time as the social venture rolled out its intervention, this information needs to be accounted for when evaluating social impact. It could be that the text message reminders in this case were not the leading factor causing improved vaccination rates but rather that transportation was. This provides critical information! In such a case, rather than (or in addition to) focusing on expanding the text message reminder system, the social entrepreneur would then focus on transportation and other factors that can have a bigger impact on the social outcome.

> You can measure your impact only if you have adequately characterized the situation before you implement your venture.

Linking to Quality

In certain cases, your intervention might entail the implementation of a certain product or procedure that is reported to improve outcomes. Let's take the case of the medical device designed to reduce neonatal deaths. To track your growth, you might decide to track the number of clinics in your target area that have implemented this device. Here, it's important to link the previous indicator to quality control indicators, to ensure that there is no room for error. If the device is used incorrectly, the number of clinics that have implemented this device will *not* be an accurate reflection of the health outcomes you are assuming. The number of clinics does not reflect the ultimate social outcome we're working toward (reduced neonatal deaths) but reflects instead a step we are taking that is necessary to get there. To link this to the social outcome we're looking for, it's important to focus on quality indicators too. Any gaps or shortfalls in linking the number of clinics to the number of deaths prevented could be addressed by working on quality of care.

Another common mistake is to measure the "number of people trained." Training people does not ensure that they will correctly execute and apply the skills they have gained, nor that they have even gained the skills you set out to train them for in the first place. Gaps between number of trainings conducted and actual learning outcomes may reflect a need to improve the quality of training or the content, or change the way participants are interacting with and applying the information and skills provided.

Inputs versus Outputs versus Outcomes

This brings us to the importance of measuring outputs rather than inputs. Training people is an input. Buying a machine is an input. Distributing a bed net is an input. The machine could collect dust in the corner of a poorly maintained hospital. The bed net could be used as a fashion or furnishing accessory rather than as a life-saving device. Inputs are the processes and steps you implement to reach a certain outcome, and outputs are the tangible results that link those inputs to your desired outcome.

If your desired outcome is a reduction in the number of malaria cases, a measurable output could be that you have increased the number of people sleeping under the full protection of a bed net. The inputs required to reach this number would be the bed nets themselves, the instruction of the end user on how to effectively use this input, and the desire of the end user to do so!

Agriculture is an easy-to-illustrate case in point. The number of agricultural tools distributed to farmers living in poverty is not an indicator of social impact; it is an input. Increased agricultural yield is an output. Better yet, increased household income (through increased sales of agricultural yield) is the ideal metric in such a case, to avoid the loophole that yield has increased but access to markets is not available. It is this metric that will result in the social outcome we are working for in this example, of eliminating poverty.

Short- versus Long-Term Goals

In the previous health-related examples, the ultimate success metric is the reduction in the prevalence of malaria cases in your target community or the reduction in infant mortality rates. These are long-term goals that need time to be reflected in the population data collected in your community. While you are working toward these goals, you can select intermediate indicators that help you measure your work so that you will have an idea of whether you are moving in the right direction. The increase in number of mothers bringing in their infants for vaccination (or decrease in number of missed appointments) and the increase in number of households with inhabitants sleeping under the full protection of bed nets are examples of success indicators that can be used to point toward the successful eradication of root causes linked to the outcome you are tackling.

Measuring Intermediate Outcomes

Such intermediate indicators point to the more immediate outcomes of our work that are hypothesized to move the ultimate outcomes in the right direction. Sometimes, it is not possible to measure the ultimate outcome right away. This is common when dealing with outcomes that take years, if not decades, to improve. You need to proceed very carefully in selecting your intermediate outcomes, to make sure that they are truly indicative of progress made toward your ultimate goal. This is where the assumptions underlying your theory of change come in handy. Don't be afraid to continue questioning the assumptions as you proceed!

This Is Where You "Cash In" the Benefits of Your Evidence-Based Solution!

In many cases, the link between correct usage of your product/service and improved outcomes has already been demonstrated, and these types of intermediate indicators are sufficient to measure social impact. For example, the solar-powered cook stoves distributed and sold by One Earth

Designs have been demonstrated to reduce exposure to indoor air pollution by replacing traditional cook stoves. Therefore, tracking the number of clients using them and conducting quality control checks are accurate methods of quantifying social impact. It may be beyond the scope of the organization to measure population health outcomes over time, such as reductions in the number of cases of pulmonary and cardiac disease, but because of the robust scientific link between these diseases and exposure to indoor air pollution (as published by numerous scientific research studies), it is sufficient to measure the reduced exposure to indoor air pollution, given the wealth of evidence on improved health outcomes associated with reduced exposure. Another social impact of solar-powered cook stoves is a reduction in greenhouse gas emissions by eliminating the burning of wood to power traditional cook stoves. This has also been quantified, and thus, it is possible to directly link the number of clients consistently using the cook stoves to the reductions in greenhouse gases.

The most classic example of this scenario is if your social venture is increasing access to a basic social good: clean water, education, healthcare, shelter, or even financial services or other programs targeted for poverty reduction. In some cases, access itself is a basic human right and the ultimate social impact. In other cases, access is linked by existing evidence to improved social outcomes and is sufficient to illustrate social impact. An important note here is to keep in mind the quality assurance aspect described previously. Providing access to clean water is only a social impact if you can demonstrate that the water is clean by a set of prespecified standards.

Direct versus Indirect Benefits

Sticking to the example of the solar-powered cook stoves, the direct benefits are improved health outcomes and reduced greenhouse gas emissions because these are the goals that drove the social entrepreneurs to found the social venture and develop these cook stoves in the first place. However, there are numerous indirect benefits that resulted from the growth of this organization. The creation of jobs is an important one. By introducing this new product to the market, the social enterprise is creating work opportunities for retail distributors and manufacturers, thus increasing their household income. (It is important to point out here that, in this example, the creation of jobs is an indirect benefit, while in another example, it could be a direct benefit and the primary goal of the social enterprise.) Increased household income often also results in increased access to other social goods such as education and healthcare for the families. If you really want to track the ripple effects, one can also point out in turn that this increased education for the children in these families will also lead to increased earning power for them in the future, thus benefiting their future families! Thus, each social venture has both direct and indirect benefits. While the direct benefits are your main indicators of success—whether you are achieving your mission—it is often valuable to also capture the many indirect benefits you are producing along the way.

Further Considerations

Valuating the Supply Chain

Because every social venture involves a supply chain (the people and processes involved in the different steps of putting together the social product or service), it is valuable to think about the social benefits incurred at each step in the supply chain. If your product is an object that is made of many parts, where are you getting the parts to put together in producing it? If it involves distribution, who is getting the product (and the parts that go into it) from point A to point B? If it involves sales, which individuals and/or retail establishments are benefiting? Many social ventures are built around building supply chains that create new jobs, empower marginalized populations, and foster change through the *process*, not just the *outcome*. For example, a social venture providing eye care is focused on the outcome. But a social venture providing average consumer goods by employing people with impaired vision is focused on the process. In this case, the number of people with impaired vision who are now sustainably employed is their success metric. Even if your social venture is focused on the product or service itself, you still need to think about the process. Both product and process should be measured: you want to make sure that you are achieving your intended outcome without incurring *unintended consequences* along the way.

Management Indicators

We've focused up until now on measuring the outcomes you're working toward, since those are your bottom line, and figuring out what success metrics you'll use to capture them. But don't forget, you are running a venture here, and you will also need to track your internal operations and performance to get there! Every company and venture needs to make sure it's doing its work right. So, while this chapter focuses mostly on outcome, here is just a shout-out for you to start thinking about your internal management systems too.

Chances are, you're not going to hit the bull's eye at the first try and reach the outcomes you're targeting. You've already seen how much prototyping, testing, and piloting are involved in building a successful social venture! In addition to measuring your impact, you're also going to have to keep track of your own internal "control knobs"—these are your internal operational indicators that will reflect what parts of the process you should adjust to get better results.

For example, you can refer to the uptake of your product or service by the target community, i.e., the number of people in your target audience who are using it. Do you need to focus on sales and marketing to have a bigger impact? Or let's say uptake is high but you're still not seeing results. Do you have the right monitoring systems in place to track whether it's being used; by whom and when and where; and whether it's being applied correctly? The latter can be demonstrated through observation or a simple checklist. This isn't adding extra steps to your work, it is your work. These are the kinds of *performance* or *operational* indicators that tell you whether you're implementing your venture in a way that is getting results.

Build Systems for Data Collection and Analysis

The metrics you are collecting are valuable not only to inform your own work and your own stakeholders but also to inform the work of others and to empower your end users by generating knowledge, information, and awareness. This creation of knowledge is an output in and of itself, which you are producing and which has a positive social impact. Let your social venture be a factory for producing information, beyond producing the specific target you are aiming for!

By building processes for data collection and analysis, building capacity in your team and your community to execute the processes, and disseminating this information widely, you are adding value above and beyond your product. One way to achieve this is to automate the data collection and analysis process, like HLC did. Investing in technologies—whether hardware, like the tablets they used in the field, or software, such as data management and analysis packages—may yield a high return in terms of your ability to produce and communicate your social impact metrics. This may also require human resources investments such as training. As you hone in on what metrics you're going to use to indicate success, step back and ask yourself how you can build a system around this so that it will be an integrated part of your venture.

One of the final pieces of the social impact metrics assembly line is communicating your results. We will focus more on this in Chapter 12. Most importantly, a feedback loop is needed to tie your assembly line together. Communicating your results to the outside world is one goal, but communicating and reflecting on your results internally are crucial to evaluating your work and strengthening your systems. In the social service sectors, these systems are referred to collectively as monitoring and evaluation (M&E).

Interview Box. Jake Harriman, Founder and CEO, Nuru International

TC: How do you measure your impact?

JH: First off, I want to say that we don't measure for the sake of measuring; we measure to get to scale. It's very much integrated into our daily work; we built measurements into our operational model and exit plan. I personally didn't know the first thing about monitoring and evaluation—this is why I hired a team leader specialized in metrics.

TC: What are some of the main challenges faced by your team in measuring impact?

JH: I think that creating and communicating a clear value-add for measuring impact is important. Otherwise, it's difficult to get buy-in for this piece because it's not as valued and is often seen as more of a box to check. If people aren't convinced that this is an important part of the company, you risk getting token efforts and token results.

TC: Do you think that we can do better in terms of innovating new ways of measuring impact?

JH: I think we have to be careful because the industry lacks standards, which makes it difficult to compare impact across different companies. We use a standardized tool because it's already been validated and because it makes it easier to compare.

TC: We've met social entrepreneurs with backgrounds ranging from law, tech, journalism, retail, to the military! What are the key qualifications that you think a social entrepreneur needs?

JH: Social entrepreneurs are a special breed; they're not defined by their background but by the way they look at things. They see a problem in the world, where people have been failed by a market gap, a failure of the government or the market, and people are suffering because of the gap. They decide to build a company around that gap with a product or service for that population. Social entrepreneurs must be laser focused on social impact too, which differentiates them from commercial entrepreneurs—Their focus is on people who are suffering.

Interview Box. Bennadette Mugita, Impact Programs Manager, Nuru Kenya

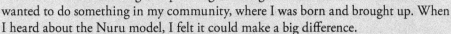

TC: Bennadette, you've been working your entire life to improve social outcomes in Kenya and other countries in Africa. Tell us how you came to be where you are today.

BM: I started out as a health-oriented person, studying nursing here in Kenya, and then community health and psychology in South Africa. At first, I worked with international NGOs such as Medecins Sans Frontiers (Doctors Without Borders) in South Sudan and Congo, responding to emergencies. But I wanted to do something in my community, where I was born and brought up. When I heard about the Nuru model, I felt it could make a big difference.

TC: What was it like living and working in these four African countries; are there similar challenges or is it very context specific?

BM: It is very different, especially in South Sudan, with the new nation and no medical supplies. Where there is war, it's so hard to improve outcomes.

TC: Nuru's model is that improving social outcomes prevents conflict. Is this something that people in your community thought of even before Nuru came into the picture, or was it a new idea?

BM: Yes and no—people know this is true but they don't have the will, desire, and drive to initiate this strategy of conflict prevention. Some leaders (especially political) use conflicts in their areas to advance their career. If the Nuru team did not come to this region, it would have taken centuries or never even happened. Most NGOs in these countries are health oriented and focus on one area such as HIV/AIDS, without taking a holistic approach in giving solutions to conflicts. After satisfying one area of need, the others lag behind and conflicts remain like never attended.

TC: Putting aside the numbers and metrics for a moment, as someone who has lived in this community all your life, are you able to observe the impact?

BM: You see and feel the changes. For me, it was especially obvious in the health area, but of course, I had to master other areas like agriculture, financial inclusion, etc. to keep pace with them in their areas of impact creation. For example, Nuru's health program with the field officers' house visits teaches Nuru farmer households 10 healthy behaviors to improve maternal child health. More people are delivering in healthcare facilities, breastfeeding for six months, immunizing their children, sleeping under mosquito nets, handwashing at critical times, having safe water treatment and latrines. The field officers sell affordable commodities like handwashing stations, sanitary towels, soap, and the uptake has increased. Most farmers have shown improvement in health, and you are able to spot these changes. You go to households, you see maize planted well, crops are healthy-looking, which is a sign promising bumper harvest for Nuru farmers compared to non-Nuru farmers. Again, you meet people who are operating businesses started using savings from Nuru Financial Inclusions groups.

TC: Do you think that this model can be applied in other communities and countries?

BM: Yes, we started first in Nuria West district and now we have expanded to Nuria East district. When we did this, we surveyed the community first, measured indicators, needs, educational level, agriculture, and scouted different counties. Next, we will scale to other districts. I think it could work in other countries, even South Sudan. You need to engage all community members to ensure maximum participation so they own the program. They identify priorities and spearhead what they want done. For example, it would be better to identify the crops the local people plant so that you support them with that but only improving the method and techniques for doing the farming.

TC: What about people who say that it's too geopolitically rooted and complex to solve?

BM: I don't think it's very complicated. We make it very clear. We invite stakeholders, talk about what we are able to offer, make expectations clear and spell out each party's roles and responsibility so that it becomes a shared common goal. We stay politically neutral, choose members well, and now, we have incorporated a cooperative strategy in Kuria East to make work even easier. It becomes complex when some leaders especially administration are left out or when a certain clan feels left out in planning and executing our goal in a certain area. We are all seeing the changes and feeling the impacts as a team and as a party in this model.

Building Your Logical Framework

Alright, so we've talked about what to look for when thinking about your social impact metrics and the characteristics you should be aiming for. Now, let's go ahead and set the actual targets! We're going to use a planning tool called the logical framework, or logframe for short. It helps you organize your inputs, outputs, intermediate outcomes, and long-term social outcomes into one unifying framework. This will help you determine what your denominator will be. You're starting from zero and hopefully working to reach 100% of your target!

Most of us have a love–hate relationship with planning tools, feeling that they dampen the entrepreneurial spirit. Ultimately, if you have a bunch of brilliant ideas and truly intend on implementing them, at one point, you're going to have to sit down and organize all your thoughts. This is the time. Let's take the vision of success that you've built and figure out how we're going to turn that into reality.

Step 1: Setting SMART Objectives

We'll start by breaking down your ultimate goal into a number of objectives, so that we can then tie each objective into one or more success metrics. Having specific and measurable objectives makes it possible to link your goal to the outputs you are going to produce. Remember, you want to keep the number of metrics manageable—this will tie back to keeping your objectives simple and finite. A helpful way to think about how to set your objectives is to make them "SMART": specific, measurable, achievable, realistic, and timely. Figure 7.1 illustrates an example of smart objectives linking an overall goal to a set of measurable outputs needed to get there.

SMART objectives include indicators. If eradicating poverty is the overarching goal, then be specific about how you're going to measure this. Your indicator of poverty could be household income: you might aim to increase household income by a specific amount. This provides a metric you can refer to that will help you assess what needs to be done and be able to say when you've done it! Household income can be measured, and health statistics can be tracked by applying a household health survey. This is just one example—you might use other indicators for other goals—and the case study at the end of this chapter provides an example of multiple indicators for the same goal.

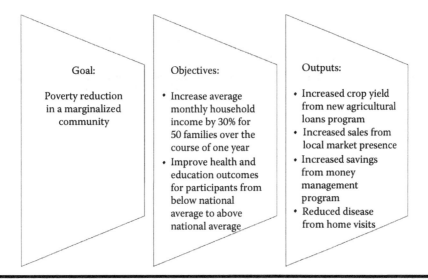

Figure 7.1   Example of SMART objectives.

Step 2: Producing Measurable Outputs

Outputs are what you need to produce through your work before you can reach your objective.

To more easily understand the difference between goals, objectives, and outputs, it may be helpful to think of a class you've taken. In a social entrepreneurship course, for example, the goal is for students to gain knowledge and skills needed to build a social venture. The learning objectives will be along the lines of… "By the end of the semester, students will be able to:

1. Generate an economically, socially, and scientifically feasible solution to a social challenge of their choice.
2. Characterize and evaluate the audience for the proposed product or service, incorporating socioeconomic and environmental considerations, including vulnerable populations, variability in population exposures, and gender analysis.
3. Develop a business plan detailing resources and timeframe required to implement the proposed solution and including a SWOT analysis of strengths, weaknesses, opportunities, and threats related to the proposed solution."

The measurable outputs produced to meet those objectives will be assignments, such as the following:

- Seven weekly in-class discussions
- Seven weekly homework assignments
- One final project: 10-page executive summary
- Social venture pitch contest
- Group participation as scored by peers

The importance of these assignments is that they can be graded by the instructor, thus providing a metric that indicates whether the student has successfully achieved the learning objectives.

Overarching goal: What is the social outcome you are working to achieve?					
Objectives (S.M.A.R.T.)	Outputs needed to reach those objectives	Activities needed to produce those outputs	Cost estimates for these activities	Time estimates for these activities	Success indicators (targets and milestones)

Figure 7.2   Example logframe template.

Figure 7.2 provides a template for you to fill in up to three objectives and list all the outputs you'll need to produce in order to reach those objectives. You can play around with it and tailor it to your needs; you might have fewer than three objectives—or conversely, a more complex framework—but give it your best shot and chances are you'll discover a lot about how to clarify what you're trying to do and how you're going to do it.

Step 3: Determining the Inputs

Outlining the Activities Needed to Produce These Outputs

What activities do you need to conduct in order to produce the outputs you need? In the case of the previous course assignments example, you'd need to read the required materials before class, research information on your topic of interest to develop your weekly deliverables, meet with your classmates to work on your group projects, write the documents/slides/etc. that will result in the measurable output, then review, edit, and submit to the instructor. In the case of the poverty reduction example in Figure 7.1 or any other social venture, it gets much more complicated. Careful planning is required to budget enough time and resources to ensure that you successfully complete the activities.

Estimating the Time and Cost of Conducting These Activities

The next step is to estimate the time and cost of these activities, which will help create a budget for your social venture. Don't forget to budget time and money for data collection, analysis, evaluation, and reporting of your social impact metrics! In the household health survey example, how will you ensure that the survey you're administering really does capture the health statistics that you're looking for? Both the content of the survey and the way it is administered matter, or a survey might not be the most effective tool—maybe spot-checking a random sample to conduct more in-depth interviews, measurements, or diagnostics is the way to go. This may include investing in experts up front, and it may include hiring a M&E officer. Or it may include investing in technology to streamline the M&E process—like the tablets HLC procured for each center and like the software that most of you will purchase or the coders you might hire. All these steps should be factored into your activities, timeline, and costs, whether you use a logframe or any other planning tool. In the next chapter, we'll talk more about assigning financial and time estimates to your activities.

Pros and Cons of the Logical Framework

All planning tools have advantages and disadvantages, and the logframe is no exception. The advantages of using a logframe are that it puts everything in one place to help assess how the different components of your theory of change will fit together as you grow it into an organized initiative. It helps you connect all the dots in terms of specifying your objectives, outputs needed to get there, activities required to produce those outputs, costs of conducting those activities, and success indicators. It uses your theory of change as a starting point, building on it and setting the stage to link the core components of your intervention to a budget, work plan, and key metrics to assess your progress. For those who need a planning tool to help develop these long-term forecasts, the logframe comes in handy.

The disadvantage of the logframe is that it can often be perceived to impose rigidity on an organization. Many social entrepreneurs feel that they need to retain the flexibility to respond to market needs and opportunities, learn by trial and error, and figure things out as they go along. Rather than decide from the outset what the work plan is, it is tempting to proceed one step at a time, depending on what information and inspiration unfolds each step of the way.

A happy medium might be to develop a logical framework (or some other equivalent or similar planning tool) and stay open to modifying it, periodically checking in to see whether the targets still make sense in each new phase, depending on what new information, inspiration, feedback, or resources become available. If you find that the logframe is not the right tool for you, there are other tools you can refer to in developing your social impact metrics. As one example, McKinsey & Co.'s Learning Driven Assessment Workbook provides an online platform using the work of the Rockefeller Foundation, European Venture Philanthropy Association, and others, in which you can enter your objectives, organize your learning questions, and come up with your own metrics.*

How to Choose Your Targets

Whether you use a logframe or other planning tool or no planning tool at all, you will still have to set your success indicators; these are the targets you'll be working toward. Having "smart" objectives helps ensure that you can measure your success—but how do you come up with the numbers to attach to these?

There is no formula for choosing your targets, but there are a number of factors that will inform your decision-making process. First, baseline information is necessary. As we have discussed, your targets are most likely comparative; i.e. you are aiming to reduce or increase the incidence of some social indicator by a certain amount. If no information on the baseline is available, one of the first

---

* This is just one example: http://lda.mckinseyonsociety.com/.

steps you can take in your intervention is to invest time and resources gathering this information. Second, using a participatory process for setting your targets will help ensure that they are realistic and feasible and that your stakeholders are as invested in reaching them as you are. Engaging your end users, suppliers, providers, collaborators, and other stakeholders in the decision-making process will help make the process less daunting.

Third, reflecting on the community attributes you have learned about during your initial and ongoing community-driven research will help inform your decisions. Depending on the assets available to you, including human, physical, and financial capital, and the efficiency of the systems you are relying on for your value chain, you can estimate whether it is realistic to set a 100% target (e.g., eradicating under five mortality in this community) or a nonabsolute target (e.g., reducing under five mortality to a specified level, taking into consideration infrastructural factors, etc.).

Benchmarking against other settings is also advisable. What were other communities able to reach? Has this challenge been completely eradicated elsewhere? What are the statistics in other populations? Last but not least, consult your own experience and the experience of your team and wider community. What could go wrong, what external factors are beyond your control, what are the strengths and weaknesses of your team? In the next chapter, we'll talk more about assessing these risks and external factors that can help you evaluate and refine your targets to ensure that they not only reflect what is physically and hypothetically possible in the best case scenario but also incorporate the most likely scenario depending on the environment in which you're operating; and to have contingency plans in place for the worst case scenario too.

To Be Ambitious or to Start Small?

Many social entrepreneurs struggle with two schools of thoughts when setting their targets: one school of thought says to be ambitious, set high goals, and if you work toward those goals, you will achieve more, even if you don't get to the ideal number you've aimed for. The other school of thought says to start small, pick a number you can definitely reach, it is better to under promise and over deliver. What you choose to do depends on your own leadership and management style, but it is definitely recommended to retain scientific integrity when selecting your targets: make it your goal to actually find the number that is likely attainable.

Remember, this is not a personal exercise; if you build your social venture in the way that you would conduct a personal project, you are at risk of failing those around you. Valuable resources, both human and financial, are being dedicated to realizing your targets. The best way to optimize these resources—and increase the chance of having more resources at your disposal in the future—is to aim for accuracy when selecting your target, neither overprojecting nor underprojecting. Both extremes are commonly observed among social entrepreneurs, and this is a common mistake, so try not to make it, for the sake of those around you if not for your own.

Setting Up an M&E System

As your organization grows, one or more team members may become specialized in the role of collecting and assessing impact metrics. Your M&E framework may start out as a simple spreadsheet sheet in which you manually enter information collected by paper surveys distributed in your community, for example, listing the names of your participants/customers/patients/end users and the characteristics you decided to collect information on (these could include gender, age, employment status, occupation, starting income, income over time, other social metrics as determined by pre/post surveys, etc.). With time it could evolve into a more automated software or system requiring more than one team member.

The first step is the monitoring, where you collect and analyze data. Setting up your monitoring system involves choosing your targets, deciding how you are going to gather information on these targets, where you are going to store this information, and how you are going to summarize and characterize your results in order to use this information in your day-to-day management. Evaluation is step two, where you compare the results against your initial targets. What did you set out to do, what have you accomplished, and how did you accomplish it? It is important to note that when you evaluate your social venture, you are evaluating not only outcomes but also processes. Did you engage the target population in a way that empowered them? Do you need a new strategy, or if you already have one, were you able to follow it, and did it work? Have your resources been used efficiently and effectively? Are there any trends or patterns over time that suggest that your operations and impact may not be sustainable? What are the stakeholder implications of your results? Indicators to answer these questions should be included in the data you are collecting.

Monitoring and evaluation aren't always discrete events. If you're able to automate your data collection and analysis, you should be able to constantly and continuously evaluate your performance and progress by monitoring both process and outcome metrics that will inform your decisions moving forward.

Assessing Your Results With Your Stakeholders

Measuring social impact isn't just about obtaining the metrics, it's also what you do with that information afterward. Decision making and reflecting on the results are some things that take place both internally with your team and with your external stakeholders. Part of your contribution as a social venture is not only the social outcome you are creating but also the knowledge you are disseminating to the world. This allows us to assess the cumulative impact of multiple social ventures working to tackle social and environmental challenges. Reporting your results, learning from the overall process, and listening to the experiences of your stakeholders before, during, and after implementation allow you to create a learning plan for where you want to go next. Exchanging knowledge with other ventures and agents of change enables you to create a multiplicative rather than an additive effect.

Summary and Next Steps

Social impact metrics reflect the bottom line of a social enterprise, which is created to produce change and positive motion. The metric is simply a tool that enables you to understand whether you've reached your goal and whether you're using your resources optimally. It enables you to communicate with your stakeholders, assess past progress, and plan for future work. At the end of the day, your social impact metrics should be easy to collect, with minimal time and resources, inherent to the operations required in your intervention, and aligned with your mission and vision.

Ensuring that your processes and outcomes are in line with your mission and vision means that your social impact metrics will accurately reflect whether you're fulfilling that mission and vision. In the next chapter, we'll complete your business plan by tying together the different components of your business model that you've created up until now: characterizing your challenge, co-creating with the community, designing your solution and theory of change, operationalizing that theory, and selecting your social impact metrics. This will empower you to tie your bottom line of social change with the support structures required to get there, which we'll cover in the last few chapters: financing, organization building, communicating, external partnership, and expansion.

Exercise: Measuring Success

You knew this moment was coming! It's time to roll up your sleeves and crank out those impact metrics. That's right, before you move on to the business planning chapter, you are going to write down what success looks like to you and how you are going to measure it:

1. What is the social outcome you are working toward? (You can pull this up from your theory of change assignment from the last chapter.)
2. Write down one or more SMART objectives that you think you can reach toward that goal. Remember, the less the better to start out, in terms of the number of objectives.
3. How will you measure your progress? Write your key impact metrics in one sentence each and summarize the processes, tools, and systems you will use to collect data for this in another sentence. (You can write down more than one sentence for each in your own records, but make sure to come back and summarize each in one sentence for this chapter challenge.)
4. What is the baseline? How much progress against the baseline will you aim for? You can choose your own timeframe in answering this question. It can be a long-term goal (10 or 20 years) or a short-term goal (5 years or less). The way to get there is to go back to the assessments you've already conducted, such as your asset mapping, talk to any stakeholders you can, and compare with what other people have been able to do in other settings.
5. What outputs will you need to produce to reach this target? List the outputs by objective. You can use the logframe template if this helps.
6. What inputs are needed to produce those outputs? For each input, estimate the cost and time needed. Include human resources, physical resources, financial, and other resources. Try to be as specific as possible. Yes, this is a huge assignment! In the next chapter, you are going to complete your business model, so be prepared!

CHAPTER SUMMARY
- In a social venture, the bottom line is the social change you are working to create. It's up to you to define what success looks like and how you'll know when you get there.
- Standardized social impact metrics exist, and it can be helpful to work with these in case you find yourself being compared with other social ventures in the future (for example, by a funder). But you don't have to—you can make your own!
- When choosing your impact metrics, find something that's easy to measure without being costly or taking too much time and that can be measured inherently as part of your work rather than as extra work.

- Although you're focusing on capturing the social outcome you're working toward, you may need to capture intermediary outcomes along the road so that you can evaluate progress, if your outcome takes a long time to change (which most do).
- You'll also need to measure the "control knobs" of how you're trying to achieve your goal, so that you can adjust these if needed. These are the process metrics, as opposed to the outcome metrics. Both are considered performance metrics, only the latter indicates social impact. Measuring inputs does not indicate impact.
- To flesh out your inputs, outputs, outcomes, and impact, it's helpful to use an organizational tool such as a logical framework. This helps you operationalize your theory of change and gets you ready for business planning.
- At the end of the day, you are monitoring your progress in order to evaluate your work, decisions, and actions—not just for the sake of it. Measure what you need.

Social Ventures Mentioned in This Chapter

Company profile: Nuru, www.nuruinternational.org.
Founded in 2008 in Silicon Valley, California.
Product/service: Nuru International is building the world's first self-sustaining, self-scaling, integrated development model to end extreme poverty. It equips the poor living in rural areas with the tools, skills, training, and guidance needed to lift themselves out of poverty.
Goal: Enable people to lift themselves out of extreme poverty in remote rural areas.
How it works: By analyzing the past 50 years of international development, Nuru has identified a sustainable development model, which includes four key phases: (1) instead of what, start with who. Nuru identifies the most promising community leaders and then mentors and equips these leaders with essential skills. (2) The leaders identify the most pressing issues, data are collected, and baselines are established. (3) The leaders are provided a toolkit of proven poverty interventions; they chose what will work best in their context. (4) Successful local business people are recruited to start businesses that will fund the poverty fighting work and scale to neighboring communities. Throughout these phases, Nuru provides world-class training and access to new markets/capital. When Nuru leaves, the community is self-reliant and sustainable.

Case Study: Nuru International

Nuru is an example of a social enterprise that was designed around evidence tried and tested in the field, centered on poverty reduction in remote rural areas. Building on the work pioneered by poverty alleviation researchers around the world, Nuru added their own business model and integrated existing impact metrics to pave the path for scale. How did all these elements come together?

It all starts with the local community. In Nuru's poverty eradication model, they start with a clean state with individuals within a village. Nuru's team spends time in the village to identify local leaders and form an on-site team. Members of the new team then undergo leadership training to equip them with knowledge and skills to thoroughly assess community needs and co-create impact programs that are locally relevant, scalable, and sustainable (Figure 7.3).

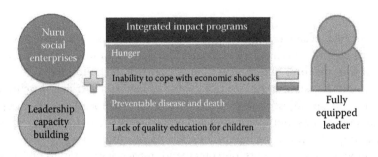

Fully equipped:
1. Able to identify gaps in four key areas of need
2. Able to design sustainable, scalable solutions based on best practices and lessons learned that create measurable impact
3. Implements, manages, improves, and scales these solutions
4. Able to innovate past challenges (redesign) as they arise
5. Access to a reliable, market-based capital source for sustained operations and growth

Figure 7.3   Nuru's impact model.

The leadership training is based on the premise that people living in poverty are marginalized by discrepancies in power and that international development programs don't work because local leaders see themselves as beneficiaries instead of change agents. Nuru's goal is for local leaders to run a community development organization that is financially self-sustaining. Nuru works with local leaders to become effective managers, solution builders, decision makers, and problem solvers. The team then works together to remove physical and psychological barriers preventing effective solutions and to design and implement impact programs that equip communities to overcome the obstacles and environmental disruptions to ensure that these solutions are long lasting.

Impact programs fall into four main themes: agriculture, financial inclusion, health, and education. As an example, in Kenya, Nuru's local team developed an agricultural program that provides a package to farmers including a farm input loan with seeds and fertilizer, technical training, extension services, and group support structures. Farmers finish repaying their loans after harvest and take their surplus produce to market with the assistance of Nuru's local team.

Nuru's local team also provides financial literacy training and one-on-one coaching to strengthen the money management skills of farmers; and supports farmers to form a savings group that creates access to basic financial services, namely, savings and loans. Nuru Kenya healthcare field officers provide home visits in which they deliver tailored information on disease prevention and offer affordable commodities such as soap, water purifiers, and bed nets. Nuru Kenya Education provides remedial education at rural primary schools, along with teacher training and curriculum development, to strengthen local schools and improve education outcomes.

These impact programs are funded by revenues from Nuru Social Enterprises, a holding company that invests in local entrepreneurs in the countries where Nuru works and incubates local business ventures that can return a profit both to shareholders and to Nuru to fund the impact programs. Examples include dairy, poultry, honey, and consumer products (Figure 7.4).

Nuru's team developed an M&E strategy with program indicators based on Nuru's logical framework. While certain parts of the logframe were easy to measure, such as the outputs, which are tangible, direct products of program activities; the long-term outcome proved far more challenging. How do we know that Nuru is achieving its goal of eradicating poverty? Nuru's M&E director, who developed the strategy, referred to this as measuring the "parts" versus the "sum

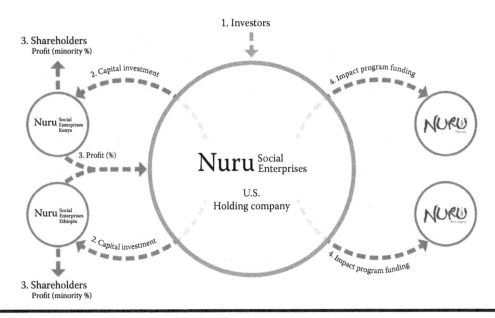

Figure 7.4 Nuru's business model.

of the parts."* The parts refer to the outputs, which are tangible, direct products of program activities. These were measured by indicators for each program area such as agriculture input loan repayment rates, savings deposits, group savings loan repayment rates, literacy and reading comprehension in children, and adoption of healthy behaviors leading to saved lives and saved money. (The latter included 12 health behavior indicators such as treating water, using a latrine, sleeping under a mosquito net, delivering in a clinic, and having newborn consultations.)

> Poverty reduction is one of the most complex outcomes to measure, because it is multidimensional.

While these outputs are already directly linked to the ultimate outcome of poverty alleviation, Nuru's team was intent on measuring the sum of the parts in order to understand and optimize the composite impact of the programs on poverty. Here, the team emphasized the importance of finding a tool that aligned with their definition of poverty. Nuru's team selected the multidimensional poverty index.† Other commonly used tools are the multidimensional poverty assessment tool‡ and the progress out of poverty tool.§ Poverty reduction is one of the most complex outcomes to measure because it is multidimensional. Social ventures such as Nuru, which tackle multiple dimensions of poverty, are tasked with assessing their impact on both the parts and the sum of the parts. Other social ventures that we will visit in other cases may focus on one pathway, such as income, health, education, energy access, etc.

---

* http://www.nuruinternational.org/blog/monitoring-and-evaluation/lessons-learned-measuring-parts-sum
-parts-poverty-alleviation/.

† http://www.ophi.org.uk/.

‡ http://www.ifad.org/mpat/resources/mpat_brochure.pdf.

§ http://www.progressoutofpoverty.org/about-us.

But measuring impact is only the first step. This is referred to as monitoring, which tells us whether Nuru has made a measurable difference. Evaluation of the program then requires assessing whether the program is on track to meet its objectives or whether it is ahead of or behind schedule; understanding why and making adjustments in the planning and implementation accordingly. It also requires constantly checking to ensure that the programs and the corresponding monitoring tools are relevant to the local community or whether they need to be adjusted.

Another part of the evaluation process is thinking about whether this program and these results are scalable. This involves asking yourself whether these could be applied to other areas of your work and in other settings and locations. Last but not least, will they last? To answer this question, Nuru's team developed a financial sustainability ratio and a leadership sustainability index (Figure 7.5).

Getting results was one thing, but making sure they would last was a whole other ballgame. To assess financial sustainability, Nuru's team compared expenses of the impact programs with profits from Nuru Social Enterprises (Figure 7.6). Operational self-sufficiency was defined as the ratio of revenues to expenses; for example, if the social enterprises achieved 100% cost recovery, then they had an operational self-sufficiency of 1. While this meant that they were able to generate enough revenues to cover their own costs, this ratio would not allow them to also support the impact programs. Thus, operational self-sufficiency requires the social enterprises to achieve more revenue than expenses so that excess revenue can be distributed both to investors and to the impact programs. The financial sustainability ratio was defined as the profit of the social enterprises (revenues minus cost) divided by the expenses of the impact programs in the same country. For example, if the social enterprises in Kenya covered all the costs of Nuru Kenya's impact programs, then the financial sustainability ratio would be >1.

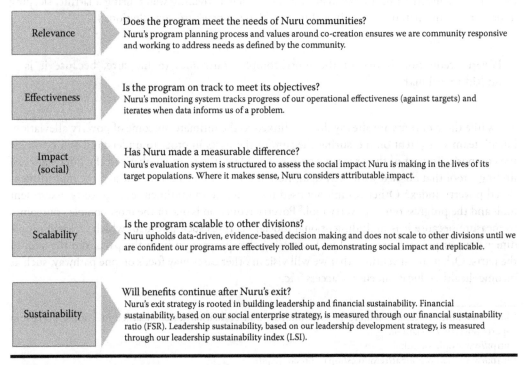

Relevance
Does the program meet the needs of Nuru communities?
Nuru's program planning process and values around co-creation ensures we are community responsive and working to address needs as defined by the community.

Effectiveness
Is the program on track to meet its objectives?
Nuru's monitoring system tracks progress of our operational effectiveness (against targets) and iterates when data informs us of a problem.

Impact (social)
Has Nuru made a measurable difference?
Nuru's evaluation system is structured to assess the social impact Nuru is making in the lives of its target populations. Where it makes sense, Nuru considers attributable impact.

Scalability
Is the program scalable to other divisions?
Nuru upholds data-driven, evidence-based decision making and does not scale to other divisions until we are confident our programs are effectively rolled out, demonstrating social impact and replicable.

Sustainability
Will benefits continue after Nuru's exit?
Nuru's exit strategy is rooted in building leadership and financial sustainability. Financial sustainability, based on our social enterprise strategy, is measured through our financial sustainability ratio (FSR). Leadership sustainability, based on our leadership development strategy, is measured through our leadership sustainability index (LSI).

Figure 7.5 Nuru's criteria for assessing impact.

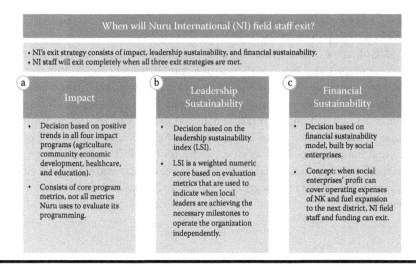

Figure 7.6   Measuring impact is only the first step.

But money isn't everything. In order for the social impact to be sustainable, local leaders must be able to operate and sustain their organization independent of international staff. This is where the central pillar in Figure 7.6 comes in: leadership sustainability. Nuru's M&E team created a leadership sustainability index, using a number of measurement tools (Figure 7.7).

Once Nuru's team has enough evidence to indicate that they had helped create the desired impact and that it was sustainable both financially and through local leadership, then they will make the decision to exit. Thus, the M&E was created to inform decision making, not just for the sake of it. To equip themselves to use these results in a systematic decision-making process, Nuru's

Data collection tool	Purpose of tool	Type of tool	Who it's administered to	When is the data collected?
Postassessment	To assess staff after leadership trainings on understanding of main concepts taught	Written test taken by staff members	All levels (levels 1, 2, and 3)	After each leadership training
Staff in-person survey	To assess staff's readiness for Nuru international's exit from the project	Oral self-report survey, administered by M&E team	All levels (levels 1, 2, and 3)	Once a year (usually in June)
Performance evaluation	For supervisors to assess staff on performance of specific job responsibilities	Written human resources assessment on staff performance, filled out by supervisor	All levels (levels 1, 2, and 3)	2×/year; June and December
Staff leadership review	For supervisors to asssess staff on various skills necessary to operate the project independent of Nuru international staff (not assessed through performance evaluations)	Written assessment on staff performance, filled out by supervisor	Field managers, district managers, and senior leadership (levels 2 and 3)	2×/year; June and December

Figure 7.7   Data collection tools to inform Nuru's leadership sustainability evaluation.

team developed a dashboard that helped their leadership visualize all the results, "the sum of the parts," to inform next steps and strategy.

Nuru's M&E director at the time, Veronica Olazabal, pointed out that assessing progress toward impact is complex and requires the use of a combination of lenses. But not everyone will need a 10-indicator composite index for social impact, complemented with two additional indices to determine the sustainability of that impact over time! Nuru's case is one of the more complex in terms of multidimensional impact measurement and evaluation. Your social venture will probably not require so many moving parts. Nuru is still a young venture and has still not reached the desired impact, although preliminary evidence indicates that it is well on its way. The reason it has been selected is to demonstrate that no matter how elusive measuring impact can seem, there is always a way to reflect success in progressing toward your goal and the social outcomes you are working to improve.

Chapter 8

Completing the Business Model

Over the past few chapters, you've been taking key steps to build your business model. This starts with your value proposition, the 5Cs and 5Ps of your market plan, the nuts and bolts of your operations and distribution, and your social impact targets. These components of your business plan have been developed with the goal of maximizing your impact while ensuring financial viability. Now, it's time to put it all together and make sure the numbers add up!

Your complete business model ties together the different parts of the equation that you've been hard at work figuring out. It answers the following questions:

- Who is your customer?
- What are you offering to them?
- How much will they pay?
- What is this costing you?
- How will this exchange take place?

There are numerous business models that other social entrepreneurs have employed before you—or you can invent your own! We'll explore some examples together, to give you a sense of how others have made it work, and then you'll find what works for you. The key is to calculate what resources are needed and what opportunities you have to cover those resources. Your business model is basically a combination of your impact model (how you make change), your revenue model (how you make money), and your cost reduction strategy (how you keep costs minimal).

Building Your Budget

The Basics

Let's start by making sure we've covered the basics of cost and revenue. In Chapter 7, you developed your organizational framework by planning ahead the various outputs you need to produce in order to meet your objectives as well as the inputs (activities, people, time, money) that will be required to produce these outputs. The next step is to create your start-up budget. A budget is simply a table that organizes the various costs.

Costing is the process of putting a number on all the resources you require. How much will it cost you to reach your objectives? Start with your first year. Who do you need to hire, what equipment do you need to buy, how much will you need for transportation, utilities, physical spaces? All you need to do is check back in with the organizational framework you created in Chapter 7, which has listed the main steps you need to take. Then ask yourself, is it missing anything? Are there any costs not directly associated with a specific output but are just general or administrative costs required to run this venture? Don't forget about communications: building a website, hiring someone to maintain your social media, etc. Legal, accounting, and filing costs should be included—if you're going to register a new organization, you'll need technical support on that, you'll need to file for taxes, and these all require a budget.

To create your budget, you simply organize your costs into a table. This is usually done in a simple spreadsheet, using basic computing software. It's helpful to organize your costs by category; for example, how much will you need for recurring costs compared with starting capital? *Starting capital* means money that will be invested upfront to get this venture going. For example, it could be buying new equipment, paying for software, website or app developers, conducting initial research, and other steps required to launch your venture. *Recurring costs* means ongoing costs required to keep it going. Salaries are recurring costs, rent and utilities are recurring costs, transportation and communication are recurring costs.

Recurring costs should be divided over time, so that you can calculate how much you will need at different stages—for example, each month, each quarter, and each year. They should also be divided into fixed versus variable costs. *Fixed costs* will recur regardless of your level of production. Examples include your rent and base salaries. *Variable costs* will increase or decrease depending on how much you are producing. Some salaries or extra payments may have to be added, for example, if more people are needed. You might spend more on utilities, communication, and transportation if you have a larger volume of work. This is good! It means your operations are growing! You just have to be sure that you've factored it in.

Planning your growth costs is also advisable at this point. Depending on your distribution model, you need to think ahead about how much each stage of growth will cost. How much will each new branch, franchise, or point of sale cost you to launch and then to maintain? Different sites might have different fixed and variable costs, depending on location and other factors. When you are forecasting your costs and revenues, it's important to think beyond just your pilot. While expanding your operations is costly, at the same time, in many cases, it's also a requirement for financial viability.

Forecasting Growth

You can create separate budget tables for each point of sale or service, as well as a central table that analyzes the combined costs and revenues to determine the overall financial viability. In most cases, your largest costs are the initial start-up costs of developing and testing your venture, and the relative cost of starting each new point of sale or service decreases over time in relation to the revenues they will bring. This is what we refer to as economies of scale. In many cases, growing and reaching large volumes are the only ways you can get your revenues to cover or exceed your costs. In other cases, it might be the other way around and your optimal operating size might be smaller. This could be the case if you grow into new markets—whether geographic or demographic—where your model is less effective. It could also happen if you grow too soon and don't have the sufficient processes and human resources and, as a result, you end up losing time and money to fix it.

Like everything else in your venture, your business model and your growth model need to be evidence based. Research each growth scenario to get the forecasted costs and revenues for your growth plan. Question the assumptions behind each forecast. You'll never have all the data you need, but at least you can do your best to make your estimates based on data from the field. This will allow you to compare different scenarios and evaluate the financial viability of each.

Cost per Unit

A useful figure to calculate is your *cost per unit*. If you are providing a service, your unit might be a person (cost per person served). If you are providing a product, your unit will be the product (cost per product served). If you want to get really creative, you can even calculate the cost per unit of your social impact metric. For example, let's say your social venture is aimed at job creation, and your bottom line is the number of jobs created. What is your cost per job created?

In most cases, you'll want to include everything that goes into developing the product or service (before it is manufactured or offered) and everything that goes into selling or providing it to the customer. Sales, marketing, transportation, communication, and distribution costs are all included. Most of the time, the more units you create, the smaller the cost per unit becomes. This is because all these costs are divided by a larger number of units. So volume is usually a good thing from the point of view of costing. And different distribution scenarios might allow you to reach different volumes—so it's not only the starting costs that you need to take into consideration but also the economies of scale over time. If you want to calculate just the cost of the good you're selling, without the development and sales cost, this might also be a useful statistic to have—we refer to it in business shorthand as "COGS" and you'll see it later when we talk about income statements.

Your costs are usually incurred before your revenues. This is simply because it will cost you something to produce your product or service before you are able to generate revenue. So you need to make sure you've budgeted enough and raised enough starting capital. This involves calculating how much revenue you think you will make, and when.

Revenue Models

Here's where it gets interesting! You've done everything you can to minimize costs, and now it's time to make sure that your revenues cover your costs. This is the make or break of a financially viable venture. The first component of a revenue model you'll look at is pricing. The interesting thing about pricing is that it's not always as obvious as it seems. Many people might assume that a social entrepreneur should price their product or service at cost, charging the minimal amount possible to keep your operations going. However, in most cases, your pricing should be informed by your market research. What did your market research tell you? How much are people willing to pay for a unit or package of your product or service?

How you bundle your offering is one control knob in your revenue model that you can play with. How people pay for it is another aspect. Will you need to finance it, or will it be an upfront payment? Are people paying in cash, or are other forms of payment more preferable in your target audience? We've learned that it's not only the product design that's piloted, it's also the pricing and revenue model. Did you roll out a "test batch" and get customers' feedback? Have you tried different price points and payment methods? These are the data that will help you build a financially feasible system around your solution.

One scenario to be prepared for is that in some cases, even if you were able to get your costs down to the lowest possible level, it might still not be low enough for your target audience. In this scenario, you would need to find ways to make up for your losses—that part of each unit's cost that won't be covered by its price. Differential pricing is one way to make up for these losses, by offering the same product or service to different audiences at different prices. We've seen this with One Earth Designs, Aravind Eye Care Systems, and many others. Diversifying your revenue streams is another way to make up for these losses, by offering a range of products or services that may be more profitable, to help cover your costs. You can also supplement your revenue from sales or fees, with other forms of revenue such as grants or donations. These are three different options for subsidizing the cost of your product or service to your target audience, if needed. But even if you have to go for one of these options, you'll still need market research to determine what the optimal price is to get your end users to value your product.

Scenario Analysis

Right now, you're probably asking yourself some very important questions. The first might be: how can I put together my starting budget if I'm still exploring various scenarios to make this all work? The answer is that it's not only *possible* to compare costs and revenues for different scenarios, it's also *necessary* that you do so at this point. This is all part of testing different prototypes for your delivery model! You already know that all the scenarios you're exploring operate within the context of your social goals—they've all been developed around the solution you've built with your end users. Comparing the costs and revenues possible for each scenario is one of the most important things you'll do at this point to assess feasibility and find a viable path to take in moving forward. You can make one table or tab per scenario, to compare the financial feasibility of each. You'll need different resources for different options; for example, branches versus franchising or manufacturing centrally or decentralization, etc. You'll also have different revenue opportunities in each scenario, and you'll need to compare various combinations of each until you find one that you feel comfortable getting starting with.

The iterative process is ongoing. Even at this stage, you might have to go back to the drawing board with many aspects of your social venture. This is not something to be discouraged by; it's something to be reassured by, that every social entrepreneur has had to do this! If the numbers don't add up, you keep innovating, designing, brainstorming, prototyping, and testing different options until they do. Assessing different revenue models can take multiple iterations before you can get the revenues to cover the costs.

Pro-Forma

An *income statement* allows you to combine your costs and revenues to see how they add up. Just like the budget tells you where you are spending your money and when, the income statement tells you where you are getting your money from and when. If you have different products or services that you're testing, different locations, or different customer segments, you can organize your revenue streams from each one. You can also note patterns and trends over time; for example, your sales might peak during certain times of the year. Income statements, like budgets, are also organized according to your *sales cycle*—the length of time it will take you on average to get your product or service to your end user, and to get paid. This describes the life cycle of each unit of product or service, telling you how long you'll need to wait between incurring costs and generating revenue. This could be by month, quarter, year, or something in between. Some smaller ventures even summarize this information on a weekly or daily basis. Preparing your income statement simply entails entering data on your sales and how much you made—think of it as a form of financial inventory! You can either manually enter this information into a simple spreadsheet using basic computing software or set up an automated system for tracking sales and automatically entering revenues (similar to those you might observe at retail and service points on an everyday basis).

Before you launch your venture, it's helpful to create a "pro-forma" income statement (Figure 8.1). This means that, although you may not have begun your revenue streams yet, you can project and estimate the revenues you will be making. You can even try out different versions to compare various options for pricing and revenue models that you may be considering! For example, what would my income statement look like if I went with option A versus option B? Filling in the numbers here will require you to make certain basic assumptions such as the number of customers you are projecting.

Again, use the evidence you've collected in the field to inform these assumptions. Try to be as realistic as possible and estimate the most likely scenario. Then, take it one step further and calculate your best- and worst-case scenarios. How do these compare to your most likely scenario based on your market research? Is it a wide margin? What can you do to prepare for a less-than-optimal outcome? While we are taking all the measures that can get you to your most likely scenario (or better!), we also need to make sure you're prepared for the worst-case scenario. It's usually recommended to make conservative estimates and to make sure that you're prepared with a financing plan to get you through lower-than-expected starting numbers.

When you are done estimating your revenues, you subtract your costs to calculate your profit. If you are using your total cost per unit sold, then the difference will be your net profit (overall

	Q1	Q2	Q3	Q4	Total in the first year
Sales	+	+	+	+	+
COGS	–	–	–	–	–
Gross profit					
Shipping and logistics	–	–	–	–	–
Marketing and customer acquisition	–	–	–	–	–
Product development	–	–	–	–	–
General and administrative	–	–	–	–	–
Total operating expense					
Pre-tax income	?	?	?	?	?

Figure 8.1 Example pro-forma income statement template.

profit) once you remove taxes. If you are using your COGS, then the difference will be your gross profit—you'll have to then subtract operating expenses and other expenses to get your net profit.* This is the last line at the bottom of your income statement, which is where the word "bottom line" originally came from!

You'll notice that the sales bring in positive cash flow, while the other lines in the income statement incur negative flows (various costs and expenses). Question marks have been placed on the bottom line of the template because you'll need to determine what the resulting *balance* will be. When you first start, your balance might be negative, which means you're not generating enough revenue to cover your costs. This is normal and healthy! As you proceed and your customer base grows, you'll start covering your costs and achieving a positive balance. Any surplus revenue can be used to fuel growth.

When you reach that point where all costs are covered, this is called breaking even. It's important to estimate your *breakeven point* in order to plan ahead and secure enough funding to fuel your own growth before the revenues start rolling in! This template provides an example for the first year, but your pro-forma will most likely need to include multiple years. Most new ventures take several years to break even; a common breakeven point is three to five years, and in some cases longer. This is because so much time is invested in getting to a point where the venture is self-sustaining.

Timeline and Phasing

Phasing refers to the different stages your venture will go through. Upon launching, your costs will exceed your revenues until you reach the breakeven point. The breakeven point is when 100% of your costs are covered by revenue. Your business plan should include a timeline indicating at what point you estimate you'll break even. Again, it's usually not realistic to expect to break even in the first or even the second year. The importance of phasing is reflected not only in your budget and income estimates but also in various aspects of your business planning as it pertains to funding rounds, marketing strategy, and organizational strategy.

Timeline and growth strategy refers to how you plan on expanding your venture before and after you break even. Some ventures will not scale their operations right away once they break even but will take the opportunity to evaluate success indicators and operational indicators and accrue income to fund expansion. Expansion might entail the production of more products/services, the cost of a marketing or advertising campaign, the hiring of additional staff. Other ventures will apply for a new round of funding to fuel the expansion, effectively pushing back their breakeven point by once more having their investments exceed their earnings, until the increased earnings come in. Yet others will have an expansion plan that pays for itself, especially in situations where increased production results in larger profit margins due to economies of scale. In this case, the breakeven point will not be achieved until you are able to expand your operations sufficiently. If this is your most likely scenario, then you'll need to plan accordingly and get the financial and nonfinancial support you'll need to make it all the way to the breakeven line! We'll talk more about these resources in the coming chapters.

Economies of scale have implications beyond the forecasting and budgeting of your growth; they are also important to consider in your everyday operations and in planning your costing

---

* In addition to taxes, you may have other considerations to account for such as interest, depreciation, and amortization. This is why you'll often see the abbreviation EBIDTA used here, referring to: earnings before interest, depreciation, tax and amortization.

and pricing. Thinking to your own personal experience, when you go to the grocery store, you will notice that if you buy in bulk, the price per unit decreases. Similarly, a venture that produces in bulk will have a lower cost of production per unit in most cases. The social entrepreneur can decide whether to keep prices constant, in which case profit will increase, or whether to lower prices if this may result in more people accessing the product or service or even whether to increase prices if this is part of the growth strategy. Some ventures can choose to start at lower prices in order to gain a market and then increase their prices for certain segments of the market if this will result in increased financial sustainability while continuing to reach the target audience, especially if they experience customer segmentation amenable to differential pricing.

Staying Lean

We've already talked about designing for affordability, about the different dimensions of poverty, and the AAAQ checklist. Remember that you are working in a setting where the market has failed to provide a solution for this social challenge. As you build your business model, operations, and other components of your social venture, keep this in mind. You need to be a lean, mean solution-providing machine!

Being lean simply means that you stretch out your resources to the max and set yourself up such that you get far with few resources. You are looking for the distribution channels, administrative setup, and other characteristics that will allow you to operate at low cost. Of course, you are also looking for revenue channels that will cover your costs and allow you to grow—it's a balancing act with multiple levers.

The coming few chapters will be infused with tips and techniques to stay lean: where to situate yourself physically, how to hire lean and outsource where possible, and how to mobilize resources creatively. For now, this is a shoutout to keep in mind while developing your business model and business plan that you don't have the luxury of building anything that is not as literally lean as possible.

Business Models

Ideally, you would like to have a revenue model that allows you to maximize your social impact while covering all your costs and more. To maximize your social impact, you would then reinvest as much of the profit into your mission as possible. In some cases, however, the nature of the market is such that profit is not possible. In these cases, the social entrepreneur needs to generate multiple revenue streams to supplement sales. In all cases, a social entrepreneur develops a business model with the goal of maximizing social impact. This is why you've invested so much time learning about the social challenge you're tackling, the population segments you're serving, the theory of change that ties your product or service to the social change you're creating, and the impact metrics that you'll follow to track and maximize this change. The business model then comes in to allow you to maximize those targets because you need money to make it happen!

Let's take a look at some of the different types of business models out there. As we learn about the different models and the thought process behind them, keep in mind that there is no one method or one correct way to maximize impact. There are different points of view, and different people have approached their own social ventures in their own ways. It is up to you to figure out what model will fit your goals and your theory of change and help you reach the social impact targets you've set out for yourself.

High-Profit Business

High-profit businesses are rare in the social sector because we are often dealing with market failures and inefficiencies that created the social challenges we're trying to improve in the first place. Most social ventures are targeting underserved and marginalized populations, trying to provide them with basic goods and services such as education, health, water, energy, information, and other needs. This is what differentiates social from commercial entrepreneurship after all! However, some thought leaders point out that profit drives scale and that if you can make even a small margin of profit multiplied by millions, if not billions, of people, then you will have a high-profit business (see Interview Box 1). One business model that can result in large profits for a social venture is a low-cost, high-volume model. This means that you're aiming to serve a large number of people at a low cost, with the profit margins aggregating to form large overall gains. If you can achieve this business model, then great! You can serve more people. The important thing is to keep in mind your number 1 goal, which is to maximize your social impact and work toward your social mission—in most cases, this will mean reinvesting the profit to grow the social venture.

Nondividend Social Business

Reinvesting the profit to grow the social venture means that you are operating a nondividend social business. This means that it's possible for the entrepreneur and supporters to recoup the costs associated with launching the venture, but it's not possible for them to use the business for their own personal gain. This doesn't mean you can't make a respectable living as a social entrepreneur—no one is asking you to live in poverty. Growing your venture will require you to attract and retain top talent, and you'll need to pay them too! It just means that all decisions are made with the goal of maximizing social impact. Most social ventures we'll learn about through the case studies in this book are designed as such: they employ business models to generate as much surplus revenue as possible within the goal of maximizing their social impact, then use the profits to fuel the continued growth of their work and their operations to have the highest impact possible (see Interview Box 2). Again, the number 1 driver of your growth should be the change you're aiming to create in the social challenge you are setting out to tackle, as specified in the theory of change and impact targets you have developed.

Not Always Mutually Exclusive

If you're able to generate enough aggregate profit to qualify for investors seeking both social and financial returns, this can be a powerful tool to fuel growth. So, the two previous business models aren't necessarily always mutually exclusive—it really just depends on the scenario. The main point is that in social entrepreneurship, profit is a means to an end—it is not an end in and of itself.

Hybrid Models

If your product or service does not pay for itself, then you are faced with a situation where you are not able to recover all of your costs. In this situation, you have a number of options. You can either diversify your product or service mix or diversify your customer segments. Some nonprofit organizations find different services they can provide in order to cross-subsidize their social mission. Others offer their core product or service to a higher-paying customer, to cross-subsidize those customers who are unable to pay the full cost of the product or service. These options are referred to as hybrid models. By combining the different revenue streams, they are able to add up to cover their costs. Most hybrid models aim to break even, using their secondary value chains to cover the costs of their primary value chains. But some hybrid models find that there is a huge opportunity to profit using their secondary chains, which can fuel the growth of their primary mission. The important thing is not to distract resources, time, and attention from the primary mission if you don't have to.

Another form of hybrid model is the nonprofit model where non-trading revenue streams (such as grants and donations) are used to supplement sales from the primary product or service. This is a highly risky business model, as grants and donations are not guaranteed. They may certainly be used to fuel your start-up costs, and often, your ongoing research and development costs. But ideally, what you would like to have is a product or service that is somehow tied to a revenue stream directly related to providing that product or service to your end user. Challenge yourself to find a business model that is based on trading activity. This means that either:

- Your end user is able to pay the full cost (or more) in exchange for the product or service;
- Another end user pays a higher price to cover the cost of your target audience;
- You have a range of products or services whose revenue streams add up to cover costs; or
- You have multiple stakeholders partnering to contribute various resources, each in exchange for a benefit to themselves (e.g., public–private partnerships).

If you are unable to cover the costs of delivering your social mission using one or more of these models, then you can supplement it with a set of non-trading revenue streams, achieved by applying for grants, securing ongoing donors, holding fundraisers, etc. However, as a general rule of thumb, the more you can minimize your reliance on these sources of revenue, the more sustainable your venture will be in the long run.

Interview Box 1. Jigar Shah, President of Generate Capital, Former CEO of Richard Branson's Carbon War Room, and Founder of Sun Edison

TC: Jigar, you use innovative payment schemes to spread the use of solar power. In developed settings, you used carbon wedges, which entails replacing existing cars or existing sources of energy. Does this also work in settings where people don't have cars and aren't on the grid?

JS: Absolutely. Take mobile phones for example. There are 5 billion people with mobile phones. In some places, they have to travel 5–10 kilometers to charge their phones. The person with the diesel generator is charging them pennies to charge their phones, the equivalent of $5–$10 per kW/hour in the US. Same for electricity inside homes. People use kerosene, charcoal, and wood; while the solar lantern is 80% cheaper, pays for itself in 6–12 weeks.

TC: Do you think that there are some populations that just can't be reached by this approach, where a non-profit approach is necessary?

JS: A lot of people say that social enterprise should reinvest all profits into the social mission. I think that if you want the private sector to have a positive impact, you need to be aware that in the private sector, profit drives scale. A nonprofit microfinance group can charge a lower interest and have a shorter payback period. But it still can't reach everyone. We've been waiting for the World Bank and others to provide essential basic human services to marginalized populations for decades and still not everyone has been reached. The private sector has to get involved. If you compare a for-profit company like Compartamos with any traditional social business, you'll see that just like the nonprofit, a portion of the interest it charges goes to cover the overhead and collection costs—the main difference is that the additional interest it charges goes to investors. Because it charges a higher interest, there is a longer payback period, but it has the same impact.

TC: What about in situations where it's just not possible to profit? How do you scale essential services in those settings?

JS: This is where the government comes in. The government can help cover risk or subsidize costs in sectors where there's not enough profit, to encourage private sector players. Nongovernmental organizations can also do this, like what Rockefeller is doing. Intergovernmental agencies have done this before. The IFC made 25% financial return on investment to spread the coverage of mobile phones. They spread mobile phone coverage by investing through funds, and the funds made 25%, 40%, 50% return on investment. Look at Mo Ibrahim [Celtel]—he set out to produce social good, and he's a billionaire. Their goal was to provide people with access to information, and that's a social good.

TC: On the design front, do you think it's possible to design social products and services for billions of people across income brackets? Your approach is that large volumes are needed. So far, most entrepreneurs target either those living in poverty or those not living in poverty. Do you think it's possible to think of it as one large market instead, or should we be stratifying and segmenting?

JS: I think we need to stratify and segment. But we need to divide it into thousands of segments, not two. You have people in certain places disassembling cook stoves and using their parts for jewelry. Products need to be customized by culture, by income, people react to them differently. The underlying technology, however, doesn't change.

Interview Box 2. Muhammad Yunus, Economics Professor, Founder of the Grameen Bank, and Recipient of the Nobel Peace Prize 2006

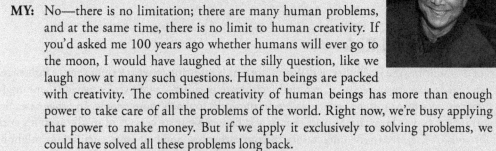

TC: Professor, you have advocated the social business model, which means a nondividend business created to solve a human problem. Do you think there are any limitations to this model?

MY: No—there is no limitation; there are many human problems, and at the same time, there is no limit to human creativity. If you'd asked me 100 years ago whether humans will ever go to the moon, I would have laughed at the silly question, like we laugh now at many such questions. Human beings are packed with creativity. The combined creativity of human beings has more than enough power to take care of all the problems of the world. Right now, we're busy applying that power to make money. But if we apply it exclusively to solving problems, we could have solved all these problems long back.

TC: Do you think big businesses can also solve social problems?

MY: They can, provided they create social businesses alongside their profit-seeking businesses. Social businesses generate profit, but owners don't take it for their use because the company is dedicated to solving human problems. In social business, owners use all their creative power and the financial power to solving problems.

TC: So there are no market-driven solutions?

MY: Of course there is. Social business is a market-driven solution. But it is a mission-driven market solution within the market which is now almost exclusively populated by personal profit seeking businesses. There is nothing wrong with the market. Investors decide what they want to achieve by using the forces of the market. Market is a playground. Players decide what game they want to play. Social business plays for changing the world. Some others play for stacking up money for themselves.

TC: What if you can't create a market because some people just can't pay? Let's use refugees as an example. How can you build a social business targeting refugees as your customer?

MY: I don't believe that there are some people who cannot pay. It is a question of giving people the ability to pay, now or later. Grameen Bank lends money to beggars. They give them the money to sell something and earn. They earn and they pay. Grameen Bank lends money to the poorest people, particularly the poorest women. The repayment is close to a hundred percent. It is all a question of how you design your business. Poor people, like all other people, are smart people. They can choose the right option. Refugees make up their own community, and their own economy, just like any other community anywhere in the world. They bring skill, experience, and connections with them. No war or violence can take it away from them.

> **TC:** Let's talk about scale. Most social problems affect millions, if not billions, of people. Can the social business model reach them all?
>
> **MY:** Global problems are nothing but accumulation of local problems. Once we find solution to a local problem, solving the global problem becomes a matter of repetition. Small-scale solution can be expanded into sustainable mega solution if it is done in a business way, particularly a social business way. In the medical world, we invent a medicine, try it out on a few people, if it works, we take the step to administer the medicine on millions of people to cure them from the same disease.

Uncertainty and Risk

Part of determining the feasibility of different options is assessing to what extent they're influenced by external factors. In some cases, external factors are positive—as we've discussed, there might be opportunities for you to leverage existing frameworks to reach more people. In other cases, it's important for you to be aware of risks that may influence your success. And in all cases, it's critical for you to characterize the uncertainty in your estimates. Some of your calculations might be relatively straightforward, such as some of your starting costs. Others might have a large range in between your best- and worst-case scenarios. When comparing different options, you're comparing not only the most likely scenario or midpoint of these estimates but also *how likely* that scenario will be and how wide the range of possibilities is.

Your decisions on which business model you'll go with are largely personal. On the one hand, your ultimate responsibility is to deliver the largest social impact possible as it pertains to the social challenge and target audience you've characterized. On the other hand, many of these forecasts have different degrees of uncertainty in them and we all have different levels of risk aversion. Things to keep in mind are the following:

■ You are already a risk taker by even getting to this point.
■ There are ways to mitigate your risks and resources to help you do so, such as the organizations and networks in Box 1.1 and others we'll explore in the coming chapters.
■ The first step is to thoroughly chart out the landscape, and then together with your team and stakeholders, you can make the decisions that feel right to you.

PESTEL Analysis

One way to start thinking about external factors is to conduct a PESTEL analysis. This framework helps you organize your thoughts into a manageable set of categories and determine what aspects of each category could be considered a threat and what aspects could be considered (or made into) a positive factor.

While you cannot address all of the external factors surrounding you, it's critical to be aware of them and to take them into account while analyzing the risks you'll face and building your organizational strategy. You need to think about what you and your team will do differently to mitigate the threat to your success posed by these factors and create contingency plans in case your goals are derailed by these factors. Sometimes, there is nothing we can do to change the nature and magnitude of external factors, but what we can do is adapt the design and implementation of our intervention to respond to our external environment, while considering the various factors we have to account for. Other times, we can be more ambitious and set an agenda to influence external factors. This usually requires a huge amount of collaboration, advocacy, and hard work over a long period. So it's important to both recognize what you're working with when you first start and put the right pieces and players in place to change it as you go along.

Political

The P goes first in PESTEL for good reason. The political environment you are working in, both at a local and at a larger geopolitical level, is an upstream factor that will influence the economic, social, technological, environmental, and legal context in which you're working.

Conflict states, transitional nations, and secure settings all have their different political nuances. If you're operating in a conflict state, the external threats posed by political factors may include your physical safety, the physical safety of your end users and other stakeholders, the security of your supply chain and thus your ability to procure and deliver goods and services; and the composition of your end users (e.g., for a social venture targeting disadvantaged populations in a conflict setting, it is easy to imagine a state of constant flux due to refugees and migrant populations). In a transitional nation (e.g., post-conflict), the physical safety of individuals and assets may not be under threat, but the political will and administrative capacities required to regulate logistics and the flow of information, goods, and services at the community or state level may be weakened. Even in a politically stable situation, political factors may often be underlying the social challenges you are dealing with. Housing inequities in metropolitan areas are a historical example. Availability of resources to support social ventures providing services to HIV patients from marginalized populations is another.

Are there any positive influences or opportunities provided by the political setting in which you're operating? Are there any policies or political debates that could amplify the visibility of your venture? An example of a social entrepreneur who seized upon an opportunity related to a new government policy in the United States is the founder of Benestream, a start-up designed around the new Affordable Care Act.* If you are working in a nation under transition, are there any positive trends that you could leverage among the political turmoil? A wealth of social entrepreneurs in Egypt created new social initiatives and community-driven organizations in the years preceding, during, and after the Arab spring to mobilize resources for social development. Two of the many examples are Hisham El Rouby, who saw youth as an emerging resource and founded Etijah to build youth networks for volunteering and civic engagement,† and Mona Mowafi, who saw the Egyptian diaspora as a resource to support local entrepreneurs and founded RISE Egypt to mobilize the global community.‡ The RISE website shares a wealth of examples of social entrepreneurs working to create new products, services, and systems in Egypt (www.riseegypt.org /entrepreneurs).

Economic

Whether your social venture is a for-profit enterprise, a nonprofit organization, or an initiative within an existing organization, it will most certainly be shaped by economic trends. You could be addressing a market need and providing a market-based solution or addressing a gap where

---

* http://benestream.com/.

† http://etijah.org/about/.

‡ http://www.riseegypt.org/letter-from-the-president/.

the market is broken and may work against you. In both cases, it is essential to understand the economic landscape around you, whether it will change over time and whether you may be able to influence the market over time. Again, just like the political landscape, the economic factors you are faced with will likely present both threats and opportunities.

The size of the market is a key factor. Are you operating in a setting where you are likely to reach large volumes? Or are you operating in a setting with a limited economy and market size? Scales of economies is just one factor; trend over time is another. You could be operating in a large market that is on the decline or a small market that is on the rise.

Another important nuance is the relationship between economic factors and other factors in your PESTEL analysis. The scale and direction of growth of the economy may change suddenly if you are operating in a politically volatile situation. How will the economy you are operating in be influenced by political changes? Political instability generally means economic instability, and it is critical to factor that uncertainty and plan for sudden change.

Economic considerations might also influence your investors. The size, trends, and volatility of the market you're operating in will determine not only how you build and structure your venture but also how you finance it. Some social entrepreneurs are working to build policies to help shape the economic and investment landscape in fragile markets, beyond providing their product or service to their target audience. One of the many examples is Willy Foote, who we'll meet in Chapter 9, who founded Root Capital and helped build ANDE* to support small and growing businesses that can help lift countries out of poverty.

Social

Cultures, religions, histories, heritages, and heterogeneity of your end users have already shaped the design of your venture throughout your research, prototyping, and testing phases. As you roll out your venture, how will these factors continue to shape it, and how will the introduction of your new venture affect the social dynamics caused by these factors?

What social norms are tied to the challenges you are addressing, and how will your intervention challenge these norms—what are the repercussions? Preparing for the social dynamics already in existence and those that will be introduced by your venture goes beyond the basic procedures such as meeting with stakeholders to ensure ownership and participation; it involves thinking in a far-sighted way to build the social networks and support systems required to produce social change.

Building women-led businesses is a great example of this. We've already heard from Libby McDonald about challenging social norms and building new systems and value chains in the waste sector in Chapter 3. These days, Libby is working on Prosperity Catalyst, a spin-off of the social enterprise Prosperity Candle, building businesses with women in conflict settings.† In this and other examples, you're not only manufacturing and marketing the product or service itself, you're also challenging social norms that are still deeply rooted in many societies around the world today. These not only affect the women leading the business but also have consequences on the perceptions and behaviors of their customers, suppliers, everyone along the supply chain, and other stakeholders.

As a first step, awareness and understanding of these social nuances help you integrate them into your business plan, operations, marketing, and contingency plans. You have to survive in

---

* www.andeglobal.org, www.rootcapital.org.
† www.prosperitycatalyst.org.

this environment in order to work in it and change it. More importantly, it helps you shape your organizational strategy and external partnerships and purposely plan your ripple effect.

Technological

Many social ventures work in low-resource settings, and technological external factors can be a barrier. Poor Internet connectivity or speed, unreliable electricity, and high telecommunications costs are some of the common barriers encountered by social entrepreneurs all over the world. These are a risk because they can slow down operations and make it challenging to communicate with end users and stakeholders. (Often, they are also related to social factors such as preference for face-to-face communication, which can require more travel and can be time consuming and expensive.)

At the same time, technological trends around the world can also be considered a positive external influence and an opportunity to introduce new solutions, increase access to information, and design and create mobile services and products. Examples are m-health interventions and telemedicine, which bring access to healthcare to remote rural settings with few doctors. Online education and online lending are also examples, as we saw with Kiva in the first chapter. New technologies can either be developed explicitly as solutions to tackle social challenges, as we saw with D-REV in Chapter 4, or incorporated into the implementation of other solutions to enhance their efficiency and efficacy, as we saw in the HLC case study.

The way people interact with social challenges is changing every day due to new technological developments such as increased access to mobile phones and the Internet. This will affect your customers, your competition, your communications, and your ability to connect with collaborators. What technological aspects are considered a challenge in the setting in which you are operating, and what are some aspects you could leverage as a positive factor, or develop new ones? How can you use existing technologies to optimize your social impact?

Environmental

How is the natural environment related to your social enterprise? If you are working in rural settings, especially in the agriculture setting, there will be many external factors related to the environment (soil, temperature, water, etc.) to account for. But even if you are working in a digital enterprise, chances are that one or more steps in your supply chain will in fact be influenced by the environment. Natural resources such as fuel for transportation are one aspect—will rising fuel prices affect your operations? Or will you leverage this external factor to introduce renewable energy as part of your venture? What about social trends related to climate change— are consumers making choices differently, in a way that will affect the number of people you are able to reach and the way in which you reach them? Is your level of competitiveness compared to other enterprises affected by changing commercial and corporate attitudes and initiatives related to the environment? Keeping your pulse on these changes will help make sure you stay ahead.

Even in a basic social enterprise, seasonal changes and patterns of behavior are important environmental factors to consider. How are the movement, activity, and spending patterns of your end users influenced by their physical environment? How does this influence demand? On the supply side, transportation, storage of goods, and other logistical factors are all related to external climate, weather patterns, and the physical infrastructure of the setting in which you are operating as it relates to the natural environment. This is where you take the time to chart out these changes and how they affect your operations, customers, suppliers, and other stakeholders.

As with all external factors, it's important to understand not only how environmental factors may affect your venture, but also the effects your venture will have on the environment. Regardless of your topic and sector, part of your impact on society will be your environmental footprint (the natural resources you require and wastes or by-products you emit). This provides an opportunity for you to quantify that footprint, and work with stakeholders across your value chain to understand and optimize your total impact on the world, finding ways to maximize your net positive effects in the social, economic, and environmental dimensions for sustainable development.

Legal

Familiarizing yourself with the legal requirements involved in setting up and running a new venture in the country you're operating in is critical to do from the start. Safety protocols, quality control requirements, and reporting and tax laws will differ not only by location but also by sector within each location. The food sector, the health sector, the education sector…each line of work has its own rules and regulations, and these vary within and across countries. So legal considerations are important from the inside out!

Legal aspects are often the last step a social entrepreneur considers, and this can potentially have devastating implications. Depending on where and how you register your venture, there will likely be legal restrictions on what you are allowed to do and how you are required to manage your finances. As we saw in Chapter 7, Nuru is an example of a social enterprise with multiple entities registered in the United States, Kenya, and Ethiopia. The different legislation in each country impacts whether the organization is even able to register as a social enterprise to start with, what goods and services it is allowed to offer, how much tax and external auditing is required, and other implications related to profit.

In many countries, a legal entity for social enterprises does not exist. In these cases, social ventures are often required to select one of the traditional commercial or civil legal forms, even if it's not the best match for them. Being aware of these legal aspects can help you plan for the necessary technical, legal, accounting, and other forms of support that alleviate the burden of navigating government rules and regulations on your own, filing the right paperwork, etc. But more than that, being aware of the legal environment will educate you on the behavior of your competitors and other stakeholders, the advantages and disadvantages of different sectors (e.g., private vs. civic), and the opportunities for you to benefit from legal structures that were made to protect you.

Beyond your own interactions with the law, it is important to understand how the legal system operates in the countries you are working in—are you working in a setting where laws are enforced, or are you working in a setting where government corruption, bribery, and lack of transparency are common? There are various developing and transitional nations in which the risks from these legal factors are too high for you to operate on your own in an efficient or effective manner. Thus, your PESTEL analysis may lead you to make strategic decisions such as partnering or working as part of an existing organization, whether it be an international or established local organization.

Last but not least, are there any legal factors you aspire to change? Who are the stakeholders working on, and affected by, the policies and regulations affecting your social challenge? Is it possible for you to incorporate a legal reform agenda into your planning, as we saw with Albina Ruiz and Ciudad Saludable in chapter three?

Know Your Limitations

Other than assessing your external threats and opportunities, it's also important to assess your internal strengths and weaknesses. We've already talked about some of the internal strengths of your social venture, such as the fact that it's user driven, tried and tested, and based on market research. Your team composition should also be built toward serving as a strength factor for your success. But there are always inherent weaknesses. No product or service is perfect! Thinking about your strong points and your natural limitations is important before you move forward. This helps you play to your strengths and make the right partnerships to complement your weaknesses.

Internal weaknesses could be technical, physical, knowledge based, or structural. Characterizing them is key in determining the feasibility and viability of your business model and in making accurate projections. No team is perfect, and no idea is bulletproof. Not knowing your own weaknesses *is* your number 1 risk! Some teams have a highly specialized degree of technical expertise (e.g., coding, for a mobile app; clinical care, for a health intervention; curriculum development, for an educational social enterprise, etc.) but less experience in financial management—this can be fixed by hiring or contracting out the right person! Others may have excellent management skills but incomplete information on measuring and maximizing social impact, understanding gender implications, or analyzing geopolitical and sociocultural factors. This is totally okay! Identifying your strong and weak points is just the first step in addressing them. You can hire or partner with new team members or external partners with diverse skills, or partner with other organizations specialized in the skills that are not your forte, thus turning these would-be weaknesses into strengths.

In some cases, your weaknesses may not be in your team or personal skills but aspects of your product or service itself. In developing your solution to meet the needs of your target population, you may have had to make tradeoffs knowing that it can't serve everyone, everywhere, at the same time. In other cases, you may have had to sacrifice sophistication for affordability, flexibility for durability, local context for scalability. This is part of the game. It helps you focus your attention on your strong points, clarify your value proposition, and clarify your target audience. You can also form strategic partnerships with other organizations or social entrepreneurs to build a supply chain that offsets these weaknesses, for example, by offering a set or system of complementary solutions.

Knowing your strengths and limitations is key to focusing your efforts, time, and resources in the right places. No social venture can solve all the world's problems. Sometimes, trying to strengthen your limitations is not the best way to focus your efforts. Rather, focusing on your strong points and recognizing your limitations may get you farther.

Tool: SWOT Table

Now that you've spent time with your team and stakeholders building your internal strengths, recognizing your internal limitations, and analyzing your external opportunities and threats, let's put them all together and see how this will play out. We call this a SWOT analysis, and it's basically a way of examining the complete landscape and assessing factors working for and against us. We've already agreed that social entrepreneurs do not operate in a vacuum. The biggest weapon you can arm yourself with is knowledge and consideration of the factors that might play out in

SWOT	+	−
Internal	Strengths	Weaknesses
External	Opportunities	Threats

Figure 8.2 SWOT.

your favor or work against you. The SWOT table (Figure 8.2) can help give you a complete picture of the pluses and minuses of your business. What are the internal strengths, internal weaknesses, external opportunities, and external threats that you are working with here? And how might they interact with each other?

Summary and Next Steps

The business planning process began the moment you started studying the challenge you're setting out to tackle. Characterizing the challenge, co-creating with the community, and innovating and designing the solution all laid the foundation for your value proposition, USP, and theory of change. Developing your social impact metrics using the logframe or equivalent planning tool allowed you to work backward from the change you're targeting, to build the framework needed to get there. In this chapter, you learned to add the costs, revenues, and timeline to this logical framework and put together the different components of your vision into a viable business model. Most importantly, you've incorporated your risk analysis, which will help you plan for and account for your internal strengths and weaknesses versus external threats and opportunities.

Exercise: Building a Viable Venture

Before you move on to the next chapter, you owe yourself the following three deliverables:

1. Develop your pro-forma income statement, using the template in Figure 8.1, or any other template of your choice. You should be able to answer the following in one sentence: How much time will you need to break even and what are your start-up costs?
2. Present your PESTEL analysis. Use bullet points with less than 250 words per point.
3. Fill out your SWOT table using the template in Figure 8.2 or any other template of your choice.

CHAPTER SUMMARY

- In this chapter, we analyze the financial viability of your venture. This is yet another step in the iterative design process. If the numbers don't add up, we go back tov the drawing board and iterate until we find a way to make it work!
- To assess your financial viability before launching, a pro-forma income statement is used to summarize all costs and revenues.
- Costs are estimated based on the information you have collected to date, such as the resources listed in your business canvas and from Chapters 5 and 7.
- Revenues are estimated based on your market research from Chapter 5, including the market size, customers' willingness to pay, promotion, and competition analysis.
- Common business models in social entrepreneurship include profit generating models, where revenues from customers add up to exceed costs; and hybrid models, where multiple revenue streams are required to subsidize the cost of service.
- Risk and uncertainty analysis is required to assess the internal and external factors that might influence your venture's viability. These are summarized using the PESTEL and SWOT frameworks. Leveraging your strengths and external opportunities and accounting for your weaknesses and external threats help maximize your chances of success.

Social Ventures Mentioned in This Chapter

Company profile: BeneStream, www.benestream.com.
Founded in 2011, for-profit model based in New York City, United States.
Product/service: BeneStream's signature product, Medicaid Migration™, helps companies identify and enroll eligible employees in free health insurance through the Medicaid expansion portion of the Affordable Care Act.
Goal: BeneStream is a mission-driven business whose goal is facilitating access to quality healthcare for low-income workers while helping businesses manage healthcare costs.
How it works: BeneStream identifies and enrolls low-income workers in Medicaid using a process called Medicaid Migration™. Medicaid Migration™ allows businesses to fulfill the employer mandate portion of the ACA while reducing their healthcare costs by moving eligible employees off of their health plans. BeneStream utilizes a proprietary screening platform to identify Medicaid-eligible employees and enrolls the employees using phone based and on-site professionals.

Company profile: Prosperity Catalyst, www.prosperitycandle.com; www.prosperitycatalyst.org.
Founded in 2010, US-certified B Corporation (for-profit) and US 501c3 (nonprofit).
Product/service: Prosperity Catalyst incubates and launches women-led businesses in distressed regions all over the world by providing the tools, training, and a community to help women thrive as skilled entrepreneurs and leaders.

Goal: Creating new opportunities for women in conflict areas, thus creating entrepreneurs and leaders to be catalysts for social and economic change.

How it works: Prosperity Candle is a social enterprise that believes in supporting women's entrepreneurship. At Prosperity Candle, every candle produced is handmade by female artisans. They began in the United States, and their partnership with Women for Women International allowed them to test their idea in Iraq. Today, they also operate in Haiti. Every candle purchased helps provide a living wage for those women, many of whom are poverty stricken or refugees working to build a better life and future within the United States. The sister organization, Prosperity Catalyst, provides the tools, training, and a community to help women thrive as skilled entrepreneurs and leaders.

Chapter 9

Pitching and Networking

Getting the Support You Need to Make This Happen

Now that you've designed the different components of your social venture and tested them out, you'll need to present it to funders and other stakeholders who will provide you with the financial and nonfinancial support needed.

There are so many resources at your disposal, and part of being a strategic social entrepreneur is going out and mobilizing those resources!

In this chapter, we'll make sure you go out there armed with the right tools and weapons you'll need. The first thing you'll need to have in your hand is a business plan or executive summary outlining the key points of your business model, how and why it works. Then we'll talk about some ways to expand your network and surround yourself with the right people and resources to help pave your path toward securing the funding you'll need.

Why Do You Need a Business Plan?

We've all heard the famous saying, "People don't plan to fail, they fail to plan." At this stage, you've failed on purpose while experimenting with different solutions in the design stage; now it's time to start succeeding on purpose! The point of a business plan is not to waste your time locking yourself in to a minute-by-minute dictation of how you will spend your time for the next several years, as many social entrepreneurs fear. First, the point is to provide a roadmap. It's that simple—having a map in your hand helps you see where you're going and the different ways to get there. You can still decide to go off-roading! It just helps you assess the dangers and opportunities ahead, and plan for adequate supplies for your journey.

Second, it helps you garner support. If you want people to help you, you'll need to show them where you're going with this. Most people don't back an idea, they back a person; that person's vision, and that person's ability to make that vision into a reality. You need to demonstrate that you are a backable social entrepreneur with not only the passion and the vision, but also the know-how to translate it into results.

At the end of the day, your business plan can and will change. You have to be responsive to the data that emerges from the field as you implement your plans, and adapt to new evidence, not to mention changing contexts. In fact, it's that responsiveness and adaptability in the end that will most likely determine your success. There are a lot of unknowns, as we explored in the last chapter. You've done a lot of work to chart out this new territory, and writing your business plan is simply a way to have a plan in your hand as you venture out. Think of your business plan as an adaptable, living and breathing plan—you can, will, and must revisit it along your journey.

How to Write a Business Plan

Guess what? You've already written the key components of a business plan. The chapters in this book so far have represented the journey you've taken to building an effective and viable solution, and the business plan simply presents those ingredients of the solution. If you haven't skipped the homework section of each chapter, all you need to do at this stage is put it all together!

You start by presenting the challenge you're facing, any key statistics that can help capture its breadth and depth and some personal stories that capture the urgency and importance of tackling this challenge.

Then you present your solution, describing how it builds on existing evidence, what others have tried before and what they haven't, how it was co-created with the community and developed through user-driven design.

You present your mission, vision, values, and theory of change. Then you go about describing how it will all work.

This includes describing your market research, preliminary results from your testing and piloting, and the dimensions of your social market strategy. Include summary information on the nuts and bolts of your operations, including distribution channels and key resources.

This is followed by your financial projections, timeline and breakeven point, and plans for growth. Last but not least, you present your strengths-weaknesses-opportunities-threats (SWOT) analysis and describe your contingency plans to mitigate risk.

A business plan provides high-level information and summarizes it in an easy-to-understand format. If you'd like to include details that you feel will alter the flow, it might be better to include these as an appendix.

Highlight your strengths and convince the reader that you and your team are the right people to make this happen! As with everything you do as a social entrepreneur, this is not something you sit down and type up alone in your office overnight. This is a living, breathing document that is co-created with your stakeholders over time and revisited as your venture grows.

Your businesses plan can come in many different sizes, shapes, and forms. It can be a document, a slide deck, a long and detailed version, or a basic nuts-and-bolts version. Go with what works for you as a start, and you can tailor it to different audiences as needed.

Right now, you're aiming for a 10- to 20-page summary document, although some business plans can be much longer. For a slide deck, you're looking at 10 slides ideally; this needs to be much more barebones than a narrative document.

Most entrepreneurs like to have both handy, because after pitching your slide deck to a potential supporter, you might be asked to then share your more detailed business plan document!

Executive Summary

Regardless of the length and format of your business plan (whether it's in document format or presented in a slide deck), you should be prepared with a one-page executive summary. This tells your reader just enough to know about the main concepts and components of your venture, highlighting key takeaways from each component of the plan without going into too much detail. You'll see in the future that many times, when you tell people about your venture, they'll ask to see a one-pager on it. So have your executive summary ready!

Business Plan Outline

Before you go back leafing through the previous chapters of the book and digging up all your homework assignments, let's take a snapshot look at the main components we're talking about here. The outline shown below in this section presents the basic components of a business plan as they should be presented. Each numbered point can ideally be captured in a written page, or a slide if you're going for a presentation format. The indented points are the details you need to elaborate on if you're writing a full business plan document, and you can also elaborate on if you have more time to give a full presentation (we'll talk more about presentation options below). Of course, you can use more than one page or one slide for each point, if needed. Remember, technical details are best added as appendices to avoid disrupting the flow.

You don't need to stick to the exact same order as the outline in the following, but make sure your business plan tells a story and follows the logic you used in developing your solution. Have you noticed how most website have different sections called "about us" or "who we are," "what we do" and "how it works"? These are the key pieces of information that people will want to see in your business plan. Think about where it makes sense to put each piece and how it combines with other pieces to convey your message. The only pointer we'll provide here is that in any social business plan it is advised to start with the challenge and the solution. The team can go sooner or later after that as you see fit, but it's not advised to put the team before the challenge and solution. Remember, this is not about you, it's about the challenge you're tackling and how you're going to change it!

Here is one way to do it:

1. Cover page: contact info, title, name of venture, logo, date of writing/presenting
2. The Challenge: What is the social/environmental challenge you are facing
   (including key statistics on who is affected, where, how, root causes)
3. The Opportunity: Where is the opportunity you have identified for change
   (including a description of your co-creation and testing process)
4. Your Solution: A description of your product or service
   (including how it works, nuts and bolts, operations, distribution, customers and market)
5. Vision, Mission, theory of change, target audience
   (a description of the components of your compass)
6. Team: Why you can make it work; skills, values, your story, how this came about
   (key positions and who fills them, why you are the best people to make this happen)
7. Business Model: How is this viable
   a. Main costs and revenues, financial projections, breakeven point
   b. Scenario analysis, competition and market analysis, threats and opportunities
8. Impact: How does it affect people, what does it change, what are the long-term effects
   a. Stakeholders and community ownership; potential partners and collaborators
   b. Short- versus long-term goals; Milestones; phasing
   c. Expansion plan: Where will you reach, how many people will you impact, how big will you grow

      d. How your team will evolve to meet the needs of a growing organization

      e. Strengths of your model and your team that will allow you to reach your target; characteristics of the market

  9. How the audience can help: What do you want from them, where can they add value

      a. Challenges you are facing: Obstacles, risks, limitations, how these are addressed

  10. End with a reminder of the vision you have for the future, and the change you will make, bringing it back full circle to the story you started within the first one to two points previously.

Presenting and Pitching Your Plan

You should be prepared to present your social venture in a variety of formats. A common slide deck pitch can be 10–20 minutes when presenting to private investors. At conferences, speakers are usually given about 15 minutes, with time for questions and answers (Q&A) afterward. If you are speaking as part of a panel, you may be allotted 5 minutes or less, with a longer discussion time. Many entrepreneurs find it helpful to have three versions prepared: the full slide deck (10–20 minutes), the abridged version (5 minutes or less), and the elevator pitch (less than 1 minute).

Your Slide Deck

Your full slide deck is something you can adapt to use in a versatile manner when presenting to funders, peers in conferences, prospective clients, and other stakeholders. It is based on your business plan and follows the same general order and outline. While the basic information inside the slides will not change from audience to audience, your areas of focus and the ordering will. We've all rearranged our CV to demonstrate a better fit to various job descriptions—the same goes for different audiences. If you're presenting to funders, you may need to spend more time going through the financial details. If you're presenting to community members whose collaboration you're seeking, you may need to spend more time going through your co-creation process, describing the feedback you received from various community members, how it was incorporated into the final product, and how you're leveraging community assets at multiple points along your supply chain.

    If time allows, it's helpful to share preliminary results, trends, patterns, and even raw data with your audience. If you're tight on time, include these as appendix slides. What are the factors that so far have affected the customer experience? How are you faring with respect to your competitors? Your audience may have questions on these points, so it's better to be prepared!

The Abridged Version

When you are given only 5 to 10 minutes to present, use an abridged version of your slide deck. What challenge are you tackling? What is your solution? How does it work? Who are your clients, and how are you reaching them? What is your business model? Where will you reach in terms of scale?

    Again, you can include more detailed information in the appendix, for discussion and Q&A. The goal of your presentation is simply for people to understand what you do, as a starting point for discussion.

Less Is More

The fewer pieces of information you use, the more information will be conveyed and retained by the audience. For example, you don't want to include all the statistics you have gathered on your social challenge. Include one photo, or one statistic, that demonstrates the urgency and need. Then move on to your solution. There is a growing body of literature on the "less is more" approach to presenting information, especially in a setting where time is limited.

Your full slide deck should be reserved for settings where people are coming prepared to settle in for a while and focus, and are looking to acquire detail about your work. Outside of those settings, your goal is not to share detail but to secure the attention of your audience. Keep the information on your slides minimal, use a simple message or photo to convey your point, and focus on making an emotional connection rather than presenting dry facts.

> If you don't have your elevator pitch prepared and practiced in advance, by the time the doors open, you'll still be fumbling for words.

Your Elevator Pitch

The elevator pitch does not involve a slide deck. This is how you present your organization verbally to someone at a networking event, conference, reception, or other social encounter. The term originates from the quite literal situation of bumping into someone in the elevator and having mere seconds to tell them what you've been up to. You need to be prepared to deliver a speedy, info-packed, answer to the question "So, what have you been up to?" And this does not mean talking fast. If you don't have your elevator pitch prepared and practiced in advanced, by the time the doors open, you'll still be fumbling for words.

When preparing your elevator pitch, take yourself back to the most basic and literal sense of the term. Imagine yourself in an elevator with someone, where you have literally seconds to explain what you do and why it's important. Can you answer this question in one sentence?

You can have a slightly longer elevator pitch of two to three sentences reserved for situations where time—and the interest of the person(s) listening—allows for a fuller explanation. But, definitely, have your one sentence version ready to go. The shorter, the better! Think back to the advice you got in Chapter 5 about stating your value proposition and writing your mission statement. The shortest version of your elevator pitch can be just that.

Some social entrepreneurship conferences and contests have "lightning" rounds of pitches. This means you have less than a minute (sometimes 30 seconds or less) to pitch your social venture to an audience or panel of judges. The term comes from the image of a bolt of lightning, which delivers a big impact in seconds, boom pow! Try watching some lightning rounds online to develop your take on what pitching might look like and feel like. Try out your own pitch to friends and family and teammates before you attempt it on others!

Pitching Tips

Find Your Balance

Perfecting your pitch ahead of time is crucial for a smooth delivery, but there is a very fine line between delivering a well-prepared pitch and sounding like a robot! While fumbling for the right words will risk losing the attention of your listeners, so will a delivery that sounds like an automatic voice recording. Sounding natural, passionate, and real is what will engage your audience. Say it like you're saying it for the first time!

Make a Connection

It's not just the words you say and how you say them but also how you connect with the person you're speaking to. Maintaining eye contact, smiling, and positioning yourself so that you're facing them and giving them your full attention will draw them in and help them give you their full attention in return.

A common mistake is looking around the room at a networking event while you're talking to someone, to see who else you should be talking to. It's hard for your listener not to notice this, and it will make them much less interested in hearing what you have to say. Make them feel like they're the only person in the room!

Similarly, if you are standing in front of a room full of people presenting your work, make each person feel as if she or he is engaged in a personal conversation with you. Look at them and hold eye contact for a few seconds until moving on to the next face. Wait to see if something registers in their face to show that they are actually listening. Find someone whose eyes look glazed over and look straight at them while delivering a line until they focus back in on you. Pay attention to the signals your audience is giving you. Are they smiling, nodding, and looking concerned about what you are saying? These are all signs that they are really listening and that what you are doing is working. Are they checking their watches or their phones or looking around the room at others? This means you have lost them and need to switch gears fast. Ask a question, take a vote, show a picture, or tell a joke!

One of the best ways to make a connection, whether in a small-group conversation or while presenting to an audience, is to research your audience ahead of time. What do you know about your listener(s)? What do they do for a living, what do they care about, why are they here today? Presenting your work from different angles will help draw in diverse audiences with different perspectives. For example, focusing on the financial aspects or the people aspects first, focusing on the geographic regions or the demographic populations first, or thinking about what will grab their attention and what they'll want to hear more about are different ways to present the same information using a different lens.

Get Them to Ask Questions

Another great way to keep your audience engaged is to share just the right amount of information to spark their curiosity and have a nugget of information or two that you hold back for "round two." This is especially the case in informal settings, where you are not standing in front of an audience who is expecting an entire presentation but rather are making conversation and networking with one individual or a small handful of individuals. Here is an example:

- ■ Scenario A
  - – Your listener: So, what do you do?
  - – You: I create medical devices to enhance maternal child health in low-resource settings. There are x children around the world who die each year and y mothers who die in childbirth. This can be solved with a simple device that does ABC. We work in geographic regions 1, 2, and 3, have served xxx people so far, and plan to scale to yyy in five years.

  In this scenario, you have probably bombarded your listener with too much information right off the bat, by delivering your entire story in one go.

- ■ Scenario B
  - – Your listener: So, what do you do?
  - – You: I create medical devices to enhance maternal child health in low-resource settings.

- Your listener: Oh, interesting...
- You: Yes, it's extremely challenging work. There are *x* children around the world who die each year and *y* mothers who die in childbirth. This can be solved with a simple device that does ABC.

In this scenario, your listener is more likely to ask you a question to keep the conversation going. She or he is probably extremely curious by now to find out more!

Know When to Ask Questions

It may be counterintuitive, but often, the best way to get someone curious about your work is to ask them about themselves. People love talking about themselves, and a great way to create a positive first impression is to show someone you are interested in them. Listening to their story will prep them for listening to yours. Plus, it helps you get that research out of the way, of knowing your audience before pitching to them! You can strategically find a way to segue back to your work by asking them about successes or challenges in their work and find commonalities you can talk about. Starting your presentation at a stage where the listeners already know they have something in common with you automatically makes them more interested in learning about what you do.

Common Mistakes to Avoid

Most of us have spent enough time listening to others present, to know the most common mistakes to avoid!

- Don't look at the ground → Do look directly at your audience.
- Don't fiddle with your hands → Do place them by your side to avoid distraction. Use them strategically when emphasizing a point.
- Don't shift your weight → Do stand strong with equal weight on each foot.
- Don't talk too fast → Do maintain a consistent pace of delivery, while livening it up with intonations, surprises, and catchy pieces of information.
- Don't make it sound like you have all the answers → Do sell your ideas while showing that you've thought out the risks and challenges and how to mitigate and address them.
- Don't stress out! → Do enjoy yourself, because you're the one who will set the tone for the mood in the room, and you want others to enjoy listening to you!

A good way to catch some of the habits you might have while speaking in public is to record yourself and play it back multiple times. The first time you view the playback, listen to yourself carefully and try to catch any habits you can improve on, such as speaking too softly or too quickly or saying things like "um" and "like." The second time you view the playback, watch your body language and try to catch any habits you can improve on, such as distracting movements, looking at the floor, or poor posture. The third time you view the playback, watch it in fast forward! This will make even the smallest of gestures and body languages painfully obvious and will help you correct them. Next, practice your new habits and take a second video recording to see how you've improved and how you can do better! Try new postures that convey confidence and authority—it turns out your body language doesn't only influence your audience, it also influences YOU!*

---

* Watch this TED talk or read the interactive transcript:
  http://www.ted.com/talks/amy_cuddy_your_body_language_shapes_who_you_are.

Advice for Introverts

Many of the most creative minds are introverts, who prefer to spend more time thinking quietly to themselves rather than talking to others. If you are an introvert, do not be intimidated by the concepts in this chapter. It *is* possible to enjoy yourself while pitching and networking! Focus on the ideas and on your work and how much you believe in it. It's not about you, nor the person you're talking to. It's about the mission.

Communication skills are something that you can learn, even if it doesn't feel like they come naturally to you. If you feel energized after working a room, then great! If you don't, that's totally okay! Knowing yourself, building in the time that you need on your own before and after social and professional engagements, and sharing the responsibility with your teammates will help make it a more rewarding experience for you. But don't shy away from it. Each and every person can play to their strengths when conveying their ideas to others—whether you are gregarious, quiet, talkative, thoughtful, charismatic, shy, or a different combination of these at different points in time. Don't try to be something you're not, and at the same time, don't give up until you find the communication style that feels right to you. And you can, if you just keep trying!

Don't be afraid to sell it.

You Can Be Humble and Promote Your Work at the Same Time

Most social entrepreneurs have a strong sense of humility because the work itself is humbling. When presenting your work, your humility will come through, and that is a good thing. Your audience will respect you for it. Just make sure that being humble about yourself doesn't mean understating your work, your ideas, and the importance of your mission. Promoting them is not the same as promoting yourself personally. And remember, you are the person who developed this mission, this vision, this product or service, and its value proposition. As much as you believe in your work, believe in yourself. Humility is an important quality in a social entrepreneur. But that doesn't prevent you from showing pride in your work. Don't be afraid to sell it.

Your greatest resource is your network.

Building Your Network

In the next chapter, we'll focus on funding, but before we talk about money, let's talk about your greatest resource. Your greatest resource is your network. Start with your current network and build outward. Many social entrepreneurs we've met throughout the course of this book have said as one of their top pieces of advice during their public speaking: use your network. Your network starts with the people you already know (peers, professors, parents, etc.) and the people they know.

Attending conferences and events is a great way to build your network. Be prepared with your elevator pitch, but don't attack people with it! Allow the conversation to naturally progress to the "So, what do you do?" question. Another great way to build your network is by conducting informational interviews. It may sound surprising to you, but many people will actually reply if you e-mail them to request an informational interview. People like talking about themselves, and if you make it clear why they should talk to you, you might just get a response. Try the tips in Tip Box 9.1 to help increase your chances of getting a response.

Once you've scheduled an informational interview, make sure you are well prepared to use your time wisely (Tip Box 9.2). Informational interviews usually take place over the phone or online conferencing, rather than in person; but if you're in the same city as the person you're meeting with, offer to come to their office for a short time slot. Suggest 15 minutes so that they will know you are aware of their busy schedule and don't want to take up too much of their time. In person meetings are by far more effective, and help establish a stronger personal connection.

Have your questions prepared, and keep them limited. No one wants to feel overwhelmed with too many questions, especially within a short period. In order to make the most use out of your limited time, make sure you've done all your research before coming to the meeting. Look up these persons online, read any articles they've posted or videos/speeches they've made. Make sure you're familiar with their personal background, their work history, and their organization. This will allow you to avoid asking redundant questions, and create an actual connection with these persons.

That said, while your goal is to make the most of your time, the last thing you want to do is rush through. Try to create a dialogue, rather than a Q&A. Save space for unexpected directions in the conversation and also give them space to ask *you* questions. A good way to keep a conversation structured is by starting out with your goals (what you want to accomplish, both in your own work and in this meeting) and looping back to them at the end. This will also help you organize your own thoughts! This skill will also come in handy when you start having one-on-one meetings with potential funders. Last but not least, make sure to ask for any recommendations they may have on other people you should talk to or actions you should take. Send them an e-mail within 24 hours thanking them and following up on their recommendations, and keep track of all your meetings so that you can build on each link in your network, one at a time.

TIP BOX 9.1   HOW TO GET AN INFORMATIONAL INTERVIEW

1. If you have a university e-mail, use it, rather than your personal or work e-mail.
2. As your subject line, write "Request for Informational Interview."
3. Keep your e-mail short. You don't need more than three sentences:
   a. Who you are and what you do
   b. Why you want to talk to that person (explain why you're interested in their work and what you want to learn from them)
   c. End with a simple and direct sentence such as "If your schedule allows, I would be grateful for 20 minutes of your time."

TIP BOX 9.2   WHAT TO DO ONCE YOU GET THE INTERVIEW

1. Have your questions prepared and keep them limited.
2. Make sure you've done your research.
3. Don't rush through. Keep space open in the conversation for unexpected dialogue.
4. Start by explaining what you hope to achieve (both with your work and with this meeting) and circle back to those goals at the end of the meeting.
5. Ask whether they have any recommendations for other people you should talk to.
6. Send a follow-up thank you e-mail within 24 hours.

Keep track of your informational interviews and any action items.

Other than informational interviews, networking opportunities come in many shapes or forms. Your career or classroom is the biggest networking opportunity. Chances are, whether you're a midcareer professional or a college student, the people in the room with you today are people you will cross paths with in the future—and have the opportunity to build things with starting now. Social events, professional events, conferences, and other networking events are abundant in your community no matter where you live. Go to where the knowledge is!

In the following sections, you will find some more tips on where you can find like-minded people and how you can expand your network to include potential funders, teammates, and other supporters. But before you foray into these networking opportunities, keep in mind the basic do's and don'ts of networking (Tip Box 9.3). While it is important to "seize the day," you don't want to sabotage yourself by making someone feel you are out to "seize" them! Recognizing the moment is a soft skill that each entrepreneur needs to fine tune over time. Easier skills to get right from the first try are the following: look people in the eye, smile, relax, and have fun! People will enjoy talking to you if they feel you are enjoying talking to them! Make sure you are well polished (practicing personal hygiene is a basic skill that cannot be overlooked!), have a nametag where possible and wear it on the right-hand side to meet the other person's eye when they reach out to shake your hand; and have a firm hand-shake but don't be too aggressive. There's a fine line between being a go-getter and making someone feel that you're out to get them!

TIP BOX 9.3   CARPE DIEM, NOT CARPE CORPUS!*

1. Remember your presentation skills: look people in the eye, smile, relax, and have fun!
2. Practice personal hygiene: you want to give the appearance of someone who is on top of things. Wear well-laundered, well-pressed clothes and definitely do not skip a shower or forget to brush your hair (or your teeth)!
3. Have a nametag where possible, and wear it high on the right side, since people read from left to right (and your right is their left).

Have a firm handshake, but don't be too aggressive!

---

* *Carpe diem* means "seize the day" in Latin. This is just a reminder that you can seize the day without making someone feel that you are out to seize *them*! (*Corpus* means "body" in Latin ☺.)

So You've Got Your Business Plan ... Now What?

Surround Yourself with Supporters

Before you seek funding, make sure you're surrounded by the nonfinancial support that you need. Your internal team should be composed of people who are in it for the long haul, just like you. Of course, once you secure funds, you will be able to hire others. But your cofounders and founding team are those who have skin in the game and are willing to take risks with you, sweat with you, and pull all-nighters with you, if needed. Asking people to put their name on a start-up means that you are asking them to have a vested interest. This applies not only to your internal teammates but also to those who you assemble around you for guidance and mentorship.

Assemble Your Advisory Board

One of the best ways to make sure you're getting the guidance you need and to start expanding your network of contacts is to ask mentors to serve on your advisory board. The advisory board is a group of people with a level of expertise in one of the areas that you need, who believe in your venture and are willing to invest their time and knowledge—and affiliate their names—with you. This is different from your board of directors or trustees, which we'll discuss in a later chapter. The advisory board has no legal or financial commitments to you but is just there to support and guide you.

Building a relationship with potential advisory board members is a process that best occurs organically; that is, these should be people whose help you genuinely need and whose interests match yours. Think about it as looking for people who, when you reach out to seek their help, will be impressed with and inspired by what you are working on. Building this relationship is a process that occurs naturally and gradually over time, so that by the time you formally invite them to serve on the advisory board, they already feel that they have been playing that advisory role.

When thinking strategically ahead about who it makes sense to reach out to, think about the different areas of knowledge, experience, and types of networks that you need. Most likely, you will need people with a mix of experience in entrepreneurship (those who have started their own ventures) and in the subject matter you are working on (whether it's health, education, environment, etc.). It is also strongly recommended to have general management advisors, whether those with experience in nonprofits if your business model is nonprofit or for-profit if your business model is for-profit. There are also people who are general networkers and have a huge pool of contacts that they can help you spread awareness about your venture to. These are the connectors we referred to in Chapter 3, those naturally gifted "people persons" who tend to make links with others and nurture those links over time.

If you start with a handful of core supporters to help you build your venture from the ground up, that core will grow as your accomplishments grow and as you are able to validate yourself as an organization or initiative. Pool your contacts with your other founding team members and see who they suggest. If you've identified a pool of individuals whom you think would be valuable resource people to you, do some background research before reaching out to them. You only get one chance to introduce yourself or be introduced by a common contact, so don't play that card until you're ready. Go to a seminar, fundraising event, or other social networking opportunity that you know that person will be attending. E-mail them in advance to let them know that you're interested in speaking and will be approaching them at the event. Find out whether you have any common acquaintances that might be able to introduce you.

While you shouldn't hesitate to try reaching out to new people, it's often advised to start closer to home. Who are you already surrounded by that can support you? Tap into your existing core network, whether peers at your learning institute, colleagues at work, professors and their contacts, or parents and their contacts. Think across generations in terms of not only your network from school and work but also the network of those you know who are a generation or two above you. These people are likely far more advanced in their careers than you are, have a larger pool of contacts, have more knowledge and experience, and probably even more time to share. More often than not, they will respond positively to the opportunity to help the younger generation (even if you don't consider yourself young!) in making changes for the future.

Start Fundraising!

Raising funds has to start at the very beginning. Before you can approach institutional investors, donors, or funds (more on these in the next chapter), you need to find a way to demonstrate your proof of concept, and this costs money! Different ways to start include the following:

1. Crowdfunding

    A popular choice at the early stages is crowdfunding, a process where you appeal to the masses to support you. If a large number of people donate small amounts, you can fund your proof-of-concept stage. Crowdfunding is not limited to small amounts, you can also get larger donations though a crowdfunding campaign, and you can appeal to people either online or offline. Some web pages have compiled information on leading crowdfunding websites around the world.*

2. Fundraising events

    Offline, holding events is one way to crowd fund. Events can help people get involved for the long-term, by building awareness and creating personal connections. Finding company sponsors in your community is one way to increase the amount of funds you can raise, whether by matching the amount of donations made, offering food or beverages, providing the venue, or other forms of support. People can either donate at the event, or you can provide the information and start building relationships which will develop over time to result in financial support for your future organization.

3. University-based opportunities

    If you are based in a university or other educational institution, you may have access to research funds, student grants, fellowships, scholarships, or awards. Most universities have various offices for student affairs, student services, community service, and related themes; many also have offices or centers for entrepreneurship and innovation. There are people whose job it is to help you identify resources—Use them!

4. Contests

    Social entrepreneurship contests are held both at universities and by other hosts, including foundations or corporate sponsors. Examples of these include the Hult prize, Dell competition, Shell competition, Microsoft contest, and various university-based social enterprise conferences and contests around the world. Find these, and apply! A few helpful links are

---

* http://www.crowdfunding.com/, http://marketingmoxie.biz/the-big-list-of-crowdfunding-sites/, http://www.inc.com/magazine/201306/eric-markowitz/how-to-choose-a-crowdfunder.html, http://crowdsourcingweek.com/top-15-crowdfunding-platforms-in-europe/, http://www.goodnet.org/articles/353.

listed here to help get you started.*,† Some universities hold campus-wide competitions, but most open their competitions to social entrepreneurs worldwide. Contests are also often part of most social entrepreneurship conferences, which we'll read more about further in this chapter.

5. One-on-one meetings

Meeting with potential funders might include philanthropists or investors looking for a mix of social and/or financial return. Either way, it's someone who believes in your vision and in your capacity to make it happen. Some fundraising experts say that when meeting with a potential funder, you should never ask for money at the first meeting. This may sound counterintuitive, but if you think about it, it makes sense. You want to focus your energy on selling your vision to them. Once they are sold, they will be asking you, how can I help, how can I get involved? Learning this is mastering one of the greatest characteristics of a leader, to make people want to follow you.

Tips for one-on-one meetings are similar to general networking tips (Tip Boxes 9.1 through 9.3), but a one-on-one meeting with a potential funder is more focused and personal. You are basically pitching your social venture to them. You need to keep in mind that a social investor is someone who wants to change the world: they have a mission of their own. Your goal in the first meeting (or before you meet them if possible) should be to find out what their mission is. Then, you focus your first meeting on making them see that your missions are aligned. (If they're not, then this investor is not the right match for you.) Ask for their advice, make them feel engaged, and invite them to come join you on a site visit to meet your team and your end users.

A key nuance can be that the way to end a first meeting may differ between philanthropists and for-profit investors. In philanthropy, it often takes multiple meetings over a long period to cultivate a relationship that leads to a large donation. Impact investors and other for-profit social investors, on the other hand, may be accustomed to a more aggressive approach and will likely be looking for an "ask" at the end.

What Is an "Ask"?

When you pitch your project, your goal is for your audience to be asking by the end of your pitch, "How can I help? How can I get involved?" They will be expecting you to provide them with an "ask." This means that you need to end your pitch with information on what they can do. Depending on your audience, you may want to provide a combination of nonfinancial and/or financial resources. For example, various asks could include the following:

■ Follow us on social media and tell your friends
■ Volunteer your skills and expertise
■ Sign up for a monthly or annual donation

---

* http://www.ventureacademy.mckinsey.com/competition, http://socialventurechallenge.asia/about/, http://www.genesis-generation.org/, http://enactus.org/, https://entrepreneurship.duke.edu/social-entrepreneurship/clubs-competitions-conferences/, http://socialimpact.umich.edu/programs-activities/social-entrepreneurship-competitions/, http://grasshopper.com/blog/startup-competition-guide/.
† http://www.ilo.org/wcmsp5/groups/public/---africa/---ro-addis_ababa/---ilo-pretoria/documents/instructional material/wcms_222474.pdf (p. 5).

Or, you could end with an ask targeting an investor or group of investors, that says something like:

■ We have an idea that could change the world. To develop our proof of concept, we need $Y. With your help, in the next six months, we aim to: A, B, C.

(Or for a more advanced venture):

■ In the past three years, we have demonstrated proof of concept, showing that our product or service does A, B, C. In the next five years, we are looking to reach X people with our solution. We are raising $Y to fund this expansion (having already shown them information on your costs, revenues, and business model). With your help, we can achieve _____ (fill in the blank, inserting your social outcome or objective).

These are just examples of what various asks could look like. The important thing is that by now, you have carefully thought of and planned out what you are going to do and what your needs are to get there. Run your pitch and your ask by friends, families, advisors, and supporters. Tailor it for each audience, and then … Go for it!

Interview Box. Willy Foote, Founder and CEO, Root Capital

TC: Willy, you've navigated a whole set of diverse resources, including both financial and human capital. What advice do you have for social entrepreneurs just getting started?

WF: I'm a firm believer that to do this work, you've got to dive in. You can't decode everything up front, so you need a license from all your stakeholders—including investors—to adapt and iterate.

TC: What was the turning point for you, when it all came together?

WF: For me, it was spending time in Mexico, the "barefoot empiricism." Hearing complaints from people, what they struggled with. I had to search for my slip stream, the guiding path that would allow me to leverage resources to tackle something as big as a market failure. For me, the slip stream was three things. The first was I realized we have to shorten agricultural value chains, remove the middlemen. The second guide path was people who carved our way—first there was banking for the poor, and now, agriculture is next. The third factor that helped it all come together was the shift of focus to agriculture among policymakers. These are the enabling conditions and slip stream that allowed Root Capital to innovate.

TC: How did you navigate all these players, from the farmers and cooperatives, to the big businesses in the coffee industry, to the governments and multilaterals?

WF: Root Capital and our clients are part of a much broader ecosystem made up of private, public and non-profit organizations—each with different motivations, perspectives and approaches. Reconciling these competing interests is not always easy, but to achieve transformative impact, it's essential that everyone is at the table. In general, we are pathologically collaborative in almost everything we do: forming networks with peers and practitioners, or joining existing ones, to push ourselves and the social enterprise sector further. For instance, Root Capital is a founding member of the Aspen Network of Development Entrepreneurs (ANDE), a group of over 100 organizations working together to find common approaches to measure impact, for example. We've also been working with our competitors to form an industry association called the Council on Smallholder Agricultural Finance; recognizing that Root Capital meets less than *one percent* of the total demand for finance among smallholder farmers, we're speaking with a collective voice to expand the supply of capital to rural farming businesses. As an organization, we have to stay relentlessly focused on our core competency and always put our clients front and center. At the same time, solving market failures this deep require many hands, and as long as we're all facing the same sector-wide challenges, it's pointless to stand in separate corners of the room.

TC: Can you give us an example of how you mobilized different networks and resources?

WF: A recent example was Root Capital's response to the outbreak of coffee leaf rust, a fungal disease that has reached epidemic proportions throughout Latin America over the past three years. This created an emergency situation in multiple countries where millions of dollars and thousands of jobs were lost. To respond, Root Capital mobilized several of our partners to launch the Coffee Farmer Resilience Initiative—a platform from which individual actors could pursue their own commercial or noncommercial interests, while also supporting the "public good" activities that had long been neglected by others. In this case, private sector partners made philanthropic donations and direct investments to ensure a stable supply of high-quality coffee and to support farmers throughout the region. Meanwhile, the U.S. Agency for International Development matched some of this private sector capital and offered a partial credit guarantee, and the Inter-American Development Bank provided grant funding to support training and capacity building. Then, Root Capital served as the lender: we designed and deployed long-term loans so that coffee farmers can replace disease-affected trees with newer varieties, and we offered intensive training on financial management and income diversification. It's an example of how to collaborate across sectors and blend capital to achieve a common goal: more stability and resilience for all actors within a particular supply chain.

TC: This was an emergency situation—how do you build on it for sustainable development?

WF: Yes, this was an emergency situation, but the writing was on the wall for decades. Leaf rust revealed the effects of decades of under investment in agriculture, and it's the proverbial "canary in the coal mine" signaling the impact that climate change will likely have on agriculture and, in turn, on the livelihoods of smallholder farmers. In that sense, the outbreak is a symptom of a much larger, chronic problem—one that is rooted in the same market failure I witnessed in Mexico fifteen years ago. To achieve long-term sustainable development, you have to work in partnership with others. You have to work across sectors and across borders in what are often messy and uncomfortable partnerships. This is what I like to call pathological collaboration.

Photo from www.rootcapital.org.

Finding Your Tribe

Being an entrepreneur can be lonely. While you may be surrounded by people most of the time, and while you're co-creating and recruiting supporters and team members, there are also days when you might wake up thinking "this is impossible" and nights when you go to bed with your heart thumping and your mind racing at the sheer burden of everything you have taken on. Social entrepreneurship can be overwhelming! It's not easy, and never at any point in time will you feel that you have all the answers. Knowing that this is normal and that others are in the same boat can help. While your main team is those immediately around you working on your venture with you, community members and other stakeholders vested in this alongside you, you might find comfort in realizing that your "tribe" is much bigger than that. Your tribe includes all the social entrepreneurs out there, working just as hard as you are to make a difference—finding them will empower you and strengthen you by putting you in your element where you can get things done best.*

That's on the soft side—on the technical side, there are also a wealth of tips, knowledge, expertise, experience and tools that you can exchange with others. This can range from bouncing ideas off someone, going to a seminar with a more seasoned entrepreneur, attending training workshops, or accessing mentorship, consulting, and advisory resources. You can learn about tried and tested methods, cases, and where to access certain needs, such as outsourcing—and you might even get discounts on these services by joining certain networks. Below we will review some of these networks and resources, which can be as valuable to you as the funding itself.

Mentors and Coaches

Finding your tribe does not just mean finding your peers. People who have been in the same situation that you are in right now and have gotten past it to succeed and move beyond the struggle you are facing today can be a huge source of support and guidance. A mentor is someone you develop a long-term relationship with, who can offer you advice and often connections, and who simply cares to see you succeed. Mentorship is one of the most valuable resources you can access, even before you try to access funding.

Finding a mentor sometimes comes naturally in a university or workplace setting. Other times, you have the opportunity to sign up for a mentor through formal channels. If you are taking a course in social entrepreneurship, then chances are your university offers resources to support students starting their own social ventures. Your mentor can be a professor, an alumnus, or a volunteer in a specialized network. Mentorship networks are often associated with universities, investor groups, events, coworking spaces, incubators and accelerators, and other training programs. However, you don't need to restrict yourself to social entrepreneurship mentorship networks to find the right match for you.

Coaches are similar to mentors but play a more short-term role focused on building a specific competency. Coaches are often provided to help you work on specific tasks if you enter a competition or join one of the various different kinds of entrepreneurship spaces described below. You can also hire a coach if there are specific skill sets you need to work on.

Coworking Spaces

Many entrepreneurs work from home, coffee shops, libraries, or other places where they can save on rent and keep their operations lean. Others use shared offices or find a corporate sponsor or

---

* A great reference on this notion is the book *The Element: How Finding Your Passion Changes Everything* by Sir Ken Robinson, Chapter 5.

other organization to donate space. Yet another option you might want to familiarize yourself with is the coworking space. This is different from a shared office because, in most cases, a coworking space is set up with the specific purpose in mind to support entrepreneurs and their start-ups, provide utilities and facilities at low costs, and provide other services that members can benefit from. Joining a coworking space can enhance your visibility and offer you access to a network of other entrepreneurs and potentially investors. Many coworking spaces are also affiliated with incubators and accelerators, which we will learn more about below. Most are often designed with a vision of providing a space that fosters creativity and inspiration. Joining a coworking space is a low-cost, high-yield way of accessing tools and services that foster innovation, while avoiding the isolation that can come from being an entrepreneur.

Incubators

Incubators are spaces where entrepreneurs can grow their ideas into reality. Usually, this entails a physical space to be shared by start-ups. Most incubators provide a package including one or more of space, supplies, technical support, mentorship, and funding. Each entrepreneur enters and exits the incubator at their own pace, creating an environment full of innovation at its various stages! For most incubators, you will have to apply and be accepted. Well-known incubators exist all over the world, representing various sectors. Most incubators include mentorship plus funding in return for equity (a share in your venture; we'll talk more about this in the next chapter).

A few examples of social entrepreneurship incubators from around the world are the Halycon Incubator in Washington, DC, Enviu in the Netherlands, Social Incubator Fund in the United Kingdom, Social Impact Lab in Germany, PACT in Singapore, and many others.*

Accelerators

Accelerators, on the other hand, are more like a class you are in, in the sense that they usually have a predefined period in which everyone enters and exits the program and a more narrow set of selection criteria. While incubators may host a wide range of start-ups at various stages, accelerators usually have a predefined program that requires that most participants fit within stringent criteria. The goal of an accelerator is to rapidly grow an existing start-up, rather than gradually nurturing it over time as an incubator does. Accelerators often offer investment capital or at least provide the social entrepreneur with access to investors through networking, pitching, and showcasing opportunities.

Some programs offer a variety of choices across the spectrum ranging from accelerator programs, "excubator programs" (nonresident incubation), mentorship programs, and boot camps. Examples are the Global Social Benefit Institute (www.scu-social-entrepreneurship.org/gsbi), the Global Development Incubator (www.globaldevincubator.org), and the Unreasonable Institute (www.unreasonableinstitute.org). Many incubators and accelerators also spun out of universities around the world, and chances are, you'll have the opportunity to participate in one in your university! An early-stage example is SEED in Cambodia (monashseed.org/incubator-program), and a more advanced example is the Agora Partnership, initially established in Nicaragua and now operating throughout Latin America (agorapartnerships.org/accelerator).

* Read this fun article about incubators in India: http://social.yourstory.com/2013/09/social-business-incubators-helping-startups/.

Boot Camps

Boot camps are often also provided by accelerators but aren't necessarily always tied to one. They are short, intense training programs that help entrepreneurs develop their ideas and prototypes. Social entrepreneurship boot camps are available at many universities around the world and through other networks. An example from Asia is the DUS-HUB social entrepreneurship boot camp (http://www.venturesforchange.com/). Social entrepreneurs can also attend general boot camps not specialized in social purpose organizations; these can still provide the creative, rapid-fire environment that you are looking for!

Other Networks

Other organizations and networks are available around the world to contribute to the social entrepreneurship ecosystem by building networks that bring people together. An example from Europe is the Start Up Europe Club (http://startupeuropeclub.eu). Alumni networks specialized in entrepreneurship are also common in various universities. Angel networks and other investor networks will also be an important potential resource for you—more on these in the next chapter.

Fellowships

Fellowships combine several of the services described by the various previous resources: they gather a cohort of social entrepreneurs, offer them mentorship and in most cases funding, help accelerate and scale their impact, and help them incubate new ideas. Fellowships are most often for slightly more advanced rather than early stage ideas, which have already been tested and demonstrated impact. Leading fellowship programs are listed in Chapter 1, Box 1.1. Most of the listed institutions, which were formed to support social entrepreneurs, are best known for their fellowship programs, which often form the cornerstone of their work. But don't stop there—universities and governments also offer fellowship programs, so make sure to check for fellowships near you!

Events

Entrepreneurship events and conferences are a great place to find mentors, investors, and potential team members. They don't need to be specialized in social entrepreneurship; there are often social impact topics at general entrepreneurship events, and even if there aren't, you are still likely to find like-minded people looking to change the world.

University-based conferences can be found in most parts of the world and are easy to identify using a quick online search. A good place to start is by seeing if there is a social entrepreneurship interest group at your university or workplace. If there isn't, you might just be the best person to start one! Non-university-based conferences are also plentiful, such as the annual Social Enterprise World Forum, Global Social Business Summit, Clinton Global Initiative, Social Capital Markets, Poptech, Net Impact, and many others. Most of the institutions listed in Box 1.1 also hold annual events and conference, so make sure to check those out.

Events other than conferences can also be found in most major cities, and even in the most unexpected places around the world. You will find business planning seminars in a coworking space in Beirut,* pitch contests in a coffee shop in Beijing,† and real-time prototyping events in

---

* http://www.lebtivity.com/event/kick-start-your-business-plan.
† http://www.1776.vc/insights/how-china-could-take-over-the-startup-world-2/.

Bihar.* Global Entrepreneurship Week† takes place each year in over 140 countries around the world and is a good place to find many of the innovation and entrepreneurship players in your geographic region. Even if you are not able to get there in person, check the website of the event nearest you and read about the various organizers, speakers, participants, and partner organizations. You may want to reach out to some of these on your own, no event needed. Conduct an informational interview, find out about their application process, and create a dashboard for yourself to determine the best timing to take this further (see resource dashboard in next chapter).

A Word of Caution

You'll notice as you start to build momentum how easy it is to get carried away with the social entrepreneurship scene. There is a lot of hype around social entrepreneurship these days! While it can be extremely helpful on many levels, for both moral and technical support, it's also easy to lose touch with the reality of your end users and the world they live in, which is a very different scene. Stay connected to the community you co-created with; make sure your mental bandwidth, energy, and thoughts are with them, not with the hype around you. Whatever you do, stay focused on your mission and your work. Remember what we talked about at the very beginning of this book: if you want to succeed, you can't make it about you. What you want to be celebrating and shouting out loud about is not you and your ideas; it's your work and the tangible progress you make toward the social impact you set out to achieve.

Summary and Next Steps

In this chapter, we've created a vehicle for you to present your work to the world by putting it all down into a business plan. With your business plan in hand, you can hit the pavement and start rallying support from potential funders, advisors, and other players in the social entrepreneurship ecosystem. Building your network, building your advisory board, and finding out what resources are available for social entrepreneurs in your area will lay the foundations for you to start talking to funders. But most importantly, it will help surround your social venture with supporters who can help you influence the outcome. In the next chapter, we'll talk about the different sources and types of funding and different social investment approaches that various funders take.

Exercise: Putting It Down on Paper

All right, it's time to put it all down on paper!

1. Using the outline provided at the start of the chapter, prepare a 10- to 20-page document presenting your social venture and how it works. Remember, you have already drafted most of the material, you just need to pull together and organize your assignments from the previous chapters!
2. Using a similar outline, prepare a 10-slide pitch deck to present your venture to potential supporters. Try your best to stick to 10 slides as much as possible or as close as you can get it. Remember, you can include preliminary data and other technical details in appendix slides, but it's important to be able to tell your story in about 10 slides if possible.
3. Record yourself presenting your elevator pitch in less than 1 minute and without using a slide deck. Pay special attention to your body language, eye contact, and movements. Play

---

* http://www.designpublic.in/.
† http://www.gew.co/.

back your presentation and watch carefully. What were your strongest points, and what points need improvement? Play it back in fast forward too. Are there any body language or movement patterns you've picked up on that need strengthening?

4. Get in touch with three to seven potential supporters and conduct informational interviews. Remember to be prepared with the information and ideas you're looking to exchange with this person and your objective for each interview. Then follow up in a timely manner to thank them and make sure to note down their recommendations and potential next steps.

CHAPTER SUMMARY

- In this chapter, we talked about how to get out there and rally support for your venture. You'll need to approach potential funders, advisors, and other types of supporters.
- The key tool in your artillery for this is your business plan. You've already been assembling the different components over the last few chapters—now it's time to organize it into a document or slide deck to present to potential supporters.
- Every social entrepreneur needs to be prepared to pitch and present his or her venture to a variety of audiences in different settings. One of these is the elevator pitch, which summarizes the key concepts in under a minute and leaves the audience wanting more!
- Once you're prepared with your business plan and elevator pitch, it's time to hit the pavement and build your network. You can do this by organizing informational interviews, attending conferences and other events, and joining networks on your subject matter or on social entrepreneurship in general.
- One of the first milestones in building your network of supporters is assembling your advisory board. This is not required but is highly recommended. Your advisory board is a group of volunteers with expertise in an area you'll need guidance in moving forward.
- Other resources that will help you build your venture include mentors, coaches, coworking spaces, incubators, accelerators, conferences, contests, fellowships, and other networks and events.

Social Ventures Mentioned in This Chapter

Company profile: Root Capital, www.rootcapital.org.
Information extracted directly from website.
Product/service: Nonprofit social investment fund that lends capital, delivers financial training, and strengthens market connections for agricultural small and growing businesses.
Goal: Building a thriving financial market to serve agricultural businesses that generate long-term social, economic, and environmental sustainability for small-scale farmers and their communities around the world.
How it works: Root Capital works in poor, environmentally vulnerable places in Latin America and Africa. Root Capital's lending is directed toward businesses that are too big for microfinance but not yet able to secure credit from conventional commercial banks, "the missing middle" of developing world finance. Root Capital provides capital and training to ensure volume and quality, and links these businesses with the global market, helping forge contracts with buyers.

Chapter 10

Funding Your Venture

Now that you've assembled your business plan and are ready to pitch it, it's time to go out there and secure resources to get your start-up going! In this chapter, we'll talk about funding options to finance your venture. Before you decide if and how to register your organization, it's important that you're able to navigate the different sources and types of funding available to social entrepreneurs and understand the different social investment approaches.

Sources of funding include private funds, individuals, governments, multilateral agencies, and NGOs. Common funding vehicles provided by these different sources include donations, awards, grants, loans, and equity. And depending on what the funder asks from you in return, there are different approaches to the who, what, when, where, and how of funding.

We'll proceed through each of these subtopics one at a time so that by the end, you'll have a complete picture. Ultimately, the funding sources you pursue should be informed by your business model—and not the other way around.

Creating Your Resource Dashboard

Before we dive in, let's make sure you have a tool in hand to help you manage all this information. With all the different resources available to you, different ways to raise money, different sources of money, funding vehicles, and investment approaches, it is easy to get overwhelmed and not know where to start. Take some time upfront to create a resource dashboard. This is a way to organize the different resources at your fingertips, to make sure to approach them in a well-thought-out and strategic manner, rather than an ad hoc manner.

Your timeline for tapping into specific resources should be based on your venture's stage of growth and level of maturity. For example, you may want to focus more on nonfinancial support such as technical expertise, networking leads, advisors, and other forms of supporters before you approach funders. You may want to flag certain people to touch base with down the line, when you are ready to make use of their area of expertise. You may also want to circle back to certain people to keep them posted, and timing is everything. Don't overbombard people with e-mails or requests for meetings, but make sure you stay on their radar with timely updates (even once a year). Remember, you are in this for the long haul.

It is important to be both resourceful (making the most use of your resources) and strategic at the same time, about *how* and *when* to make use of your resources. Especially when meeting with potential funders, you only get one first impression. While it's crucial to get enough funding early on to avoid running out before you're self-sufficient, you also don't want to approach prospective funders before you're ready for your next stage of growth or at least have information about what the next stage(s) will entail and when.

Your dashboard may look something like the sample template in Figure 10.1. The different tabs contain information on resources available to you for your proof-of-concept stage, for when you launch your venture, and for your later growth stages. This way, when you come across information now on resources available to mature social ventures, you can file it away for later. Most importantly, it's need-driven, so you write down your venture's needs first and then go out there and find the resources to meet those needs (Figure 10.1).

In the funding world, the three stages represented in the different tabs in Figure 10.1 are often referred to as the seed-funding, series A, and series B funding rounds. Different investors are specialized in different stages of maturity, so using a resource dashboard can help you figure out and keep track of which sources of funding you qualify for at each stage, and keep this information on your radar as you progress. You can either use this template or create your own, but in either case, it's crucial to keep track of all resources you come across (whether people, events, deadlines, sources of expertise, or sources of funding) and organize your timeline to make the best use of resources at the optimal time.

Tab 1: Proof of concept	Tab 2: Launch	Tab 3: Growth
Expertise needed	People to talk to	
-	-	
-	-	
-	-	
-	-	
Funding needed	Prospective funders	
-	-	
-	-	
-	-	
-	-	
Targets for each stage	Tools and resources for Each Target	
-	-	
-	-	
-	-	
-	-	
What does your product or service look like after each stage?		

Figure 10.1 Resource dashboard template.

Sources of Funding

Multiple sources of funding are available to you at multiple stages throughout your venture. Depending on your stage of maturity and the activities you intend to implement, you could be eligible for more than one of the following sources. Let's start by going through them one by one, and then we'll talk about the different funding vehicles and approaches found across the different sources of funding.

Governments

Government agencies may provide funds for research and development in specific subject areas and also in some cases seed funding for new ventures. *Research funds* are often earmarked for researchers based in universities, research institutions, or smaller organizations specialized in a specific subject. For example, the US Environmental Protection Agency allocates research funds to a range of researchers including university-based, non-profit-based, and even those based in private consulting firms. If you are a smaller social venture, a strategic way to increase your competitive edge when bidding for government funding is to partner with university researchers with a longer track record.

Government agencies may also provide *start-up funds* and other resources to encourage new ventures, whether commercial or social or both. There are an increasing number of government agencies and programs specialized in innovation. These can sometimes exist within the framework of a subject-specific agency or within the framework of a subject-agnostic program specialized in fostering entrepreneurship. Check for programs available in your country to support social entrepreneurs domestically. Don't forget that there could be both nationwide programs (like Start-up Britain* in the United Kingdom or the Spark Programs† in the United States) and more local programs (like Green Economy Malaga‡ in Spain).

In addition to fostering social entrepreneurship in their own country many governments also extend funding to social entrepreneurs in other countries through their international aid agencies. Most governments have a specialized agency to disburse funds for international development. A few examples include JICA, DANIDA, SIDA, and Norad (Japan, Denmark, Sweden, and Norway, respectively); Italian and Dutch Development Cooperation Programs, USAID and UK-DFID, India's DPA, and China's MOFCOM, to name a few. In recent years, there has been an increase in the availability of aid monies to social entrepreneurs as part of an international development strategy to empower citizens, so be sure to check for such resources in the country you are working in.

Multilateral Agencies

Beyond the resources provided by individual governments in their home countries or abroad, multilateral agencies bring together funds from multiple governments around the world, to allocate to specific causes. For this reason, they are also often referred to as intergovernmental agencies. The World Bank and UN agencies are among two of the largest and most well-known examples. The World Bank focuses on poverty alleviation and provides financing and programmatic

---

* http://www.startupbritain.org/.
† http://www.state.gov/e/eb/cba/entrepreneurship/spark/239681.htm.
‡ http://greeneconomy.bio/.

support to governments for sustainable development. Its regional equivalents are the Inter-American Development Bank, African Development Bank, and Asia Pacific Development Bank. The European Bank for Reconstruction and Development and the Development Bank of Latin America are other similar examples. While these funding institutions often finance large-scale private-sector enterprises, they increasingly are supporting initiatives to foster social entrepreneurship in emerging markets all over the world. The UN Development Group includes specialized agencies focusing on specific social challenges. These include UNICEF, UNDP, UNEP, UNESCO, and ILO. Multilateral agencies are responsible for disbursing funds from their member governments within the context of each agency's mission and scope; this often involves partnering with local actors such as social entrepreneurs.

NGOs

Social entrepreneurs may also turn to NGOs for funding. NGOs include any private association organized by individuals having a common purpose. (This includes many social enterprises in fact!) NGOs can either implement their own programs, products, and services or they can provide funding to other implementing organizations to help fulfill their mission. (Some do both!)

As an example, let us look at two organizations based in the United States and United Kingdom, respectively, and operating worldwide. MercyCorps is a US-based NGO tackling poverty and injustice by building safe and productive communities.* MercyCorps operates internationally and its staff implements various programs related to social determinants of poverty and injustice. At the same time, it provides funding to local organizations and entrepreneurs worldwide to help fulfill its mission in the local context. Oxfam is an international NGO headquartered in the United Kingdom that also implements a multitude of programs related to poverty reduction and social justice. Oxfam also partners with local organizations and entrepreneurs in countries all over the world to create solutions to these challenges.†

Numerous NGOs around the world focus on various sustainable development goals and may offer funds to local organizations that can help them deliver their mission. Usually, they will advertise such funding opportunities through civil society media, newsletters, and listservs, so make sure you familiarize yourself with these media outlets in the area you are operating.

Foundations

There is one type of NGO that you should especially be familiar with.

Foundations are nonprofit organizations that were formed for the purpose of funding and supporting other social purpose organizations.‡ This is a type of philanthropy, the practice of promoting and supporting social welfare. Historically, some foundations have been formed by individuals or families and have commonly been referred to as private foundations; well-known examples are the Ford, Rockefeller, MacArthur, Hilton, Moore, Gates, Hewlett, Dell, Clinton, Qatar, and Nuffield foundations.§ Other foundations have been formed by public entities or communities and are com-

---

* http://www.mercycorps.org.
† https://www.oxfam.org.
‡ http://grantspace.org/tools/knowledge-base/Funding-Resources/Foundations/what-is-a-foundation.
§ For more UK foundations, see "A review of UK foundations' funding for international development," available at http://www.nuffieldfoundation.org/sites/default/files/files/NUF1272_Global_grantmaking _FINAL_18_01_12.pdf.

monly referred to as public foundations; these are often location specific, aiming to support a specific geographical community* or, in some cases, a subpopulation.[†] There are also many foundations that were formed for a specific cause, such as the Ms. Foundation, Sierra Club Foundation, and STARS foundation, which focus on working with women, nature, and children, respectively. Increasingly, corporate foundations are also becoming major players in the nonprofit world, as many large corporations dedicate resources to increase their social impact. Common examples from everyday companies include Coca Cola, Pepsi Cola, Starbucks, Nike, Shell, and Google Foundation.

Investment Funds

Investment funds can be private or public, profit driven, or nonprofit. Individuals can come together to form investment funds, pooling their resources and dividing the profits. Banking institutions also have their own investment funds, which individuals or organizations can choose to put their resources in. There are many different approaches to investment, and this chapter will focus on social investment, which we'll talk more about in a further section, but for now, it's important for you to be aware that there are private sources of funding for social entrepreneurs. It's also important for you to be familiar with the traditional sources of funding for commercial entrepreneurs, to understand the full spectrum of financing for start-ups and the different ways in which it is practiced. One of these is venture capital (VC).

VC firms focus on financial growth, not social returns to investment. In most cases, if a VC fund invests in your start-up, they will own a certain percentage of it and will have decision-making power. This is to ensure that they can influence the direction in which the start-up grows, leveraging the experience and expertise of the venture capitalist to help the entrepreneur achieve as much scale as possible and usually as fast as possible. The venture capitalist is taking a high risk in investing in an entrepreneur and takes this risk because there is a chance of high financial return. VC is a much sought-after source of funding for commercial entrepreneurs, but not so much for social entrepreneurs. Private equity is another form of funding you will hear about in the commercial world, but unlike VC funds, private equity funds target larger companies, not start-ups.

Other forms of funding that are more tailored to social entrepreneurs, such as impact investing and venture philanthropy, have developed over the years and have stemmed from VC approaches. We will learn more about these later in the chapter. Many venture philanthropists and impact investors begin their careers working in VC and finance, and then go on to apply those same techniques (analyzing risk, maximizing reward, and systematically collecting data to inform decisions) to social impact.

Individuals

Individuals can be sources of funding for social entrepreneurs, whether philanthropists seeking social return on investment or investors seeking both social and financial return. During early stages of developing your social enterprise, two types of individuals you may want to approach include the following:

■ **Angel Investors and Philanthropists**
   An angel investor is another type of private sector investor commonly sought after in the world of commercial entrepreneurship. This expression simply refers to the idea that an angel

---

* http://foundationcenter.org/findfunders/topfunders/top25giving.html.
[†] http://en.cydf.org.cn/OurHistory/.

investor is an individual with the means to support an entrepreneur, who might be willing to take a chance on you and your idea. It is different from the types of investors listed previously because it is a person, not an organization. These persons have the discretion to decide whether and how to use their own money. They are always on the lookout for people out there to change the world, who they can support, and help make it happen. Angel investors sometimes form networks to bring angels and entrepreneurs together but still operate at their individual discretion rather than as a company. Angel investors usually operate in the world of commercial entrepreneurship, but some are increasingly interested in supporting social entrepreneurs. Most ask for a financial return on investment.

Philanthropists are similar to angel investors but do not ask for a financial return on investment. Their goal is simply to create something new, not to make money. Most philanthropists operate through a foundation (whether their own family or corporate foundation or simply by donating through an existing foundation), but you might still find individual philanthropists willing to support your social venture directly. We will delve into more detail about the different kinds of philanthropists in the social investment section.

■ **Friends and Family**

Smaller start-ups may choose to start with a small round of friends and family funding. This is usually for the proof-of-concept stage of testing out the idea and demonstrating that it works with a small pilot, after which outside funding can be secured. The founders literally approach their friends and family to become investors, usually in return for a share of the financial value of the venture.

Advantages of friends and family seed funding are that it is more easily accessible than some of the institutional routes, and some entrepreneurs find it less stressful, carrying less pressure. However, other entrepreneurs are quick to point out that it can in fact be more stressful to ask for money from people you know, and can carry a different type of pressure and emotional burden.

Some entrepreneurs are tempted to self-fund. They believe in their cause and in their solution so much that they are willing to carry the financial burden themselves, with the belief and conviction that it will succeed and they will be able to recoup their investment. However, this is highly advised against. Not only is it financially risky, but it's also an important part of your journey to success to be able to rally supporters, stakeholders, and shareholders in some shape or form! You need to be able to find enough people who believe in your vision and your ability to implement it enough to invest in you. This is only the first hurdle of many that you will be challenged to overcome.

CSR

Approaching a corporate partner is another option for both financial and nonfinancial support. Corporate Social Responsibility (CSR) is an increasingly common approach practiced by many larger companies and increasingly even by smaller and medium-sized enterprises. Both privately and publicly held businesses might be open to sponsoring or partnering with a social venture. This is based on the premise that in addition to their financial bottom line, they would also like to increase their contributions to the social and environmental bottom lines. Thus, they allocate resources, whether financial, human, or structural, to growing their social and environmental impact in a positive direction.

When looking to approach a corporate partner, think about which business might have a vested interested in your line of work. Look for mission alignment, common interests, resources, and practices related to your venture. For example, a company focusing on the distribution of beverages worldwide may be open to venturing into increasing access to clean drinking water.* An insurance company would be your best bet for partnering on a risk reduction scheme for small-hold farmers.† Large companies often launch specialized foundations to fund and focus on their CSR work, providing financing, expertise, and other inputs.‡

Types of Funding

The types of funds allocated by the previously listed organizations and individuals can come in various shapes and forms, which we refer to as funding vehicles. The most common types are:

Donations

Donations are sums of money given by individuals or organizations to support a cause. Donations can be given in small amounts, like in crowdfunding, or in larger amounts, like in the different forms of philanthropy described previously (whether from individual philanthropists or through foundations). Donations can be given on a one-time basis or on a repeating basis such as monthly, annual, etc. Usually, donations are given to nonprofit organizations, initiatives, or people who are implementing something specific such as a program, service, awareness campaign, or lobbying for a certain cause. In return, the social entrepreneur often reports back to donors, but this is not always required. Donations do not require a financial return, only a social impact.

The word *donation* is often used to describe a hands-off approach whereby the donor provides the money but does not usually get involved in implementation. When an institution provides money in a more structured way carrying more requirements, we then refer to it as a grant.

Grants

A grant is a sum of money given to an individual or organization for the purpose of achieving a specific aim. Grants are commonly given by foundations and other NGOs, multilateral organizations, governments, and aid agencies. In some cases, these are given out for research and development purposes, in other cases for implementation of proposed programs, and yet in other cases for evaluation and dissemination of information. Grants are usually structured in a way that requires the recipient to propose a specific budget, letting the funder know what the money will be used for and by when.

Grants usually require a proposal process, which can vary in length and intensity depending on the funding institution. Usually, this starts with a call for proposals, which is circulated and advertised in the networks of the funding institution and on its website and social media. Networks include mailing lists, development websites, subject-specific journals, etc. Calls for proposals can be open ended (this is sometimes referred to as a rolling application) or can have a fixed end date.

Many grant-giving institutions issue a call for proposals once a year and have a fixed review schedule, similar to a university application process. Others have a less regular schedule depending on their funding and budget situation or their organizational strategy. For example, Rockefeller Foundation has a proactive strategy whereby it actively scopes prospective grantees, depending on subject-specific initiatives. Gates Global Challenge also has subject-specific challenges, but issues

---

* http://www.coca-colacompany.com/stories/slingshot-inventor-dean-kamens-revolutionary-clean-water-machine.
† http://www.trust.org/item/?map=kenyas-urban-poor-feel-the-rural-pull-as-insurance-helps-makes-farming-viable/.
‡ http://google.org/, http://www.legofoundation.com/.

these through an open call for proposals each year. Alfanar has a biannual cycle, with calls for proposals in the fall and spring and sometimes reserves funds for unsolicited pitches which meet its criteria. Governmental and multilateral agencies may issue requests for proposals more frequently than that, depending on programming, congressional budgeting, and other considerations.

The grant application process usually requires the applicant to present a budget explaining what the granted funds will be used for in detail and a corresponding timeline. Indicators to measure outputs produced by the budgeted activities are also a common requirement. Grants are usually found in subject-specific program areas (e.g., health, environment, education, financial inclusion, and gender equity) but can also be found in programs aimed at fostering innovation and entrepreneurship across topics. The most common duration of a grant is one year, but shorter grants and multiyear grants are also common.

Pros and cons of grants depend on the organization they are coming from. Some organizations require a heavy reporting process, especially government agencies and multilateral agencies. A commonly heard complaint among social entrepreneurs is that more time can sometimes be required to fulfill these reporting requirements than to do the actual work! Especially when combined with the lengthy application process and staggered timelines of various grant-making organizations, many social entrepreneurs may find that this can become overwhelming and counterproductive. However, many grant-giving institutions also provide nonfinancial support such as technical guidance and expertise, and these can be found to be a huge advantage. In addition, grant-giving institutions often seek to develop a long-term relationship with the grantee (as opposed to a one-time award), which can also be an advantage.

Awards

Awards lie somewhere in between donations and grants, in the sense that, on the one hand, they carry fewer restrictions and commitments and, on the other hand, they are received at the end of a structured process whereby candidates are systematically compared and assessed based on predetermined criteria. Awards are usually given at the end of social enterprise competitions or in association with specific events. Two examples from different parts of the world are the Clinton Global Citizen Award and the King Abdallah award for youth innovation and achievement.* While the former is a ceremonial recognition that can help to highlight a social entrepreneur's work, the latter is a financial award that resembles a grant. Banks and other commercial institutions are increasingly offering such awards. They are most often awarded as a one-time gift. Awards can also come in the form of free consulting—this is commonly found in social entrepreneurship contests, which are held by universities and other organizations.

Awards are similar to donations in that they are less likely to be associated with specific budgets, targets, and timelines like grants are. However, they are similar to grants in that they are awarded in return for a competitive process, whether the social entrepreneur is assessed for an early-stage idea or a later-stage development that has already shown results.

Loans

A loan is a sum of money that is given to an individual or organization and must be returned. This is commonly referred to as credit or debt. Loans usually carry interest, which means that in addition to repaying the original amount (also known as the original capital), you need to pay an

---

* https://www.clintonfoundation.org/clinton-global-initiative, www.kaayia.jo.

additional amount in the form of a percentage. The percentage can range widely. Sometimes, it is matched to the rate of inflation so that the lender is neither gaining nor losing money. (Because the value of money decreases over time due to increasing prices, otherwise known as inflation, by the time the loan is repaid, it is worth less than when it was issued.) This is often referred to as a low-interest loan. Lenders specialized in the nonprofit sector may also issue a zero-interest loan, which only requires the original capital to be returned.

In most cases, the interest is larger than inflation because the lending institution or individual is relying on this loan to generate an income. However, funders specialized in social ventures usually minimize the interest because their goal is to grow your social impact and they are wary of putting you at a financial disadvantage.

Many social entrepreneurs have a fear of loans because it is money that they are required to return to the funder. Certain cultures around the world are more credit-averse than others.* To qualify for a loan, you must demonstrate to the creditor (the individual or institution issuing the loan) that you have the capacity to generate enough revenue to pay it back. Regardless of the success of your venture, you are still obliged to return the loan.

However, the advantage of a loan is that it can give you more freedom than other forms of social investment such as grants or equity. You are accountable to paying it back, but you are also usually free to use it as you see fit to achieve your social mission while generating the required financial return for your venture and for your creditor.

Equity

Equity refers to a financing mechanism whereby the funder owns a part of your venture, often proportional to the amount of money they have given you. Equity investors are referred to as shareholders. A share simply refers to a part of the company, and a shareholder is someone who holds a part of the company. Types of funders most commonly associated with equity investment include venture capitalists, private equity firms, and individual investors (whether angel investors, or friends and family). Regardless of who your funder is, if you're working with equity the basic core processes are more or less the same.

First, the venture is valuated. This means an estimate is made of the financial value of the proposition you are offering. How much is your venture financially worth? This is calculated according to projected future revenues. Let's say your venture is valuated at $1 million. If a funder invests $10,000 in your start-up, they will own 1% (i.e., 10,000 divided by 1 million). Next, a term sheet is drawn up that sets out the agreement between the funding and funded party. This is similar to a grant agreement and a loan agreement. The terms of the agreement specify for how long the equity is initially held (e.g., three to five years while the venture is growing). After this initial period, the funder may have the option to hold onto their share, if they desire to maintain ownership; or cash out, if the entrepreneur is able to buy back their share by paying them the same percentage value of the company's current worth at the time. This may or may not equal the initially forecasted value. If the company grows more than was projected, the funder will take away a larger financial sum than they invested, and if the company grows less than projected, the funder could end up losing their money. The funder also has the option of selling to another investor, other than selling back to the social entrepreneur.

---

* http://www.ssireview.org/blog/entry/fueling_financial_innovation_in_the_middle_east.

The most striking difference between loans and equity is that loans must be repaid, regardless of the outcome. Whether the venture succeeds or not, the entrepreneur is held liable for the loan, and the funder will get the money back. For equity, however, the funder is not guaranteed to get the money back. The funder simply owns a part of the venture; so if the venture succeeds, they have the option of selling this ownership for cash, but if it does not, then there is no financial return. Another characteristic of equity is that ownership often confers decision-making power (unless this is waived). Of course, in the previous example, 1% ownership does not give much power to the individual funder. However, in many cases, the group of individuals investing in a company can add up to a large percentage of ownership, so that they can influence outcomes and decisions made. Also, some equity investors may impose stringent criteria before getting involved, such as the larger impact investing firms. Therefore, some entrepreneurs would rather take the risk of having to pay back a loan rather than share ownership with funders. Others might prefer the support of equity versus the liability of loans.

Interview Box. Sir Ronald Cohen, Chair, Portland Trust; Chair, Global Social Impact Investing Steering Group; Cofounder and Former Chair, Big Society Capital

TC: Sir Ronald, I was hoping you could tell us a little bit about the latest developments in financing for social entrepreneurship.

RC: It's a revolution in the making, aiming to improve the lives of those in need. The G8 Taskforce, which I chaired, has been succeeded by a Global Steering Group, which includes 13 countries. I've just come from one of its meetings, and what is clear across these countries is the extensive efforts to measure results and to remunerate social entrepreneurs for social outcomes. This is the fundamental idea behind social impact bonds (SIBs).

TC: Tell us more about SIBs.

RC: SIBs are a vehicle for achieving tangible outcomes—improved enrollment rates, improved employment rates, etc. Governments, corporations, foundations, and others can target social challenges through social impact bonds. If the social entrepreneur achieves results, the investor is reimbursed and receives increasing interest according to their success. This has been used by countries all over the world to tackle various challenges such as reducing higher education dropout rates, reducing the rate of diabetes and other chronic diseases, and many other topics. It's replicable and applicable across sectors.

TC: How are SIBs and other new financing mechanisms influencing social entrepreneurship worldwide?

RC: Social entrepreneurs up until now have tended to focus on raising grants and donations. The big change that has occurred since 2010, when the first SIB was launched in the UK, is a realization that if you can deliver social improvements, you can repay your investors. This effectively means that social entrepreneurs can create their own balance sheets to support their efforts by monetizing the social improvements they bring. At the same time, the measurement of impact has led social entrepreneurs using a profit-for-purpose model, as opposed to a not-for-profit one, to define impact objectives alongside financial ones. We've come to define impact entrepreneurship as encompassing two avenues: not-for-profit organizations and profit-with-purpose businesses. SIBs are mainly for nonprofits. Profit-with-purpose businesses can access equity and debt, to pursue opportunities that deliver both financial and impact returns, often innovating through models that allow lower price points for the consumer and require lower capital investments.

TC: What are some examples of innovative financing from around the world?

RC: The best example is the UK. The government used unclaimed assets: they took bank accounts that had been separated from their owners for 15 years and allowed the funds, 400 million pounds, to go to Big Society Capital to invest in organizations funding frontline social organizations. This was supplemented with 200 million pounds from banks. So, an entrepreneur in the UK is now able to go to scores of organizations and social investors to raise money—a range of choices. Japan is now also releasing $800 million in unclaimed assets from banks. Australia is making an effort to set up a financial wholesaler of capital for social impact. So there is a bubbling of activity, which feels a bit like the early days of VC.

Photo from http://www.portlandtrust.org.

Social Investment Approaches

These different funding vehicles and sources can be combined into different investment approaches, depending on the goal of the social investor. You'll be hearing a lot about these different social investment approaches, so you'd better familiarize yourself with the basic definitions of each and some of the major players.

As we discussed in Chapter 1, social entrepreneurship lies on a spectrum between traditional charity and traditional commerce. Where traditional charity involves giving away money for social impact, traditional commerce involves making money without necessarily considering the value of the social and environmental outcomes produced. Social investment refers to the different approaches that lie between traditional charity and traditional commerce, in terms of fueling social entrepreneurship, with regard to both financial and nonfinancial resources.

All of the funding vehicles described previously are considered different forms of social investment. All of the funding sources described also consider themselves social investors. When they provide you with funding or other forms of support, they are investing in you as a social entrepreneur. They are adding their resources (whether money, social networks, or technical know-how) to yours to help you get to the results you're aiming for. It's important that you understand the world of social investment and the different players in order to be able to navigate that landscape.

Crowdfunding

Before we dive into large-scale investors, it is important to mention the crowd. Ordinary people who do not have large amounts of money can still think of themselves as social investors. They can *lend* money to people living in poverty to help them build small businesses (such as Kiva.org, which we talked about in Chapter 1), *donate* to help support an inspiring idea come to fruition (such as the crowdfunding websites described in Chapter 9), or invest their money in social ventures through the increasing number of crowd investing platforms (such as the new Vested .org, which allows investments of as little as $20). All these activities and funding mechanisms are considered social investment: putting resources into a social venture to help it grow and create change. If your social venture appeals to the crowd, then this can be an important source of funding for you. In fact, some social ventures have built their business model entirely on the assumption that crowdfunding is a sustainable source of revenue (see, for example, www .crowdfundhealth.org).

Philanthropy

Philanthropists are individuals who donate large sums of money to help create something that didn't exist before, or help sustain or grow an existing venture or initiative. Philanthropists can help create or support new movements or institutions like universities, museums, theaters, hospitals—or they can support a person or group of people in their work, like artists, scientists, activists, or social entrepreneurs. As mentioned previously, many philanthropists donate through a foundation and others donate individually to different causes. While philanthropists are in it for the social change and not the money, they may sometimes ask you for a financial return on their investment so that they can then invest in other social entrepreneurs as well. There are specialized approaches in philanthropy, with some huge similarities and some key differences.

Strategic philanthropy refers to the practice of philanthropy to achieve predetermined goals by studying what milestones are needed to reach those goals and taking an active role in making sure that those milestones are achieved. Strategic philanthropists are working toward specific social outcomes and thinking about how to invest their money to best achieve those outcomes. We use the word *invest* here to demonstrate that strategic philanthropists evaluate the return on investment in terms of what social outcomes will be produced if they support something. Many foundations practice strategic philanthropy, raising funds from individual or institutional investors (including governmental, multilateral, or private) and channeling those funds to support social ventures, often providing nonfinancial resources such as technical support to help recipients produce a larger impact. Grants are the primary funding vehicle in the large majority of cases. Recipients are required to produce social outcomes, but they are not always required to generate financial revenue, so strategic philanthropy can be a helpful funding source for nonprofits. Along those same lines, *catalytic philanthropy* refers to an approach whereby the philanthropic organization takes responsibility for the outcomes, mobilizes others and uses all available tools, generating actionable knowledge to develop the field further.* Examples of foundations practicing catalytic philanthropy are the Gates Foundation and Rockefeller Foundation, among many others.[†]

---

* http://www.fsg.org/approach-areas/catalytic-philanthropy.
† http://www.gatesnotes.com/About-Bill-Gates/Catalytic-Philanthropy-Innovating-Where-Markets-Wont.

Venture philanthropy refers to the practice of providing financial and nonfinancial support using a hands-on approach over a long-term investment, with predefined exit criteria that the organization is working to achieve before the investor withdraws support. Venture philanthropy organizations (VPOs) maintain a portfolio of investments—social ventures receiving support from them—and evaluate the impact of their portfolio, reporting back to their investors. Investors can include individual philanthropists or institutions (including government, multilateral, and private institutions). Most VPOs require that their investees (the social entrepreneurs and organizations they invest in) generate a financial return; however, the return is intended for the investee to grow, not for the VPO to generate a financial return on investment. Examples of VPOs from around the world include New Profit in the United States, Social Ventures Australia, and Alfanar Arab venture philanthropy; numerous multiple VPOs in the United Kingdom and Europe can also be found under the umbrella of the European Venture Philanthropy Association.* Depending on the organization, financial vehicles used in venture philanthropy can include grants, loans, and equity.

Impact Investing

Impact investors require both a financial and a social return on their investment. This can take place in the form of either debt or equity. Some impact investors, like Acumen Fund and Echoing Green, are nonprofit organizations that reinvest the financial returns into other organizations and expand their impact without distributing any financial gains to their donors. Other impact investing firms operate in a for-profit capacity, distributing financial return to their investors in addition to reporting on their social impact. Private impact investing firms are sprouting up all over the world, where individuals and institutions pool their money for both financial gain and social impact. In between the two is also another type of nonprofit organization that leverages private capital for social impact and returns financial gains to investors, and then reinvests any remaining profits for social impact rather than distributing dividends. A good place to read about the wide spectrum of impact investors is the Global Impact Investing Network (www.thegiin.org).

Private investors are willing to put their money in ventures that may generate less financial return than the commercial averages, in favor of generating social and environmental returns. Impact investors valuate the total output produced: financial, social, and environmental. This is in contrast with traditional commercial investors which valuate only the financial outputs of investees. Each part of the world uses different terminologies and legal frameworks, but the core concepts are the same. In Europe, an investment fund qualifies as a Social Entrepreneurship Fund if at least 70% of its capital is invested in social businesses, defined as having a supply chain or end user composed of vulnerable or marginalized, disadvantaged, or excluded persons.[†]

Socially Responsible Investors

Socially responsible investing is a domain inhabited by investors who come from the commercial sector but want to make sure that their investment activities are not producing social and environmental harm. They are looking for investments that can generate large financial returns (larger than impact investing would) but they are also looking for information on the corporate social

---

* http://evpa.eu.com (includes both VPOs and foundations practicing venture philanthropy among other activities and program areas).
[†] http://www.oecd.org/sti/ind/social-impact-investment.pdf.

responsibility of their investees. They want to make sure that the companies they're supporting have policies and practices in place to ensure that they are reducing their carbon footprint, contributing to their communities, and providing social benefits to their employees. While this is a slightly different field of practice than what this book focuses on, it has huge implications for social entrepreneurs. Socially conscious investors and socially conscious customers who want to know more about the products they are buying play a powerful role in shaping the market.

Finding the Right Approach for You

The social investment vehicles and approaches described above are not mutually exclusive. You can combine more than one at the same time, and you can leverage different approaches at different points in the life cycle of your venture. Awards and donations might be more helpful during the seed stage of your venture, when you're still prototyping, testing, and establishing proof of concept. Grants, loans, and equity will come into play when you want to formally launch your venture. In Chapter 11, we'll talk about different registration options for formally launching your venture. If and when you reach a stage where you need to invest in growth, whether by opening new sites or expanding existing operations, you may need to go for additional funding rounds.

As you grow and your revenue becomes more predictable, investors at the tail end of the social investing spectrum will become more interested. If you can generate enough financial return for both your social goals and your investors, then impact investing could be a good fit for you. This is often the case in environmental entrepreneurship, whereby you are solving a problem that impacts people in both high resource and low resource settings. The volume and distribution of the challenge you are tackling enable you to generate significant financial revenues while implementing your solution and in order to reach those volumes you need to be fueled by large scale investors. On the other hand, if you can generate enough financial return for your organization to function sustainably, but not to generate profit for yourself or anyone else, than you are more likely to find support from a VPO. Many social entrepreneurs may not even qualify for a VPO if they employ a business model that relies on donations and grants to a large extent rather than trading activity; in this case, a foundation employing strategic philanthropy might be your best bet. Depending on where you lie along the social entrepreneurship spectrum between traditional charity and commerce, you will find your match along that same spectrum on the social investment side.

Many social entrepreneurs start on one side of the spectrum, closer to traditional charities, and slowly inch forward along the spectrum until they are closer to traditional commerce. Such examples might benefit from different social investment approaches at different stages along the way. In fact, some VPOs make it part of their job to help you increase your cost recovery; for example, you could start out as a venture that relies largely on grants and donations, and by the time they exit, you might have reached, passed, or approached breaking even.

What you decide to do with your profits will be a huge part of your decision on which funders to approach. Many social entrepreneurs believe strongly that they want to focus all their energy, creativity, and resources toward producing social outcomes and that all profits will be reinvested toward those outcomes. Others feel convinced that profit will drive scale. There is no right answer. The important thing is to find a social investor whose mission and approach is aligned with yours and who can support you in reaching your goals without trying to drive you in a different direction than where you set out with your vision.

Summary and Next Steps

The sources and types of funding and the different approaches available to you depend on your business plan, your end goals, and how you intend to get there. Whatever your model, you will find the right fit to fund it. Be wary of changing your model to become the right fit for funders—you've invested a lot of time, resources, and work (both your own and your stakeholders') to find the best business model to reach the social outcome you're working for. You need to believe in your solution and make others believe in it too. The social investing landscape is complex and dynamic, with different approaches sharing overlapping characteristics, and various combinations of funding vehicles and sources. Navigating this landscape can feel overwhelming, and the surest way to maintain integrity to your business plan is to take a needs-based approach as outlined in your resource planner. Most importantly, make your decisions along with your team, advisory board, and other stakeholders.

How you formally set up and register your social venture will also depend on your business model: your revenue streams and what you plan on doing with surplus revenues are key factors in determining the legal form your organization takes. This in turn can affect the sources and types of funding you're eligible for. In Chapter 11, we'll examine different options for formalizing your venture, whether within an existing organization or by registering a new organization.

Exercise: Funding Your Venture

1. Create your own resource dashboard starting with the template in Figure 10.1 and tailoring it to your needs. Start by populating it with the nonfinancial resources you explored in the last chapter. Next, add the funding sources, noting the different types of funding each source provides. Which resources are available to you right now as you develop your venture? Which will you be eligible for in the early years after launching, before breaking even?
2. Share your results with your team and advisory board. Are they familiar with any of these sources, vehicles, or approaches? Do they know additional ones you can add?
3. Conduct informational interviews with five to seven potential funders, either in person or virtually. This will help you determine whether their approach and requirements are a good fit for you and how you might prepare yourself to qualify as a strong candidate.
4. According to your pro forma, do you expect enough financial returns to qualify for social investors requiring both social and financial return on investment? Incorporate potential funders into your scenario analysis in terms of where your surplus revenue will go if you pursue loans or equity. How will this affect your financial estimates, timeline, and phasing?
5. Do any of the funding sources, vehicles, or approaches specify certain requirements or restrictions that might affect your legal registration options?

CHAPTER SUMMARY

- Social entrepreneurs have a wealth of funding opportunities to choose from and more importantly can catalyze new opportunities. One way to explore your various options is to examine the different funding sources, vehicles, and approaches.
- Sources of funds can range from individuals and private investment funds to corporate funding, government funds, multilateral organizations, and NGOs, including foundations.
- Types of funding vehicles include donations from individuals or awards from institutions, which are usually given with no strings attached; grants from institutions, which are given for specific objectives; loans, which can be provided by either individuals or institutions and must be repaid; and equity vehicles, which confer partial ownership to the individual or institution providing funding.
- Social investment is a growing field in which individuals and institutions apply a wide range of approaches to support social ventures. Depending on the objectives of the funder and what they expect to receive in return, social investment can include more than one of the above sources and vehicles. All social investors require a social return on investment, and some require a financial return on investment too.
- Your social venture may qualify for more than one of these options at the same time or over various stages in its life cycle. The key is finding the right fit for you and your stakeholders, based on the business model you've co-created.
- Like everything you do as a social entrepreneur, don't assume that the status quo of social investment is the way things have to be. Bring together new players, catalyze new conversations, and find new ways of mobilizing financial and non-financial resources.

Social Ventures Mentioned in This Chapter

Company profile: Crowdfund Health, www.crowdfundhealth.org.
Product/service: Online platform linking people who need funding for a health service with people crowdfunding that service by giving as little as $10 per person.
Goal: Remove barriers to treatment by funding medications, transportation, testing, and healthcare for patients in resource-poor settings.
How it works: The business model is premised on the assumption that there are enough people out there willing to crowdfund health services for others and that this is a source of revenue that can be counted on. Health services are delivered by a possible, nonprofit healthcare company that delivers high-quality, low-cost healthcare in low-resource settings. A network of partner organizations manages the financial platform, social media, and other communications.

Company profile: Vested.org, www.vested.org.

Product/service: Online platform where you can make impact investments through Calvert Foundation's Community Investment Note®.

Goal: Fund nonprofits and social enterprises around the globe.

How it works: Calvert Foundation pools individual investments to make loans to organizations including non-profits, microfinance institutions, and social enterprises. Investors earn financial and social returns, receiving annual interest and reports on the social impact their investments create.

Chapter 11

Building the Organization

Now that you've developed a sense of the various funding opportunities available to you, it's time to start thinking about how you will build your venture and institutionalize it for sustainability. The different options available to you will depend on the country you're operating in and on your business model of course. In this chapter, we will explore various legal structures and other components of institutionalizing your venture, including your internal governance and composition.

Legal Structure

When to Register

Before launching your venture, it's worth stopping and asking yourself whether you really need to register and build an entire organization starting from scratch. Is it possible to launch your venture from within an existing organization? It could be a new department, program, or project of a larger organization; a new branch; a joint venture; or a variety of other creative setups. If you're able to identify someone else who's working toward and dedicated to the same mission as you, then why are you starting your own organization?

Setting up an organization is costly. It requires time, resources, cash, legal expertise, paperwork, and ongoing tax and maintenance fees. Not only the setup but also the ongoing costs required to run an entire organization are not to be underestimated. Your brain space alone is a valuable piece of real estate, and if there is any way to free it up from the start, then it is advisable to at least explore this option.

A large part of this chapter will be dedicated to learning about legal options to register an organization and other aspects of creating and growing a new organization. But before we start, know that this is not your only option. In fact, many established and successful entrepreneurs and serial entrepreneurs have advised against it in their public speaking.

This is especially the case for social ventures that will seek out grants and donations as part of their revenue stream. The market will determine whether there is a space for a for-profit venture, and funders seeding the start-up costs of a for-profit are not likely to support it if they do not believe there is a market to keep it going. Too often, however, passionate individuals raise donations to start a nonprofit, without having a vision of whether the work can be achieved without investing all the time and money required to build an organization. Their cause draws attention, but they struggle to build and sustain the organization.

If you are starting a new nonprofit, ask yourself first what value you are adding that cannot be achieved by working under the umbrella of an existing organization, whether it be a nonprofit, government, private, or academic institution. Who has started similar organizations before, and does it make sense to join forces with them? Nonprofits often compete for valuable resources when they could be joining forces to more effectively garner them—whether it be people's attention or funding.

A third option is to incubate within an existing organization and then spin out on your own. This can provide valuable time and resources to test and refine your product or service—time that would otherwise be spent in the red if you are out on your own, before you are able to scale and generate enough revenue to be self-sufficient.

Can you test your proof of concept under the umbrella of a host organization before you spin out on your own? Riders for Health is an example of an organization that was started out of MercyCorps and then later spun out on its own when it became more financially sustainable.* During this time, it benefited from the human resources and existing infrastructure that MercyCorps provided. This included administrative, legal, logistical, technical, and a host of other resources. Even raising money may be more effective if done with a larger organization.

When you reach a stage where you need to register and open a new organization because you will gain something tangible and crucial, then take that step. But don't register and open a new organization just for the sake of it.

Legal Options

If and when you do decide to register, your legal form will most likely reflect your business model. If you are a nonprofit organization, then the most likely legal form for you will in most cases be a charity or association, depending on the country (more later in the chapter). If your organization is a for-profit, then depending on your country or state, you will need to either choose from one of the traditional for-profit setups or register as a social enterprise if that option is available to you.

Many social entrepreneurs aspire to run a for-profit business that reinvests all its profits into growing its social impact after distributing any required returns to its investors. While you may argue that this operation is not for profit, legal requirements in your country may not be developed enough in the social entrepreneurship direction for you to qualify for certain registration options. At the end of the day, many social entrepreneurs feel that it becomes more of a taxation issue and less of a reflection of their business model and social impact model. Whatever the requirements in your country are, let's go through the basics first so that you can get a picture of how it works in most places and then definitely make sure you get a few different opinions from specialized legal professionals.

Charity

In many countries, the legal structure of a charity is suitable for nonprofit organizations, including those that generate revenue. For those with less than 100% cost recovery (that is, where revenue

---

* www.riders.org.

generated is less then expenditure toward the social mission), this is the most commonly chosen legal option.

Each country has its own version of the mainstream charity organization legal form. In the United States, the most common form of registering a charity is the 501c3, which you will find for the majority of nonprofit organizations. In the United Kingdom, there are four main types of charity structure: unincorporated associations, charitable incorporated organizations, charitable companies, and trusts.* Checking for the type of legal registration of leading nonprofit organizations in your country is one way to find out what setups are common in your country—usually, this information will be clearly stated on the nonprofit's website and printed materials. Each country also has its own nuances, and it is important to understand the pros and cons of each option before you proceed.

One of the main advantages associated with registering as a charity in most countries is that if you need to raise money to supplement your revenue-generating activities, having a charity status facilitates this type of fundraising. When individuals donate to charities, they receive tax deductions; this was set up by most governments in order to encourage people to give. Similarly, when businesses and other institutions support social enterprises, they too receive tax deductions, which provide an incentive to help catalyze these types of transactions. Most social entrepreneurs aspire to have enough revenue generated on their own to not require donations at all. But many still rely on this form of funding, at least partly, and especially toward the start of the venture. Others find that tax incentives can make or break their business model! We saw an example of a social enterprise that leveraged this option as a resource in the Daily Table case in Chapter 5.

Some social ventures are able to generate enough revenues to equal or exceed their costs. In most cases, this margin of profit (revenue minus cost) is reinvested in the social mission, i.e., spent on growing the organization toward achieving more of its social impact. If this is accounted for in the annual paperwork of the organization (reports, accounts, government filing), then it can be shown that in fact this is not a profit-making organization because all revenues are directed toward new costs that are incurred to achieve more of the mission. In this case, a charity registration might still be possible in certain settings. In other cases, it may behoove you to explore more options.

Social Enterprise

Social enterprise legal options are nascent and limited in many countries. In the United States, two options have emerged out of the most commonly found for-profit legal options, the traditional LLC and C-Corp structures. The traditional LLC is a limited liability company; this is a for-profit venture designed to attract private investment and is common for commercial start-ups. The newer L3C is a low-profit LLC, which is not designed to maximize profit; its primary mission is charitable but it is still free to distribute profit to the owners. This type of social enterprise has the flexibility to generate profit while being driven primarily by its social mission.

The traditional C-Corp structure on the other hand is common for larger corporations (most major companies) and is different from the LLC because it is taxed separately from its owners. The newer B-Corp has the same tax status but with a purpose of creating public benefit, thus its title as a "Benefit Corporation." The formation of this newer legal option was driven by social entrepreneurs with the purpose of promoting accountability and transparency by legally defining three bottom lines for the organization: financial, social, and environmental. Not all states have

---

* https://www.gov.uk/charity-types-how-to-choose-a-structure.

L3C and B-Corp options. The Flexible Purpose Corporation is another newer option that has passed in California and Washington (where it is called the Social Purpose Corporation). This legal form requires boards and management to agree on one or more social and environmental purposes with shareholders, while providing additional protection against liability for directors and management.

In the United Kingdom, a common legal option for social enterprises is the community interest company (CIC).* This was created specifically for social enterprises and is regulated by the government to ensure that it does not deviate from its social objective. The CIC provides tax benefits to social enterprises that have prespecified restrictions on the distribution of profits. In the United Kingdom, for example, a CIC provides tax benefits to hybrids that agree to limit their distributions to investors. A CIC, once given governmental approval, has its assets "frozen" and designated for general community benefit. Investors can receive capped dividends on their investment, but the principal is never retrieved. Another option is the "group structures with charitable status," which recognize that the organization not only has a charitable mission but also generates revenue and may want to retain some surplus for strategic purposes to sustain and achieve its long-term mission.

For-Profit

The most common legal structure for commercial business in the United Kingdom is the "Companies limited by guarantee or shares." This is similar to the LLC and C-Corp options in the United States. Across countries, some social ventures choose to stick with the traditional business structure offered by these legal options because they allow for more flexibility in the company's internal governance structure and in getting investment. In these cases, in order to ensure that the company operates as a social enterprise, the founders draft their own internal governance structures by incorporating the social mission into the paperwork, whether in the form of a constitution, articles of association, rules, and memorandum depending on the country. For example, a social enterprise registered as a for-profit company will take the responsibility on its own—without government regulation, if it chooses this option—to specify in its internal governance that a certain percentage of profits will be reinvested into the social mission. This percentage can range widely, from less than 10% to 100%.

In most countries around the world, social entrepreneurs do not have many options tailored to them, as specific legal structures have not yet been created for social enterprises. Thus, creating their own clear-cut internal policies and procedures and incorporating these into their legal papers and registration (regardless of whether they choose a charity status or a for-profit status) are their pathway to creating their own legal structure.

Hybrid Setups

Many social entrepreneurs also opt for a hybrid model whereby they register one for-profit and one nonprofit entity. The rationale behind registering two separate organizations is that it provides more flexibility and allows the entrepreneur to benefit from a larger range of funding options, from venture capital to charity donations. This option might make sense for those organizations with a hybrid business model, as discussed in previous chapters. However, the hope shared by many social entrepreneurs is that new forms of legal structures will emerge and grow, which will

* https://www.gov.uk/set-up-a-social-enterprise, http://www.socialenterprise.org.uk/.

provide the same kind of flexibility and consideration for their needs, rather than having to rely on these two traditional options or a combination thereof.

In some cases, social entrepreneurs launch their start-up with a charity registration, and over the years, as they grow and scale, they move on to start a for-profit. This was the case for One Earth Designs, whom we met in a previous chapter. Initially registered as a 501c3, the social enterprise later went on to register as a B-Corp to sell to the commercial market (oneearthdesigns .com) while retaining the charity to support sales and distribution in low-income settings (one earthdesigns.org). Another example is Embrace, the infant warmer, which also began as a 501c3 (embraceglobal.org) and later registered as a for-profit social enterprise for rapid scale of its manufacturing and distribution (embraceinnovations.com). In both cases, the nonprofit owns part or all of the for-profit, a setup that gives the nonprofit power to control the activities of the venture while protecting its social mission.

If a hybrid were to register as a nonprofit only, it could not access equity capital markets because it can't legally sell ownership stakes to investors. But if a hybrid were to incorporate as a for-profit only, it couldn't offer the same tax benefits to donors as registered nonprofits do, even if these approaches lead to the most effective social solution.

Cooperatives

Other options available in most countries include the cooperative structure, whereby the organization is owned by a number of individuals or groups of individuals, known as members. Cooperatives are common in the agricultural sector but are increasingly growing in other sectors, including the service, credit, consumer, and housing sectors. In the United Kingdom, the two main cooperative, legal structures are the industrial and provident society (IPS) cooperative and the IPS community benefit society, also known as "bencom" or "society for the benefit of the community." The former is set up for the benefit of its members (in the agricultural sector this would be the individual farmers) and the latter is set up in a way that it can benefit others in the community, even if they are not members.* While by name the Bencom appears to be structured similarly to the B-Corp in the United States, in practice, it has more stringent requirements to qualify for registration as a society and not as a company, such as including a provision requiring that its benefits will be returned to the community and not its own members. This is not to say the United Kingdom and United States are the only countries with cooperatives! In Kenya, cooperatives are responsible for almost half of the gross domestic product, operating the vast majority of the coffee market, cotton market, and other national production. In Argentina, up to a quarter of the population is a member in a cooperative, and in Columbia, the majority of microcredit is provided by cooperatives. In France and in Japan, 9 out of 10 farmers are members of a cooperative. In Denmark, more than a third of the consumer retail market is held by consumer cooperatives, and in New Zealand, three quarters of wholesale pharmaceuticals are held by cooperative enterprises.† In China, farmers' specialized cooperatives benefit from tax exemption from selected tax categories such as the value-added tax.†

---

* http://knowhownonprofit.org/basics/setting-up-a-charity/legal-forms-for-non-profits-1/industrial-and-provident
 -societies.
† http://www.bsr.org/reports/FYSE_China_Social_Enterprise_Report_2012.PDF.

Variations around the World

Some social entrepreneurs choose to register their organization in the country where they will be fundraising (whether philanthropic or private investment funds) to facilitate these financial transactions. Funders sometimes require this in order to ensure that the investee is abiding by reporting requirements specified by law in certain countries. Social enterprises registered in the United States or United Kingdom but operating in Sub-Saharan Africa or Southeast Asia are common. This is because many funding organizations and impact investors are based in the United States or United Kingdom and have made it their mission to support entrepreneurs around the world.

However, many other options and legal forms are available in different countries. Sometimes, these are still emerging into the social enterprise dialogue and entrepreneurs are not familiar with them. Other times, they are set up by the government in order to encourage social entrepreneurship but have not yet been fully developed to meet entrepreneurs' needs and are not fully adopted. Civilian run nonenterprise units and social welfare enterprises in China are examples of options that have not been leveraged as much as traditional for-profit enterprises yet. In the Middle East and North Africa, social entrepreneurs in most sectors are confined to the traditional for-profit or nonprofit structure, but in the education and training sectors, they have the option of registering the equivalent of a social benefit company.* In India, nonprofit trusts or societies have been historically prevalent in the social landscape, but social entrepreneurs are increasingly turning to for-profit options, such as the Private Limited Company.† A comparison of some of the most commonly registered legal forms from various countries and regions is presented in Table 11.1.

Many entrepreneurial social ventures have built their own structures and groups of structures within these existing options, finding innovative ways to manage the different requirements and tradeoffs of each. One example is the Groupe SOS in France, an association that consists of a number of nonprofit organizations, which own subsidiaries with commercial activities. The commercial activities are built to provide livelihoods for marginalized populations, and profits are used to fund complementary social programs. The organizations formed an executive board with representatives from each of the founding nonprofits, as well as a management alliance to help optimize management across the different bodies, in areas such as finance, accounting, human resources, communication, and other aspects of organizational health.‡

Weighing the Pros and Cons

While many entrepreneurs appreciate the freedom and creativity of forming their own internal structure to define their social venture, others point to the disadvantages conferred by having to choose between a charity status or for-profit status, which is the case in most countries that do not yet have a social enterprise specific legal form. For example, auditing requirements, tax requirements, and other legal specifics will not take into account that the venture is a revenue-generating impact-first organization. This can handicap the organization and have negative implications for its growth.

---

* Jamali, D., & Lanteri, A. (2015). *Social Entrepreneurship in the Middle East*. Palgrave.
† http://intellecap.com/sites/default/files/publications/intellecap_landscape_report_web.pdf.
‡ http://www.groupe-sos.org/en/387/organisation.

Table 11.1   Comparative Overview of Social Enterprises in Nine World Regions and Countries[a]

Region or Country	Common Organizational Type	Outcome Emphasis	Program Area Focus	Strategic Development Base
United States	Nonprofit/ company	Sustainability	All nonprofit activities	Foundations
United Kingdom	Social enterprise	Social/economic benefit	Human services/ employment	Government/civil society
Europe	Association/ cooperative	Social benefit	Human services/ employment	Government/EU/ international donors[b]
Southeast Asia	Small enterprises/ association	Sustainable development	Employment/ human services	Mixed
MENA	Nonprofit[c]/ company	Social/economic benefit	Human services/ employment	Human services/ employment
Zimbabwe/ Zambia	Microfinance institutions/small enterprise	Self-sustainability	Employment	International donors
Argentina[d]	Cooperative/ mutual benefit	Social/economic benefit	Human services/ employment	Civil society/ international donors
Japan	Nonprofit/ company	Social/economic benefit	Human services/ employment	Government
China	Company/ cooperative	Sustainable development	Employment	Mixed

Source: Adapted from Kerlin, J., *Voluntas* 21, 162–179, 2010, and additional sources.

Note: EU, European Union; MENA, Middle East and North Africa.

[a] The listing of regions versus countries table is based on the original analysis of Kerlin (2010). Europe was combined as one region; MENA was added as a region because countries share similar registration options; China was added as a country because legal setups are unique compared with those of other countries in the region.

[b] International donors category applies for East and Central Europe, while Government category applies for Western Europe.

[c] Nonprofit organizations are commonly registered as charities, associations, or civil society organizations and are often referred to as NGOs.

[d] Kerlin uses Argentina as a representative of common registration forms and activities in Latin American countries. Social enterprise legal guides for other select countries in South America can be found at http://issuu.com/nesster.

Investing in a lawyer is crucial when registering your venture. It may be possible to recruit a pro-bono lawyer who is willing to give their time at no cost, or at reduced costs. It may also be possible to obtain legal counsel, or at least information on lawyers specialized in social entrepreneurship, through one of the many organizations that support the formation of social enterprises that we discussed in Chapter 10. Universities also often have legal clinics with reduced fees that are open to students working on registering a new organization.

Interview Box. Catlin Powers, Cofounder and CEO, One Earth Designs

TC: Your organization started in the Himalayan Plateau and has now expanded worldwide. How did you manage this growth?

CP: To be honest, we struggled to meet the demands of a growing worldwide organization. We started off working with nomadic groups in a very specific setting, and we were bootstrapping at the start. The only reason we registered in the US (as a charity, 501c3) was because people wanted to donate and we had to open a bank account! We won awards and grants for our work, and registering a nonprofit organization was a straightforward way to use these resources. But we quickly learned that there are some regions, China included, where government suspicion towards nonprofits hinders can hinder charitable missions. So we set up a for-profit traditional limited company in Hong Kong, which would be allowed to work in China. We chose Hong Kong because we wanted this new company to be 100% owned by the original nonprofit, which would not have been allowed in China. We now have a US subsidiary of this company, which allows us to sell online in the US too.

TC: So the nonprofit came first, and then you went the for-profit route. How does this affect your original target audience?

CP: It helps us reach more people on the Himalayan Plateau and other low-resource settings because revenues from the for-profit businesses subsidize the nonprofit organization. Our US subsidiary is B-Corp, which reinforces our social mission. It's taxed the same as the traditional C-Corp, but the incorporation documents outline optimizing social, environmental, and financial impact as opposed to the traditional C-Corp, which says you're beholden to shareholders to maximize profit. Our nonprofit still sells to rural customers and foundations serving refugees and other marginalized populations all over the world. At the same time, we sell to customers in middle- and higher-income settings who want to use solar power, and we use differential pricing for the different customer segments.

TC: Were there any stages where you struggled to meet the demands of your customers while investing in growth?

CP: We experienced rapid growth in demand for our products, which motivated us to set up a formal manufacturing line to meet demand. To do so, we needed capital. We wanted to engage with impact investors, and in order to do so, we created a sister company which allowed us to expand our operations in China while maintaining strong corporate transparency and responsible practices.

TC: Were there any advantages and disadvantages of operating in all these different places?

CP: Each setting has its advantages and disadvantages. In Hong Kong, we first started out paying 13–15% profits tax, while in China the concurrent laws at the time would have had us paying 33% profits tax with other taxes on top of that, for a total of 45% corporate tax. Right now, we're in the process of expanding our for-profit line to Europe, which presents a whole new set of challenges. Recent changes in European VAT regulation have resulted in different tax rates, and we're required to register in each country.

TC: What advice do you have for social entrepreneurs building their organizations right now?

CP: I want them to know that no social entrepreneur has ever had everything figured out right from the very start. We all just do our best with the information and resources we have at each decision point.

Photo reproduced with permission from Dr. Powers.

Organizational Health

Whether you register your social venture as an independent legal entity or as an initiative within an existing entity, you can still apply the concepts presented in the following sections to yourself, your work, and your team. The main idea behind the concepts presented in this chapter is to think of your social venture as an organism. It is a living, breathing, being and it's up to you to ensure that it's provided with the support system, environment, and nutrients that will nourish it and allow it to grow.

Reflecting on your own life, when you go to the doctor or take your children to the doctor, the doctor examines you and asks you questions and diagnoses you. She or he may give you a mark of good health or may warn you that certain aspects of your health need strengthening. She or he will ask you various questions about your activity patterns and your nutritional patterns and will measure your physiological health indicators and mental health indicators.

So too should you as a social entrepreneur observe and strengthen the health of your organization. In the following sections, we will discuss key points that reflect a healthy organization and how you can ensure that all these factors are in place (Figure 11.1). What does a healthy organization look like?

What does a healthy organization look like?

Vital signs:

✓ Governance
✓ Financial
  health

✓ Institutional
  memory

✓ Transparency and
  accountability

✓ Human resources
✓ Legal and
  tax health

✓ Information and
  communication
  systems

Figure 11.1   Diagnosis: all systems clear for social impact!

Financial Health

A healthy organization has healthy financial systems. What does this mean? We have already discussed the importance of having a solid business model in place, specifying your revenue streams and expenditures. Ensuring that you are well equipped with financial planning, reporting, management, and accounting systems is essential in tracking and managing this flow of revenues and expenditures.

Financial planning means being prepared ahead of time for the flow of cash and other resources into and out of your organization. The reason it is crucial to be prepared is that inflowing and outflowing resources may not always be synched in the same schedule. Depending on your industry and sources of revenue, resources might cycle into and out of your venture at different times. Knowing ahead of time when you're expecting revenues and how much (whether from funders or end users) and when you're expecting to make payments (whether monthly salaries, utilities, service costs, manufacturing costs) will help make sure you don't run out of resources.

Budgeting is a huge part of financial planning. Having annual forecasts is important not only before you start but also for the duration of your venture's life cycle. During the start-up phase, you might be in the red, and that's completely normal. It's important for you to have a plan on how you're going to get yourself to the point where you're finally financially sustainable. And when you do get to that point, you may want to consider having reserves of financial resources on hand to serve as a safety margin. Last but not least, financial planning is critical in helping you determine your growth strategy. Expanding your operations can be a huge investment; sometimes it can feel like being a start-up all over again!

Financial management entails a lot more than planning. It also entails the ongoing management of resources, ensuring that all expenditures and revenues are accounted for and making sure that your venture is abiding by legal requirements. On the accounting front, building systems to facilitate the tracking of revenues and expenditures can be as simple as buying an accounting software platform in which you can enter each item as it comes in or goes out. Some of the newer software allow you to take photos of receipts from your phone and these are automatically entered into a spreadsheet, which you can then manage.

It is highly advisable to have a specialized person take care of the accounting needs of your organization. If you try to do everything on your own, it can not only overwhelm you and distract you from other components of your work, it also can result in less-than-optimal results and hurt your social impact in the long run. Specialized accountants can be either outsourced (i.e., paid for a concrete task, without entering your payroll and becoming an employee in your organization) or as your venture grows, you can have one or more persons join the team to handle your finances.

Financial management as a whole is not something you can do alone. Unless one of your cofounding team members is specialized in this subject area and has previous experience, you are putting yourself and your venture at a huge risk if you don't hire, contract, or outsource this service. Moreover, it can be quite time consuming. First, different funders and investors will have different reporting requirements. Second, as you grow, checks and balances will need to be put into place to ensure that there is no room for corruption. Who is responsible for writing checks? Who manages cash accounts and tracks receipts? How many signatories are there on your accounts? These are all details you will have to keep in mind.

Last but not least, as your venture develops, your financial needs will change. The person who will help you fill out that initial accounting software system is probably not the same person who will help you broker high level deals with banks! Like everything else in your organization, your financial systems and team will evolve over time.

Taxes

Taxes are a topic spanning multiple categories—financial health, reporting, legal requirements, and registration options. As mentioned by Dr. Powers in the interview box, understanding the tax requirements of different countries and different legal forms within each country will likely be part of the decision you take on how to register. This underscores the importance of consulting with legal experts at that stage of decision making. Once you register, staying on top of your tax requirements takes on a whole new level. Not to mention, it affects your balance sheet and cash flow. Managing all this is not something you can do alone, nor should you. It is time consuming and requires you to stay up to date on tax law and other moving parts. Using a certified tax specialist working closely with your accounting person or team is critical. This will *not* add a huge expense to your annual budget and will be well worth the investment.

Reporting

Different legal registration forms have different implications for reporting requirements, with charities and nonprofits often bound to stricter requirements than privately held for-profit businesses. However, regardless of your technical legal specification, as a social venture, it behooves you to share information with the outside world, demonstrate transparency in your financial and social inputs and outputs, and account for your activities and use of resources as they pertain to fulfilling your social mission.

Many social ventures post their annual financial reports on their websites, to account for all sources of revenue and funding, including trading activity and donations, as well as expenditures. Social ventures also report their impact, not only for their own internal M&E purposes but also to communicate to all stakeholders what they are doing and whether it is working. There are various reporting frameworks that social ventures can use, and these can often be found online depending on your industry and location. At the end of the day, it is not which reporting template you use but rather the fact that you are holding yourself accountable to sharing your organization's ins and outs with the world that make you a stronger social venture.

Internal Governance

Regardless of the legal structure of your venture, it is important to have internal governance documents and guidelines. These outline the key principles, policies, and procedures that your venture adheres to and holds everyone accountable to them. Chances are, in the past, you've been involved in a volunteer group or student group at one point in your life. These groups have constitutions that outline the make-up of the organization (officers), the decision-making processes (voting), and the rules by which all members should abide (by-laws). Just like a nation has a constitution that serves as the basis for policy-making and legislation, your organization also needs a constitution. It can be called "articles of association" or might have another name depending on the type of organization and the country you're operating in. The nomenclature is less important than the basic principles, which require you and your founding team to lay the foundation for your organization's growth and well-being.

Your business plan already contains a huge portion of the information required for your internal governance. It states what you'll do with profits, describes your organization's mission, and lays out how all your work will reflect the mission. What remains to be added in your internal governance documents are the rules and processes that will govern the execution of these guiding principles. How will decisions be made? Is it just up to the founding members to decide what is best for their organization? How will new people be hired and other resources be added and procured—do they need to fit certain criteria?

> Transparency is not one component to check off your list but rather a characteristic that is engrained in all parts of your organization.

Transparency

Transparency refers to the flow of information both within the organization and in exchange with the outside world. Transparency in decision making means that all stakeholders know in advance what criteria are being used to make decisions, and by whom. Transparency in accounting means that there is no hidden information on certain costs and revenues. Transparency is a value and an approach that is applied across components of the organization: it is not one component to check off your list but rather a characteristic that is engrained in all parts of your organization.

Accountability

Accountability within your organization refers to "who is in charge of what." As a group, you are all jointly accountable for working together to achieve the social outcomes you've set out to create for your end users. Within the group, layers of accountability refer to the notion of having checks and balances in the decision-making process. This means that there are ways of double checking important decision points to make sure that they were made in accordance with the organization's internal guidelines and having the ability to balance out one person's viewpoints and contributions—whether positive contributions or potential mistakes—to ensure that the organization is moving in the direction specified by its mission and its values.

Specific officers are responsible and accountable for specific tasks and outcomes. For example, finance officers may be in charge of the organization's budget. However, the chief executive is also responsible and accountable for the outcome, and so is the board. If a budget officer makes a mistake, he or she has to answer to it and is held accountable, but it is also the organization's leadership that takes responsibility. Ultimately, the team and its leadership are accountable to its stakeholders and end users. But you're also held accountable to each other, because at the end of the day, you're all bound to your mission, and your job is to get it done together.

Decision Making

Part of building a healthy organization is having clarity on key decisions that have to be made as part of your process map and what the procedures for going about this decision-making process are. In a small enterprise, the owner is free to make decisions as she or he pleases. In a clinical setting, different decisions are made by different people—certain clinical decisions by physicians, others by nurses, and others by administrators. Once you have fully developed your own organization's process map, you will have an idea of the main decisions that need to be made on a regular basis in order to smoothly operate your venture. You and your team need to be in agreement on who makes these decisions, what information is needed, who provides the information, and what the key criteria are for making the decision. This is crucial to an efficient, effective, and transparent organization. The board is usually responsible for making long-term, strategic decisions that can affect the direction of the organization, along with the chief executive. But the information that informs these decisions comes from the troops on the ground. Being clear on what steps must be taken before a decision can be reached will help manage the process and the time frame.

Documenting Institutional Memory

Manuals

The internal governance documents (whether a constitution or other high-level document) refer to the basic principles that guide an organization's direction. But documentation and institutionalization of the main practices involved in running the organization on a day-to-day basis are a whole other beast. This is often managed by creating a set of manuals. Examples include operations manuals (there can be one or more depending on what the organizations' operations are like), human resources manuals (these include guidelines for hiring and firing as well as ongoing monitoring and evaluation of human resources), and training manuals (how to go about preparing newcomers for their roles—this can also be part of the human resources manual in some organization's).

Just like a car comes with a manual, so does an organization!

Depending on what the organization's operations are—what products or services are offered and what the steps required to produce these are—there can be one or more operations manuals. This is usually tied to the size of an organization. For example, procurement is sometimes considered part of operations. Procurement means the process of buying things that are needed for your supply chain. In a small organization, procurement is one step that one person makes. In a large organization, procurement might require an entire department! In this case, it would need its own manual, while in the smaller organization, it would be mentioned in the overall process map, and most likely, there would be one comprehensive manual. Similarly for human resources and training, these might fall under the same manual or be two (or more) separate manuals.

The goal of manuals is not to build bureaucracy and paperwork, but rather to provide written documentation of guidelines and best practices. Just like a car comes with a manual, so does an organization! You have put a lot of work into figuring out the best way to do things, and the next step is for you to document them. Then, they can be revised and updated, and improved upon in the future.

Policies and Procedures

Policies and procedures may be included in either the higher-level internal governance documents or various other manuals, depending on the policy or the procedure in question. Sometimes, these fall into a neat category: for example, we are all familiar with return policies that specify when a purchased item can or cannot be returned from a retail store. This type of policy would be found within an operations manual and would be accompanied by a set of procedures to operationalize it and serve as guidelines for the person implementing and enforcing it. Child protection policies, antidiscrimination policies, and antiterrorism policies often also fall underneath the umbrella of operations but are more likely to be found as clauses within an organization's basic articles of association or other high-level documents because they apply to all components of your work. Standard templates for these documents are available online and examples can be viewed by visiting the website of any large, well-established organization and comparing a few. Spend some time with your team thinking about how these basic principles and values can be incorporated into various steps of your work to ensure that there is no room for unintentional adverse outcomes on these fronts.

Depending on your line of work and the setting you're working in, there may also be policies and procedures that are required by law. Human resources is an example, to ensure that no one is discriminated against. You may not be aware of all the nuances, so it's important to get legal advice while working on your organization's policies and procedures. Sector-specific requirements are also important, such as safety and hygiene checklists. As your organization grows, it's critical to ensure that you have a steady grasp on all requirements and, more importantly, that all incoming staff members receive training on them.

The Board

Why You Need a Board

Having a board in place helps provide some of the checks and balances needed for a healthy organization and adds support to ensure that all its vital signs are stable and thriving. Different organizations use different terminologies for their board depending on the type of organization and the country in which it is registered; it can be referred to as the board of directors, board of trustees, or board of governors. Regardless of its name, the board serves a central purpose, which is to oversee the organization and ensure that it stays true to its mission, uses its resources ethically and efficiently, maximizes its social impact, and follows sound practices in its policies and procedures.

Having a board in place is a legal requirement for any organization that is not privately owned, whether it is for-profit or nonprofit.* Most funders and investors also require you to have a board, and many also require you to give them a seat on the board. This is their way of ensuring that they can be involved in the venture's decision-making processes, directions, and outcomes. Regardless of your legal registration and your funders' requirements, it is your obligation as a social entrepreneur to take the steps on your own to formalize the structure of your organization as a social enterprise. These steps include creating internal governance documents that require a transparent and participatory process for decision making, to ensure that all decisions are made to the benefit of the target audience and are in line with the mission.

Note that the board of directors/governors/trustees is different from the board of advisors we talked about in previous chapters. While the former are responsible for overseeing the direction of the organization, its governance, and decision making, the latter serve as an additional volunteer corps to share their technical expertise, social and professional networks, and other resources.

What to Look for in the Board

The board can be one of your greatest assets—and sometimes one of your greatest headaches! Whether you are a for-profit or a nonprofit, the board can play a combination of roles. Board members can support the chief executive in contributing diverse perspectives and in building new relationships through their social networks and their leadership position in the field, in the multiple sectors that they represent. Having board members from industry, from government, from academia, from business, and from civil society will ensure that you are well represented in different social and professional circles and that you benefit from different points of view when making decisions for your organization. It will also help you benefit from the unique insights and experiences offered by various fields of practice, and integrate best practice from different fields of work.

As a starting point, you want to make sure that your board members have strong track records in leading and governing organizations. Then, when you are thinking about recruiting board members, ask yourself the following questions:

- ■ Who do I want to find out about my work and join forces with me?
- ■ What resources do I need to gain access to?
- ■ What technical know-how do I need advice on?
- ■ What skills or strategies would help me achieve my goals?
- ■ What experiences or perspectives would complement my own and my team's?

Then ask yourself where you can find those people who can help provide these needs and make these links. Meet with business leaders, thought leaders, chambers of commerce, nonprofit organizations, think tanks, foundations, and government agencies. Start with your existing network and build out from there. Your existing network includes classmates, colleagues, friends, family members, and their networks (think outside your own generation). It includes your professors, managers, mentors, parents, and their networks too. Start by meeting with people you think can help, have specific questions prepared for them, and ask them who else they'd recommend you meet with.

---

* http://corpgov.law.harvard.edu/2012/04/15/nonprofit-corporate-governance-the-boards-role/.

Building up to a board relationship takes time and care. Asking too many people to join your board may make it difficult to manage. Moreover, it is important to ensure that board members "play well" together. The last thing you want is for internal politics and power dynamics to develop between your board members, which would interfere with their primary task of supporting and ensuring good governance of your venture. Organize a series of meetings between yourself and prospective board members, and between prospective board members themselves before inviting each to join. This will have the double benefit of ensuring that they feel engaged and giving you the opportunity to experience what it's like to work with them.

Like any role within your organization, write a job description for your board members.* This is used for your reference, to help you think about what characteristics you are looking for in a board member, and for their own reference, to be clear on what is expected. What are you asking for? Typical requests include attending a minimum number of board meetings per year (e.g., quarterly), organizing events to promote awareness about your work, and oftentimes also making a financial contribution, although this is not necessarily always the case and can differ in different countries.

Ultimately, the role of the board is to hold the chief executive accountable. All social entrepreneurs, founders, and other leaders are held accountable to themselves and their teams because they are the ones who set out to achieve their social mission in the first place; but having a body of senior board members to answer to certainly helps to ensure that the risk of drifting from the mission is mitigated, that other risks in general are mitigated by having people both to support you and to question you, and that all views and all potential pathways are explored rather than relying on the judgment and the decision-making power of one person. Accountability means that you have to answer to someone other than yourself. When you report to your board on a regular basis, whether quarterly or annual or whatever schedule you agree on, you will be grilled—they will ask you questions about what you have accomplished and what you have not, why you made certain decisions, and what you intend to do moving forward. They will help you set the bar high and at the same time be realistic. They will make you sweat, and they will make the next board meeting loom like an ultimatum in the forefront of your mind. These are all good things! Just like you study the most before a final exam, having a board to answer to will push you harder.

One of the most important things to keep in mind is to look for diversity in a board. If you fill it with members who have the same characteristics as yourself, you are not adding as much value to your organization. Look for people who have something to offer you that you don't already have. Do they have experience to refer back to that will add to yours? Do they have knowledge and skill sets that you don't? Do they have contacts they can introduce you to? Think of your board as your army; they are the people who will back you and your team members up.

Leadership beyond the Founders

The purpose of taking the steps recommended in this chapter—building systems, processes, and people—is to set up your social venture in an organizational framework that can last without you. As your venture grows, it needs to be tightly managed; this is where hiring the right team members and having solid operational and governance systems and structures come

---

* Sample job descriptions can be found at www.bridgespan.org.

in. While you as the visionary behind the venture were a driving force in making it happen, it's your responsibility to set things up such that they can go on without you. Whether you prefer to be out in the field interfacing with the customer or at the back end setting strategic directions, or both, the everyday and every-year running of the organization cannot be managed by you.

There is a whole field of writing about leadership versus management, and we will not go into that here. Suffice it to say that leadership and management are two separate skill sets and that both are required to grow an organization or initiative. Leadership skills and behaviors are those that focus on setting the vision and garnering support from stakeholders, both within and external to your own team. Management skills and behaviors are those that focus on producing the measurable outputs and the resulting social impact and financial growth systematically over time. These are not mutually exclusive but can be found and fostered in each one of us.

Summary and Next Steps

The goal of this chapter is to make sure you set strong foundations for a healthy organization. Your first goal is for this organization to flourish and thrive and for all its vital signs to remain stable as you roll out operations and start growing so that the structure will be strong enough to withstand pressure. Then, once you've demonstrated that it's a stable healthy organism, you can start thinking about growth. In the coming chapters, we'll talk about options for growth and how to expand your impact. But first, it's important that you be able to demonstrate your impact and demonstrate that you're a viable organization.

Exercise: Reflections

1. Is it possible for you to carry out your work within the umbrella of an existing organization? Is it absolutely necessary for you to start your own organization from scratch to do this work? What are the pros and cons of each?
2. Look up the legal registration options available to you in the country you're working in. What advantages and disadvantages does each confer to you? Would you benefit from registering in more than one country?
3. If you have decided to register a new organization and have chosen your registration form, look up the legal requirements specific to this type of organization. What are the taxation and reporting requirements? What are the industry-specific standards you need to be aware of?
4. If you were a doctor diagnosing the health of your venture, how would you score yourself? Which of the vital signs and systems we discussed in this chapter do you have under control; which are flourishing, which need strengthening, and which are nonexistent? Put together a work plan for yourself: list the steps you need to take and a timeline for each step.
5. Write out a job description for your board members. What would you need from them? What do you want them to hold you accountable for? Make a list of your "dream team" board members. Who are the first five people you will invite, and what is your action plan to recruit them?

CHAPTER SUMMARY

- Starting a new organization is not a given. In many cases, you can achieve your goals by working with others and skip the headache and the overhead of running an organization. Make sure you've explored this option and considered potential partnerships before you open up your own shop!

- If you do need to start your own organization, weigh the pros and cons of different legal registration forms in your country. Talk to more than one lawyer; get a second and third opinion. Registration options specific to social enterprises are rare in most countries, and you'll have to start with the existing legal structures. Learn how they affect what you're allowed to do, how you're allowed to grow, and your tax requirements.

- An organization is a living, breathing organism with several crucial systems working together to keep it all going. Take the time and care to assemble these systems into a healthy structure, since it is the body that will carry you forward in the journey ahead.

- Make sure you know what vital signs will tell you how each system is functioning and what back-up structures you can build to support the smooth functioning of each system. These include financial systems, governance, legal and tax, human resources, and accounting systems, and many others.

- One of these structures is a board. Boards require careful management—be strategic about who you invite to serve on your board, what you expect from them, what you want them to hold you accountable for, and how you'll go about managing these expectations.

Social Ventures Mentioned in This Chapter

Company profile: Riders for Health, www.riders.org.
Founded in 1989, social enterprise registered as charity in England and Wales, US 501(c)3 nonprofit organization, country programs registered as local NGOs.
Product/service: Helps to make sure all health workers in Africa have access to reliable, well-maintained transportation so that they can provide regular health care to the most isolated of peoples.
Goal: Strengthen rural health systems and truly achieve equitable healthcare in Sub-Sahara Africa by providing transportation and logistical assistance.
How it works: Riders for Health manages and maintains motorcycles, ambulances, and other four-wheeled vehicles used in the delivery of health care across seven countries in Africa. By focusing on the "last mile," they ensure health care truly reaches the most isolated. They partner with ministries of health, NGOs and community-based organizations to maximize the local impact and charge those partners a not-for-profit fee to secure their own sustainable progression. They also build on local capacity by providing training and employment opportunities on preventive vehicle maintenance. The emphasis is to educate and communicate that keeping a vehicle running efficiently over time is often more cost effective than repairing one that has broken down completely. Riders for Health are currently ensuring that 21.5 million people in Africa can be reached with reliable health care.

Company Profile: Embrace, www.embraceglobal.org, www.embraceinnovations.com. Founded in 2008, Hybrid Model: US 501c3 and for-profit United States, India.
Product/service: Infant warmer to help save the lives of low birth weight and premature infants in conjunction with education programs to help address the root causes of neonatal hypothermia.
Goal: Advance maternal and child health by delivering innovative solutions to the world's most vulnerable populations.
How it works: Embrace Global forms partnerships with clinics, governments and NGOs in areas were low-birth-weight and premature infants occur in high volumes. They donate warmers to under-resourced communities, and provide training on hypothermia and care for under-weight infants, at each program site. Embrace Innovations is a VC-backed company that is responsible for product innovation, manufacturing, and sales and marketing. They sell products through channel partners to both private hospitals and governments in developing countries at scale. Revenues are also augmented through a branded consumer product e-tailed in the US. Embrace Innovations sells units to Embrace Global at a guaranteed best price for programs, and pays a royalty for every unit sold otherwise.

Company profile: Groupe SOS, www.groupe-sos.org.
Founded in 1984, French nonprofit "Association Loi 1901."
Product/service: A group of multiple social ventures providing social services and job opportunities in the fields of youth, employment, health, solidarity, and seniors.
Goal: To fight against social exclusion.
How it works: Groupe SOS has incorporated numerous social ventures over 30 years in above five programmatic areas. Examples include nursing centers, retirement homes, children's centers; social business serving those in transition from addictions, homelessness, and other challenges; production units and various service businesses run by those with handicaps or disabilities. Operating in 20 countries, the group includes 300 different structures and serves over 1 million people each year. A central innovation is the sharing of resources across these structures to professionalize their activities, pool their expenses, and develop synergies to maximize social outcomes.

Chapter 12

Communications

Communicating Your Venture

Communications are integral part of your organizational development and have already been an integral part of your work from day 1. Communications means a lot more than pitching and networking—it also means creating feedback loops, finding ways to keep listening to your stakeholders, and influencing others. Communications includes the exchange of information within your team, other stakeholders, and most importantly your end user!

Social entrepreneurs are often intimidated by this aspect of their work. But what they don't realize is that they have already done it in so many ways, shapes, and forms! Co-creating your solution is a form of communication itself, requiring the exchange of information in multiple directions. Listening can be one of the most important parts of communicating. Brainstorming with your team and developing your first few prototypes also involved another form of communication to exchange and catalyze ideas. Testing your prototypes then required getting feedback from your end users, again, giving them something to react to and listening to their responses. So, you are already pretty good at this communications stuff. Don't forget that! Because with the gift of confidence and the art of listening, you are already halfway there.

Communicating your impact and deciding on what metrics you'll use to capture and convey that impact are also key components of your communications strategy. How will you make sure that everyone (including your end users, yourself, your funders and other stakeholders) knows exactly what your impact is? The metrics you set in Chapter 7 are communications tools in and of themselves! Writing a business plan—no matter what length, shape, or form you decide to make it—is a form of written communication. It requires you to organize your thoughts and structure and convey them clearly. The business plan is intended for your own benefit, to provide a blueprint for your work, but it will also be shared with your team, your potential successors, and various supporters along the way, whether funders or board members. As we've seen, sharing it with others can take place in different ways, depending on with whom, where, how, and why you are sharing it.

In this chapter, we'll discuss the different components of a communications strategy and make sure that you're using your resources wisely in conveying the right information, to the right people, in the most effective way, and at the most effective time.

What Are the Different Components in Your Communications?

Let's take a moment to step back and think about the various players we need to exchange information with and the different approaches and skill sets needed to communicate with each one. Like everything you do, your communications are strategic. That is, you set a goal and use communications as a tool to reach that goal. Before you start, think about the outcome you're aiming for, for each one. Let's explore the different categories of audiences we might need to communicate, and the different purposes for which we're communicating with each one.

The "Who" and the "Why"

Communicating with Your End Users—Selling Your Product or Service

You've already been communicating with your end users to *develop* your product or service. Now, how are you going to *sell* it? How do you get the word out? How will you compete with all the other products and services that various end users are spending their attention, time, and money on? This involves specialized marketing skills, which include branding, messaging, and advertising. We'll delve into these more deeply when we get into the "what" and the "how" further in the chapter.

Also, once you do attract a customer, how do you keep them? How do you ensure that your customer service and feedback systems and protocols make your end users feel they're being heard? Future iterations of your product or service, adding new products or services to your offerings down the line, and ensuring that your team is constantly responsive to your end users' needs and can convey them to your management and other stakeholders are all part of communicating with your end users. Thus, this is a two-way exchange of information: both getting the word out and listening to others.

Communicating Internally—Information Flow within Your Team

Internal communications is also an essential component of getting your job done right and making progress toward your mission and goals. Internal communications can take place within team members horizontally and can take place vertically in terms of providing feedback from management to the frontline and vice versa, providing information to the board of directors, and making decisions.

How can you ensure that information is exchanged across all the different lines that make up your workforce? Recruiting, hiring, and training team members involve a certain form of communication to help convey your mission and ensure that your values and vision are internalized by each person. As your team grows, other forms of communication become essential. Communicating from the frontlines to the management is essential to ensure that the customer's voice is heard and that all decisions are made with the customer's best interest in mind. This means that the people providing the product or service to the end user (those at the frontline) need to have a way to get information to the people making strategic decisions and garnering resources to build the venture (those in executive positions). Conversely, the executive team members need to make it part of their job to solicit information and feedback from the frontline when making decisions.

Keep in mind that the number 1 experts are the end users and that those directly interacting with the end users have the largest opportunity to understand their needs and preferences. The role of the management is to gather, synthesize, and analyze information about what the end users want and need—not to make their own decisions based on their own opinions and assumptions. The least "social" your venture can be is to have a setup where decision makers spend their time sitting in the board room discussing among themselves and exchanging their own opinions and making decisions accordingly. It is crucial to be evidence based all the way, and it is everyone's job to gather this evidence. Everyone has a role to play. The most strategic approach you can take is to build feedback systems in your organization so that information flows from the end user to the decision maker, and not the other way around.

How to do this? To make sure that your team members are empowered to share their own feedback as well as feedback they have received from end users, open channels of communication need to be built into your organization from the start. This can be achieved through regular meetings, events, and surveys to make sure that everyone has a voice. Comment boxes, online forms, random samples, and other data collection vehicles can help make sure you are able to reap this valuable information within your organization as it grows. Even the layout of your office can impact the exchange of information! Open spaces, shared facilities, and other design aspects can help people interact more regularly, and this can be extremely valuable not only in exchanging feedback but also in sparking new ideas!

Most organizations have an annual review whereby employees are evaluated: there are two opportunities to improve upon this process. The first is to increase the frequency; for example, conduct these reviews quarterly. They don't have to be elaborate or time-consuming, it's just an opportunity for people to share feedback. The second is to make them 360° reviews, which means that everyone is given the opportunity to review others and the review doesn't only happen from the top down.

Communicating with Stakeholders—Reporting Back

Traditionally, in commerce, reporting to shareholders has meant conveying information on your financial performance, which is the bottom line that you are accountable to them for. In a social venture, your stakeholders are not necessarily people who hold a share in your company and are positioned to benefit financially from it. The financials are secondary to your stakeholders. You want the world to know your social impact because everyone who has supported you along the way has done so in order to reach the social outcomes and end goals you have set out to achieve.

Thus, reporting back to funders and other supporters involves tracking your impact using the metrics you've identified in Chapter 7 and also conveying to them the voices of your end users, which are harder to capture using statistics. Make it personal. Don't forget that your supporters include all the stakeholders who made your work possible from the start.

Remember, the word *stakeholder* literally means anyone who has a stake in your venture: when you first set out to co-create your venture, you met with local leaders, most likely including local government, potential opponents, and various parties. These are people you need to continue to communicate with along the way.

Reporting on your impact, your progress, your successes, and your lessons learned is key. Let people know what's working, and let them know what you could still use their help with! This is the best way to keep people engaged. Support is not something you get once at the start; it's something you need to keep garnering throughout your journey.

Be very clear on all evidence and data gathered. Reporting is an opportunity for you to not just show off your successes but also share with the world the valuable information you've collected along the way. This will cause a ripple effect, whereby your work will influence the work of others. This ripple effect is something that has to happen consciously. Think about how you can get information out there that you want others to adopt and propagate, and message it accordingly. This in and of itself will have a huge social impact!

> Think about how you can get information out there that you want others to adopt and propagate.

Communicating Externally—Advocating and Spreading Your Impact

Beyond communicating the work itself to those who have a direct interaction with it, as part of achieving your mission, you'll most likely need to exchange information with people who can influence the field you are working in. Your collaborators, supporters, partners, suppliers, team members, and end users are already part of your value chain. But what about those who influence your work by making (or blocking) policies that affect your ability to reach your target audience?

Thinking back to Chapter 2, we talked about identifying the various pathways and root causes that affect the social and environmental challenges we face. These are complex, and you can't tackle them all in your work. But there are a multitude of opportunities that you can look for—and that you can *create* together with others in your value chain—to influence the social, environmental, political, and economic determinants that underlie, propagate, mediate, or block these pathways. There is a much wider audience to your communications strategy than you may at first think. This includes lobby groups that can work for or against your cause, policy institutes and think tanks, politicians, advocates, and others.

As with all other audiences in your communications strategy, the flow of information needs to go in more than one direction. What information do you need to get to these people and parties? And what information do you need to get *from* them? Pay attention to what they are saying and doing at all times because these will influence your work and your ability to reach your goals. And you may have the opportunity to influence them in return; this is why this target audience is an important part of your communications strategy that cannot be overlooked.

Building a Goal-Oriented Communications Plan

As you can see from the previous discussion, everything you do, say, and share is with a goal in mind. This is why we talk about building a communications *strategy*. Your communications cannot be ad hoc and sporadic. It needs to be well studied and well thought out, planned in advance, and crafted with specific objectives in mind, just like everything else you do!

This is why each target audience mentioned above has been listed according to *why* you are trying to reach them. If your goal is to sell the product or service, you are trying to reach the prospective end user. If your goal is to spread the word about the importance of the social outcome you are working toward, you are targeting other stakeholders and decision makers who can influence policy and other determinants of social infrastructures and outcomes. Other goals include keeping your team well informed so that they feel a sense of ownership and buy-in toward the processes (how we do things) and the outcomes (what we're trying to achieve) and receiving their input and feedback in order to improve both your processes and outcomes in return. Reporting back to existing supporters and managing relationships with prospective supporters—or even trickier relationships such as those who stand against you—are all separate objectives with separate target audiences. Thus, we need to craft different contents for each one: this is where the "what" aspect of your communications strategy comes in.

Interview Box. Laila Iskandar, Cofounder, Mokattam School and A.P.E. Rug Weaving Center (former); Minister of Urban Renewal and Informal Settlements, Egypt (current)*

TC: Laila, you've played many roles over the past 30 years. How did your work evolve from the grassroots level to the policy-making level?

LI: The work itself hasn't changed, but what's evolved has been the awareness and contribution of multiple players over multiple sectors. The challenge was to build the quality and the business model. The rag pickers I started working with in the early 1980s were already there doing work long before they formed a social enterprise. Multiple stakeholders were mobilized to support the "learn and earn" rug weaving center created with the Association for the Protection of the Environment. Later, we formed the Mokattam School with the NGO Spirit of Youth through my consulting firm CID, partnering with multinational companies. This required not only obvious barriers such as raising capital but less obvious barriers such as convincing people of the added value!

TC: How did you go about messaging for different stakeholders, from multinational companies to government representatives and policymakers?

LI: They key is to get people to see past the end of their nose. Many stakeholders in different sectors had a myopic view of what an added value would look like for them. They only wanted quick solutions. The key is to demonstrate that some solutions might need more investment but would bring greater value to them, alongside others. Most people won't work with you just to help others or to help the environment. It has to have an added benefit for them too.

TC: What advice do you have for social entrepreneurs on where to focus their communications?

LI: Build quality in your work before you approach stakeholders. Careful monitoring and evaluation of results is needed. There is a huge potential to create solutions with multiple benefits for multiple stakeholders, if entrepreneurs can bring the different ingredients together. The different resources are already there; they just need to be mobilized and well managed. It takes an entrepreneur to catalyze. But more than that, we need to break silos and see things through a social lens. We need to re-define what business and profit looks like. If it's not social, it's not sustainable.

Photo Source: https://www.flickr.com/photos/foreignoffice/9136952666. Open license under creative commons.

---

* At the time of writing (previously Minister of Environment).

The "What"

Exploring your objectives and your target audiences is only the first step in building your communications strategy. The next step is to figure out the message you need to convey to each one.

Just like you've tailored your solution and its delivery and pricing around your end user, you'll also need to craft tailored messages to each stakeholder.

Messaging

We've already seen that there are many different stakeholders who form a part of our multi-dimensional marketing strategy. We have to position ourselves for collaborators to understand our added value, in addition to our customers. Just like you've tailored your solution and its delivery and pricing around your end user, you'll also need to craft tailored messages to each stakeholder. The trick is to maintain clarity, be concise, be compelling, and be *consistent*. There's a fine line between tailoring your message to effectively get your message across to different stakeholders and maintaining integrity to your core story. Let's talk about some of the important things to keep in mind while crafting each message.

What Action Do You Want Each Audience to Take?

The information you present to each audience needs to be packaged in a way that will get across the key message that you're looking to convey that will result in the actions you would like them to take. For end users, you want them to buy your product or service. For your internal team, you want them to own and inform the process and the results. For other stakeholders, you want them to understand why it is that what you do is so important and how they can support you.

What's in It for Them?

Your messaging is based on your value proposition to each audience. What will the end user get out of this? Why should your team do what it is they're doing, to help get the results you're looking for? What do other stakeholders have to gain if you achieve your social mission—what is their vested interest? Understanding the motivations, needs, and preferences of each party is a key informant to your messaging, so it's important that you dig back to the information you gathered and the analysis you conducted during the co-creation process and throughout your journey.

Stakeholder Ladder

In the world of marketing, a common concept is the stakeholder ladder: this suggests that each target audience will follow multiple steps after they are exposed to your message (Figure 12.1). First, they will be suspicious. "What is this new idea? Why should I adopt it?" they might be asking themselves. If you get the messaging right, they will become prospects. Hmm, they might start thinking, this sounds like it might be interesting to me or benefit me in some way. Once you nail down your marketing, they will become sold on it. For the end user, this is when they become a customer. But this is not where it ends!

Follow-Up

To get them to come back, you need ongoing communication—and it has to be tailored to repeat customers, who require different messaging than prospective customers. Once you can get them to

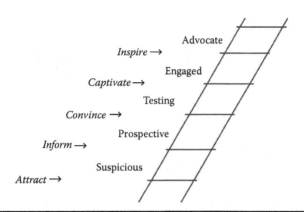

Figure 12.1   Stakeholder ladder.

come back repeatedly, they become clients. And if you can keep your clients satisfied—more than satisfied, delighted—they become advocates and get others to join as well.

This applies not only to end users but to other stakeholders as well. After the suspicious and prospective stages, they test out your ideas and then become fully engaged. The important thing to keep in mind is that your communication strategy needs to incorporate tailored messaging and timing for each of the previous stages.

Multidimensional Messaging

A tool to help you organize your messaging is shown in Figure 12.2.* Here, you list all your different audiences and then create multiple columns for each: Attract, Inform, Convince, Captivate, Inspire. What does it take to grab the person's attention? Where do they read, watch, shop, buy, listen, go? Then, what information do you need to provide to them? Write down at least one key message that this audience needs to know about your product. It most likely will not be a description of your product but rather a description of how it can change their lives for the better. Again, this

Who/Why /→ What	Attract	Inform	Convince	Captivate	Inspire!
End users					
Internal team					
Existing stakeholders (reporting)					
Prospective stakeholders (advocating)					

Figure 12.2   Multidimensional messaging.
Inspired by the Messaging Matrix of the Social Enterprise Marketing Toolkit, with many thanks!

---

* Check out this valuable resource and others at www.enterprisingnonprofits.ca.

is where the importance of understanding each target audience comes back. What do they aspire to? One frequently emphasized social marketing tip is to appeal to people's emotions. How do they want to feel? This is how you'll attract and retain them as long-term stakeholders! Don't describe the features of your product. Do show how it will make that person's life easier, happier, better.

The "How"

Okay, so we've talked about who we're targeting and what we need to do to build the right. But how will we get these messages across to them? Here, we need to talk about the different communications channels.

The "who" and the "why" will determine the "what," which will then help you decide *how* you are going to get your message across. You have many options, and in most cases, you'll end up using a variety of different communications channels, which we refer to as the media mix. The medium is the vehicle or channel through which you get your message to your target audience. Examples include the following:

- Social media: These include your website, Facebook page, Twitter account, and other social media.
- Multimedia and interactive media: Videos and other audiovisual content, usually posted through your social media, can also be on more traditional media such as the television.
- Publications: These include both print and online publications. Print publications include brochures, which are still very important. These explain what you do, how you do it, and how people can get involved (either as an end user or other stakeholder). Other publications include reports, research, thought leadership, articles, and blogs.
- Mailing lists: Maintaining an updated and active mailing list is a must, and this usually includes both electronic and paper mail.
- Face time: You also have to just get out there and talk to people. This can take place through conferences or other events, through smaller group meetings, and through one-on-one meetings.
- Surveys and feedback forms: Some communications channels are specialized in getting information *in* as opposed to *out*. This is how you build systems to help make sure you keep listening and responding to your customers and other stakeholders. Nothing beats face time, but you can't meet with everyone, so these other forms of gathering input are needed.

What you should know about each one of the above communications channels:

Social Media

Social media can be tricky because it can just as easily work against you as it can work for you. Marketing gurus always point to the importance of carefully managing your content and thinking about unintended consequences of everything you put out there for the whole world to see. The crowd can go either way! Social media is not something you should be doing yourself. When you first start, the cofounders may well be posting their first few updates. But as you grow, as soon as possible, it is critical to get someone specialized in social media to join your team. This person can be part time, or a consultant, or might even be a volunteer. They need to have specific skills to achieve specific outputs, such as the following:

- Grow your number of followers and likes.
- Respond to both positive and negative feedback.
- Strategically post content for various target audiences, to get them to move up the stakeholder ladder.
- Collect and synthesize real time information, updates, and photos from the field, co-creating the content with the people who matter the most!
- Manage and balance the different types of information and the different sources and make sure that all your social media are "synched" in terms of being regularly updated and consistent with each other yet complementary rather than repetitive.

These require specialized skills and social media can be challenging to maintain and manage, so make sure you've got someone supporting you on this! One of the trickiest things about social media is how rapidly it is evolving. While this book might refer to Facebook, Twitter, Instagram, and other forms of social media, by the time it is published and you read it, these might be outdated, and there will be others grabbing people's attention! So make sure you have the capacity you need to stay up to speed on social media.

Multimedia and Interactive Media

Short videos are a powerful way to get your message across and can often be part of your social media strategy. Podcasts, whether audio or audiovisual, are another medium that you can leverage. Conducting interviews on television and posting videos from the field online are also examples of leveraging multimedia. Again, it is important to have specialist guidance in creating and disseminating these materials. Incorporating the most effective music, messaging, length, and punch line requires a special talent and skill set!

Your website is one of the most powerful communication channels you might come across. All other channels will point to your website. People will search for you online and visit your website when they hear about you. So make sure it is interactive. Your website cannot read like a brochure! It needs to have updates from the field, blogs from your team and end users if possible, photos, videos, testimonials, news updates, thought leadership, research, and publications. Ideally, you might want to have a live chat function so that people can make inquiries and receive responses in real-time. Someone on your team needs to be in charge of maintaining your website at all times. Most likely, this will be your social media person to start. As you grow, you may likely have more than one person involved in communications. Ideally, you'd like to have a communications strategist thinking about what needs to get out there, to whom, and why. This person can then be supported by one or more team members who are in charge of implementation—posting, updating, and making sure that everyone is kept up to speed.

Publications

As part of making your media mix interactive, you need a publication plan. First, make sure you have a good old fashioned brochure to put in people's hands. Some people just need to have something printed that they can hold in their hands! Your brochure should be simple and streamlined and include specific examples of what you offer—like a menu—but not too crammed with information. It needs to contain contact information and "action points" that people can take if they want to get involved, whether as an end user, supporter, advocate, supplier, or other form of stakeholder.

Then, start thinking about what else you can publish. You are out there on the cutting edge of the field, generating new ideas and finding new ways of doing things. This is called thought leadership. While your work most certainly speaks for itself, you have an opportunity to create a ripple effect not only through your own work but also by informing and inspiring the work of others. Sharing blog posts from the field, discussing what you are struggling with, what works, and what doesn't, is as important as the more official quarterly or annual reports you release. Publishing articles on your website, on other websites, and in journals is another way to get information out there, although this requires more work and careful review. This is another point when it becomes crucial to have a communications strategist supporting you. Publications will always remain out there for everyone to read, so another pair of discerning eyes is a must.

Mailing Lists

> While your work most certainly speaks for itself, you have an opportunity to create a ripple effect not only through your own work but also by informing and inspiring the work of others.

Yup, mailing lists are old school, but they still work! If someone sees a post from you out there on social media, an interview on TV, and a video online, those are all great—but it's not the same as seeing your name in their inbox. Both electronic and print newsletters could be helpful to convey information and to give people a sense of being part of your community, depending on the setting you're operating in. Three important points to keep in mind here are that it's important not to overdo it (neither in the frequency of mail-outs nor in the content included), that timing is everything, and that an action item is required.

Annual, biannual, or at most quarterly mail-outs are advised. In very rare cases are monthly mail-outs advisable. Or, mail-outs can be scheduled according to special events and calendar dates that are specific to your work. Examples are holidays and subject-specific days when the international community focuses on one topic such as earth day, children's day, women's day, etc.* If you're starting a new phase of growth or reaching a new milestone, then this could also be a strategic time for a mail-out, especially when fundraising needs are anticipated.

In terms of content, keep it simple and catchy. A photo is a must. Bold points of the key messages are highly recommended. Last but not least, give people an action item. Whether it's buying something, donating, sharing with friends, attending an event, taking a survey, let people know what they can do to help. Thanking them for their support (even if they haven't given it yet!) is always recommended—positive reinforcement is an effective route to getting and keeping people engaged.

> Positive reinforcement is an effective route to getting and keeping people engaged.

---

* A list including these and many more can be found at http://www.un.org/en/sections/observances/international-days/.

Face Time

No, we're not talking about the iPhone app. We're talking about good old-fashioned handshakes and looking people in the eyes. You've got to pound the pavement! Speaking at or attending conferences and other events, organizing smaller group meetings such as panels or round tables, and proactively scheduling one-on-one meetings are all part of your communications strategy.

Matching this and following up on this with other channels of communication is a must. E-mailing people after you meet with them, sending them newsletters (whether electronic or print), sending them free samples, inviting them out to the field…these are all examples of ways to engage people, retain their attention, and build their level of interest over time, until they are committed supporters.

Interpersonal interaction is one of the most important channels of communication, and although it takes the most time, it is part of what makes your venture a social venture: interacting not only with prospective supporters but also with your end users. As your organization grows, make sure you still find the time to get back to where it all started—with your end users. Spending time with the people you're serving is one of the most important parts of any communications strategy.

Creating that experience for others is also an effective way to garner support. Rather than telling stakeholders about your work, show it to them. Videos are great, but if you can get someone out to the frontline, do it.

> Creating that experience for others is also an effective way to garner support. Rather than telling stakeholders about your work, show it to them.

In other situations, it might help to bring people together to discuss your work. Creating your own conferences, workshops, round tables, fundraisers, or other events is part of your communications channels and these are different ways of reaching and interacting with different stakeholders. Just make sure to keep in mind the objectives you've set—these will drive the time, resources, and content you put into each interaction.

Surveys and Feedback Forms

While nothing can replace face time, it is impossible to meet with each and every stakeholder. This is why it's crucial to create systems to gather feedback to complement interpersonal interaction. Simple tools you can use to invite input from your end users, supporters, or other stakeholders include surveys and feedback forms. These can be disseminated online or in print. Your M&E team will play a crucial role in developing and implementing this part of your communications strategy.

Evaluate Your Communications

Just like every other component of your social venture, your communications need to be evaluated. What are the intermediate indicators that you're trying to reach? How is each one tied to your end goal, the social outcome you're working to change? Are you trying to get more followers and likes on social media as an indicator that you're increasing awareness of your work? And what is your target—how many followers and likes, and by when? In most cases, your targets will stem directly from your market research, for example, building on the potential first-time customers and repeat customers you're aiming for. Make sure to check in regularly to evaluate the outcomes of your various communications messages and media. Setting targets as part of your communications strategy will help you track and evaluate your progress. If you are putting a lot of time and paying someone a lot of money to work on something but it's not getting the results you need to help you meet the objectives you set, then maybe you need to rethink it!

Over time, each social venture will gather its own communications data to learn what works best for its topic, audiences, and objectives. Throwing an annual event might work for one organization, while sending letters in the mail might work better for another. This is why it's important to set objectives for your communications strategy—why are you communicating with each target audience, what do you need them to do in order for you to reach your ultimate goals—so that you can go back and measure progress toward those objectives and determine whether you're going about reaching them in the most effective ways.

> Whatever setting you're working in, don't try to import ideas from the outside. Look around you and see where people spend their time, money, and attention.

Different Strategies Needed for Different Settings

Reaching audiences in an urban setting is completely different from reaching audiences in a rural setting. In the first, most people are overstimulated and constantly bombarded with information, and it's hard to get their attention! They're also more likely to use electronic resources rather than print. In the second, you may experience completely different challenges. It might be really hard to get the word out!

It also varies by culture and by parts of the world. One social enterprise started printing its ads on calendars and distributing the calendars when they found out that people in their community loved calendars! Another used a traditional troubadour to help spread the word. Yet others used outdoor events, plays, and music to reach their end users.

Whatever setting you're working in, don't try to import ideas from the outside. Look around you and see where people spend their time, money, and attention. What brands are considered desirable? Get to know what people believe in and what they trust and make sure your product or service, and the messaging and branding that goes with it, embodies those values.

> Get to know what people believe in and what they trust, and make sure your product or service, and the messaging and branding that goes with it, embodies those values.

Different Skills Needed for Different Stages

As you've probably noticed by now, communications are not something you can execute on your own! You need to hire skilled talent that will differ for each component of your strategy. The first step is developing that strategy! One of the most valuable investments you can make is to work with someone specialized in developing communications strategies. This is the CCO we talked about in Chapter 6. If you don't have that person or that skill set on your founding team, you might want to consider working with a consultant.

Once you've developed the strategy, you'll also need specialized support to implement it effectively. When you're first starting, it's a good idea to outsource specific tasks or deliverables on a part-time or consulting basis to people specialized in each need. As you grow, you may want to start considering hiring specialized officers, but keep in mind that it's not every person that can have all the different skills required for the various components of communications.

Skills needed can be divided by communications channels and by communications goals. As we've seen, different communication channels include social media, awareness campaigns, events, individualized/tailored outreach efforts, short films, and physical advertising products. Different communications goals include building awareness, gaining customers, securing stakeholder collaboration, fundraising, advocating for policy changes, or internal exchange of information. And the latter can be for multiple purposes too, ranging from training to internal coordination for operations, to M&E, financial/social/environmental assessment, etc. The person who is going to get your number of Twitter followers up from 1,000 to 10,000 is not the same as the person who is going to organize a gala dinner to raise a six-digit sum of money—and this in turn is not the same as the person who is going to produce a short and catchy film for crowdfunding!

You will need these various skill sets at different points along your journey. This is why it's important to have a well thought-out communications strategy and work plan, to know what action is needed and when, for you to reach your goals.

Social entrepreneurs and founders can be thought of as "evangelists" promoting their cause,* and part of the communications strategy entails developing a work plan to conduct meetings with high-impact individuals and institutions who can help further the cause. But the founding team can't be everywhere at the same time and have other functions to fulfill in addition to rallying support for their venture. This is why it's so important to invest time and money in recruiting and retaining top talent to help develop and implement your communications strategy.

Most social entrepreneurs are focused on the social change they're working to produce and don't have the skills needed for branding and communications: you need to entrust yourself to a skilled professional for communications, just like you have for legal advice, financial management, accounting, and other components you may not necessarily be specialized in. Many design firms can manage the entire branding process for you, from the identity (name and logo) to the website, letterhead, brochures, business cards, etc. Some specialized firms offer discounted rates for social entrepreneurs, and some might even do it at no charge, what we refer to as pro bono. Others might hold "Brandathons," where they offer start-up organizations an opportunity to compete for their services for free. In most cases, you'll be able to secure discounted or volunteered resources, but even if you aren't able to, this is one of the best investments you can make.

Tips and Pointers across Audiences, Media, and Messages

Be Positive

Key tips from the marketing world are to always keep it aspirational and tell a story. People are more likely to respond to positive inspirational stories that make them feel that change is

---

* http://www.ssireview.org/articles/entry/freeing_the_social_entrepreneur.

possible, rather than depressing news. Sounding an alarm will be less likely to invoke action than sending out a well thought-out, positive message. Think about how you would respond to a headline reading "Climate change is out of control!" compared with a headline reading "Did you know that by following these simple steps you can make a huge difference?" While the first is alarming, the second is calming. The first evokes a negative feeling; the second evokes a positive feeling. Rather than feeling anxiety, a sense of foreboding, perhaps even irritation and anger at the state of the world today, the recipient feels empowered to do something about it.

> Most of the people you're trying to get any message out to don't have the full picture the way you do—any information you share with them is simply a snapshot that they ingest and try to build a picture around.

Be Thoughtful

One of the main reasons underlying the importance of developing a communications strategy is the importance about being very careful about what you communicate and to whom and when. Social media is not the only mode of communication that can turn against you!

Most of the people you're trying to get any message out to don't have the full picture the way you do. Any information you share with them is simply a snapshot that they ingest and try to build a picture around. So you need to be very, very careful about how you present information, how you create context, and how you preempt any misunderstandings or miscommunication.

This is another opportunity for you to co-create communications materials with your stakeholders. What do your end users have to say? What do your teammates have to say? What do other stakeholders have to say, and what do they think about the content you have drafted? Bounce your ideas off people, take suggestions, run any messages or materials by multiple audiences, and test them out—like everything else that you do!

Keep It Personal

Another pointer is to focus on a person and tell his or her story. While numbers are absolutely critical in helping you to formulate your solution, sometimes they can feel overwhelming to others when you issue a call for action. If a person is told that millions of children are dying before the age of five, they will more likely than not feel extremely depressed, hopeless, and frustrated. But if they are told that a child named Maya who lives in a town named Victoria survived to celebrate her fifth birthday because of your work, they are more likely to become supporters. People don't like feeling down! They might even start avoiding you and ignoring your calls for help. So tell them what they can do to help, and make them feel great about it! This applies to your team members, your end users, and people you are trying to rally for support.

Keep It Simple

This is a tip you have heard before: less is more! Don't bombard people with information. This applies both to the frequency and content of your communications. Of course, this varies across communications channels and across audiences as well. An obvious example is the frequency of social media posts, which can be multiple times per day, versus mail-outs, which can be a couple of times a year.

> People are already bombarded with so much information that they are constantly screening things out. So keep it simple—otherwise you might just get screened out.

When in doubt, go back to the key messages from your matrix in Figure 12.2. What are the top one to three messages that you want people to retain? Adding more information might prevent them from focusing on the most important points you want them to think about. People are already bombarded with so much information that they are constantly screening things out. So keep it simple; otherwise, you might just get screened out.

One exception might be internal communications, where the value of transparency and a participatory approach could indicate that the opposite could be true at times. This is important to build a sense of ownership and buy-in across the team, all the way up to the board. Still, even in such scenarios, it's important that information is carefully curated and presented in a way that meets your objectives. You always still need to think about what key messages you want your audience to retain, without exception. A great way to balance this out is to offer more detailed information (such as the raw data) in a separate channel (like an appendix, a separate file, or a detailed report that can be downloaded separately) and focus on highlighting the key messages more proactively. Passive versus active recipients are important to think about here. For passive recipients, highlight key messages. For active recipients, make more information available.

> You always still need to think about what key messages you want your audience to retain, without exception.

Evoke Emotion

Many of you know the famous quote by the author Maya Angelou, who said, "People will never forget the way you made them feel." Information is easily forgotten. Data, statistics, facts, and figures are hard to retain and remember. But emotion is something that stays with us. Inspiring people, making them feel hope, making them feel useful, that they are making a difference are the best ways you can get them involved. Whether you are thinking about garnering support or selling your product or service, ask yourself this question: How do people want to feel?

Most people just want to feel happy. If they feel that your product or service will generate happiness for them and their loved ones, then you are connecting it to the most basic need of the human race. And that is what social entrepreneurship is all about.

Summary and Conclusions

Your communications strategy determines what, why, when, how, and to whom you exchange information (Box 12.1). Writing your business plan and sharing it with others are part of your communications strategy! Co-creating with the community in a constant and evolving way and gathering feedback from end users and teammates and other stakeholders in your value chain are all also part of your communications strategy! Presenting your work to potential supporters, opponents, or the general public is something that you are now starting to do after these previous preliminary stages. So make sure you have the right communications team to help you do this in a goal-oriented, effective manner.

There are a wealth of resources specialized in communications and marketing that you can refer to for more information. To prevent you from being overwhelmed by everything a quick Internet search will have to offer, a few favorites are shared in Box 12.2. These have been selected because they are fun, simple, to the point, and largely tailored for social entrepreneurs (Box 12.2). The goal of this chapter is not to make you a messaging expert but rather to make sure you're aware of the different forms of communications you need to think about and the different skills needed. No chapter—and no book for that matter—could possibly teach you all the communications skills you need for every communication function! And you shouldn't be the one doing all this on your own in the first place. For now, use the framework described in this chapter to help you get started in building your communications platform and team.

Exercise: Your Communications Strategy

Use the framework in Box 12.1 to outline your communication strategy:

1. For what purposes do you need to exchange information with the outside world and within your venture? List the different objectives of your communications.
2. For each objective, list the audience. Who do you need to exchange information with to reach this objective?
3. For each audience group, what are the key messages you need to get across? List one to two key messages for each audience group.
4. Now step back and assess whether the same audience group has been listed multiple times in your previous outline. Extract the key messages you are trying to get across to them. Are there any missing pieces in your messaging for each audience group? Review Figures 12.1 and 12.2 to determine whether your strategy is complete for each audience.
5. How will you get the message across at each stage? List the different channels and media mix for each message. Indicate the timing and frequency of each: when and how often will you deploy each message?
6. Once you have evaluated your messaging needs and channels for each audience, go back and reorganize them chronologically. Make a work plan for each month, by week. Who will be responsible for implementing different parts of the work plan?

BOX 12.1 WHAT DOES A COMMUNICATIONS STRATEGY LOOK LIKE?

1. Objectives—the "why?"
   Why do we need this information to be exchanged? What are we hoping to accomplish?
2. Audiences—the "who?"
   Who are the different stakeholders we need to exchange information with?
3. Messaging—the "what?"
   What are the key messages we need to reach each audience for our objectives?
4. Media mix—the "how?"
   How are we going to get these messages across? This includes timing—the "when"

Cross-cutting guidelines: create feedback loops so that the exchange of information flows in, out, within, and across your social venture. This includes evaluating the implementation and results of your communications strategy and whether it is helping you achieve your goals.

BOX 12.2 RECOMMENDED RESOURCES—A FEW FAVORITES

Marketing strategy:

"Marketing for Social Entrepreneurs: A How-To Guide" by UnLtd* (see p. 5 for more resources)
"Social Enterprise Marketing Toolkit," with video modules and downloadable worksheets[†]
"The Universal Marketing Structure"[‡]

Social media tips:

Five tips for social entrepreneurs, from a team member of Ashoka Changemakers[§]
Measuring benefits from social media[¶]
Tips for nonprofits (applicable to for-profits too!)[**]

Bonus: Pitching and presenting:

http://www.sethgodin.com/freeprize/reallybad-1.pdf
http://unreasonable.is/your-elevator-pitch-is-way-too-long
http://women2.com/2014/07/16/10-tips-5-million-dollar-demo-day-pitch-google/

---

* http://www.setoolbelt.org/system/files/resources/marketing_1934.pdf.
[†] http://www.socialenterprisecanada.ca/en/toolkits/strengtheningtoolkit/nav/Marketing.html.
[‡] http://www.huffingtonpost.com/ira-kalb/marketing-the-missing-ing_b_6973658.html.
[§] http://www.theguardian.com/social-enterprise-network/small-business-blog/2013/may/23/social-media-five-lessons-entrepreneurs.
[¶] https://hootsuite.com/resources/white-paper/8-tips-for-social-business (note: this is not an endorsement of Hootsuite).
[**] http://www.nten.org/article/21-social-media-tips-for-nonprofits/.

CHAPTER SUMMARY

■ As a living, breathing organism, your social venture has various communication needs. Exchanging information with your end users, internal team, suppliers, supporters, and other stakeholders takes place at various points in your life cycle and operational cycle, using multiple modes of communication.

■ As a strategic social entrepreneur, you need to develop a proactive communications plan. This includes identifying the different purposes and objectives you aim to reach with these exchanges of information. Why are they needed, and who are the different audiences for each one? What are the different messages needed for each audience to achieve each objective? How and when will you get these messages across?

■ Messaging is tailored to each audience within each objective. The same audience might have different messages tailored to them at different stages of your relationship. This is how people move up the stakeholder ladder and become drivers of success for your venture. This applies to everyone who is already in your value chain and to those who are not yet but whom you are aspiring to work with.

■ A combination of different communication channels is needed to convey these different messages at different points in time. Depending on the media mix and skills required, you'll need different team members to help build and implement your strategy.

■ General rules of thumb across messages and channels are to focus and tailor your messages, keep it simple, keep it personal, and evoke emotion. Combine the power of data with the power of the human story. If you can make people feel that they can be part of creating positive change, then you will be well on your way to reaching your goals.

Social Ventures Mentioned in This Chapter

Company profile: A.P.E. Rug Weaving Center, www.ape-egypt.com.

Product/service: Hand-loom rugs and patchwork items created by recycled textiles.

Goal: Provide learning opportunities in conjunction with earning opportunities to women who were not able to complete school because they left to work the garbage route in Mokattam "garbage village" in Cairo, Egypt.

How it works: Built as a project within the Association for the Protection of the Environment in Egypt, the Rug Weaving Center was funded by profits from a predecessor composting project. Partnering with the private textile sector in Egypt to secure rags, the project trains mothers in creating high-quality marketable products, alongside literacy classes, health awareness training, and empowerment to deal with culture-specific matters such as female circumcision, early marriage, and others. Trainees graduate and go on to produce from their homes.

Company profile: Spirit of Youth, http://soyzabaleen.blogspot.com.
Product/service: Education and livelihood opportunities for youth garbage recyclers in Cairo, Egypt.
Goal: Educate marginalized youth to earn income and improve their environment through playing constructive roles in their communities.
How it works: Founded by several sons and daughters of garbage collectors in the same garbage city as Kamel's rug weaving center, Spirit of Youth is an NGO that has formed numerous collecting companies through strategic partnerships with other recycling communities in Greater Cairo. The NGO works with youth recyclers to provide certified literacy training and has recently launched an e-waste recycling venture providing computer assembly and repair using electronic waste. The recycling school was established by CID Consulting four years before Spirit of Youth NGO was established. It was housed in an existing NGO in 2000 then moved to Spirit of Youth in 2004. It was designed around the recovery of shampoo containers that were refilled in the fraudulent low income popular markets.

Chapter 13

Managing Growth

Once you have set up a healthy organization and feel confident about its vital signs, you can start thinking about taking the next step and pushing your impact further. Now, we enter the growth stage. Growing your impact means graduating from your initial piloting and launching stages; scaling your operations, your volume, and your reach; and more importantly reaching beyond the confines of your own operations to build strategic partnerships with others, to collectively transform together the face of the social challenge you set out to change.

PART ONE: ACHIEVING SCALE

Dimensions of Growth

The first dimension of growth is scaling your existing operations. Let's say you reached 100 people in your pilot. What happens next? You may have set ambitious targets for yourself while planning your venture, but what considerations do you need to be aware of when the time comes to implement your growth plan?

Growing your impact is not always as simple as increasing your level of activity to reach more people. First, the increase in activity is not always linear in proportion to the increase in impact. For example, hiring a new person or opening a new point of service does not mean you will provide the exact same number of products or services as did the last person you hired or the last point of service you opened. Second, there are so many directions you can grow in. This could mean expanding your geographic scope (reaching different places) or expanding your demographic scope (reaching different people), both of which will expand your *breadth* of impact. It could also mean expanding the range of your products and services, which could expand the *depth* of impact (Box 13.1).

Third, moving beyond these dimensions, you will most likely wish to consider expanding *outside* your own venture. This means partnering with others, thinking about ways in which your work and your goals can influence different stakeholders, and maybe even venturing to tackle some of the different pathways or root causes related to the challenge you are addressing. Creating networks to lobby or advocate for social policy is an example of expanding your impact outside your own venture. These are all considered different dimensions of growing your impact.

BOX 13.1 WHAT DOES IT MEAN TO GROW YOUR SOCIAL VENTURE?

Expanding your venture can happen in different ways:

- Increasing the number of people you reach.
- Increasing the impact you have on each person you reach.
- Increasing the scope of your social impact, beyond your direct end users.

Expanding the breadth and depth of your services can happen through multiple pathways:

- Increasing your market share in your existing market.
- Adding new products or services for your existing customers.
- Entering new markets, whether new geographies or new target populations.

How to determine which pathways are right for you:

- Collecting feedback from your existing customers and other stakeholders.
- Surveying the market of customers you have not reached yet.
- Testing out different options through small pilots, just like when you first started.

Things to watch out for when planning and measuring growth:

- Growing your inputs and operations does not necessarily equate with growing your impact.
- Growing too fast can sometimes put the quality of your work at risk, resulting in long-term reductions in overall impact.
- Growing too soon can strain your resources and decrease your chances of success.

Just like your pilot was based on an evidence-informed solution, so should your steps toward growth be based on evidence. When you were designing your solution, you looked into all the different pathways and factors related to the challenge you're tackling and its root causes. By collecting information and by co-creating with your community, you made a conscious decision about which aspects you could tackle most effectively and focused on those. The same applies to growth. Trying to do too much, too soon, or stepping on the gas pedal without a well-thought-out strategy may strain your resources or cause you to grow in the wrong direction. Revisiting your mission and your theory of change, examining your internal organizational and operational vital statistics, and consulting with your team and your board and other external stakeholders are all steps that you need to take at this point in time and on an ongoing basis in the future.

Let's start with the first dimension first: scaling your operations.

Scaling Your Operations—What to Assess

Scaling your operations means producing more of your product or service, which you've already demonstrated to have a measurable social impact. The goal here is to reach more people and have a larger cumulative impact. At what stage are you ready for scale? You'll need to have preliminary data on your social impact and demonstrate financial viability with respect to your business model. You'll need to have charted out the technical and marketing skills required to cope with the needs of expansion and set in place a team and a plan to meet those human resource requirements. You'll need to have conducted sufficient market research to develop an evidence-based marketing plan, which may hold different insights from your pre-launch marketing plan now that you've collected data from your own customers. Growing too soon can be detrimental to your venture, if you haven't built the tools and muscles needed to carry it out.

Here is one of the key points in the life of your venture when you will reap the rewards of data collection. You have been gathering two main types of data: (1) social impact metrics and (2) organizational and operational performance metrics. Both types of data will tell you whether and to what degree you have been succeeding in meeting your internal targets and your stakeholders' needs. The second will also tell you how your organization's vital statistics are doing and whether its systems are running smoothly, in order to withstand growth.

What is the rate of growth of your customer base? This can be calculated by plotting the number of people you have served over time. By now, you might have automated software, databases, or data analytics to help you do this, but even if you don't, this is one example of a very basic and easily accessible statistic. As an example, a low-cost way of assessing your growth to date is to maintain a spreadsheet. You can choose your time units by specifying days, months, or quarters (during the start-up stages, it's not recommended to use time units larger than that, but you can most certainly use smaller time units such as hours and then aggregate or add them up). These are usually listed in the first column of the spreadsheet. In the adjacent columns, you can list the information you've collected about your end users. Sometimes, this can be detailed information, such as in the case of a health venture, whereby name, age, gender, personal details, education, occupation, income, insurance, and address details may be collected. At the other extreme, it may be simply a count of the number of users. Scanning a large amount of information visually is difficult and the patterns or trends may not immediately stand out to you. Plotting functions are available in the most basic spreadsheet software and allow you to chart the data points on an axis, for example, with time on the *x*-axis and number of end users on the *y*-axis. This will allow you to assess trends over time (Figure 13.1).

Has your user base been growing at a steady rate? Has the growth tapered or increased? Were there any dips or peaks, and what could you hypothesize were behind these (seasonal changes,

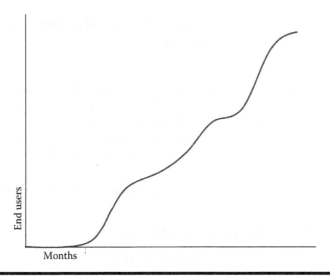

Figure 13.1 Example of a chart plotting growth over time.

changes in your staff, external influences or newly implemented policies and procedures)? What is the overall length of time you are assessing here? If it's two months, it's not likely you'll be able to draw any conclusions to inform your starting point for growth. If it's two years, then it's more likely these trends will be able to inform your growth decisions.

What other information have you been collecting? There's a huge difference between assessing total customers and breaking it down into new and returning customers. Were your returning customers asking for more products or services, were they returning for maintenance on existing products purchased, were they following up with positive results or negative results?

Revisiting your process map is a key step in preparation for scale. Are there any steps being taken that have not been included in the process map? Examine each step being taken in your organization and ask yourself: is this needed? If no, how can it be eliminated or automated? If yes, how can it be incorporated into a system, to standardize it across sites and staff? One of the components that benefits the most from standardization is the M&E. The success metrics that you collect, how and who collects them, serve as a carrot that drives the behavior and performance of each site and each subteam, so make sure you've got the golden standard for these!

> Examine each step being taken in your organization and ask yourself: is this needed? If no, how can it be eliminated or automated?

Most importantly, what do the results say about social impact? The number of people reached doesn't necessarily signify that you've achieved the desired impact. They simply reflect the growth trend. You'll also need to evaluate the success metrics you set when you designed your logic model or other blueprint for operationalizing your theory of change. Do the data indicate that the desired outcome was achieved for each end user? For example, tracking the number of patients presenting at your community health center does not necessarily indicate that health outcomes have improved, unless you have the evidence to demonstrate it.

> The number of people reached doesn't necessarily signify that you've achieved the desired impact. They simply reflect the growth trend.

Growth patterns and related outcomes are objective, usually quantitative measures that can inform your decision to scale your operations. Next, look into the qualitative measures. Talk to your team. What has been their experience? Do they feel that the infrastructure is in place to allow them to take on a larger volume? Have they experienced a need to increase the *range* of products or services or to expand the same core offering to different geographic places, or perhaps to different target audiences? You are not able to interface with each end user, nor to experience every aspect and element of running your venture, and you are not able to make decisions on scaling alone.

Scaling Inputs versus Outputs versus Impact

What does it mean to design for scale? As we saw in Chapter 4, part of what it means to design for scale is that you've created a product or service, and a set of processes and mechanisms by which it's delivered to the end user, that you can then expand on to reach as many end users as possible. In

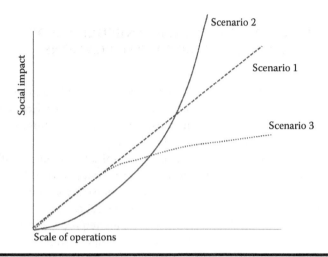

Figure 13.2 Example growth scenarios.

order to scale, the organization needs a strong logistical structure that can carry the added demand of delivering more impact. There are a couple of different ways in which growth can play out for your venture in terms of impact delivered versus resources needed (Figure 13.2).

The first route happens when a social entrepreneur is not able to design for scale. In this scenario, the ratio of resources to impact remains constant as the venture grows. That is, the venture is not able to reach economies of scale. This doesn't mean you can't scale; it just means the resources you put in will remain proportional to the social impact you get out. You don't gain economies of scale by growing, but you can still grow if you have the resources.

The second route happens when the venture is designed such that the amount of input does not increase proportionally to the amount of output. That is, the marginal amount of input required to produce more impact decreases as you grow. This is called achieving economies of scale. The more people you serve, the less it costs per person. This is ideal for growing your impact! Most of the social entrepreneurs we met over the course of this book relied on economies of scale to reach both their social impact targets and their financial viability targets.

There is also a third scenario, which can happen if you're not able to scale effectively. In this scenario, the burden on the organization actually increases per unit output as you grow. This could happen if you grow into new markets—whether geographic or demographic—where your model is less effective. It could also happen if you grow too soon and don't have the sufficient processes and human resources and as a result you end up losing time and money to fix it. In order to avoid this ad hoc emergency type of situation, let's make sure that you spend enough time, thought, and resources in preparing for expansion (Box 13.2).

What we have learned above is that elements of success in expanding the operational aspects of scaling your growth include the following:

■ Designing a scalable product or service
■ Building the processes and capacities to deliver on a large sale
■ Strategically planning expansion to increase the chances of success

There are two nuances in these. The first is that the relationship of input and output does not always stay the same as you grow. Ideally, you would like it to decrease. The second is that the

**BOX 13.2   INFORMATION NEEDED BEFORE
YOU CAN SCALE YOUR OPERATIONS**

- Is your organization financially viable? Has your pilot indicated that costs and revenues are trending in accordance with your initial financial projections?
- Has your social impact been demonstrated? Have the results from your initial M&E met the social impact targets you set before launching?
- What does the feedback collected from your initial customers indicate? Is there demand for, and satisfaction with, the product or service you're offering?
- Have you collected data on potential customers outside your initial pilot? You need evidence to inform piloting your product at the next site.
- What will be the technical and managerial inputs required to scale? What physical and financial resources are required? Do you have these resources?
- What strains will this place on your venture, and what investments do you need to make upfront to ensure that your organization can handle these strains?
- Have you considered the risks of expansion? Are there different PESTEL considerations in your new market? What steps can you take to address these threats and mitigate risk?
- Also consider what new assets might be available to you at your new sites of operations. Revisit, continue, and build on your initial co-creation process at each step of expansion. This is the number 1 investment you can make that will help ensure your success.

relationship between output and impact may not always stay the same either. Even if you're able to produce the outputs necessary to deliver your product or service, it may not have the same effect in different places and different populations.

Chart out your best-case, worst-case, and medium-case scenario. Ask yourself what it would take to get to each of those places. What does success look like, and what would failure look like? What are some different ways that you could fail? You did this already at the first design stages—conducting a premortem—the opposite of a postmortem! Next, ask yourself what you and your team are capable of and willing to do. What would it take to make you do more (or less) than you are aiming for right now? What is your limiting factor in scaling? Is it supply, is it demand, is it logistics? How will you address it?

Gathering New Information and Innovation as You Grow

Whatever options you choose for your growth strategy, one part of the template that should be included for any strategy is gathering new information and innovations as you grow. For one, each new site or market or product or service is a source of information to help you assess performance, impact, and potential for further growth. Second, there will be many unexpected twists in the plot as it unfolds, and these will allow you to glean invaluable insight to improve your product or service, your processes, value chain, and needs for next steps. A growing organization is, after all, a snapshot of increasingly larger pilots, in the sense that you are creating something new every step of the way. As your experiment matures, your knowledge will catch up to your unknowns, but each new phase will present new unknowns and new opportunities for both success and failure.

Listen to your customers, and this may mean potentially delegating more resources for feedback and signaling in your organization, to compensate for the growing distance between you and the frontline.

> A growing organization is, after all, a snapshot of increasingly larger pilots, in the sense that you are creating something new every step of the way.

How can this information be used to drive new innovations within your organization, ways of doing things better? Are there feedback loops from different sites, teams, product lines, internally versus externally facing components? Size can be an advantage from the point of view of economies of scale and of number of people reached, but it can also present disadvantages from the point of view of ease of information flow and innovation.

> Giving due time and attention to data—whether positive or negative—is your biggest weapon as you grow.

Disadvantages and Tradeoffs

While growing your operations may allow you to reach more people, some of the steps you've taken to get there may have placed a ceiling on the extent to which you can impact each person you reach. Standardization, automation, and expansion of products, services, and processes can sometimes make it harder to increase the depth of impact. What can you do to counter this? Just like your growth package may have some standardized components that will be replicated across sites, you can also factor in some local, tailored, or flexible components. Which parts do you want to leave up to the manual, and which parts do you want to leave up to your local team, providers, clients, and other stakeholders? Leaving a margin of flexibility will allow your venture to adapt to the local context—in effect, it allows local market forces to shape your work and your impact on top of the larger trends that you're counting on to grow.

Managing this margin of flexibility may be as simple as conducting regular calls with site managers or product managers, having a reporting system that allows space for local innovations to be shared, or bringing together teams from different parts of your enterprise in an annual gathering like a conference. Having a rewards system to recognize innovations that increase your impact will help to both identify and encourage them, allowing you to maintain a culture of innovation beyond your initial founding or piloting teams.

Threats of Expansion

Expansion presents an opportunity, and it also presents a set of threats. It has the potential to make you stronger by creating economies of scale, building your team, increasing your evidence base, and strengthening your impact. It also has the potential to lead you off track, presenting the risk of bureaucracies, inefficiencies, and increased distance between the management and the frontline. While the founders and executive team are often the most glorified in any venture, it behooves you to think of your foot soldiers as the most valuable members of your team because they are the closest to your end users. They have the best access to data and it is through them that you will implement any changes you make in response to the data. They are the ones providing the product or service and in many cases also collecting customer feedback. These are the community health workers, the teachers, the sales representatives, and the field coordinators. As you grow, more distance is created between you and them.

When the team first starts out small, each person is responsible for multiple tasks. As you grow and division of labor occurs, some team members become specialized in outward-facing tasks, others in decision making, and yet others in roles such as budgeting and planning. It is up to you to make sure that as these various roles are introduced into your venture, this doesn't have unintended consequences that may adversely affect your social impact. These may include delays in responding to customer feedback, disproportional time spent on processes not directly linked to outcomes, and loss of the voice of the foot soldier.*

Is It Possible to Outgrow Your Mission?

When your product or service becomes valuable to a target audience that was not your originally intended audience, or in a mechanism that was not what you'd originally designed, one possible consequence of growing in that new direction is that it may distract you from your mission. Another possible consequence is that it may add to your mission and impact. Your first impulse will be to protect your mission, which is perfectly normal and most of the time recommended. But don't close your eyes to opportunities that may add to your mission and to your social impact. Not every expansion is necessarily a threat to reaching your goals.

Nobody will argue that staying focused on your path is a key to success. Some people refer to this as "putting on your horse blinders" or "keeping your head down," meaning that it's crucial to avoid distractions and stay focused on your path. And while it is true that focus is critical to success in any venture, it's also true that once in a while, it's important to take those blinders off and look around you. While it may feel at the time that the last thing you need is a new idea to consider, and you already have your plate full, don't discard unforeseen or unexpected opportunities for expansion without considering them and bringing them to your team's attention.

Don't forget, you aren't making these decisions alone. You have the support of your board, advisors, staff, and network. Most importantly, you have the voices of your customer. You've developed this from the start along with these and other stakeholders, and making this decision is one more step in the process that you will take together. It's important to look inside yourself and determine how you feel about this, and at the same time, it's important to be open to what others have to say and how they look at it, even if that means stepping outside of your comfort zone. Ultimately, it's the end users who decide. If there is a pull in a certain direction *from the end user*, then this is the direction you will be assessing.

Disclaimer

Many people in the social entrepreneurship ecosystem talk about scaling as the number 1 most important factor in determining whether social entrepreneurs are making a measurable difference in our world. While scaling is in fact the determining factor in creating a large magnitude of social impact, that is not to discard the importance of small social ventures that make a transformative

---

* http://www.bain.com/publications/articles/founders-mentality-westward-winds.aspx.

difference to a specific community that could not otherwise have been reached by a scalable venture. Yes, if we can design solutions for scale, then we can reach the billions of people affected by social and environmental challenges today. However, each situation is different, and some situations might only be solved by designing a very specific and very tailored solution that might not be the most scalable.

There Is No Black and White

Like everything else in social entrepreneurship, this is not a black or white issue. In some cases, a social venture may be designed for scale and may be replicated or expanded to reach millions. In other cases, it may be more tailored to a specific community with specific needs. And, in many other cases, it may be something in between.

Identifying what parts of your model are scalable and what parts aren't can help determine where on this spectrum your social venture lies. In many cases, the core elements in your approach could be applied to different settings, while leaving room to adapt other elements to the local context.

PART TWO: BEYOND SCALE

What Does It Mean to Reach Your Goals?

Don't confuse scaling with reaching your goals. Was your original goal to scale as much as possible? Or was it to reach as many people as possible within a certain hard-to-reach population? In some cases, scaling means leveraging market forces to reach as many people as possible. But in many cases, in social entrepreneurship, it might mean something very different.

If your goal is to reach the most underserved communities, then you might not be able to get there using *existing* market forces. The existing market forces might take you somewhere big, allowing you to reach a very large number of people, this is true. But just make sure, are these the people you set out to reach when you first approached your social challenge? If yes, then great! You have found it.

If no, then don't despair, there are still other ways to reach your goals. They just involve the same skills you used at the beginning while developing your venture. Listen. Test. Deliver. Listen. Test. Deliver.

There is nothing wrong with leveraging market forces to reach as many people as possible; this is a good thing, as long as you don't forget about the people you set out to reach. It is them you are working for. If your product or service is in demand by others too, then great! Use that. It can fuel your efforts to reach the most difficult and challenging populations that haven't been reached before. There is a reason they haven't been reached. This is because the market as it functions today has failed them. So what you need to do is create a new market. And it's not likely that it will be a one-size-fits-all market that can reach billions of people. You need to listen, test, and deliver in each market (Figure 13.3).

That is not to say that you can't modify and replicate to reach diverse populations; this is strongly recommended. The important point to understand here is that market forces as they currently function might sometimes take you in a very different direction than where you set out to go, and you owe it to your own mission and your original target audience to deliver to them. You will come across huge challenges in financing, distribution, and reaching the last mile. That is why

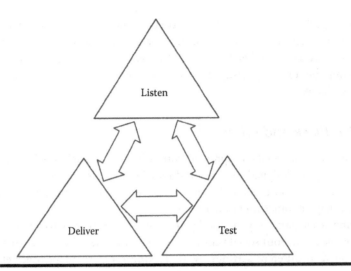

Figure 13.3   The iterative cycle of working to reach your goals.

these challenges exist in the first place, and don't forget that you took it upon yourself to tackle them! It can be done, as others have demonstrated before.

As Muhammad Yunus mentioned in his Chapter 8 interview, selling out to large multinationals might help you scale, but only if they adopt a new approach to reach your target population—otherwise, they would have been reaching them long before you came along! You have the power and the leverage to make sure this happens. Your goal is not to cash in on your product the way a commercial entrepreneur would. That is the simple difference between commercial and social entrepreneurs. Reaching only a part of your target population, and then moving on to answer the call of the market, is not enough. This is where the market failed before.

Go to them.

Don't Get Swept Away

As the Aravind case in Chapter 6 illustrated, it is often our tendency to draw conclusions about why things haven't worked. There must be something wrong with the target population. They don't want our product or service. They don't know it will improve their lives and don't have the decision-making capacity to follow through. These are some of the learning objectives of the Aravind case as taught by business schools around the world initially. How can we improve the marketing of Aravind to better convince people to take up this service? The rural poor need special marketing; that's the best way to reach them.

In the end, it turned out that Aravind's team had dropped the ball, in Thulsi's own words. They weren't listening. They weren't getting out there to where their target audience was and doing things on their terms.

Reverse the Tide: Changing the Way Business Is Done

Have you ever read about those environmentalists who keep saying that their dream is for everything not to be green? The point they are trying to make is that the mere fact we are using this

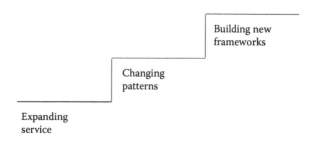

Figure 13.4 Expanding beyond your venture.

word to describe something that is "green" means that it stands out from other things that are not green. Ultimately, we would like "green" to be the standard, so that this terminology becomes obsolete.

Same thing with social entrepreneurship. Our goal is not to differentiate between social and commercial entrepreneurship. The dream is for there to be no distinction so that the term *social* entrepreneurship ceases to exist. Building business for marginalized communities is not what we want to be doing because we don't want for there to be any marginalized communities.

In both cases, for both the green and the social, this requires behavior change. It requires existing companies to alter their way of thinking and their standards. And it requires governments and the citizen sector to push for that from both sides.

Changing the Field You're Playing In

As every single social entrepreneur interviewed in this book emphasized, you can't do it alone. This is where you need to step outside your own venture and work at multiple levels (Figure 13.4). If existing policies, legal frameworks, spending patterns, consumer behaviors, attitudes, and priorities are propagating the social challenge you're tackling, then these need to change. No matter how innovative and effective your product or service is, you need to look outside your venture to change your field.

> If existing policies, legal frameworks, spending patterns, consumer behaviors, attitudes, and priorities are propagating the social challenge you're tackling, then these need to change.

Expanding Your Scope of Impact

Growing the scope of your impact is not something that has to happen within the confines of your venture. Let's venture outside the borders of your product or service for a moment. Think about the PESTEL factors you assessed while building your venture: the political, economic, social, technological, environmental, and legal barriers and opportunities. How have you built your venture to work within their context, and how have you in turn shaped these factors?

Growing your social venture's "footprint" happens at multiple levels (Figure 13.5). Delivering your solution will always be at the core of your work, but you can also change the way people interact with the social challenge you're tackling at other levels. Building awareness, advocacy, and

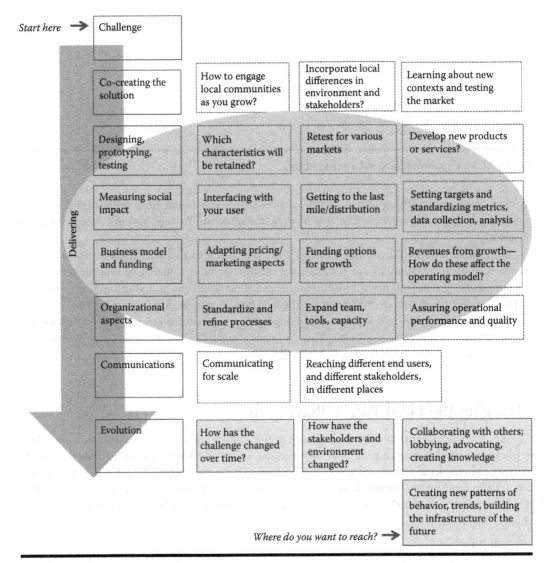

Figure 13.5 Continuum of growth.

policies are a whole other ballgame, and guess what—you are now a key player. Influencing the mobilization of resources, the collaboration within and across sectors, and getting others to step up and accept responsibility for social challenges is all part and parcel of your work.

Seeing the Forest from the Trees

There's only so much impact you can reach by growing inside your venture—you alone are not going to be able to reach the entire spectrum of change that you are aspiring toward. The first step toward collective impact is stepping back and inviting others into your dashboard. By now, you might have really gotten sucked into the nuts and bolts of your own social venture! Now that you've grown it, let's take a step back and look at the big picture once again, right where we first started.

This textbook has encouraged you to build your venture from the very root of the challenge. Now that you're well on your way, how can you zoom out from the grassroots perspective to see the forest from the trees? Are there ways for you to combine your view with that of other social entrepreneurs working in a focused and steadfast way on their own initiatives? If you can step back and exchange perspectives, together, we can build a wider lens that might allow for a multiplicative, rather than an additive, effect of all our positive actions.

Inside vs. Outside Your Venture

So in thinking about reaching your goals, it's not enough to question whether you're reaching your target population, it's only the first step. What you can accomplish alone is most likely a drop in the ocean compared with what you can accomplish with others. You may be saying, "But I have already engaged external stakeholders at every step of the way in developing and implementing my venture." This is true, but now it is time to think beyond your venture. What can you do *beyond* the activities listed in the previous sections? How can the cumulative impact of your work and the work of others be multiplicative rather than additive? To completely transform the challenges you are tackling, you need to step outside of your own venture.

> To completely transform the challenges you are tackling, you need to step outside of your own venture.

This may sound counterintuitive or tricky, but in fact, it is something you've been thinking about since you first characterized your problem, formulated your solution, laid out your mission and vision, and tested your theory of change. You've recognized that there are multiple pathways to reach the ultimate social outcome you are envisioning and that the product or service you are providing is only one small part of the solution to what is most likely a very multifaceted challenge. How can you expand your impact as it pertains to the other pathways?

Mechanisms for Expanding beyond Your Venture

There are many different ways that this can happen:

Setting New Trends

By tackling your social challenge and introducing a new way of doing things, you're already setting new trends in the market and changing the behavior of your end users and other stakeholders. It's important to realize that this trend-setting can and must affect the pieces of the value chain upstream and downstream of your venture. This is how you create a ripple effect! What patterns are you a part of and what patterns do you want to change?

For example, an organization working on providing sanitary pads for school-aged girls and young women to improve their attendance at school and, thus, their educational outcomes and job opportunities in the future has a vested interest in gender equity in this community. Changing norms and trends (like not prioritizing education for girls, like allocating fewer resources for girls' education outside of the school—such as school supplies, books, transportation—and like discrimination toward hiring women and discrimination in wages) are part of the changes that need to take place in the ecosystem in order for this organization's work to be truly impactful. If a student has full attendance and perfect scores at school but does not have any opportunities to apply his or her knowledge and skills outside of school, then the impact on his or her life and his or her household will be gravely reduced.

Health is another example. If your social venture is working on improving the supply chain for medications or reducing the use of counterfeit drugs, then part of maximizing your social impact is looking to influence others outside your venture. How can your work be used to leverage communication channels and create awareness and to put pressure on others (especially government and business leaders) to ban these practices or allocate more resources toward the reinforcement of existing legislation banning these practices?

The pioneering efforts of the Daily Table Team demonstrate that if you put together the right ingredients (pun intended!), you can create a market where none existed before, and markets speak for themselves. Once there is enough demand in these neighborhoods, more health food ventures are likely to open targeting low-income populations, and the food desert will begin to be chipped away at.

Collaboration with Other Organizations

Just as we have seen Aravind eye hospitals provide technical support and consultations to other hospitals in different parts of the world, each organization finds different ways of spreading their method and reaching more people. Similarly, HLC and other education ventures make their materials publicly available and rely on other organizations to spread their work. Nuru aims to make their poverty eradication model open source for other organizations to implement in other locations worldwide. Without this kind of collaboration, it would not be possible for them to reach these entrepreneurs' visions of educating every child, treating every case in need, and eliminating poverty worldwide. More than just sharing your material, proactively creating partnerships and pushing and supporting others to take on your work will allow you to have a greater collective impact than your organization alone ever could.

Government Adoption

Adoption by the government is the ultimate way to take a successful social venture and apply it at a much larger scale, institutionalizing key components. While this may need to be adapted for large-scale government application, the potential is enormous. Using the independence and flexibility associated with social entrepreneurship, you can create and demonstrate best practices and impact and either partner with the government to grow beyond your own venture or have your methods adopted and adapted for widespread implementation.

A successful case example here is BRAC. Originally founded as the Bangladesh Rehabilitation Assistance Committee, it is now the largest NGO in the world. Often cited as the social venture with the most impact worldwide, BRAC operates several social businesses within an overall nonprofit framework.*

BRAC's approach is that large-scale change comes only by partnering with government, collaborating with other organizations, and through advocacy and policy-making at multiple levels:

---

* www.brac.net.

Figure 13.6 **Venturing beyond scale → reaching your goals.**

local, national, and global. As such, advocacy and policymaking can be seen as the last stages of scaling beyond your venture and reaching your goals (Figure 13.6).*

Advocacy and Policymaking

Influencing the way things are done outside of your venture can be viewed as the last step of scaling, as illustrated by BRAC's approach and others. You alone cannot reach all the people or all the situations that would benefit from your intervention. How can you contribute to changing policies that influence the work of others, not just your own work?

Building your advocacy platform is a key step. Once you have been able to demonstrate results in your own measurable outputs and related social outcomes, you are now positioned to influence the way others do things. Beyond providing your core product(s) or service(s) to your target audience, what do you want to change about the world? Legislation and government policies related to your work itself or to the social outcomes you are working on are one important example.

Different ways to do this include joining forces with other stakeholders to lobby for policy changes and for the allocation of resources to tackle the challenge you are addressing—and its root causes—on a larger societal level. Creating and disseminating knowledge and other resources based on what you have uncovered along your path can facilitate the spread of information, ideas, and know-how. Engaging your end users in both of these tactics will amplify the results. For example, organize a forum that brings together decision makers and other stakeholders or publish your findings or viewpoints and have your end users and other stakeholders also contribute to the writing or other forms of media. Albina Ruiz and Ciudad Saludable wrote the national policy that changed the way local governments deal with waste management and with people living in slum areas who started out as waste pickers—and are now service providers. Thirty years ago, if you had asked whether this was imaginable, most people would have replied that it's impossible.

---

* This figure summarizes BRAC's approach as documented in Ahmed, S., and French, M., Scaling up: The BRAC experience, BRAC *University Journal*. III(2), 2006, 35–40.

Together, we can build a wider lens that might allow for a multiplicative, rather than an additive, effect of all our positive actions.

Collective Impact

Creating collective impact requires as much strategy and planning as you have committed while growing your own organization (Figure 13.7). Identifying other organizations working in the same field, strengths and weaknesses of each one, common versus complementary characteristics, and joint networks will allow you to assess the range of targets you could jointly set. This requires the formation of tangible alliances and networks beyond just general cooperation and cheerleading of each other's efforts. Setting an agenda, allocating resources, and agreeing on accountability for each organization involved will boost your ability to grow your cumulative impact beyond your separate organizations.* This allows the sum of your joint impacts to be greater than the parts that each organization alone might achieve.

Interview Box. Sir Fazle Abed, BRAC Founder and Chairperson

TC: Sir Fazle, your organization is cited as the largest NGO in the world. What advice do you have for social entrepreneurs working on growing their ventures?

FA: We can never reach every person through direct service. It's important to change how people think so it can be a self-propagating change. Take poverty alleviation for example. There are millions of children without access to quality education. BRAC works both to solve individual needs for education and also to advocate for universal primary education.

TC: Tell us more about how you approach these different levels of service.

FA: It is very difficult to provide quality education. In Bangladesh, 95% of children enter school and 20% drop out before finishing primary school, so only 75% are receiving sustainable primary education. Advocacy work is needed to get all children into schools. But it's more than that; education is not just going to school. Are they learning? Is it effective quality or repeating rote learning? We need to look at how the schools are performing. If students can think for themselves, they become a catalyst for change.

TC: What has been the most effective way of creating large scale change in your experience?

FA: You need partnerships with 3 others in order to have impact. Government is a big actor to scale your own solution. We work with other NGOs for advocacy and policy change; civil society needs to unite. It cannot be about each one doing his own work without looking at the big picture. We need to put our energy and resources to alter the systemic problem on a large scale.

---

* http://ssir.org/articles/entry/channeling_change_making_collective_impact_work.

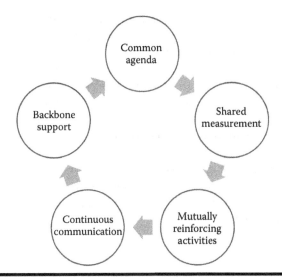

Figure 13.7   Conditions of collective impact.
(From Hanleybrown, F., Kania, J., and Kramer, M., Channeling Change: Making Collective Impact Work, Stanford Social Innovation Review blog, 2012.)

Building a Culture of Change

We've talked about building, maintaining, and nurturing a culture of innovation inside your own organization. But how can you venture outside your own walls to foster and nurture a culture of change, a movement of change outside of your venture? Well, this actually involves many of the same approaches it took to foster innovation within your own work! Embrace failure—fail on purpose, as Doug Rauch said. Fail in order to learn; test things until they reach their breaking point, as we learned from Umesh Malhotra. Exchange knowledge, and build knowledge by bringing together different perspectives, as Libby McDonald shared with us. We saw how Jake Harriman found others to help him with the parts he himself didn't feel equipped to tackle; we saw how Willy Foote brought together different players from completely different ecosystems to create one new ecosystem working together for positive change. We heard from Thulsi Ravilla how you have to constantly test your own assumptions. As Catlin Powers and Laila Iskandar pointed out, no one has the complete picture when they first start. You just do the best you can, and share your successes and failures along the way.

Sharing Failures

Please remember what we talked about in Chapter 4, when you were designing your solution. Failing is part of succeeding; it's the first several attempts required to get you to that next try where success is finally reached. Sharing your failures is as important as sharing your successes. When you're first designing your solution, deciding on your distribution channels, fleshing out your theory of change, building your process map, and all these many moving parts that you've accomplished throughout this textbook, you're basically just trying things out. It might look perfect on paper, but when you come to implement it, it might turn out completely different. This is okay! You tried your best to increase your chances of success at that first attempt, by co-creating with the community, developing user-driven designs, using various planning tools and templates, and building the best team you possibly can. The rest is up to trial and error—there's no denying that this is a huge part of it. Take the leap! And if you land in the wrong place, don't be ashamed to brush yourself off and start all over again.

Just make sure you document your trials and errors, not only for your own internal records but for others to build on. This is how we incrementally push forward the boundaries of human knowledge. Scientists conducting an experiment note in detail the steps they took and the outcomes of each, and keep detailed logs so that they'll be able to replicate if and when needed, and so that others can too. So too should a social entrepreneur take on this additional burden of tracking and reporting herself.

Knowing which variables you combined leading up to your success—or your failure—will allow others to figure out for themselves whether those variables might work in different scenarios. Perhaps a factor of your failure, if altered in a different setting, could make that failure into a success for the next social entrepreneur.

Sharing Successes

Similarly, can you create a "testing package" for others so that they can test out whether your successes might work for them too? Imagine the ripple effect you could have if your own model could serve as a prototype for others to build on (Figure 13.8).

Don't Forget the Underlying Theory

Don't forget, you have built your social venture around a specific theory of change, which has a number of underlying assumptions. If your venture works, it's because those assumptions hold and your product or service will create the intended outcomes for the target audience and entry point you've identified. All these moving parts may not hold in other settings! This is why it's important to think about what parts of the theory of change are transferable or generalizable and what parts are context specific. Then, before others try to replicate your work, they can test out the assumptions in their own specific context that they're working in.

Don't Forget to Celebrate Your Successes!

If you've made it all the way to this paragraph, this is where you'll receive a huge congratulations. To get here, you've been required to put away your fears, look at the world through completely

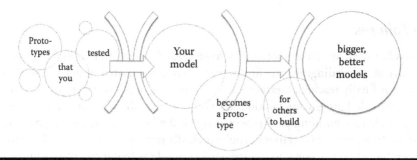

Figure 13.8 Collective learning and iterating.

different lenses, push yourself to try different things, and try to find answers to seemingly unsolvable problems. You have only just begun. By taking the first step, you have joined the ranks of social entrepreneurs working to change the face of the social challenges we face in today's world. The more people we can recruit and train into this force for good, the more we stand a chance at leaving behind positive change.

Avoiding a Bubble

How can we avoid unintentionally creating a bubble around ourselves? We have watched as various bubbles have burst for those before us—most readers will remember the "dot com" bubble of the late 1990s when everyone thought that Internet start-ups were all the rage. Remember what we said in the pitching and networking chapter: don't get swept up in the hype. Stay focused on what is true and tangible, stay connected to the people you are co-creating with, and stay in touch with *their* reality.

The best way to avoid a social entrepreneurship bubble is to recognize its limitations. Social entrepreneurship is not a prescription to solving all the world's problems; there are many problems that need to be solved by governments and by the larger private sector being more responsible. We are not practicing social entrepreneurship for the sake of it. It is a means to reach an end, which is to create positive social outcomes. The goal is not to create parallel systems, but to provide a tangible, effective, scalable solution. If governments and other sectors can work together to offer our solution and penetrate more widely and deeply, then that is the golden standard. Better yet, if our solution effectively zaps at the roots and the challenge ceases to exist—or has been transformed into something positive—then we have reached our ultimate goal. We have become obsolete.

Remember, penetrating more widely and deeply requires that solutions be adapted and replicated to work in multiple different situations. There are no one-size-fits-all problems nor one-size-fits-all solutions. The most likely outcome is that the solution we offer will need to be tailored to each local context and added to; supplemented and complemented; tracked and monitored and evaluated. We need to be prepared for this by mobilizing local and global resources and capacity to do that in a timely manner. At the end of the day, it's about the people you are co-creating this solution with. Whatever doesn't make sense for them doesn't make sense to pursue.

Recap

So, now it's your turn to tell us, what does social entrepreneurship mean to you? At the beginning of this textbook, you were challenged to find new ways of doing things, to think like a child, to question all assumptions. That includes questioning and building upon the framework presented to you in this book! Can you find a better way of doing it? Chances are, you already have! Or, hopefully, you are well on your way.

As a reminder, this framework has been built upon the collective experience of other social entrepreneurs before you, and presented to you to help you get started in taking the first steps of your social entrepreneurship journey. There's no reason to start from scratch; it's good to stand on the shoulders of those before you. But don't forget when you get up there to look around you and ask yourself how things could be done better. Then brace yourself to support others in climbing up even higher!

Taking the Next Steps Together

Social entrepreneurship as captured by the principles and frameworks presented in this book is not the be all and end all of solving the world's challenges. Social ventures can't solve everything. The biggest and most striking example of that are the humanitarian crises we face every day, where immediate relief is needed and people just have to help each other. Social entrepreneurship is just one more way we can make a difference, and it has the potential to make a huge difference. It's just important to know your limitations alongside your potential. Above all, it's important to be humble. Don't play God. Look for every opportunity to learn from your mistakes or your lack of knowledge to fill in the gaps. The social entrepreneur is one tiny person. One tiny person can make a difference. But she or he cannot do it alone. The more people you can mobilize, the more systems and sectors you can bridge together, the larger scale and depth your impact will have.

Keep questioning, and don't get complacent. Questioning all assumptions means questioning yourself too, not just the status quo. Look for any evidence that might indicate you are mistaken. Incorporate it into your work. Keep collecting as much evidence as you can. The only thing we can know for sure is that we'll never have all the answers. But eventually, hopefully, collectively we'll find as many answers as possible.

Exercise: Fueling Growth

After building a healthy and viable venture, it's time to focus on growth. Let's explore the multiple dimensions and directions in which you can grow your impact to reach your ultimate goals:

(250-word limit per question unless otherwise specified. You may need to write more for your own records, but come back and summarize here.)

1. Within the scope of your theory of change, how can you grow to reach more people? What data are needed to determine the right timing and directions? Do you have these data?
2. How can your impact on each person be greater in magnitude and duration? What do your preliminary results indicate are the most impactful components of your solution?
3. What ripple effects is your solution having on society? How can you actively and consciously grow these?
4. What do you need to produce to fulfill your response to the first three sets of questions? Is it more products or services, more scale, more follow-up with customers, more involvement in external activities outside your venture?
5. What does the communication strategy you prepared in the last chapter require in terms of advocacy? What policies exactly are you advocating for, and who are the key players you need to mobilize in order to change these policies?
6. How can you look beyond your own venture to create collective impact with others, such that the whole is greater than the sum of the parts? What might be some potential common agendas, shared measurements, mutually reinforcing activities, communication needs and other resources needed? (800-word limit total for question 6, use bullet points)

CHAPTER SUMMARY

- Growing your social venture is about more than growing your operations. It's finding new ways to reach your target audience and to create ripple effects in the community. It's also about venturing outside your own work to join forces with others.
- Careful assessment of your preliminary data is needed to help determine when and how you can grow your products, services, or reach.
- But most social entrepreneurs will not be satisfied by simply scaling. They envision something much bigger than a linear path that goes up, up, up. What most social entrepreneurs see is a multidimensional growth path that disrupts everything in its way!
- Growing outside your social venture means partnering with other organizations, leaders, and stakeholders to change the frameworks that you and others operate in.
- Mechanisms for expanding beyond your venture might include government adoption, collaboration with other organizations, advocacy and policymaking, planning for and measuring collective impact.
- It's important to share and celebrate your successes and also to share your failures so that others can build on them.
- Most importantly, keep questioning. Don't get complacent, and don't get comfortable. Remember the social challenge you set out to tackle, and remember that you need others, to truly make this obsolete.

Social Ventures Mentioned in This Chapter

Company profile: BRAC, www.brac.net.
Founded in 1972; Bangladesh.
Product/service: Multiple social businesses and programs operating worldwide including a rural credit and training program launched in 1979, which paved the path for Grameen and other subsequent initiatives.
Goal: To empower people and communities in situations of poverty, illiteracy, disease, and social injustice.
How it works: Based on the premise that poverty is a system and its underlying causes are manifold and interlinked, BRAC provides people with tools to fight poverty across all fronts. They have developed support services in the areas of human rights and social empowerment, education and health, economic empowerment and enterprise development, livelihood training, environmental sustainability, and disaster preparedness. They operate social enterprises and create value chain linkages that increase the productivity of members' assets and labor and reduce risks of their enterprises.

Index

This index includes the preface and author's page. Page numbers with b, f, n, and t refer to boxed texts, figures, footnotes, and tables, respectively. Readers are referred to the case studies, interviews with specific social entrepreneurs, and specific social ventures for the examples of concepts discussed in this book.